The Rise of the Russian Democrats

STUDIES OF COMMUNISM IN TRANSITION

General Editor: Ronald J. Hill
*Professor of Comparative Government
and Fellow of Trinity College,
Dublin, Ireland*

Studies of Communism in Transition is an important series which applies academic analysis and clarity of thought to the recent traumatic events in Eastern and Central Europe. As many of the preconceptions of the past half century are cast aside, newly independent and autonomous sovereign states are being forced to address long-term, organic problems which had been suppressed by, or appeased within, the Communist system of rule.

The series is edited under the sponsorship of Lorton House, an independent charitable association which exists to promote the academic study of communism and related concepts.

The Rise of the Russian Democrats

The Causes and Consequences of the Elite Revolution

Judith Devlin

Department of Modern History,
University College, Dublin

STUDIES OF COMMUNISM IN TRANSITION

Edward Elgar

Published by
Edward Elgar Publishing Limited
Gower House
Croft Road
Aldershot
Hants GU11 3HR
England

Edward Elgar Publishing Company
Old Post Road
Brookfield
Vermont 05036
USA

British Library Cataloguing in Publication Data

Devlin, Judith
    Rise of the Russian Democrats : Causes and
    Consequences of the Elite Revolution. -
    (Studies of Communism in Transition)
    I. Title   II. Series
    320.947

Library of Congress Cataloguing in Publication Data

Devlin, Judith, 1952-
    The rise of the Russian democrats : the causes and consequences
    of the elite revolution / Judith Devlin.
        p.   cm. — (Studies of communism in transition)
    Includes bibliographical references (p.   ) and index.
    1. Post-communism—Russia (Federation)   2. Democracy—Russia
    (Federation)   3. Political parties—Russia (Federation)   4. Russia
    (Federation)—Politics and government—1991-   5. Glasnost.
    6. Soviet Union—Politics and government—1985-1991.   I. Title.
    II. Series.
    JN6692.d48   1995
    321.8′0947—dc.20   94-48417
                                                                         CIP

ISBN 1 85898 251 0

Electronic typesetting by Lorton Hall
Printed and bound in Great Britain by
Hartnolls Limited, Bodmin, Cornwall

Contents

Acknowledgements

This work could not have been written without considerable intellectual and material assistance. In the first place, I wish to express appreciation to the President and Governing Body of University College, Dublin, for awarding me a Newman Scholarship and to Aer Rianta, Ireland, for their generosity in funding the scholarship and thereby enabling me to pursue my research.

I am indebted to the staff of several libraries and institutions in Moscow, who gave me much practical help. In particular, I would like to thank the Institute of Sociology, Academy of Sciences; the Russian Humanitarian State University; the INION Library; the Lenin Library; the Moscow Bureau of Information Exchange; the State Public Historical Library; Mr Michael Smallman and the library of the Queen's University, Belfast; and the INDEM Centre, Moscow, which kindly invited me to Moscow in the Spring of 1992.

I am grateful to many Russian friends, scholars and intellectuals who gave generously of their time and tried to enlighten me about Russian politics and recent Soviet history. They include Anatoly Ananiev, Yuri Afanasiev, Yuri Burtin, Alexander Bek, Leonid Batkin, Nina Braginskaya, Igor Chubais, Vadim Damie, P. Fedorov, Vyacheslav Igrunov, Evgeny Ikhlov, Natalya Ivanova, Boris Kagarlitsky, Alexander Kalinin, Vladimir Kardailsky, Dmitri Kataev, Elem Klimov, Vitaly Korotich, Vladimir Kostyshev, Igor Kliamkin, Andrei Kolganov, Anatoly Kryuchkov, Pavel Kudiukin, Boris Kurashvili, Vera Kuznetsova, Asya Lashiver, Vyacheslav Lyzlov, Igor Minutko, Andrei Maximov, Mikhail Malyutin, Andrei Mironov, Tatyana Mikhailskaya, Nikita Okhotin, Stella Oleinikova-Volkenstein, Valentin Oskotsky, Nikolai Novikov, Anatoly Pristavkin, Alla Parayatnikova, Vladimir Pribylovsky, Lev Ponomarev, Evgeny Proshchechkin, Georgi Satarov, Natalya Setyukova, Ilya Shablinsky, Mikhail Shatrov, Vyacheslav Shostakovsky, Oleg Sosnin, Igor Surikov, Mikhail Topalov, Lev

Timofeev, Nikolai Travkin, Oleg Witte, Sergei Zalygin, Sergei Zimin, Vladimir Zharikin and Sergei Zinchenko.

The assistance and hospitality of friends in Moscow did much to make the practicalities of research easier and more enjoyable. I would especially like to thank Tom and Kiki Russell, Conor O'Riordan and Tanya Vargashkina in Moscow, Helen Browne in New York and Deirdre MacMahon in London.

I am especially grateful to Dr Theodore Zeldin, St Antony's College, Oxford, and Professor Ron Hill, Trinity College, Dublin, for reading different versions of this book and for their unfailing advice and encouragement. The shortcomings of this work were perpetrated despite them. I should finally like to thank the Irish Department of Foreign Affairs for posting me to Moscow in the mid-1980s, at one of the great turning-points of modern history. Above all, I should thank my mother, who enabled me to bury myself in my study and emerge only to eat and sleep while I was writing this book.

Judith Devlin
December 1994

List of Abbreviations and Glossary

PUBLICATIONS

AiF	*Argumenty i fakty*
IHT	*International Herald Tribune*
Lit.Gaz.	*Literaturnaya gazeta*
MN	*Moscow News*
NG	*Nezavisimaya gazeta*
NM	*Novy mir*
NYRB	*New York Review of Books*
RFE/RL	*Radio Free Europe/ Radio Liberty Reports*
SK	*Sovetskaya kultura*
SR	*Sovetskaya Rossiya*

POLITICAL TERMINOLOGY

Apparat	Higher Party and State officials
Apparatchik	Member of the *apparat*
CC	Central Committee of Communist Party
CPSU	Communist Party of Soviet Union
Glavlit	Chief Censorship Board
Gorkom	City Party Committee
Goskino	State Committee on the Cinema
Goskomizdat	State Committee on Publishing
Komsomol	Young Communist League
NEP	New Economic Policy (in which some private enterprise was tolerated) pursued 1921–28
Nomenklatura	List of key appointments and suitable candidates, controlled by the CPSU

Obkom   *Oblast'* or provincial Communist Party committee

Plenum   Meeting of the full Central Committee

1. Introduction

The decline and fall of the Soviet empire between 1989 and 1991 were hailed, more in hope than with confidence, as a revolution, as a triumph of liberal and democratic ideals in the heroic mould of the nineteenth century.[1] Following the dramatic defeat of the August 1991 coup, a new Russia, led by its first democratically elected president and freed from the tyranny of discredited ideas, policies and persons, set out to effect the economic transformation that would underpin the political revolution. But, in the light of recent developments, uncertainty has replaced euphoria. Were we mistaken about the nature of the political changes in Russia?

Russia is preeminently a land of illusion, a world through the looking-glass, an upside-down world. The now extinct art of Sovietology recognized this: one of its first rules was that things are not what they seem. Until the 1990s, it was customary to scan speeches to see what they did not say, to find the signals which alerted the knowing reader to the significance tucked away behind the apparently innocuous platitude, the real meaning which was often entirely at variance with the apparent sense. Similarly, photographs were studied for absences and deceptive appearances. Perhaps for this reason, the West's relations with Soviet Russia have been beset by misapprehensions – from the German who had the unhappy idea of bringing Lenin back to Russia, to the fellow-travellers of the 1930s and the warm reception of Brezhnev: should the celebration of Russia's democratic revolution now be added to this list?

The West's early enthusiasm for Gorbachev and *perestroika* was based on something of a misunderstanding. It was not just a natural

---

1 See A. Roxburgh, *The Second Russian Revolution* (London, 1991), p. 3; F. Fukuyama, *The End of History and the Last Man* (London and New York, 1992), p. 31; J. Dunlop, *The Rise of Russia* (Princeton, 1993), p. 282 for examples, qualified by Dunlop's own doubts.

response to reassuring changes in foreign and domestic policy: it betrayed the assumption that when the lid was finally lifted off Soviet society, nothing too unpleasant would be found in the pot – in short, that an embryonic replica of a Western society would be revealed. However, the cauldron was found to be bubbling with nasty ingredients – the proto-fascism of *Pamyat'*, anti-Semitism, numerous and competing chauvinisms and a legacy of private and public lawlessness and crime, much of it unpunished. It was a combination which overwhelmed Gorbachev and which his successors have shown little capacity to overcome. The turbulence and unpredictability of events make it not inconceivable that the West may come to regret the passing of the old regime, much as later generations came to look back nostalgically on the Austro-Hungarian Empire as a guarantor of order.

The feeling is now widespread – especially since Autumn 1993 – that Russia's democratic revolution has run into the ground and that Russia's democrats are unrepresentative both of the political class and of Russia in general. Is this an accurate assessment and if so, what happened to the democratic revolution? Did it ever take place? No reform from above can ever expect to be entirely successful: it requires collaboration from below to be carried through. Until recently, analyses of *glasnost* and the independent movements in the former Soviet Union suggested that the reform leadership of the CPSU had successfully elicited (indeed, too successfully for their own good) a popular and powerful reform movement.[2] Most recently, however, this thesis has been questioned: Richard Sakwa, Jonathan Steele, and Victor Sergeyev and Nikolai Biryukov have argued that democracy has failed to put down deep roots in Russia, and some have suggested that the reasons for this are to be found in Russian political culture.

This argument reflects a school of thought which can be traced at least to the early nineteenth century. It suggests that Russia is an essentially Eastern or Asiatic country and, consequently, that the individualistic and libertarian culture of the West – and its political and economic offshoots – are fundamentally alien to it. The idea that

2 G. Hosking, *The Awakening of the Soviet Union*, rev. ed. (London, 1990); G. Hosking, J. Aves and P. Duncan, *The Road to Post-Communism* (London, 1992); M. Buckley, *Redefining Russian Society and Polity* (Boulder, CO, 1993).

Russia and the West are fundamentally antithetical has long been argued both by Russians and foreigners. Russian nationalists (and a long line of left-wing revolutionaries from the nineteenth-century populists to twentieth-century Stalinists) held that it was a mistake for Russia to try to emulate the West's pattern of development and social organization. The Slavophiles of the late 1830s and 1840s were the first to hold that the Russians were by nature a collectivist, apolitical people – more preoccupied with spiritual than with secular and state affairs, with inner freedom than with political liberty (a theme taken up over a century later by Solzhenitsyn). Authoritarian rule, they believed, suited the Russian temperament and mores. The fact that the Slavophiles' ideas about the Russian national soul and identity owed more to German philosophy than to historical reality did nothing to diminish their appeal.[3] Their ideas recurred throughout the nineteenth and again in the twentieth century, both among Russian *émigrés* and, later, in official circles, where, after a summary reworking, they informed the ideology of the later Stalinist and Brezhnev eras.[4] Among the *émigrés*, a group of scholars known as the Eurasians held that Russia and its Muslim dependencies formed a distinct cultural entity (Eurasia) which had to find its own, separate path of development. Some of the Eurasians ultimately found refuge as teachers in the USA and were thus well-placed to popularize their ideas.[5] The totalitarian interpretation of the Soviet Union, which held sway during the Cold War, was a variation on this theme: it was not just the case that Russia laboured under a dictatorship – the

3 See A. Walicki, *The Slavophile Controversy* (Oxford, 1975).
4 See A. Koyré, *La Philosophie et le problème national en Russie* (Paris, 1929); E. Thaden, *Conservative Nationalism* (Seattle, WA, 1964); M. Petrovich, *The Emergence of Russian Pan-Slavism* (New York, 1956); H. Kohn, *Le Pan-Slavisme: son histoire et son idéologie* (Paris, 1963); D. Treadgold, *The West in Russia and China*, vol.1 (Cambridge, 1973); T. Masaryk, *The Spirit of Russia*, rev. ed., vol.2 (London, New York, 1968). On nationalism in the Soviet period, A. Yanov, *The Russian New Right* (Berkeley, CA, 1978); J. Dunlop, *The Faces of Contemporary Russian Nationalism* (Princeton, NJ, 1983); V. Shlapentokh, *Soviet Intellectuals and Political Power* (London and New York, 1990).
5 See O. Böss, *Die Lehre der Eurasier* (Wiesbaden, 1961); P. Milyukov, 'Eurasianism and Europeanism in Russian History' in *Festschrift T.G. Masaryk* (Bonn, 1930), part 1, pp. 225–36; L. Dupeux, *National-Bolshévisme*, 2 vols (Paris, 1979); and M. Agursky, *Ideologiya natsional-bolshevisma* (Paris, 1980) for another largely anti-Western strain of Russian nationalism after the Revolution.

dictatorship was held to be somehow congenial to the Russians, or at least consonant with their political traditions.

Confronted with the evidence of contemporary Russia's shaky democracy, several writers have turned again to Russia's history – citing not merely its practical, institutional and organizational consequences (weak legal culture, absence of an effective, impartial administration, poor social infrastructure, an atomized society) but above all its psychological legacy. Russians' deep-rooted and unconscious attitudes are, it is suggested, inimical to liberal democracy. According to Sergeyev and Biryukov, Russian popular culture is deeply penetrated by the spirit of *sobornost* (a term invented by the Slavophile thinker, Khomyakov, to describe the unique Russian collectivist *Volksgeist* and which Sergeyev and Biryukov understand as the myth and cult of the people and the priority accorded to the rights of the people over those of the individual). Sergeyev and Biryukov see *sobornost* as having been integrated into Soviet political culture and, thus, as having survived to the present. They interpret the speeches of the conservative deputies in the USSR Congress of People's Deputies as evidence of the continuity and strength of this collectivist, authoritarian tradition.[6] Jonathan Steele has also emphasized the importance of Russia's historical legacy in undermining modern attempts to reform.[7]

The conclusion, for some modern analysts, is that the Russians are politically passive and, as the Slavophiles contended, inclined to authoritarianism:

> Most ordinary Russians [...] put their faith in the Tsar or Stalin to provide order and justice [...] *Perestroika* [...] could not change attitudes quickly. How often did we hear the phrase 'We believe in Gorbachev [...]' or 'We believe in Yeltsin [...]' The word in Russian – *'verit''* [...] is more than a matter of trust. It [...] has the quality of faith, the submissive belief in a saviour with all the religious overtones that go with that.[8]

Even some Russians (notably in the Westernizing intelligentsia) agree. Galina Starovoitova believes that 'The consciousness of the people has remained "tsaristic": the people adore a charismatic leader'.[9] A

6 V. Sergeyev and N. Biryukov, *Russia's Road to Democracy* (Aldershot, 1993), p. 130.
7 J. Steele, *Eternal Russia* (London, Boston, 1994), p. 45.
8 Ibid., p. 272.
9 G. Starovoitova, *NG*, 30 July 1991.

number of Russian intellectuals (in both the democratic and the nationalist camps), having rediscovered Eurasianism, have declared Russia a peculiar Oriental – essentially undemocratic and illiberal, egalitarian and imperial – culture.[10] Many Western writers agree: how could it be otherwise, they argue, in the absence, historically, of democratic structures, of a middle class, of a civic society?[11]

The attempt to put contemporary Russia in historical perspective and to take into account factors other than the superficial interplay of high politics is laudable. But the thesis that the East in general and Russia in particular is imprisoned in or uniquely inhibited by an authoritarian mentality raises a number of questions. The first is whether the collectivist religio-political mentality (*sobornost*) posited by Sergeyev and Biryukov and their predecessors ever existed in historical fact as opposed to the imagination of intellectuals. The fact that most Russians lived in and were controlled by a peasant commune does not mean that this arrangement was necessarily popular and unchallenged. Nor is it clear that the primitive egalitarianism of its dispositions was essentially different from the egalitarianism of traditional peasant communities elsewhere (where democracy nonetheless emerged) or that it precluded the development of more individualistic sentiments (as the response to Stolypin's reforms might suggest). Until the Russian historical record has been subjected to the same detailed analysis as that – for example – of France, the case remains to be proved. As for popular and traditional cultures in the twentieth century, both their lack of autonomy and the assaults on them make sustainable generalizations even more problematic. Contemporary Russians' political passivity and indifference, their longing for strong leadership to deliver them from the chaos into which their country is sliding, can hardly be called unique: in Western Europe, the political system is beset by a crisis of confidence, marked by popular scepticism, apathy and calls for firmer and more inspired political leadership.

10 Yu. Afanasiev, *NYRB*, 31 Jan. 1991, pp. 38–9; Round table in *Den'*, 12–18 April 1992; see J. Dunlop, *The Rise of Russia* (1993), pp. 290–91 for similar reorientation by Sergei Stankevich.
11 See for example R. Sakwa, *Russian Politics and Society* (London, 1993), pp. 394, 402, 427; J. Steele, *Eternal Russia* (1994), p. 49; R. Pipes, *Russia under the Old Regime* (London and New York, 1974); and T. Szamuely, *The Russian Tradition* (London, 1974), are classic statements of the general argument.

In general, the emphasis on Russia's unique (and perverse) culture tends to overlook the difficulty with which the transition to democracy was achieved elsewhere. The history of Germany, Italy and Spain exemplify its protracted and problematic nature. Countries where the development of democratic institutions and culture were relatively easy are the exception rather than the rule. It has been customary to view Tsarist Russia as particularly backward, both politically and economically. However, it is possible to see in *fin de siècle* Russia signs of an emerging civil society and middle class, soon matched by the uncertain rise of constitutional politics: it was not so much Russian traditional collectivism that put an end to these trends as the Great War.

It is perhaps worth drawing the comparison with that apparent paragon of liberty and democracy, France. The history of nineteenth-century France was once taught as that of a country mesmerized by revolution. Yet for all that it celebrated liberty in its political rhetoric, France remained a profoundly conservative and authoritarian country for most of the nineteenth century and it retained a strong authoritarian tradition into the twentieth century (in government, with Pétain and the Gaullist presidency, and, in popular opinion, with the *Action française* and communism). This was true especially at an institutional level. Civic liberties (freedom of the press and association) lagged behind the right to vote and were won definitively only at the end of the nineteenth century, in two instalments: in the 1880s and the early 1900s. Political parties – in the sense of organizations as opposed to schools of political thought and congeries of statesmen and conspirators – were established only in the first years of the twentieth century. In formal terms, therefore, Russia (whose civic liberties and political parties also date from the first decade of the twentieth century) was neither as anomalous nor as anachronistic as Russians themselves believed.

The modern Russian revolution was not, in my view, subverted by the Russians' alleged collectivism and authoritarianism but vitiated by its purely formal and rhetorical character: the political culture of the liberal elite failed to integrate with popular culture, for reasons that have less to do with the Russians' political mentality than with time-scale, the balance of power within the democratic movement and the economic and political crisis into which the country was plunged.

Nor would it be reasonable to expect a new public culture to be formed so quickly: the process is too complicated and profound to be effected within a few years.

The Russian revolution of 1989-91 in some ways resembles its nineteenth-century liberal and democratic predecessors. The 1830 and 1848 revolutions witnessed an almost accidental coincidence between the political discourse of the elite and popular discontent: their heroic popular victories were quickly shown to be illusory and they represented not the definitive conquest of democracy but a stage on the road towards it, an episode in a more protracted and profound process. Similarly, the modern Russian revolution was essentially a revolution of the elite. It was launched by the old political leadership, carried forward by major figures in the cultural establishment and ultimately taken over by the *Realpolitiker*, officials and technocrats more interested in wielding than in transforming power and whose commitment to reform and modernization was essentially pragmatic. Society at large, however, remained ambiguous and amorphous in its response to these changes.

Some comments on terminology may be helpful here. One of this book's central theses is that the Russian intelligentsia played a disproportionate role in the formation of the democratic movement – above all, in exploiting the tentative civic liberties of both press and association in the late 1980s. While there has been endless debate over the meaning of the term intelligentsia,[12] it is used here not – as in Soviet sociology – to denote white-collar workers but to designate intellectuals. The term intelligentsia has been retained, however, because the Soviet Russian intellectual elite were distinguished from their Western counterparts by a peculiar *esprit de corps* and character, generated by their singular history and position within the regime.

The pro-reform, anti-Stalinist intelligentsia are often referred to in this book as democrats, to distinguish them from their authoritarian opponents in the CPSU and in the cultural establishment. What did

---

12 G. Fischer, 'The Intelligentsia in Russia' in C. Black (ed.), *Aspects of Social Change* (Cambridge, MA, 1960), pp. 253-74; M. Malia, 'What is the Intelligentsia?' in R. Pipes (ed.), *The Russian Intelligentsia* (New York, 1961), pp. 1-7; R. Pipes, 'The historical evolution' in *ibid.*, pp. 51-5; C. Read, *Religion, Revolution and the Russian Intelligentsia* (London, 1979), pp. 1-5; N. Zernov, *The Russian Religious Renaissance* (London, 1963), pp. 2-3; L. Churchward, *The Soviet Intelligentsia* (London, 1973), pp. 3-7; V. Semenov *et al.* (eds), *Klassy, sotsialnye sloi i gruppy v SSSR* (Moscow, 1968), pp. 136-43.

they stand for? The reformers' demands evolved. At first, in 1987, they were concerned with the Stalinist heritage: establishing (within the permitted parameters) the historical record and lamenting the conditions which had enabled Stalin's tyranny to be exercised led to discussion of the need to end arbitrary rule, introduce legal norms and establish a civil society. By the middle of the following year, the need for the codification of civic freedoms had become inescapable and was acknowledged by the Party.

From 1987 on, radical intellectuals also supported Gorbachev's calls for greater democracy within and outside the Party: but this support was initially muted and generally conceived in terms of collaboration rather than of competition with the Party. Until 1989, few anti-Stalinists argued for full political pluralism and representative government as a realistic option. Most advocated a form of democratic socialism, in which the economy would be reformed to admit some freedom of enterprise and a more tolerant CPSU would continue to dominate political life, while allowing different opinions to be expressed so long as they respected existing economic and political structures. Only when the strength of the Party *apparat*'s resistance to these calls became apparent, as the Party leadership began to vacillate in its commitment to reform and as public expectations soared, were the anti-Stalinists radicalized to the point where they began to call for democratic constitutional change and, as a remedy for the country's growing economic plight, for the introduction of market reforms. The democrats' message therefore evolved and was far from being fully democratic in content in the early stages of *perestroika*.

The anti-Stalinist intellectuals faced growing opposition. It took time for the battlelines to be clarified. However, divisions within the ruling party, the CPSU, were of cardinal importance in shaping the country's political life. If two broad tendencies (for and against reform) became evident soon after Gorbachev took over, by mid-1989 and early 1990 fragmentation had proceeded apace, with commentators distinguishing up to eight currents of opinion within it.[13]

13 B. Kurashvili, 'Kriticheskaya faza' in M. Vyshinski (ed.), *Pravo i vlast'* (Moscow, 1990), p. 40; V. Vyunitsky, 'Ot "diki" mnogopartiinosti', *Dialog*, 1990, no. 17, pp. 34–5; V. Parol', 'Mnogopartinost'', *Obshchestvennye nauki*, 1990, no.1, pp. 118–19; M. Malyutin, quoted in A. Trusov (ed.), 'Neformaly yest'', in V. Pechenev *et al.* (eds.),

Predominant within the Party's higher administration or *apparat* and at the top of the army were those who, vehemently opposing reform, favoured retaining the old empire (or Soviet Union and areas of hegemony in Central and Eastern Europe) and the centralized command economy, with its emphasis on heavy industry and large defence budget. To this end, some of its members were ready to join forces with nationalist intellectuals in an attempt to seduce public opinion. Others, more taken with ideological orthodoxy, favoured a kind of populist Stalinism, which, while ostensibly respecting more democratic structures, hoped to exploit popular poverty in order to wrest power away from the reformers. Because of their opposition to reform, they are sometimes called conservatives in this work. A large body of opinion in the Party, both in the rank and file and at the centre, was reluctant to challenge either the system or the Party leadership, but was ready to compromise and accept modest reforms. It was with the Party hardliners rather than with the centrists that the democrats fought their sharpest battles. The authoritarian and nationalist right wing in late Soviet Russian society will be the subject of a separate volume: here they figure simply as the democrats' antagonists.

This book attempts to analyse the democratic movement, its strengths, weaknesses and ultimate impact. It is concerned not so much with the democratization of Russian society as a whole, with the new civil society, as with the emergence of new democratically-inclined political formations and their contribution to the political culture of contemporary Russia. It focuses on the Russian Federation, rather than on the Soviet Union, since – despite the links between the Russian democrats and some of the republican nationalists – the dynamic of change was very different in the former republics of the Union and Russia itself and developed in response to local pressures and separate cultural and historical traditions, which are beyond the scope of this work.

Neformaly: kto oni? (Moscow, 1990), pp. 260-61; 'Partiya i novye obshchestvennye dvizheniya', *ibid.*, pp. 316, 320-21.

2. The Social Context

A joke told during the Gorbachev years about *perestroika* illustrates contemporary attitudes to the regime and its projects:

> The train of communism is trundling across the field of life one day, when the engine splutters and dies. Comrade Stalin wakes up. 'Shoot the driver', he suggests. Comrade Khrushchev demurs. 'Rehabilitate the driver', he argues. Comrade Brezhnev settles back comfortably in his seat. 'Let's just pull down the blind and rock from side to side', he says. 'Then no one will know the train has stopped'. Finally, Comrade Gorbachev leaps to his feet. 'You've got it all wrong!' he shouts. 'What we need to do is to get off the train and all shout together: the train isn't working, the train isn't working![1]

The black humour of the Brezhnev and Gorbachev years – an offstage irreverent echo of the regime's pompous rhetoric – was symptomatic of attitudes hitherto marginalized but which, with the introduction of Gorbachev's reforms, were to resonate through Soviet society and politics.

If Gorbachev's reforms unleashed a democratic movement in Russia in the late 1980s, it was ultimately because Soviet Russian society had become more sophisticated since the previous attempt to reform under Khrushchev in the later 1950s and early 1960s. It was more diverse and discriminating than the appearances – of conformity, repression and backwardness – suggested. The Thaw, the relative affluence and security of the Brezhnev years and the spread of education left the Russians more detached and demanding than ever before in Soviet history.[2] A middle class of sorts had come into

---

1 Cited in G. Hughes and S. Welfare, *Red Empire: The Forbidden History of the USSR* (London, 1990), p. 200.
2 As Brezhnev put it in his speech to the Twenty-Third CPSU Congress: 'The present generation of boys and girls has not passed through the hard schools of revolutionary struggle and trial experienced by the older generation. Some young people would like to circumvent the fullness of life': cited in Boris Lewytzkyj, *Politics and Society in Soviet Ukraine* (Edmonton, 1984), pp. 129–30.

existence and it was receptive to the arguments of the reform leadership and the intelligentsia in favour of change.

THE INTELLIGENTSIA AND ITS AUDIENCE

By the mid-1980s, Russian society was more complex, its demands and interests more various than they had been twenty-five years earlier, during the Thaw, but political and state structures had not kept pace with these changes.[3] Between 1959 and 1989, the urban population (mainly of European Russia) had almost doubled (increasing from 100 to 186.8 million) and the bureaucracy and services had replaced agriculture as the major employer. People were better educated: while the secret census of 1937 revealed that 38 per cent of the population were illiterate and while a majority of the population in the late 1950s had not completed their secondary education, by the late 1980s the number of people with a higher education had grown dramatically: from 1.2 million in 1939, to 8.3 million in 1959, to 21 million in 1987. White-collar workers with a technical or professional training numbered around 35 million in 1987 and the number of white-collar workers doubled between 1960 and 1987.[4]

Living standards improved significantly under Khrushchev and Brezhnev. R.J. Hill notes that, on an index of 1940=100, per capita real income rose to 298 by 1965 and to 602 by 1982. Lower-paid workers and collective farmers benefited most from this development[5] but overall wages rose, pensions and social security benefits were introduced or extended.[6] Salaries could now procure the necessities of life and money was left over to put towards televisions and fridges, or even jeans, cassette tapes and *samizdat*. Between 1956 and 1970, 126.5 million people were rehoused in separate flats, instead of in the

---

3 A. Fadin, a member of Democratic Perestroika, participating in a round-table discussion on the informal movement in the Higher Party School, in 1990, in S. Yushenkov (ed.), *Neformaly, sotsialnye initsiativy* (Moscow, 1990), pp. 58-9.

4 D. Lane, 'The Roots of Political Reform' in C. Merridale and C. Ward (eds.), *Perestroika: The Historical Perspective* (London, 1991), pp. 99-100, 102-6; see also G. Hosking, *A History of the Soviet Union*, rev. ed. (London, 1990), pp. 402-3.

5 R.J. Hill, *Soviet Union* (London, 1985), pp. 165-6.

6 G.B. Smith, *Soviet Politics* rev. ed. (London, 1992), pp. 274-6.

squalid communal apartments or shacks that had hitherto been the rule.[7] Soviet citizens, in the late 1970s and early 1980s, were therefore far better off than their parents had been.

Paradoxically these achievements – instead of increasing the regime's prestige – encouraged new, more demanding attitudes in society. This better-educated, urban population had different expectations and outlook on life from the generation of the Thaw, with their naive belief in Soviet socialism and hopes for reform – and still more from the generation of the 1930s, with their mix of faith and opportunism. This more prosperous generation expected more of the government and assumed their living standards would continue to rise – a belief unwisely encouraged by the Party's propaganda about the advantages of developed socialism. When, in the late 1970s and early 1980s, the rate of economic growth slowed down and as the economic crisis deepened, these expectations were bitterly disappointed.

One might be tempted to conclude that a kind of urban middle class had emerged in Russia in the Brezhnev years. However, while these social groups might be described as middle class in education and occupation, they were not on the whole economically a middle class: although statistics are an unreliable guide to Soviet living standards because they do not include hidden benefits and privileges, the decline in the living standards of these white-collar workers, in relation to manual workers, was a source of discontent.[8] In addition, social problems – the rising incidence of alcoholism, divorce, illness due to pollution, declining mortality rates – all pointed to a deteriorating social environment.[9]

This constituency of comparatively well-educated but poorly remunerated state employees might be expected to have been dissatisfied and thus sympathetic to proposals for radical change. Many were responsive to the reformers' calls for change: they accounted for much of the dramatic increase in the mass readership of

---

7 Smith, *Soviet Politics* (1992), pp. 259-60; B. Kerblay, *Modern Soviet Society* (London, 1983), pp. 63-4.

8 D. Lane, 'Roots' in Merridale and Ward (eds), *Perestroika* (1991), pp. 109-10. Office workers earned 50 per cent more than manual workers in 1932 and, on average, 20 per cent less in 1986. See also Shlapentokh, *Soviet Intellectuals* (1990), pp. 11-14.

9 J. Dunlop, *Contemporary Russian Nationalism* (1983), pp. 95-102; Hosking, *History* (1990), pp. 396-401.

the liberal journals[10] and they also formed the backbone of the informal movement.[11] Nonetheless they did not take the initiative or in any sense dictate the initial reforms. Gorbachev, as Catherine Merridale points out, was not 'somehow generated' by the social context.[12] As Alexander Yakovlev has observed, the public response to the promulgation of reform by the Party was much less enthusiastic than it had been under Khrushchev to the Thaw, and the expected popular support failed to materialize.[13] This relative passivity may be ascribed to a profound change in public consciousness: the passage from optimism to scepticism, that may be explained by the higher general level of education, the failure of previous attempts to reform the system from above and by the growing indifference to the Party's claims and rhetoric, following long experience of inefficiency and corruption.[14]

Another factor which inhibited the effectiveness of this constituency, when it finally intervened politically, was its diversity. The Russian – and still less the Soviet – middle class was not homogeneous. It was divided culturally between the intellectuals – employed in the academies, the arts and journalism – and office workers, technicians and economic managers, between those privileged to live

10 See Shlapentokh, *Intellectuals* (1990), p. 265, for statistics on the popularity of liberal papers.

11 In 1988, sociological surveys suggested that one in three participants in the informal movement was an engineer, technical or office worker, one in four was a student and one in five a worker. In Novokuznetsk, in an area famous after 1989 for the radicalism of its workers, 50 per cent of those involved in the informal movement were students or office workers and 38 per cent were manual workers: V. Churbanov and A. Nelyubin, 'Neformal'nye ob"edinyeniya' in V. Kuptsov (ed.), *Demokratizatsiya sovetskogo obshchestva* (Moscow, 1989), p. 241; see also, on the predominance of young scientific technical workers and students, O. Alexandrova, *Informelle Gruppen* (Cologne, 1988), p. 5; B. Kagarlitsky, *The Thinking Reed* (London and New York, 1989), p. 353. V. Berezovsky and N. Krotov, in their *Neformal'naya Rossiya* (Moscow, 1990), p. 25, point to the predominance of the lower and middle intelligentsia, office workers and students, all of whom were experiencing a declining standard of living in the mid-1980s. Also, interview with A. Kalinin, deputy of Mossoviet, 9 July 1990; L. Gordon, 'Working Class', in Merridale and Ward (eds), *Perestroika* (1991), p. 85.

12 Merridale, 'Pluralism' in Merridale and Ward (eds), *Perestroika* (1991), p. 20. In this, she is at odds with D. Lane, 'Roots' in ibid., pp. 106–11, who believes that *perestroika* was somehow 'pushed' from below.

13 A. Yakovlev, interview in *Lit.Gaz.*, 25 December 1991, p. 3. This was a common observation by those who lived through both periods.

14 See S. Stankevich, 'Trudnosti stanovleniya demokratii' in Yushenkov (ed.), *Neformaly* (1990), pp. 136–7.

in Moscow or Leningrad and the provincials, between the intellectual elite (the Academicians, famous artists and writers) and the obscure researchers who thronged the institutes of Russia's great cities. Although Soviet sociology lumped them all together in one category (the Soviet intelligentsia), the differences ran deep, Soviet society being far more caste-ridden than the egalitarian ethos of the regime would lead one to expect. The differences are important because the intellectuals played an important role in the reforms but never really managed to win solid and unambiguous support for their ideals in wider social circles.

What were the peculiar traits of the intellectuals? How could one define their political culture? There are two competing definitions of the intelligentsia: one insists on its political and moral function and traditions, the other on its social composition. Soviet sociologists expanded the term intelligentsia to cover all categories of white-collar workers. Thus, not only schoolteachers and doctors but also factory technicians, clerks, bureaucrats, industrial managers and even Party workers and propagandists were presumed to share the attitudes, values and behaviour of artists, writers, journalists and actors. Underlying this approach was the idea that there was nothing special about intellectual work: it was somehow equivalent to manual labour; behind toilers at the coal-face and at the factory bench (the governing working class) came labourers in the fields (the Soviet peasantry) and workers in the office and at the desk (the intelligentsia). Orthodox Soviet sociologists would have been loath to suggest that the intelligentsia had anything to do with the independent generation of ideas or, horror of horrors, with their critical assessment. Implicitly, all three categories of Soviet society were united in the goal of their activities – the building of socialism. As a result of these assumptions, official estimates of the size of the intelligentsia were high – 38 million out of a population of 280 million.[15] Such a definition is so broad as to be meaningless.

15 V. Semenov, Rutkevich *et al.*, *Klassy, sotsialnye sloi i gruppy v SSSR* (Moscow, 1968), pp. 136-43; A. Koval'chuk and T. Naumova, 'Mesto intelligentsii' in A. Amvrosov (ed.), *Problemy nauchnogo kommunizma* (Moscow, 1984), vol.18, pp. 85-7; L. Ivanova (ed.), *Sovetskaya intelligentsiya* (Moscow, 1987), p. 50; P. Amelin, *Intelligentsiya i sotsializm* (Leningrad, 1970), pp. 14-15, 45-6; L. Churchward, *The Soviet Intelligentsia* (London, 1973), who follows the Soviet line. For contemporary Russian intellectuals' heroic view of their vocation, see T. Tolstaya *et al.*, *MN*, 6 August 1989, p. 3; Roxburgh, *Second Russian Revolution* (1991), p. 110.

If one does not accept the Soviet definition of the intelligentsia, can one talk at all about a modern Russian intelligentsia? Were the artists and writers of modern Soviet Russia in any sense a caste, with recognizable values and mores of their own? Was their role and place in society in any way different from that of intellectuals in other countries? I would suggest that the Soviet Russian intellectual elite formed a self-conscious social group, sharing a characteristic lifestyle and, to some extent, attitudes in a way their counterparts in the West did not and they were thereby placed in a unique position to respond to the Party leadership's political reforms and to form an articulate political caucus.

Russian intellectuals were seen as heirs to a special tradition. According to this view, Russian writers and thinkers defended the ideals of human freedom, dignity and spirituality from the incursions of political authority. The term 'intelligentsia' was first used in Russia in the nineteenth century to designate the class of revolutionaries – the consumptive, long-coated haunters of the cellars of St Petersburg and the cafes of Zurich. Historically, it was seen as a specifically Russian phenomenon. Berdyaev – famous for his critique of the intelligentsia's nefarious influence on cultural and moral standards – offered a classic definition:

> The intelligentsia should really be compared to a monastic order, to a sect with its own, peculiar very intransigent morality, with its own binding conception of the world, with its own mores, customs and even a characteristic physical appearance. The intelligentsia thus formed an ideological, not a professional or economic grouping and was recruited among different social classes [...][16]

In short, the intelligentsia was, as Tibor Szamuely pointed out, 'a social category based on certain criteria not of class but of consciousness, upon a certain set of moral, ethical, philosophical, social and political values' and above all upon hostility to the existing social order.[17] The intelligentsia tended to be seen historically as a band of heroic freedom fighters, struggling against the tyranny and injustice.

This ideal or myth of the intelligentsia (although it did not go

16 N. Berdyaev, *Les Sources et le Sens du Communisme Russe*, rev. ed. (Paris, 1963), pp. 30–31.
17 T. Szamuely, *The Russian Tradition* (London, 1974), p. 192.

unchallenged)[18] to some degree influenced the Soviet Russian intelligentsia. A small number of heroes and martyrs, such as Pasternak and Solzhenitsyn, consecrated the myth in the Soviet period. It also helped to inspire some Soviet intellectuals. These, however, were the exceptions for the modern Russian intelligentsia was widely believed to have compromised itself in its dealings with the political authorities – to have sold its soul to the devil. It was partly for this reason that the Westernizing intelligentsia championed the cause of liberal reform so vehemently as soon as the opportunity arose: they were anxious to redeem themselves for the abdications and concessions of the past.[19] Myth and tradition none the less enhanced the prestige of intellectuals and distinguished them from the rest of society.

The modern intelligentsia's unique character derived not only from its public image and the mythology surrounding it but also from its unique institutions. The Soviet authorities created prestigious organizations, which both supervised intellectuals and rewarded the subservient. These organizations had the effect of creating a world apart, in which the established intellectual lived and worked. In the West, membership of a college, university or club affords the principal opportunity for the like-minded to congregate on a regular basis and to establish, in relation to society, a sense of common identity and purpose. In the Soviet Union, an analogous role was played by the creative unions and the Academy of Sciences – with the difference that these institutions were more intrusive and inhibiting than their Western counterparts. The unions and Academy created an acknowledged intellectual elite, which lived according to rules unlike

---

18 Controversy surrounded the role of the intelligentsia from the start: Berdyaev and his friends' indictment of its reductive and utilitarian materialism in *Vekhi* (1909) was anticipated half a century earlier by Turgenev's *Fathers and Sons* (1862). Berdyaev believed that the intelligentsia, in embracing revolution, had undermined cultural freedom. Julien Benda took a not dissimilar view in *La Trahison des Clercs* (1927), in which he criticized French intellectuals' flirtation with totalitarian politics: see N. Berdyaev *et al.*, *Vekhi*, rev. ed. (1990); J. Benda, *La Trahison des Clercs* (Paris, 1927).

19 See Shlapentokh, *Soviet Intellectuals* (1990), pp. 94–104, 179–85. Interview with I. Minutko, Moscow, 25 November 1990. For arguments in favour of continuity of cultural tradition, despite the eclipse of the pre-revolutionary intelligentsia see R. Pipes and L. Fischer in R. Pipes (ed.), *The Russian Intelligentsia* (London, 1961), pp. 53–5, 253; I. Berlin, *Personal Impressions* (Oxford, 1981), pp. 161ff; M. Schatz, *Soviet Dissent in Historical Perspective* (Cambridge, 1980), p. 12 – who sees dissidents as the heirs of the classical intelligentsia.

those applied to the rest of society – by virtue of the privilege and power they dispensed to the conformist. Another characteristic institution of the intelligentsia was the 'thick journal' – the literary and polemical magazines.[20] In the nineteenth century, not only were many of the great novels first published in these magazines, such public debate as there was took place in their pages. This tradition was renewed in the Soviet period: during the Thaw, some journals were renowned for their espousal of clearly discernible political and moral positions, a trend which was accentuated under Gorbachev. During *perestroika*, the publishing houses and editorial boards of these magazines functioned as a form of political association, in an otherwise largely fragmented society. Within these structures – the creative unions, the academic institutions, the publishing world – distinct groupings emerged, known for their commitment to the equivalent of a platform. In the Gorbachev years, the intellectual establishment split into two bitterly opposed camps: the liberal reformers and the nationalist neo-Stalinists.

Of course, many intellectuals did not belong to this elite. Some were openly or privately critical not only of the regime but also of the establishment to which the intellectual elite belonged: these dissident circles too had their conventions, recognizable lifestyle and ethical code. They were united by an *esprit de corps*, a network of friendship, acquaintance and rivalry. Finally, there was, in the capitals, a large intellectual proletariat of academics, writers and artists, not yet rewarded or recognized, critical but not dissident in orientation. Many of these were anxious to share the privileges of the elite and some were ready to pay the price for doing so. Many of the activists of the democratic movement were drawn from these circles.

Broadly speaking, however, Soviet Russian intellectuals were distinguished both by their lifestyle and by their pretensions. The intellectual elite was characterized by its exclusiveness, the extent it was organized into corporations, the degree of political pressure to which it was subjected and its social, intellectual and ethical ethos (sectarianism, clannishness, intensity). These characteristics were generated by the restrictive social and political system in which the elite lived and magnified by the fact that such a high proportion of the

---

20 As R. Pipes observes of the nineteenth-century intelligentsia in *Russia under the Old Regime* (London and New York, 1974), p. 264.

intellectual community was concentrated in Moscow or Leningrad. As a result, Russian intellectuals tended to lead a life removed from that of the rest of society and from the ordinary white-collar workers and provincial technicians and civil servants with whom Soviet sociology assimilated them. By virtue of their special position, the Russian intelligentsia was uniquely placed to respond to the Party leadership's calls for support: they were less fragmented, better organized than other social groups and they subscribed to a shared ethos or myth – which emphasized the intelligentsia's political and moral role in society. When the constraints were finally lifted, liberal intellectuals were anxious to prove the intelligentsia's credentials. Many, in the Gorbachev years, drew inspiration from the traditions of the old Russian intelligentsia, whose political and moral vocation they hoped to recover.

ORIGINS OF THE CIVIL SOCIETY

The liberal intellectuals of the elite initially gave Gorbachev important support and preached the cause of reform, albeit within the parameters set by the Party. Their message won a measure of approval among the public and especially among the wider intelligentsia – measured by the increased circulation of liberal papers and journals and the burgeoning political clubs.[21] This response could hardly have been elicited, however, had there not been a discrepancy between the official accounts of social attitudes and relations and the reality. Alongside the official face of Soviet society, a subculture of disenchantment and independent values and ideas existed.

The emergence of unofficial cultures or subcultures – particularly among the intelligentsia and the young – was one of the most important developments in Soviet society, after the death of Stalin. Social circles, which were independent of the Party and dedicated to pursuits and ideals not endorsed by it, began to appear. The growth of alienation from the regime, which while not going as far as open and unambiguous protest, indicated the declining hold of the official ideology over society. Alienation was most dramatically expressed

21 Shlapentokh, *Soviet Intellectuals* (1990), pp. 81–3; 'Ob itogakh', *Izvestia* TsK KPSS, 1989, no.1, pp. 138–9.

from the late 1960s on, in political and religious dissent, but it could assume other forms – such as membership of the informal clubs or circles devoted to unofficial art and culture, to unorthodox values and lifestyles.

Alienation

One of the effects of the long reign of the lie and hypocrisy and of the Party's monopoly on politics and decision-making was alienation. A classic *samizdat* essay, entitled 'The Split Consciousness of the Intelligentsia', argued that it was the distinguishing trait of the Russian intelligentsia.[22] Nor was alienation confined to the intelligentsia; it had become so widespread and resulted in such social passivity and disenchantment[23] that the Party leadership was even provoked to advert to its harmful effects.[24] Under Stalin the dangers and under Brezhnev the sanctions attendant upon expressing one's opinion led to the development of a split consciousness, of double standards and a sharp distinction between public and private life. Russians were accustomed to saying and doing one thing in public and another in private.[25] At work, at the Party cell and Komsomol, the factory or institute meeting, they would conform to what was expected of them; what they might think or say to their friends was another matter. The very intensity with which issues of public policy and morality were discussed in private – in the famous kitchen talks[26] – derived from the impossibility of speaking one's mind in public or of having any influence on events. The way in which Russians referred to those in power expressed this alienation: *oni* as opposed to *my* (or 'them' and 'us'). '"We" are the vast majority of the people, the receivers and

22 V. Kormer, 'Dvoinoe soznanie russkoi intelligentsii', *Voprosy filosofii*, 1989, no.9, pp. 65–79.

23 It ranged from petty theft, malingering and absenteeism to engaging in unapproved activities, such as listening in *magnitizdat* to the songs of Vysotsky.

24 See Gorbachev, Speech to CPSU Plenum, 27 January 1987, *Izbrannye rechi* (Moscow, 1987), IV, p. 305.

25 Berezovsky and Krotov, *Neformal'naya Rossiya* (1990), p. 14; Shlapentokh, *Soviet Intellectuals* (1990) pp. 83–4, 88–9; Y. Glazov, *The Russian Mind since Stalin's Death* (Boston, MA, 1985), pp. 74–5; D. Shipler, *Russia: Broken Idols, Stolen Dreams* (London, 1983), pp. 113–17; R. Khasbulatov, *Byurokraticheskoe gosudarstvo* (Moscow, 1991), pp. 198, 214.

26 See G. Hosking, *The Awakening* (1990), p. 20.

evaders of orders, passive, sporadically obedient and inwardly resentful or resigned. "They" are the givers of orders, a relatively small group.'[27] The terms *oni* and *my* were used as shorthand for a state of mind, in which the leadership was put at a remove from the citizen and which was not untinged with a hint of hostility.[28]

The public persona fitted into official life, and might even occupy public office and join the Party. The private persona often belonged to a subculture which departed from official norms. This subculture could assume various forms, ranging from the apparently innocuous to the borders of dissidence. It has been suggested that Russian high culture – especially Russian classical literature – enjoyed such prestige and was cultivated so assiduously under Soviet rule precisely because it mediated values other than and essentially opposed to those promulgated by the regime.[29] The reading of *samizdat* was by no means confined to dissidents.[30] Autonomous civil life became a private, semi-legal affair and was confined to the domestic circle of family and friends and clubs of a semi-underground character.[31]

The *kruzhok*, or circle, was a typical Russian phenomenon of the Russian intelligentsia.[32] A semi-underground gathering, it was bathed in an aureole of heroism – being associated with a long tradition of resistance to oppression.[33] The circle consisted of a group of like-minded friends, meeting privately at home usually to discuss forbidden topics and advance unorthodox views. The circle, as a tradition, reemerged after the death of Stalin and provided the principal means through which non-conformists could meet, orientate and express themselves in a wider group. It was the basic social unit of non-conformist or unofficial culture.[34] It explains not so much the

---

27 R. Hingley, *The Russian Mind* (London, 1977), p. 140.
28 Malyutin in round table discussion in V. Pechenev and V. Vyunsky (eds), *Neformaly: kto oni?* (Moscow, 1990), p. 246.
29 R. Pipes, 'Historical Evolution of the Russian Intelligentsia', in Pipes (ed.), *The Russian Intelligentsia* (New York, 1961), pp. 54–5; Kagarlitsky, *The Thinking Reed* (1989), pp. 94–5.
30 Berezovsky and Krotov, *Neformal'naya Rossiya* (1990), p. 8.
31 Ibid., p. 18.
32 Shlapentokh, *Intellectuals* (1990), pp. 128–9.
33 P. Kropotkin, *Memoirs of a Revolutionist*, rev. ed. (London, 1978), pp. 213–32; A. Herzen, *Ends and Beginnings*, rev. ed. (Oxford, 1985), pp. 160, 181.
34 N. Belyaeva believed that these circles helped 'to preserve little islands of free-thinking' in Brezhnev's Russia; unofficial groups enabled the rebellious or non-conformist to survive as a breed: see Miloslavsky, *MN*, 40, 1988.

fragmentary nature of unofficial culture as its incestuous and sometimes sectarian character. Its legacy was evident in the political clubs
of the informal movement, where the same small group of people
surfaced continually in a variety of capacities and organizations.

The subculture of alienation developed, in its modern form, under
Khrushchev. By the mid-1950s, people had relaxed enough to form
wide circles of friends, who now dared to tell jokes, mock the
inadequacies of the system, listen to the irreverent and critical songs
of Galich and his peers on the cheap tape-recorders which had
appeared on the market and tune to foreign broadcasts on newly
available radios. These 'entirely loyal citizens', Alexeeva suggests,
gradually became more critical of the regime as they were exposed to
new ideas. This process was hastened by *samizdat*, which began to
circulate in these circles in the 1960s. So great was the demand for
unofficial publications that people were expected to read a book in
one night: whole families and even friends might be invited to take
part in the reading, sitting together and handing around the pages as
they read them.[35] The spread of cheap consumer goods – especially
'Comrade Transistor' – was, as Boris Lewytzkyj observes, a 'major
threat to the party's monopoly of education' and and a channel of
'"bourgeois" ideological influences'.[36]

Another element in the subculture of alienation and discontent was
identified by Alexander Zinoviev. He predicted – correctly – that the
most effective opposition to the regime would come not from
ideological opponents, like the dissidents, but from those whose
objections were social. Discontent and alienation – manifested in
drunkenness, laziness and corruption – were widespread, he argued,
but these phenomena were too amorphous to form the basis of an
opposition movement. However, this discontent was distilled in a
more narrow, competitive milieu, which Zinoviev called Moscovia.
Moscovia meant Moscow society, those who competed for survival
and influence within it and that part of provincial society which
identified with it and wished to live in it. (It should be noted that
resentment of Moscow and Muscovites was widespread in the old
Soviet Union for economic, social and political reasons.) This social

35 L. Alexeeva, *Istoriya inakomysliya* (New York, 1984), pp. 247–8.
36 B. Lewytzkyj, *Politics and Society in Soviet Ukraine* (1984), p. 130; reference by
    courtesy of Professor R.J. Hill.

nexus fed on the hidden anti-Stalinism of elements of the establishment.

Moscovia included the most exploited group in Soviet society. This was not, he contended, the working class, but the most talented and gifted members of society: young scientists, researchers and economists, who, although highly qualified, were frustrated on account of their poor pay and career prospects. Opposition, he predicted, would be Moscow-based and led by this disgruntled, well-educated but by no means miserable and outcast younger generation. They would aim not to destroy the system but to win a better place within it. Democracy would eventually be included in their aims as a means to an end. A sort of 'sub-society' was forming, he believed, with its own way of life, outlook, criteria of judgement and relation to official culture, power and the West.[37]

This analysis was uncannily prescient. The informal movement – the first political clubs, which ultimately provided many of the leaders of the democratic movement – emerged from precisely the milieu described by Zinoviev. It was based in and dominated by Moscow and Leningrad; a large proportion of its members were drawn from the disgruntled, younger researchers of the Academy and its institutes, who initially wanted to collaborate with, rather than challenge the authorities.

Dissent

The subculture of alienation, which underpinned the Brezhnev years, found its most systematic expression in dissidence. While both the Soviet authorities and Western commentators emphasized the exceptional and eccentric nature of dissidence, dissidents themselves were always at pains to contest this approach, stressing instead what they had in common with their fellow citizens. Dissidence was one end of a spectrum of attitudes to be found throughout much of Soviet society. Ideological indifference and passivity, dissatisfaction with living standards and doubt about the claims of Soviet socialism were at one end of this scale of alienation. Scepticism (manifested in jokes and songs), refuge in 'internal exile' (outward conformity and private dissent), detachment and disagreement (suggested by non-

37 A. Zinoviev, 'Ne vse my dissidenty', *Kontinent,* 44, 1985, pp. 175–86.

participation and lack of assiduity in Party activities) were in the middle of the range. Finally, open dissent was at the outer limits of the scale. Reading *samizdat*, belonging to an unofficial group or circle, retailing irreverent jokes, listening to the songs of Galich or Vysotsky were all indicative of a degree of dissent and were often indulged in by the dissident, by the closet critic and by the person who was simply fed up with the shortages, exhortations and hypocrisy.

To isolate the dissenter purely on this account is, therefore, misleading: some of his attitudes and activities – including those for which he was liable to be imprisoned – were not peculiar to the dissident at all but were common to much of society. The fact that his attitudes were not entirely exceptional was an admission that the authorities were unwilling to make; they were anxious to singularize the dissident precisely because his attitudes were becoming more widespread in the Brezhnev years. Hence, in some ways the dissident was representative of new trends in Russian society. Nonetheless, he was distinguished from the rest of society if not so much by his ideas at least by his behaviour in relation to authority: he was ready to speak out. Consequently, he was subject to the hostile attentions of the KGB. This had the effect of isolating him, of confining him to a narrow circle of friends and like-minded acquaintances, for few people were now ready to take the risk of associating with him.[38]

Estimates of the number of dissidents vary widely.[39] In 1977, Roy Medvedev thought that there were up to 4000 active dissidents, including prisoners, in the Soviet Union. However, Medvedev pointed out: 'Every dissident has his own nucleus of friends and followers, who give him their sympathy and help, even if he doesn't issue statements.'[40] The world of formal dissidence was, therefore, confined to a tiny proportion of the total population, even if some of the dissidents' attitudes, beliefs and behaviour were shared by a

38 R. Medvedev, *On Soviet Dissent*, rev. ed. (New York, 1985), p. 1.
39 Estimates usually range from 300 to 2000 as they are based on divergent definitions of dissent and, sometimes, on misleading information. One arrives at a low estimate if one equates dissidents with political prisoners (those detained under Articles 190-91 and 70). However, this overlooks those who were convicted under the criminal code (usually for insignificant offences), those detained in psychiatric hospitals and those temporarily at liberty: if all these categories are included (in so far as they can be estimated) the number increases significantly.
40 Medvedev, *Dissent* (1985), p. 50.

considerably larger section of society. As far as the social profile of the dissident movement is concerned, dissent was expressed initially, in the 1960s, by intellectuals but, in the 1970s, as greater pressure was brought to bear on the regime's critics and on the intelligentsia, more manual workers became involved.[41]

Dissidence had its origins in the Thaw which followed Stalin's death.[42] Khrushchev's denunciation of Stalinism, the liberation of prisoners from the camps and the stirrings of independent thought provoked a mood of unprecedented optimism in society and the belief, widespread among the young and among intellectuals, in the possibility of a liberal, democratic reform of Soviet socialism. A generation of Party officials was infected with a vision analogous to that which, in Czechoslovakia, was known as the Prague Spring. Students, artists and the young engaged in earnest public debate and furnished an enthusiastic audience for the new literature – some of it critical, some harrowing, some romantic and lyrical – and joined in demands for a greater measure of artistic freedom, truth and sincerity. Poetry and song were especially popular and in the late 1950s and early 1960s, public readings of the poetry of the young Yevtushenko, Bella Akhmadulina and others drew large crowds to Mayakovsky Square in Moscow, which became one of the first public meeting points for those who wished to discuss literature, art and philosophy. Russia's religious and rural heritage began to be explored and celebrated and, implicitly, Soviet socialism's social and cultural experiments to be criticized.[43]

The State's response to these developments was erratic, varying from the crass and oppressive – as in its treatment of Pasternak, when he was awarded the Nobel Prize for *Doctor Zhivago* – to the surprisingly tolerant – as when Khrushchev sanctioned the publication of *One Day in the Life of Ivan Denisovich*. In these circumstances, people began to clarify their views and to express them publicly: differences of opinion and orientation began to emerge within the elite,

---

41 L. Alexeeva, *Inakomysliya* (1984), pp. 351–2.
42 For various chronologies of dissidence see Glazov, *Russian Mind* (1985), pp. 105–6; Alexeeva, *Inakomysliya* (1984).
43 See Dunlop, *Contemporary Russian Nationalism* (1983), pp. 180–85, for a sympathetic account; A. Yanov, *The Russian New Right* (Berkeley, 1978), for a critical analysis by a Russian émigré; T. Beeson, *Discretion and Valour*, rev.ed. (London and Philadelphia, 1982), pp. 75–7, 81–8.

principally in the intelligentsia.[44] It was from the liberal socialists –
who were tolerated for most of the 1960s and who even believed,
until about 1966 or 1967, that they might make a positive contribution
to the evolution of State policy – that many leading human rights
campaigners and dissidents of the late 1960s and 1970s were drawn.[45]

In short, the Thaw encouraged many intellectuals and young people
to express their views in the belief that they could change things for
the better. The swing, under Brezhnev, away from reform towards
conservatism and narrow authoritarianism isolated many of them,
exposing them to political persecution. As a result, many of the 1960s
reformers became closet liberals, hiding their true allegiances until the
late 1980s, when they reemerged as supporters of Gorbachev's
reforms. Others persisted in their protests or found themselves
stranded in dissent. But for all their apparent isolation, the dissidents
were unrepresentative of their generation not because of their ideas –
which had found considerable support during the Thaw – but in their
readiness to express these ideas openly in defiance of the powers and
in their reluctance to compromise. The cultural world of dissidence
was not as peculiar as either the regime or Western commentators
sometimes suggested: many of its ideas and concerns were shared by
dissidents' more timid or shrewd contemporaries. Thus, the dissident
movement both testified and contributed to the 'culture of the
catacombs' in Brezhnev's Russia.

Youth Subculture

Less political in orientation but still indicative of the limits of
ideological and social homogeneity was the semi-underground youth
culture.[46] In its modern form, it developed after the Twentieth Party

---

44 Three strands of opinion have been identified in reform opinion of the period:
   neo-Leninism, which favoured a return to the social and political norms supposedly
   adopted by Lenin and distorted by Stalin; 'technocratism' and liberal socialism, which
   had Marxist and liberal democratic wings, represented, respectively, by Roy Medvedev
   and Andrei Sakharov. The liberal socialists argued for more individual and economic
   freedom and saw the need for some measure of political pluralism, see Shlapentokh,
   Soviet Intellectuals (1990), pp. 149-59.

45 For information on the human rights movement see Schatz, *Soviet Dissent* (1980), pp.
   131-4; see Shlapentokh, *Intellectuals* (1990), p. 192, for descriptions.

46 For its origins see M. Pashkov, 'Zolotoi vek' in V. Levichev (ed.), *Neformal'naya
   vol'na* (Moscow, 1990), pp. 4-10; V. Semenova, 'Sotsial'no-istoricheskie aspekty' in

Congress of 1956, when social life began to revive after the years of the Terror. It began as a rejection of dull and intrusive official organizations, particularly the Komsomol, and the social norms these enforced. Thereafter, the young, while apparently conformist, read *samizdat* and *tamizdat* to rags, handing it around among friends, and devoured verses, songs, notes on history, ironic anecdotes and black jokes about contemporary life. This alternative youth movement quietly worked out a paradigm for informal behaviour and activities, which was a form of passive protest. It was a state of mind and culture awaiting the signal of liberalization to make its public appearance.[47]

The first wave was characterized by a new romanticism, associated with poetry and song.[48] The bard or unofficial song movement began to develop in the late 1950s, when amateur song clubs were formed in several higher education colleges in Moscow. In 1958 and 1959, students started to organize meetings of enthusiasts and composers of a new style of popular music: satirical and irreverent songs or lyrical celebrations of love, nature and the simple life. Hitherto, there had been little room in Soviet culture for the expression of private feeling. The popularity of the unofficial song movement was due partly to the novelty of its themes and style and to the scope for self-expression, both in music and lifestyle, which it afforded.[49]

The first-wave clubs also evinced a strong interest in conservation and ecology, which was soon to be deprived of any spontaneous outlet.[50] The ecology movement dates from the late 1950s and early

ibid., p. 27; V. Tolz, *Multi-Party System* (New York, 1990), pp. xv, 5: Tolz denies that this tradition was suspended by Stalinism; I. Sudiniev, 'Nashchestvie marsian' in Yushenkov (ed.), *Neformaly* (1990), pp. 4-7; A. Gromov and O. Kuzin, *Neformaly* (1990), p. 14. S. White, *Political Culture and Soviet Politics* (London, 1979), pp. 143-54, points to nationality as another focus of political culture.

47 Berezovsky and Krotov, *Neformal'naya Rossiya* (1990), pp. 7-14. Bestuzhev-Lada, writing of the modern youth movement, stressed that it was a counter-culture, opposed to the values and orientations of modern Soviet society: see S. Plasky, *Molodezhnye gruppy* (Moscow, 1988), p. 35.

48 This tendency, associated with such figures as Galich, Bukovsky and Yevtushenko, was finally forced underground or into compromise or dissent. For the new ideals of love authenticity and the simple life, see I. Sudiniev, 'Neformal'nye molodezhnye ob'edineniya' in *Sotsiologicheskie issledovaniya*, 1987, no. 5, p. 57.

49 N. Krotov *et al.*, *Rossiya: partii* (1991), I(i), pp. 50-53.

50 Sudiniev, 'Nashchestvie' in Yushenkov (ed.), *Neformaly* (1990), pp. 6-7; also Shlapentokh, *Intellectuals* (1990), pp. 128-9.

1960s, when the student ecology movement and the official ecological-cultural movement (VOOPIK) were founded.[51] The cultural wing of the conservation movement rapidly assumed a nationalist hue, with the formation in 1964 of *Rodina* (Motherland), a student society devoted to the study and conservation of historic monuments, and in 1965 of VOOPIK, the Society for the Preservation of Historic Monuments. The latter was closely associated with the 'village writers', who celebrated the culture and traditions of rural Russia.[52] As a result of these developments, by the mid-1980s, there was an extensive network of voluntary societies in the country (100 all-Union, 200 republican and 800 local public organizations) with different tasks and structures. Their independence of the Party was, however, only nominal: they were ossified captives of higher political authorities, neither reflecting their members' concerns nor capable of fulfilling their ostensible functions.[53]

It was in the 1970s and early 1980s, in response to the failure of the hopes for a relaxation of Party control over society and for greater self-fulfilment, that the second-wave informal movement – the hippies and fan clubs – developed. Some took refuge in alternative culture, others in sport or hobbies. The so-called *Sistema*, or Russian hippy movement, developed in the early 1970s. Russian hippies, like their Western counterparts, proclaimed pacifism and free love, rejected the existing social order and were recognizable by their long hair and eccentric dress. They were linked by a network (known as the System) through which they got to know and helped each other. Members of the System were young and often well educated. Many were interested in religion and mysticism.[54] Alexander Altynov explained the appeal of the System to a Soviet journalist in terms of independence: 'The System is a quest for freedom [...] The System helped me to survive morally. I think it's the same for everyone else.'[55] A member of the movement in Moscow agreed:

51 Sudiniev, 'Nashchestvie' in Yushenkov (ed.), *Neformaly* (1990), pp. 20-21.
52 Dunlop, *Contemporary Russian Nationalism* (1983), pp. 65-81.
53 Gromov and Kuzin, *Neformaly* (1990), pp. 15-16.
54 Ibid., p. 19; Alexandrova, *Informelle Gruppen* (1988), pp. 16-18; Razumov *et al.*, *Samodeyatel'nye ob"edineniya molodezhi* (Kiev, 1989), p. 5; Plasky, *Molodezhnye gruppy* (1988), p. 33.
55 S. Nenashev, *S'Affirmer: les Informels de Léningrad* (1990), pp. 5, 10.

The System isn't an organization or a party and therefore everyone can simply be himself. The System is a society within a society. There can be no laws here, each person lives just according to the laws of his own conscience.[56]

The System, therefore, unlike official culture, respected diversity of outlook and belief, offered an atmosphere of cultural tolerance, giving the individual the freedom to express his personal feelings, opinions and inclinations without fear of censure or interference. It afforded the possibility of meeting like-minded people, who offered moral and where necessary material support to the non-conformist. Inevitably, in the Russia of the 1970s and 1980s, this network and the attitudes it supported took on an underground character.

The early 1980s saw several other attempts to form unofficial cultural[57] and feminist groups in Moscow and Leningrad. They were nipped in the bud and banned. *Kommunist* condemned these efforts by 'anti-social elements' to found clubs, theatres, societies and seminars, from which Lyudmila Alexeeva concludes that they must have been quite common.[58] However, it was not until the mid-1980s (especially 1986–87) that the number of informal groups and clubs grew dramatically. By the end of 1987, over 30 000 groups were estimated to exist.[59] They covered all sorts of interests and activities – rock music, fashion, sport, ecology and conservation.[60] Most of those involved were young.[61] By 1987, Muscovites had almost ceased to be

56 Gromov and Kuzin, *Neformaly* (1990), pp. 19–20.
57 See O. Rumyantsev, 'Pereraspredelitel'naya model'' in Yushenkov (ed.), *Neformaly* (1990), pp. 209–10.
58 Alexeeva, *Inakomysliya* (1984), pp. 353–4; S. Tsvigun, 'O proiskakh imperialisticheskikh razvedok', *Kommunist*, 1981, no.14, pp. 98–9.
59 *Pravda*, 27 December 1987. Over 1000 groups were thought to exist in Moscow alone by August 1987: see W. Laqueur, *The Long Road to Freedom* (London, 1989), p. 260. In 1986, the Ministry of Culture reckoned the number of amateur cultural groups at 100 000: Churbanov and Nelyubin, 'Neformal'nye' in Kuptsov (ed.), *Demokratizatsiya* (1990), p. 241. Tens of thousands of groups with millions of members existed by the end of 1989 according to Gromov and Kuzin, *Neformaly* (1990), p. 5. By 1990, 60 000 youth groups existed: V. Berseneva, *Razvitie samodeyatel'nosti* (Moscow, 1990), p. 4; Tolz, *Multi-party System* (1990), p. 11.
60 Plasky, *Molodezhnye gruppy* (1988), pp. 26–34. By 1986–7, amateur and leisure groups accounted for 60 per cent of all informal groups: A. Razumov *et al.*, *Molodezhi* (1989), p. 11. Gromov and Kuzin put the proportion of leisure groups at 90 per cent of informals. The Komsomol had identified 70 different kinds of activity being pursued by these groups at the end of the 1980s: Churbanov and Nelyubin 'Neformal'nye' in Pechenev and Vyunsky (eds), *Neformaly* (1990), p. 18.
61 In Spring 1987, one survey showed that 60 per cent of senior secondary students, 80

shocked by the *punki*, *metallisty*, *rokery* and *lyubery* on the streets, sporting green hair and pins in their noses and aggressively proclaiming an alternative outlook and values.

Youth subculture, like dissent and unofficial art, testified to the resilience of a Russian tradition whereby the private sphere assumed some of the functions of public life. Small gatherings of friends – which in other societies would have been purely private and insignificant – in Russia came to have political significance: as one of the few forms of association and channels of communication not formally subject to official interference and control, as an alternative, micro-society. It was on these micro-societies that the democratic movement, under Gorbachev, was to build. The social basis of disaffection, criticism and potential opposition to the regime was, therefore, quite complex and by no means confined to the dissident movement.

CONSTRAINTS ON THE SUBCULTURE

What prevented this subculture from breaking through the ice until the late 1980s? One of the reasons was the legal and practical restrictions on sociability. A regulation of 1932 prevented the emergence of any kind of public association or activity outside the Party's control for almost half a century. This situation only began to change with the adoption in 1986 of a new regulation governing amateur clubs and groups. It was far from being liberal in inspiration, but represented some progress in that it acknowledged the effective right to exist of non-Party public groups. It seems likely that the new regulation was inspired not so much by an enthusiastic endorsement of liberalism as by a recognition that a large subculture of independent groups already existed and that something needed to be done to bring them under the Party's control. Legal status was granted only after registration, the procedures for which were daunting and

cent of college students and 70 per cent of other young people were involved in the informal movement: V. Dobrynina *et al.*, *Samodeyatel'nye initsiativnye* (Moscow, 1990), p. 20. At the end of 1988, about half the population under 25 took part in informal clubs: Plasky, *Molodezhnye gruppy* (1988), pp. 6–7; Alexandrova, *Informelle* (1988), p. 5; Churbanov and Nelyubin, 'Neformalnye' in Kuptsov (ed.), *Demokratizatsiya* (1989), p. 241.

cumbersome.[62] Not surprisingly, many groups failed to cross all these hurdles successfully and it was commonplace for political clubs to be refused registration. In 1988, a first attempt was made to draw up a new law on association. Copies of the draft became available to the informals who debated it and even discussed it with officials in February 1988.[63] However, no agreement could be reached even within the Party about the law and several versions were rejected between 1987 and 1989 as unsatisfactory.[64] Not until June 1990 was a new law on association promulgated, which gave the informals full legal rights.[65]

Hence, the absence of any legal basis for the activities of informal groups and the concomitant penalties for being involved in them discouraged the development of a civil society. The fact that it was impossible openly to seek out people who shared one's outlook and interests led not just to the development of subcultures and underground activities, but also to the fragmentation of public life, to its disintegration into little isolated circles of people and activity. As Leonid Gordon pointed out, the absence of a civil society in Russia meant that no system of free contacts between people developed and hence that there was no tradition or habit of political self-organization in communities. Only in small enclosed professional groups (such as existed among the higher intelligentsia of the capitals, where the academic structures and creative unions, for all their shortcomings, served as channels of communication) was the pattern of contact and sociability characteristic of a civil society retained and indeed, it is in precisely these circles that Gordon locates the most active early support for reform.[66]

---

62 Official organizations, such as the Komsomol, trade unions or schools, were to sponsor the association which wished to register: it then had to be approved by (a) the local district authorities, (b) the cultural department of the local soviet, and (c) the next level up in the hierarchy of its sponsoring agency: Gromov and Kuzin, *Neformaly* (1990), pp. 51-2.

63 O. Rumyantsev, *O samodeyatel'nom dvizhenii* (Moscow, 1988), pp. 17-18; Berezovsky and Krotov, *Neformal'naya Rossiya* (1990), p. 242; Izyumova, 'Unofficial social movements', *MN*, 19, 8 May 1988, p. 10; MBIO Informal Archive: Folder on *Perestroika 88* includes a draft law on association, prepared in the club, in the context of this debate.

64 Tolz, *Multi-party System* (1990), p. 35; *MN*, 34, 20 August 1989.

65 R. Sakwa, *Gorbachev and his Reforms* (London, 1990), p. 210; I. Zaramensky, 'Opyanenie svobody', *Dialog*, 1990, no.15, p. 17.

66 Gordon, 'Working Class' in Merridale and Ward (eds.), *Perestroika* (1991), p. 89.

The disintegration of society and the resultant isolation of the individual partly accounts for the eerie emptiness of Soviet cities in the evenings. 'It is an unhappy lot to inhabit Petersburg', Dostoevsky observes in *Notes from the Underground*, 'the most abstract and the most premeditated place in the world.' The loneliness and bleakness of modern or reconstructed Soviet cities, however, which also derived from planning, far surpassed that of St. Petersburg. The paucity of congenial meeting places, in the shape of cafes, beer cellars and pubs, or heated halls open to the public, was deliberate and discouraged crowds from thronging the cities at night or groups and clubs from gathering or meeting.

Indeed, outside the capitals in provincial Russia, as an Estonian analyst has observed, it may be misleading to talk of cities in the sociological sense. Many provincial towns and cities, it has been suggested, were more like the urban fiefs of one or two big local factories (which monopolized local power and resources) than to modern cities. The factories owned the housing, provided most local employment, child-care facilities and special deliveries of consumer goods but were in turn subordinated to the central ministries in Moscow, which determined the local standard of living.[67] Given the power of the factory director over his staff and given that housing, pay and food depended on the factory, the local employee had little scope for independent behaviour: he had too much to lose and it was too easy to keep track of his activities.[68] It is questionable whether the city – in the sense of a community characterized by considerable autonomy and social and economic diversity[69] – existed in Russia to the extent that the scale of urbanization would suggest and it could be

67 Cited in Urban, *More Power to the Soviets* (Aldershot, 1990), p. 147.
68 Khasbulatov, *Byurokraticheskoe gosudarstvo* (1991), p. 195, affirms that the provinces were even less democratic than the centre and that the further one went from Moscow, the greater the extent of personal rule by the local Party chief. B. Yeltsin, *Against the Grain* (London, 1990), p. 57, remarks on the absolute power of the provincial Party first secretaries, a power tempered only by the need to maintain good relations with the ministries in Moscow; he also notes the physical isolation of many of the cities he ruled, some of which were several days' train ride even from Sverdlovsk and to which there was no adequate road – a factor that would have inhibited the exchange of ideas and the development of social life.
69 Max Weber observed: 'It is not altogether proper to call localities "cities", which are dominated by trade and commerce. [...] More than anything the ancient and medieval city was formed and interpreted as a fraternal association': Weber, *The City* (New York, 1966), pp. 66, 96.

argued that this inhibited the development of independent social and political life. Indeed, the democratic movement was largely confined to a small number of big cities in European Russia (above all to Leningrad and Moscow). As for the countryside, it was in the thrall of the Party, in the shape of the local collective or State farm chairman: on him depended not only employment, relative tranquillity and the few small comforts and perks available to the rural population, but also permission to travel within the country, for all but the briefest of trips, as internal passports were given to farm workers only with his permission. In addition, the rural population of Russia was composed of a disproportionate number of women and elderly people – generally more passive social categories. As a result, the democratic movement made negligible inroads in the countryside.[70]

These three factors – repression, isolation and the absence of a developed social life – combined to inhibit the emergence of a civic society and the public expression of alienation. Why then did public movements supporting democracy appear when they did? For all the complexity of late Soviet society, it was the Party's moves towards democratization and openness which were decisive in enabling the emergence of a democratic caucus in Russia.

---

70 Interviews with L. Ponomarev, 16 July 1990, and A. Kalinin, 9 July 1990, both of whom stressed the passivity of the countryside.

3. The Party and Reform

REASONS FOR CHANGE OF POLICY

Management Crisis

When the team headed by Gorbachev came to power in April 1985, the country faced a crisis. The growing inefficiency and backwardness of the economy made it more and more difficult to maintain the USSR's great power status especially in view of the additional pressures generated by Reagan's armaments programmes, notably the Strategic Defense Initiative. The new leadership was well aware of the need to modernize the economy but this presupposed being able to control it. In fact, the Brezhnev years had witnessed a decline in central power both over the economy and over the *apparat*.

A key element in the *pax Brezhneviana* had been the understanding between the Party cadres and the leadership that officials would not be subjected to rotation, brave new experiments in government or threats to their personal or material security: the iron discipline, based on the threat of violence, which under Stalin had assured order in the Party and in the country at large, was eroded. In return for quiescence and conformity, the Soviet population was rewarded with rising living standards. Unfortunately, higher levels of consumption were not matched by output and production and, thus, the rise in living standards was not sustainable.

The inbuilt distortions and inefficiencies of the economic system established under Stalin meant that it was always difficult to meet the ambitious targets set in the Plan, even when force was a significant stimulus in achieving higher output. When the threat of violence was removed, discipline among the workforce diminished and the temptation grew for the management to indulge in the long-established national tradition of the fabrication of statistics.[1] A tale recounted by Vitaly Vitaliev illustrates the phenomenon. The education ministry in Moscow decided in the 1970s that an agricultural college in the provincial town of Tula should open a branch in a remote district town. The project was not greeted with enthusiasm by the officials responsible for carrying out this order: the problem of resources, energy and effort seemed insuperable. So they came up with a solution worthy of Gogol: they invented the establishment, equipping it with an imaginary curriculum, staff and student body. Moscow was satisfied and paid the necessary subvention towards running costs, while the ingenious bureaucrats in Tula pocketed the proceeds.[2]

Hence, one of the effects of the decline in discipline was the growth of corruption. Planning had never envisaged balanced growth: some sectors (light industry, services, agriculture) were neglected and performed badly. The temptation to compensate for the deficiencies in supply by siphoning goods out of the official economy and establishing a second network, more attuned to people's actual needs, was overwhelming. Under Brezhnev, the second economy flourished alongside the official economy, greatly enriching elements in the Party *apparat* (district secretaries, factory managers etc.) who were best placed to control the flow of goods. The ultimate effect of these practices was to undermine further the already inefficient official economy, depriving the State of income and production, and to subvert the Plan - as it became increasingly difficult to control an economy whose real dimensions, mechanisms and flows were unknown.[3]

When Gorbachev and the new leadership took office in 1985, it was believed that inefficiency and corruption could be eradicated by

1 G. Hosking, *A History of the Soviet Union*, rev. ed. (London, 1990), pp. 377-8, 382, 386-7 for a short summary of these difficulties; T. Colton, *The Dilemma of Reform in the Soviet Union* (New York, 1986), pp. 32-57.
2 V. Vitaliev, *Special Correspondent* (London, 1990), p. 41.
3 H. Gelman, 'Gorbachev's Struggle' in U. Ra'anan and I. Lukes (eds.), *Gorbachev's USSR* (London, 1990), pp. 45-7; H. Ticktin, 'Political Economy' in *Critique*, 2, n.d., p. 7; S. White, *Gorbachev in Power* (Cambridge, 1990), pp. 85-7; Sakwa, *Gorbachev* (1990), pp. 82-5, 268; interview with V. Shostakovsky, 20 November 1990; A. Åslund, *Gorbachev's Struggle for Economic Reform* (London, 1989), pp. 13-21; P. Hanson, 'Industry' in M. McCauley (ed.), *Gorbachev and Perestroika* (1990), pp. 49-50.

increased pressure from above.[4] The programme to which the CPSU committed itself in February 1986, at the Twenty-Sixth Party Congress, did not envisage the dismantling of the centralized, planned economy, nor were its provisions on democratization and its calls for increased initiative and participation anything more than hortatory, in that they did not commit the Party to institutional reform. Reform was proclaimed rather than launched by the Congress, which limited itself to measures which, it was hoped, would get the existing economic system to work.

The problem was that nothing changed after the Congress: the economic indicators remained, for the key sectors, as low at the end of the year as in previous periods; the first attempts to revive the economy did nothing to boost either production or public initiative; old methods of work and planning, in the central agencies, ministries and institutes continued as before.[5] It became clear that not only was the system inherently difficult to improve and that more radical changes were necessary but also that there was considerable resistance to reform – not so much from the population at large as from the middle level of Party officials and managers, who should have implemented it.[6]

During the relaxed years of the *pax Brezhneviana*, Party discipline declined. By the early 1980s, the provincial Party first secretaries and republican leaders ran their regions largely as they saw fit.[7] Some commentators even considered the political and economic management of the country feudal.[8] The new leadership, which came to power in 1985, was soon to discover that the eradication of corruption, the tightening of discipline, the fight against the black economy and the improvement of the command economy (the initial reform platform, encapsulated in the term *uskorenie*, or acceleration) could not be achieved simply by issuing decrees and delivering long

4 S. White, *Gorbachev* (1990), pp. 23–4.
5 Åslund, *Gorbachev's Struggle* (1989), pp. 84–7, 111ff.
6 Gorbachev, Speech to January 1987 Plenum, *Izbrannye rechi* (Moscow, 1987), IV, pp. 304, 317ff; Khasbulatov, *Gosudarstvo* (1991), pp. 225–6.
7 Voslensky, *Nomenklatura* (London, 1985), p. 149; Yeltsin, *Against the Grain* (1990), p. 57.
8 See Yakovlev, *Lit.Gaz.*, 25 December 1991, p. 3; Afanasiev, interview with L. Karpinsky, 'Too free too soon', *MN*, 21 September 1990; R. Tucker, 'What time is it in Russian History?' in Merridale and Ward (eds.), *Perestroika* (1991), pp. 35–7.

exhortations. Everyone paid lip-service to the new policies but this outward conformism was not followed up with effective compliance. More than any other, it was this conundrum which forced the leadership (or one wing of it, led by the General Secretary, Gorbachev) into contemplating ever more radical measures.

The Erosion of Power

It was clear, therefore, that the fundamental problem concerned not merely the economic model adopted by the Soviet Union but its political model. This was the problem on which Khrushchev had foundered: the reluctance of the *apparat* to envisage change and the absence of any other levers of power or counterweight within the system. The difficulty was that the highly centralized Soviet system, devised so as to ensure total control of society, was predicated on the principle that strict discipline prevailed within the Party, that the orders of the centre would not be countermanded, ignored or sabotaged. By its very nature, the Party's power structure included (at least officially) no alternative chain of command, and, of course, no mechanism enabling external pressure groups to influence the way the country was run. This meant that where Party officials ignored the central authorities' instructions, government policy was effectively frustrated.

The problem which Gorbachev failed to solve, and which also frustrated the democrats after his fall, was thus one of power, or more exactly, of the difficulty encountered by the centre in imposing its will on the country.[9] This difficulty was not a new phenomenon, the result of growing sophistication and rebelliousness on the part of the ruled. On the contrary, students of Russian literature and history are

9 Shlapentokh, *Soviet Intellectuals* (1990), p. 7, makes this point. H. Ticktin, 'Political Economy', *Critique*, 2, p. 12, suggests that the administration's inability to make the economy deliver points to a general lack of control over society. R. Laird, *The Soviet Paradigm* (London, New York, 1970), pp. 109-15, pointed to the limitations which the enormous and conservative bureaucracy placed on the absolute ruler's power. T. Zaslavskaya, 'Korenny vopros perestroiki', *Izvestiya*, 4 June 1988, observed that the key problem in *perestroika* was power and that unless power were redistributed from the bureaucracy, which opposed reform, to the people, *perestroika* would fail. A. Nazimova and V. Sheinis, 'Vybory' in *SSSR: demograficheskii diagnoz* (Moscow, 1990), p. 670, cite Klyamkin's observation that the Party leadership had unlimited power to uphold what already existed but did not enjoy full powers where change was concerned.

familiar with the problem: the great distances and inadequate infrastructure, the power and attractions of inertia, the impracticability of central directives, corruption and a culture (both among the governed and the governors) which encouraged people to see the law as the embodiment of central arbitrariness, to be, as far as possible, ignored, got around or subverted.[10]

Western analysts have proposed a number of theories about how power was actually exercised in the Soviet Union in the post-Stalin period.[11] Some analysts argued that the Soviet Union was a totalitarian State, in which power was monopolized by the central leadership. The various proponents of pluralism pointed to the undue simplification of the totalitarian model, observing that the Party and higher echelons of State were not homogeneous but contained diverse interests and outlooks. What is more doubtful, however, is their suggestion that the power structure itself admitted or formalized any significant degree of pluralism. There was no formal mechanism for sharing power outside the highest Party organs (the Politburo and the Central Committee) and this made the capturing of key positions a prerequisite for exercising significant and consistent influence. Decision-making was limited to an entrenched and privileged minority: only the upper echelons of the Party *apparat*, and to some extent the research institutes, could expect to participate in the formulation of policies. They could not however organize themselves

10 Gogol remarked of this problem: 'A decree, no matter how precise and well thought out, is no more than a blank sheet of paper if there is no desire at lower levels to implement it in the right way': quoted in V. Shchepotkin and I. Karpenko, *Proryv v demokratiyu* (Moscow, 1990), pp. 208-9. The difficulty still exists. Ruslan Khasbulatov observes that local authorities who opposed a new law or order, instead of resorting to open resistance, simply issued implementing or interpretative instructions to their staff which contradicted the spirit of the original decree: Khasbulatov, *Gosudarstvo* (1991), pp. 225-6.

11 Five broad theories have been identified, among them the totalitarian model; the idea that interest groups were able to form but actually exercised little influence over an ideologically motivated *apparat*; and the theory of institutional pluralism, according to which different groups fought it out among themselves and the leadership merely mediated between them: see M. Macauley, *Politics and the Soviet Union* (London, 1977), pp. 151-67; see also S. White, *Political Culture* (1979), pp. 84-112, 143-90; D. Lane, *State and Politics in the USSR* (Oxford, 1985), pp. 257-64; M. Voslensky, *Nomenklatura* (1985), pp. 148-58; M. Djilas, *The New Class*, rev. ed. (London, 1957), pp. 37-69; H.G. Skilling and F. Griffiths, *Interest Groups in Soviet Politics* (1971); L. Schapiro, *The Communist Party of the Soviet Union*, rev. ed. (London, 1970), pp. 619-29.

formally around platforms or into groups of like-minded officials: the Tenth Party Congress in 1921 had specifically outlawed the formation of factions and this ban was reinforced by the Party's organizational rules, which forbade the formation of Party branches outside the workplace or place of residence and outside its strictly hierarchical framework.

The power system that resulted consisted of a network of informal alliances, based on patronage, shared interests and ideas and confined to a small elite. It was, therefore, neither strictly monolithic nor pluralistic, but competitive and clannish: the interests at stake were, in social and ideological terms, comparable rather than diverse. In fact, the lack of any formal mechanism for influencing policy appears to have bred inertia, with office rather than ideas at the centre of most of the players' concerns. Conditions in which it was impossible to organize openly around policies tended to de-ideologize politics. Perhaps even more than in the West, Soviet politics was power politics.

Power was exercised through an unofficial system of personal alliances, on the one hand, and the official Party and State machine, on the other. The former came into play to obtain office and define policy; the latter was supposed to promulgate and implement policy. By definition, the administration was politicized, as it consisted of competing networks of alliances or interest groups, which exploited their position for purposes of entrenchment or self-advancement. This nexus of interest groups tended to emasculate the power wielded by those at the top. No leader could ever hope to be entirely effective against these networks and his real power – or ability to translate his decisions into reality – was limited, above all, because he governed not with the aid of administrative machinery but through a heterogeneous political machine. Only to the extent that the leaders' policies coincided with the interests of this machine would his policies be implemented.[12] As Alexander Yakovlev commented: 'From the start of the 1970s [...] the Central Committee to all intents and purposes reigned but did not rule.'[13] Furthermore, no leader could hope to implement any set of active policies entirely successfully,

---

12 Zaslavskaya, *Izvestiya*, 4 June 1988, refers to the opposition to *perestroika* of clans formed by those involved in trade, the *apparat* and the black economy. Yeltsin insists on the importance of corruption as a force uniting bureaucrats and Party officials opposed to reform: Yeltsin, *Against the Grain* (1990), pp. 82-3, 96-7.

13 A. Yakovlev, *Predislovie, obval, posleslovie* (Moscow, 1992), p. 135.

because it would be impossible to buy off and reward all the competing networks in the system. There would always be those who would seek to exploit the unsettling effect of new policies to increase their power.

The result was that that it was easier to preside over the system than to attempt to govern through it. Any attempt to innovate – particularly if innovation threatened the interests and privileges of the *apparat* – created an automatic opposition, an opposition that was, furthermore, capable of frustrating the leader's rule. The clan system ensured that politics, under Brezhnev, was anything but dynamic. When Gorbachev tried to modernize the economy, he discovered that the real power system prevented any significant reform.[14] Under the existing system of power, the country was essentially unreformable. Had the system been pluralistic in the manner Jerry Hough seems to have believed – that is had different groups been able to determine policy – there would have been no need to envisage democratic reform. But the power system was closed and its pluralism entailed no more than competition between groups in the elite for office and its perquisites. In other words, the structures of power and the way they operated neither reflected the differences in outlook and orientation within the governing elite itself, nor enabled the dominant elite to rule effectively.

Change in the Party

The leadership's dissatisfaction became more acute throughout 1986, when it became clear that the modest management reforms already adopted were ineffective and the economy was not responding to attempts to revivify it. The greater the resistance of the Party managers to the reforms, the more sluggish the economy and the greater the need to envisage more radical measures. This in turn exposed the fault-line running through the new leadership – and indeed through the Party as a whole.

14 Alexander Yakovlev explained the origins of democratization in these terms: 'We wanted to solve the cadres problem because it was they [managers in enterprises and Party and State bureaucrats] who were acting as a brake on economic development and *perestroika*. But during the preparation, we came to the conclusion that it had to be much wider and include political reform – that is, democracy': cited in A. Roxburgh, *The Second Russian Revolution* (1991), p. 55.

There were two main alternatives: a return to a form of neo-Stalinism (more authoritarianism, central control and economic growth at the expense of the consumer) which had the support of one wing of the Politburo; or modernization based on a relaxation of central control. A number of factors inclined Gorbachev to the second option. Firstly, the information provided by the research institutes about the social preconditions necessary for a technological revolution and about the greater sophistication of Soviet society, as well as about the likely response of world opinion to the Stalinist option, inclined reformers in the leadership to try new, more sophisticated solutions.[15] Secondly, the Party itself had changed. The higher echelons of the *apparat* and institutes were no longer staffed, as under Stalin, by men like Suslov, Malenkov and Khrushchev, promoted from obscurity and poverty to high office, but in many cases, by the children and even grandchildren of that generation: privileged, sophisticated, well-educated – second- and third-generation experts.[16] They saw not only the untenability of the Stalinist alternative but also its likely consequences for their own positions and prerogatives. Thirdly, in the immediate group of advisers around Gorbachev were men who had been through it all before under Khrushchev and who were determined, this time, to succeed.

The Brezhnev years are frequently represented as having put an end to the innovations of the Khrushchev period and to the Party's tentative attempts, between the Twentieth and Twenty-Second Congresses, to recover its authority by renouncing Stalinism and defining a new identity and role for itself. But rather than annulling the experiment, the Brezhnev years suspended it. More exactly, they forced *apparatchiki*, who had come of age in the Khrushchev years and who had been infected with the hopes and illusions of the Thaw, underground or into uneasy collaboration with the Party's new line. Among these figures were Fedor Burlatsky, Georgi Arbatov, Oleg Bogomolov, Alexander Bovin and Georgi Shakhnazarov, who had served together in the Central Committee *apparat* in the early 1960s,

15 For the famous 1983 report by Zaslavskaya and Aganbegyan's arguments in favour of reform, see Sakwa, *Gorbachev* (1990), pp. 27, 50. Åslund, *Gorbachev's Struggle* (1989), pp. 4-6; Roxburgh, *Revolution* (1991), pp. 14-20, 33-4; Legostaev, 'God 1987', *Den'*, 14 July 1991.
16 See R.J. Hill, *Soviet Union* (1985), pp. 75-8, for the high proportion of Party members in the educated elite; G. Smith, *Soviet Politics* (1992), pp. 101-2.

before reemerging as advisers to Gorbachev in the mid-1980s.[17] That these so-called children of the Thaw played an important role in encouraging the leadership to move in the direction of democratic reform seems indubitable.[18] There was, in short, an influential body of opinion in the higher echelons of the Party that favoured liberal innovations and which, confronted with the resistance of the *apparat* to change, urged the adoption of more radical policies. The first of these was *glasnost*.

THE REFORMS

The Party and *Glasnost*: 1986–89

The first real change in the Gorbachev years came neither in the economy nor in the political system, but in culture and the media. Until the Nineteenth Party Conference, in the Summer of 1988, it was *glasnost* alone, in internal affairs, which made Gorbachev's reformist pretensions and his foreign policy initiatives credible. *Glasnost* – rather than any other area of internal policy – suggested that the new leader was serious about reform and it betokened a new era of relative liberalism, unparalleled since the time of Khrushchev. From the first tentative cracks in the absolute conformity in the press and cultural life, in 1986, *glasnost* developed into an overwhelming flood of information and debate by 1988 and, by late 1989 and early 1990, into freedom.

1. Origins
When Gorbachev adopted *glasnost*, he did not suddenly promulgate freedom of the press, as even a brief perusal of the Soviet papers in this period suffices to confirm. Three main theories have been advanced as to why *glasnost* was adopted. The first suggests that Gorbachev's economic advisers – led by Abel Aganbegyan – advised that without allowing society a modicum of initiative and information,

---

17 I. Podshivalov, 'Elected by Colleagues', *MN*, 22 April 1990, p. 14.
18 They furnished part of the contingent of academics who broached the need for a measure of democratic reform in the 1960s and 1970s: see R.J. Hill, *Soviet Politics, Political Science and Reform* (1980).

the economy could not be revitalized.[19] However, in the year between the June 1985 Plenum on the economy and the accident at Chernobyl at the end of April 1986, few concessions were made towards opening up society and reducing the strict controls on it. The second theory suggests that *glasnost* was prompted principally by Chernobyl, when the disastrous consequences of the delay in admitting the accident exacerbated its environmental and human costs, eroded the Party's standing in the Ukraine, and undermined the USSR's international prestige and Gorbachev's new foreign policy. According to this theory, Chernobyl revealed the damage which excessive secrecy could wreak on the Party, its policies and authority, and strengthened the hand of those, in the Party leadership and among its advisers, who argued for a less restrictive approach.[20] The third explanation for *glasnost* relates the new policy to the conventional use of information in Russia to discredit rivals and eradicate inefficiencies: in other words, *glasnost* may best be interpreted as a political tool in the hands of the new leadership.[21] In fact, all of these pressures and considerations played a role in generating *glasnost*. Paramount among them, however, was the political impact of information.

2. *Glasnost* and structures of control

That *glasnost* was not to be confused with freedom of the press and that it was a policy shrewdly used by Gorbachev and his supporters to strengthen his authority and lend weight to his arguments and policies is shown by the way *glasnost* developed. There was a clear divergence of views within the Party leadership on any change of policy on culture and the media. Resistance to reform was led by Yegor Ligachev – who reportedly opposed releasing any information about Chernobyl[22] – when he was number two in the Party hierarchy and Central Committee Secretary for ideology. This post placed Ligachev in a powerful position to frustrate liberal policies emanating from other quarters. Ligachev constantly stressed the importance of

19 Sakwa, *Gorbachev* (1990), p. 65; G. Smith, *Soviet Politics* (1992), p. 186; Smith goes on to point out the political uses to which Gorbachev put *glasnost*, ibid., pp. 186–7.
20 See 'Second Russian Revolution' (BBC television), 1990.
21 R.J. Hill, '*Glasnost'* and Soviet Politics', *Coexistence*, 26, 1989, pp. 319ff; Hill stresses, however, that *glasnost* was used also to win public support and strengthen the leader's authority.
22 Roxburgh, *Revolution* (1991), p. 41.

maintaining ideological purity, in all its vigour, as a mainstay of the regime. In this, he was supported by KGB chief Viktor Chebrikov, and, in the early days, by an absolute majority of the broadly conservative Politburo. This disposition of forces limited Gorbachev's freedom of manoeuvre: even had he wished to liberalize more quickly, he would have been unable to do so, for want of agreement within the Secretariat and Politburo. However, Gorbachev himself was to adopt a largely prescriptive approach to culture and the media and there is little evidence to suggest that he felt uncomfortable with the general organization of work in this area. Whether from constraint or temperament, Gorbachev made no attempt to dismantle the mechanisms of control over the media and culture but moved instead to capture them for his own lieutenants.

There were five main institutions through which the Party controlled the press and culture. These were: the Central Committee Secretariat and its departments; the Ministry of Culture and the State Committees for Publishing (*Goskomizdat*), the Press and Radio; the creative unions; the censorship board (*Glavlit*); and finally, the KGB. Ultimate control of intellectual life was in the hands of the Secretaries of the Central Committee and, on a day-to-day basis, of the Central Committee department chiefs, charged with supervising the arts and journalism. Chief among this constellation from the time of Mikhail Suslov was the Party Secretary for Ideology, who, since the early 1960s, had been a Politburo member and second in command of the Party. Suslov was a narrow-minded and dogmatic purist of authoritarian instincts, who successfully stifled culture and free expression from the mid-1960s until his death in 1982. Ligachev, when he inherited the ideology portfolio in 1985 (which he held until Summer 1988), conformed in both instinct and outlook to this pattern.

Within the Central Committee *apparat*, there were two main departments, from the mid-1960s on, which dealt with public opinion and the arts: the department of culture and that of propaganda and agitation. In July 1985, Gorbachev brought in Alexander Yakovlev, previously Ambassador to Canada (a position to which he had been banished for tangling with neo-Stalinist nationalists in the early 1970s) to head the propaganda department of the Central Committee. A series of personnel changes were gradually introduced as Gorbachev engaged in a long tactical battle against the emerging opposition to liberal policies in the Party leadership. In February 1986, Yakovlev was appointed to the Secretariat of the CPSU (that is, to the second rung of the leadership); his political ascent continued with his promotion, in January 1987, to candidate membership of the Politburo and, the following July, to full Politburo membership.[23]

Between 1986 and 1988, control of policy towards the arts and media was disputed between Yakovlev and Ligachev. Yakovlev was by professional background and temperament at odds with Ligachev, who had spent his life in the stifling atmosphere of the Party *apparat* in Siberia. Ligachev, with his full Politburo status and ideology portfolio, had a watching brief over the whole range of policy in the arts and the media. Not until July 1987, when he was promoted to the Politburo, was Yakovlev in a position to challenge Ligachev, and even then he was of lower rank. Until then, Yakovlev was technically subordinate to Ligachev, answerable for ideological deviations in the press and creative life. These tensions led to inconsistencies in the Party's line on *glasnost*.

The remit of the Central Committee in the field of cultural and press policy was broad. The press and media were controlled by the Propaganda Department (headed by Yakovlev) while the creative unions were under the care of the Cultural Department (and, once he attained Secretariat rank, also subordinated to Yakovlev). The departments maintained control in two main ways: firstly, through supervising the daily running of the press and unions; secondly, through appointments to key jobs (the famous *nomenklatura*). In the press, this meant that editors were in frequent contact with the Central Committee department, which periodically issued general guidelines and regularly intervened on delicate points with 'advice'. Phone calls, attendance at editorial board meetings and written instructions were the routine forms of supervision. From time to time, the editors of all the main papers would be summoned to the Central Committee to hear Party leaders outline the parameters within which they were expected to work. In instances where editors had exceeded their powers, they were apt to be summoned to the Central Committee to explain themselves, be reproached and, sometimes, be sacked. A further

23 Further changes included, in 1986, the replacement of Vasily Shauro, head of the Cultural Department for twenty years, with the relatively innocuous Y.A. Sklyarov and the removal of Brezhnev's long-standing Minister of Culture, Petr Demichev.

element of control was introduced by the news service TASS which on its internal network (for Soviet editors) circulated instructions on how internal press stories were to be handled. For example, internal TASS instructed editors at the end of October 1987 not to carry material on the Party Plenum in which Yeltsin attacked Ligachev and resigned, although this was hot news for the foreign press.

Generally, the Party ensured that its policies were unchallenged by appointing the editors of all papers and journals – the Central Committee nominating the editors of the main mass circulation papers, provincial Party committees controlling local papers. The State Committees for the media and the Ministry of Culture helped to implement the Party's policies, adding an extra layer of bureaucratic control, which, particularly in the arts, helped to frustrate any attempt at significant innovation. The censorship board, *Glavlit*, issued all publications with a fat book of instructions on forbidden topics and, until June 1986, every article had to be passed (and stamped) in advance by the Censor's office, which had a representative in every newspaper and magazine.[24] Finally, the KGB was present in all Soviet organizations, usually in the chancellery (or department responsible for handling incoming and outgoing mail) and in the department dealing with relations with foreigners.

A similar system applied to the arts and culture. Here, the Central Committee and its accessories (the Ministry for Culture and the KGB) worked mainly through the creative unions (which embraced all the arts, from cinema to architecture). These bodies had for the most part been established under Stalin to regiment the country's writers, artists, musicians, actors and film-makers. Their structures were virtually identical: they were run by a board composed of Party bureaucrats, assisted by compliant artists, and were subject to the constant supervision of the cultural department of the Central Committee (although other Central Committee departments might also get involved in their work). Membership of the union was essential for anyone interested in pursuing a career in the arts, as it alone guaranteed fame, privilege and livelihood. Without it, income, publication and access to the public were denied. To those who were members, however, the unions offered privileged housing, medical care and holidays; a form of social insurance; prestige, political

24 Interview with N. Ivanova, 29 November 1990.

influence and even the chance to travel abroad. Once within the embrace of the union, therefore, the threat to his well-being posed by expulsion or by deprivation of the not inconsiderable privileges the union afforded, was usually enough to curb any taste the artist might have for rash experimentation or unorthodox deviation.

The fundamentals of this system were not initially altered by Gorbachev and Yakovlev, although ultimately, between 1989 and 1991, their policies led to its collapse. At first, however, their intention seems to have been to gain control of the system, using it to advance their own policies, rather than to dismantle it. Once Yakovlev had been elevated to the CPSU Secretariat, in February 1986, he was able to appoint his own nominees to several key positions within the system. Within the claustrophobic world of the creative unions, the first stirrings of a new atmosphere were felt. In May 1986, the Union of Cinema Workers held its Congress in an atmosphere of unprecedented rebelliousness. The old leadership of the union was replaced, with Yakovlev's nominee – the film director Elem Klimov, some of whose films had in the past been banned – being elected First Secretary in a secret ballot.[25] Gorbachev emphasized his support for this trend by summoning selected writers and editors to the Kremlin, on 19 June 1986, to stress the need for more democracy and openness and the importance of the writers' support for these policies. 'We have no opposition', he is reported to have said. 'How are we then to control ourselves? [...] Through *glasnost.*' He thus encouraged the writers to become a loyal opposition.[26] The proceedings of the Writers' Union Congress, held shortly afterwards on 24–28 June 1986, provoked public amazement, with sharp debate dividing the conservatives from the pro-*perestroika* liberals in the union.

Following the Congresses, a wave of new appointments consolidated changes made earlier in the Spring. A series of new editors and media chiefs were appointed between February and Autumn 1986: chief among these were Vitaly Korotich, appointed to the magazine

25 Roxburgh, *Revolution* (1991), p. 45; Christie, 'The Cinema' in J. Graffy and G. Hosking (eds.), *Culture and the Media in the USSR Today* (London, 1989), pp. 44–5; interview with Klimov, 6 May 1992.
26 'Entretien', *Cahiers du Samizdat*, 125, February–March 1987, pp. 2–5; J. and C. Garrard, *Inside the Soviet Writers' Union* (London and New York, 1990), pp. 205–7, point to the political implications of this meeting.

Ogonek, and Yegor Yakovlev, who became editor of *Moscow News*.[27] These figures were not daring radicals but shrewd political players or cautious liberals, who pursued new controversial editorial policies, which were, however, broadly defined, as before, in the Central Committee. Before long, an appreciable – and in some cases, radical – difference in their publications' treatment of information and handling of material became evident.

Responding to the desire for change widely expressed by the intelligentsia in early Summer 1986, Yakovlev removed some of the constraints under which creative intellectuals had hitherto laboured. In June 1986, *Glavlit*'s political censorship functions, traditionally exercised *de facto* rather than *de jure*, were withdrawn. Articles no longer had to be submitted to *Glavlit* in advance, but the office continued to function until mid-1989, monitoring security questions.[28] In November 1988, its director even argued in *Izvestiya* for its necessity.[29] This did not mean that political censorship ceased to exist, but simply that editors' political antennae had to be more sensitive than hitherto and that direct contacts with the Central Committee became more frequent. Even the most radical editors (Yegor Yakovlev and Vitaly Korotich) were in regular contact with the propaganda department, the latter even boasting of his direct phone link with Alexander Yakovlev's office.[30] On all delicate matters most editors took advice from on high – 'publish and be damned' was not an attitude commonly adopted, even by the heroes of *glasnost*.[31]

Other changes affected the workings of the theatrical and cinema world, hitherto inhibited by the extraordinary maze of bureaucratic procedures elaborated since Stalin's time. In April 1986, following criticism from theatre directors, an experiment giving theatres more freedom to decide their repertoires was announced, to take effect the following year. The theatre had hitherto been overwhelmed by bureaucracy. Theatres had to work to a plan agreed with the Ministry

---

27 Others included Mikhail Nenashev appointed to Goskomizdat, Ivan Frolov to *Kommunist*, Grigory Baklanov to *Znamya* and Sergei Zalygin to *Novy mir*: see J. Graffy, 'The literary press' in Graffy and Hosking (eds.), *Culture and the Media* (1989), pp. 107-8.
28 Roxburgh, *Revolution* (1991), p. 44.
29 *Izvestiya*, 2 November 1988, p. 3.
30 Interview with V. Korotich, 6 December 1990.
31 Interview with Igor Klyamkin, 15 May 1992.

of Culture and the Central Committee department. If a company wanted to introduce a new work, it had to consult about a dozen different committees, some of which also depended on other agencies. So many approvals were needed and so many people had to read the play, one Soviet critic commented, that if by some chance it were approved, the director might well have died or resigned. The theatre had thus almost no right of initiative or room for manoeuvre. The pay of its staff was unrelated to their popularity or to the quality of their work. On the contrary, the system encouraged the production of bland, safe and boring works.[32] The Leningrad director Georgi Tovstonogov recalled that on one occasion a play he proposed to produce on the small stage of his theatre was inspected by a three-man commission from the Ministry of Culture, which made 164 separate comments on it, concerning not politics but artistic interpretation. Even the title was changed.[33] The limited experiment announced in 1986 was thus warmly welcomed.[34] The inanities of the existing system also prompted the reorganization of the theatre world with a new Theatre Workers' Union emerging headed by the conformist but pro-*perestroika* actor, Mikhail Ulyanov, in December 1986. The new union, it was hoped, would protect the artistic freedom of directors and theatres and help actors, particularly the young, with their material problems.[35]

A similar system prevailed in the film world, where it required great patience, skill and good connections to get a script approved. In many cases, where permission had been granted, it was ultimately rescinded by one of the many instances involved – from the direction of the centralized studio, *Goskino*, the relevant Central Committee department. As a result, many films had been shelved, as offensive to the canons of artistic or ideological orthodoxy proposed by the Party. With Klimov's election to the board of the Cinema Workers' Union, many of these decisions were reversed and several controversial films were finally released (not, at times, without political battles that

32 Goncharov, *SK*, 16 January 1986; Tovstonogov, *Lit.Gaz.*, 25 December 1985, p. 8 for similar comments; Yefremov in *Pravda*, 21 February 1986, p. 3.
33 SK, 9 December 1986.
34 For a caustic assessment of its effects, see M. Glenny, 'Soviet Theatre' in Graffy and Hosking (eds.), *Culture* (1989) pp. 82–3.
35 Lavrov, *SK*, 6 December 1986; Laqueur, *Long Road* (1989), pp. 99–100.

required the intervention of Alexander Yakovlev).[36] The result of these policies was twofold: by introducing a measure of artistic and intellectual freedom, they won for Gorbachev the support of much of the Moscow- and Leningrad-based intelligentsia and educated opinion at large; and they enabled new themes to be broached which legitimized the leadership's new policies.

3. *Glasnost* as a political tool

The word *glasnost* is not a new one. It was modish in the early 1860s when its ambiguities provoked the irony of contemporary satirists. Under Gorbachev, many writers and journalists observed that 'openness' or 'publicity' (the nearest equivalents of *glasnost* in English) was not synonymous with freedom of the press but meant merely that the government might now tolerate the publication of previously banned material, when that was convenient.

This was amply borne out by the initial workings of *glasnost*. From 1987 on, the truth about Stalin's crimes and those of the Brezhnev period was gradually allowed to emerge. This policy was determined in the first place not by principle but by expedient. 'Filling in the blank spots', as Gorbachev called it, was not initially a question of uncovering what really happened in history, truth for truth's sake, but an exercise designed to legitimize the latest policy departure. At first, the corruption of Brezhnev's associates was exposed, for both practical and tactical reasons, partly as a pretext for dismissing them and replacing them with political allies.[37] This practice had been not uncommon in the provincial press before *perestroika* and now became widespread. Shocking revelations were also made about the inefficiencies of the economic system under Brezhnev and about the social decline - reflected in the rise of alcoholism, infant mortality and abortion and in the decrease in life expectancy, due to an ill-funded health system. Soviet society now had to digest unwelcome truths, such as that prostitution, drug abuse and, ultimately, AIDS were not the exclusive preserve of decadent capitalism but existed in the USSR

36 Interview with E. Klimov, 6 May 1992.
37 See R.J. Hill, '*Glasnost*'', *Coexistence*, 26, 1989, pp. 320-31, who sees *glasnost* as part of a broader reformist policy as well as a proxy weapon.

also.[38] The net effect of this was to shake the Soviet public's faith not only in the old guard, as Gorbachev intended, but ultimately in the system itself (which he did not).

Similarly, when it was decided that a measure of private enterprise should be introduced into the Soviet economy, it was politically necessary to find a precedent for this – to show that it was not an ideological diversion. The precedent was the NEP, approved by Lenin, and whose principal apologist was Bukharin. The introduction of the first batch of laws promoting enterprise in June 1987 was accompanied by the gradual rehabilitation of the NEP and the restoration of Bukharin to the pantheon of socialist leaders and theoreticians, early the following year.[39] Other famous victims of the show trials of the 1930s were rehabilitated as the campaign for the establishment of a law-abiding state gained momentum. Similarly, the horrors of collectivization continued to be ignored or referred to in ambiguous language (sometimes being called 'mistakes' or 'distortions') because of Ligachev's resistance to the reform of agriculture. Not until after the Nineteenth Party Conference was Gorbachev's position strong enough to allow him to introduce long-term land-leases and family contracts in agriculture – a measure which was finally accompanied by the first high-level condemnation of the cruelties associated with collectivization. In the context of this ebb and flow of political forces, history became a pretext, as *glasnost* was a tool, in the tactical battle for power. *Glasnost* – in so far as it involved the publication of the truth about the past and about present corruption and inefficiency – made the conservative position more and more difficult to defend.

It is not surprising, therefore, that editors found themselves receiving occasionally contradictory instructions and exhortations from the Central Committee and that Gorbachev encouraged them to

---

38 See S. White, *Gorbachev* (1990), pp. 60–72 for a survey of some of this literature. Even a perusal of the plays that caused a stir in 1986 indicates this: *Speak*, about local Party leaders trying to improve the lives of and motivate ordinary people; *Silver Wedding* (A. Misharin), also about the dilemmas of Party life; *Dictatorship of the Conscience* (Shatrov); and *Two Views from One Office* (Burlatsky) on debates between two Party Secretaries on the problems of reform. Biting satires of the system such as Bulgakov's *A Dog's Heart* had to wait until 1988.

39 See Curtis, 'Literature' in Merridale and Ward (eds), *Perestroika* (1991), p. 177, who relates the permission given to stage Shatrov's *Brest Peace* to this and observed that Gorbachev turned up at the premiere and embraced the author.

be open, while Ligachev reminded them of the limits of toleration.[40] It is easy to understand why most editors were cautious about testing the limits of official toleration. As the parody of Pushkin, then doing the rounds in Moscow, had it:

> Comrade, believe me, it won't last,
> This so-called *glasnost*,
> And then you'll see the KGB
> Will remember your names eternally.

Few journalists or writers in the official press anticipated the nod given from on high. In short, the concessions made to the press, rather than representing a conversion to liberalism, reflected a political battle within the Party leadership. Editors, journalists, writers, film directors and theatre companies were inevitably drawn into this battle. As *glasnost* developed, differences in orientation between radical and anti-reform papers and literary journals became more acute, reflecting the sharp polarization of opinion both within the Party leadership and the intelligentsia.[41]

Despite these changes, *glasnost* still did not amount to freedom of the press. The limitations on freedom of information were evident throughout this period until 1990: foreign affairs, defence and security policy were largely exempt from *glasnost* until the democratic reforms of 1989. Gorbachev did not intend to allow foreign policy, an area on which he concentrated particular attention between 1986 to 1988, to be openly challenged or criticized in the press. Nor did Gorbachev take to criticism of his person: when *Argumenty i fakty* published an opinion poll, in May 1989, which rated Gorbachev's

40 In speeches and statements of February, July and November 1987 Gorbachev called for more openness: Gorbachev, *Izbrannye rechi*, III, p. 162; IV, p. 373; V, pp. 397–402. In articles in *Kommunist* in April 1987, in *Problemy mira* in July 1987 and speeches of August 1987 at Elektrostal and February 1988 to Plenum, Ligachev attacked *glasnost*; in September he demanded the resignation of Yegor Yakovlev, the editor of *MN*: Ligachev, *Izbrannye rechi* (1989), pp. 189, 202, 206–8, 246–7, 277.

41 The radical papers and magazines were *Ogonek*, *Moscow News* and *Argumenty i fakty*, with *Izvestiya* and *Komsomol'skaya pravda* following a left of centre line; *Pravda*, *Trud*, *Sovetskaya Rossiya*, *Sotsialisticheskaya industriya* and *Krasnaya zvezda* showed little receptivity to the new approach. Among the literary journals *Oktyabr* and *Znamya* (with a small circulation) led the radical wing, followed by *Druzhba narodov*, *Novy mir* and *Yunost'*, while the right wing was occupied by *Nash sovremennik* and *Molodaya gvardiya*.

popularity below that of leading radicals in the Congress of People's Deputies, he carpeted the editor Starkov and threatened to dismiss him.

The limitations on *glasnost* were illustrated most dramatically by Chernobyl and by the Nina Andreeva affair. Andreeva, a teacher in an institute in Leningrad, printed a sharp attack on *perestroika* and *glasnost* from the vantage point of Stalinism, in *Sovetskaya Rossiya* on 13 March 1988. Gorbachev was at the time abroad in Yugoslavia and Ligachev had profited from his absence to have the Andreeva letter given particular prominence. Lest editors miss the point, he summoned them to the Kremlin to hear his plaudits of the article and to urge them to reproduce it. For three weeks, *glasnost* was suspended. None of the daring editors of the left risked challenging Ligachev's instructions. It was not until Gorbachev's return and the issuing of a sharp rebuke to Andreeva and denunciation of her views in *Pravda* on 5 April 1988, that the liberal intelligentsia and editors again ventured to express themselves. The episode served to show that *glasnost* was not irreversible and that the press – whether liberal or conservative – continued to be controlled by the Party and to take its line from it. The need for a press law, to guarantee press freedom, was now clear to all liberals, but although the Nineteenth Party Conference in July 1988 adopted a resolution on *glasnost*, the introduction of a press law had to await the convocation of the semi-democratic parliament and was not promulgated until June 1990.

4. From *Glasnost* to freedom

When, then, did *glasnost* become effective freedom of the press? Not until the Party's own structures of government had been radically altered and authority had been transferred from the Party to partially democratic State structures. Igor Klyamkin dates the change from May 1989, when – on the wave of the euphoria which accompanied the defeat of the Party *apparat* in the elections – a new mood swept the country.[42] The radical editors who had worked under the guidance of Yakovlev had freedom thrust on them: there was a general expectation that they would support the radicals in the Congress, that

42 Interview of 15 May 1992.

they would be no less daring than their parliamentary colleagues. To have retreated into caution at this point would have meant to lose face. Besides, the old Central Committee structures had been revised – with the propaganda department reduced in size and merged with other departments, under a new and largely emasculated Central Committee Ideology Commission, chaired by the cautious Vadim Medvedev. Given the tendency of political developments and the thrust of the reforms, it required no overwhelming courage to pursue more or less independent editorial policies. Many editors now looked forward to new conditions in which they and their staff could take over their newspapers and journals and run them as independent companies.

The net effect of Gorbachev and Yakovlev's reforms on intellectual life should not be underestimated. They deliberately broadened the scope of public debate and comment, realizing that otherwise their attempts at economic reform would be defeated. Even if liberty was not the initial goal, it was – as the conservatives understood better than Gorbachev – the likely result of the cultural ferment that followed. Even if Gorbachev himself did not at first see how far he would have to change the way the press and cultural life were run, it gradually became apparent that, for his policies to succeed, the press needed ever-increasing doses of liberty. Hence, for all his own early statements about the need for an intellectual freedom that did not challenge socialism, he came to accept that socialism needed democracy and liberty.

Democratic Reforms

It is by no means clear that the leadership intended to introduce a multiparty parliamentary system (a model that was proposed by only a tiny minority of dissidents). Within the institutes, various alternatives for democratic reform were advanced, for example by B.N. Kurashvili in the Institute of State and Law, but none went so far as to suggest the dismantling of the Party's hegemony.[43] Gorbachev himself seems to have been in sympathy with Bukharin's

43 For an account of this debate, see S. White, *Gorbachev* (1990), pp. 29-32.

relatively liberal views on public life and to have believed that political pluralism was compatible with rule by the CPSU.[44] The concept of socialist pluralism was to become Party orthodoxy between June 1988 and February 1990, when it was reluctantly abandoned in the face of mass pressure. It was the promulgation of this concept of socialist pluralism at the Central Committee Plenum in January 1987, and again in June that year when the Party committed itself to calling a Party conference to discuss its application, that enabled the development of an independent political movement.

The Plenum of January 1987 committed the Party to increased democratization of Party and State structures. Speaking to the Plenum, Gorbachev argued for the need to underpin economic and political reform with an element of control from below.[45] He promised that the elections to the local Soviets, which were to be held later that year, would be conducted in a new atmosphere. In March 1987, it was announced that, to improve on this system on an experimental basis, several candidates would be offered to the electorate in a small number of multiple-seat constituencies. Although this only affected about one per cent of constituencies and four per cent of candidates, it nonetheless represented a significant departure from earlier practice – when only one candidate ran for each seat and voting procedures discouraged a negative vote. As usual, the Party organized nominations and ran the campaigns of the candidates but the element of choice made it harder to control matters and a number of inside candidates failed to get elected.[46] This form of election met with some popular approval.

However, these tentative measures in no way suggested that sweeping constitutional and electoral reforms were envisaged by the Party leadership. The evidence suggests that there was considerable disagreement within the Politburo about how to proceed and not until the conclusion of the Party Conference, in July 1988, were sweeping democratic reforms announced. However, throughout the

44 Gorbachev, Speech to February 1987 Trade Union Conference, *Izbrannye rechi* (1987), IV, p. 431.
45 Gorbachev, Speech to Plenum, 27 January 1987, *Izbrannye rechi* (1987), IV, pp. 316–29.
46 White, 'Political Reform' in Merridale and Ward (eds), *Perestroika* (1991), pp. 3–13, for a succinct account of changes in the system of local elections in 1987; see also Urban, *Soviets* (1990), pp. 22–3, 41–2; Andryushchenko, *MN*, 1989, no. 3, p. 8, on the limits and shortcomings of this exercise.

intervening period, Gorbachev constantly reiterated his commitment to democratization,[47] while other members of the leadership made clear their opposition to any moves towards political pluralism.[48] The Winter of 1987-88 showed how determined the conservatives were to resist reform policies. Boris Yeltsin's indiscretions, in the Autumn of 1987, gave them their opportunity to stage a comeback.[49] Between October 1987 and April 1988, they were in the ascendant. To avoid Khrushchev's fate, Gorbachev introduced fundamental constitutional reforms at the Nineteenth Party Conference.

Despite being packed with conservatives, the Conference, which was held between 28 June and 1 July 1988, was remarkable on a number of counts. It inaugurated a series of institutional reforms, which, by making the soviets (parliaments) to some degree representative and responsible, laid the foundation for the new democratic structures in the country. It prepared a shift in the focus of political activity (if not in the actual balance of power) away from the Party to the soviets. It gave Soviet citizens a sense that new parameters governing political activity had been set.

The Conference was manoeuvred by Gorbachev – in a stroke of tactical genius – into committing itself to a tight timetable for the sweeping democratization of Party and State structures.[50] The main changes, as they emerged from the constitutional reform promulgated between 29 November and 1 December 1988, involved the creation of a new supreme legislative body – the first more or less democratically elected, permanent legislature in Soviet history, the Congress of People's Deputies – and a new electoral law, providing for competitive elections. Steps were to be taken to create an independent judiciary and to democratize the Party, by introducing a system of

---

47 Gorbachev, *Izbrannye rechi* (1987), IV, pp. 357-8, 316-31.
48 Ligachev, *Izbrannye rechi* (1989), pp. 174, 200-201, 210, 246; Chebrikov in speech on 104th anniversary of Felix Dzerzhinsky's death, *Pravda*, 11 September 1987; Shcherbitsky's apologia for Stalinism, *Pravda*, 26 December 1987.
49 For this affair, see Yeltsin, *Against the Grain* (1990), pp. 9-12, 142-57; J. Morrison, *Boris Yeltsin* (London, 1991), pp. 57-73. *Moskovskaya pravda*, 13 November 1987; M. Poltoranin, 'Besuch bei Boris Jelzin', *MN*, German edn, 1988, no. 2; K. Devlin, 'Soviet Journalist', *RFE/RL* 206/88, pp. 1-9; Ligachev interview with M. Tatu and D. Vernet, *Le Monde*, 4 December 1987; Roxburgh, *Revolution* (1991), pp. 72-8.
50 It was only as the Conference was about to close that Gorbachev drew a handwritten note from his pocket; it apparently contained the rough draft of a resolution committing the Party to a strict timetable for the implementation of the reforms: Roxburgh, *Revolution* (1991), pp. 101-2.

internal elections to replace the nomination of officials from above. An element of openness and accountability was to be introduced into the Party's activities, while the Party's administrative and executive functions were to be separated.

The most dramatic change was the institution of an All-Union parliament or Congress of People's Deputies. It was to consist of 2250 deputies: 750 elected from constituencies reflecting the actual distribution of the population in the USSR; 750, as before, from national territorial constituencies (designed to secure adequate representation for the nationalities); and 750 from public organizations. The Congress would elect a working legislature, the Supreme Soviet, of 542 full-time deputies which would meet for two three- or four-month sessions a year. The Congress would elect a Chairman, to be combined with the leadership of the Party.[51]

It has been suggested that this reform was achieved by diverting attention away from the depth of the changes envisaged and by compromising on the reforms themselves. Another explanation may be that opponents expected to be able to filibuster indefinitely and that the Conference was manoeuvred into committing itself to a tight timetable for implementation almost unawares. The system was far from being fully democratic. A number of filters were included in the electoral system, through which the Party elite seemed likely to be able retain decisive control over the elections and the new institutions.[52]

The key element in the reform package involved electoral and parliamentary reform. The old soviets were parliamentary assemblies in name only: in practice, they were subservient bodies constructed and controlled by the Party. The composition of the old soviets was therefore determined not by the electorate but by the Party. Although participation levels were recorded at 99.4 per cent and 99.8 per cent, personation and fraud were thought to be widespread and actual participation levels were thought to be closer to 75 per cent – not that this had much meaning when candidates were commonly unknown to voters: one survey conducted in 1988 showed that only five per cent of electors could even name a candidate. The old soviets were

51 Ibid., pp. 117ff; Urban, *Soviets* (1990), pp. 4–10, 45–6; Sakwa, *Gorbachev* (1990), pp. 133–6.
52 Urban, *Soviets* (1990), p. 49.

therefore powerless and subservient bodies. Until 1987, the only time a dissenting vote had been recorded on any proposal put to the Supreme Soviet was in 1955: in the intervening years, unanimity had prevailed. The result was a parliament that neither could nor would show any capacity for critical activity. In any case, the soviets met so infrequently as to be unable to fulfil any policy or monitoring function. The old Supreme Soviet met for three or four days a year and its members worked in the soviet on a part-time basis.[53]

One of Gorbachev's democratic innovations was to allow the nomination of candidates from below, by meetings of 500 ordinary citizens assembled at their place of residence or at work. This provision for the first time enabled Soviet citizens to nominate candidates. Hitherto, by providing only for nominations from the workplace, the law had enabled the Party to impose nominations, because of the dependence of the workforce on the factory management. The new possibility of nominating candidates from place of residence enabled the promotion of independent candidates (that is candidates not sponsored by the Party). These independents were also entitled to funds to conduct their campaigns and to pay a small electoral team (of ten agents), another helpful novelty.

However, this right of nomination was eroded by the creation of electoral commissions, in practice controlled by the Party, whose task it was to supervise the local elections and screen and register candidates. Frequently, these commissions prevented the registration of independent candidates, either by refusing or ignoring alternative nominations, or, when it had been impossible to refuse a public meeting of electors to register the candidates, by packing the hall with subservient audiences. These procedures ensured the elimination of numerous democratic and independent candidates, before the electorate had had a chance to vote.

A final distortion in the 1989 elections to the Congress of People's Deputies consisted of the right of public organizations to nominate a third of all deputies to the Congress. In this way, the Party was able to 'elect' 100 deputies (in fact, the Politburo nominated itself and other members of the Central Committee) and Party-dominated bodies

53 S. White, 'Political Reform' in Merridale and Ward (eds.), *Perestroika* (1991), pp. 3–13; Andryushchenko, *MN*, 1989, no. 3, p. 8; Nazimova and Sheinis in *SSSR* (1990), p. 654; Ivanova (ed.), *Intelligentsiya* (1987), p. 210.

– such as the trade union organization, the women's committee, the farmers' organization – were able to nominate a solid rump of conservative deputies. The intelligentsia, however, rebelled and the Academy of Sciences and creative unions ultimately elected many democratically inclined representatives.

Only in March 1990 was this structure completed by the election of republican parliaments (under a now fully democratic electoral system) and the transformation of the role of Chairman of the Congress into the executive State president, with powers of nomination of the government and other leading officials, a suspensory veto on legislation and the right to rule by decree. The creation of the Presidency seems to have been prompted, above all, by the Party's loss, if not of hegemony, at least of its political monopoly in February–March 1990.

The thrust of the reforms launched by the Conference was to allow freer competition within the Party, thereby breaking down the old power structures in the CPSU and creating new bases of authority and power in the Party at local level. Its aim was to weaken the power of the *apparat* and to enable the reform leadership to introduce the necessary changes to the system of economic management. What appears to have been envisaged initially was not undiluted popular rule and formal political pluralism (as the reforms did not introduce a fully democratic system) but a broadening of the basis of and scope for competition for power within the Party and the encouragement of wider participation in Party rule. Between January 1989 and January 1990, however, the divergences of view and interest within the Party became manifest and spilled out of the Party into wider public life, fuelling both the democratic and nationalist, neo-Stalinist, movements. The Party may be said to have prompted and formulated the democratic reforms, both through its shortcomings (which made reform necessary) and through its more enlightened members, who saw the need for change. However, it failed to control the changes it introduced, partly because the CPSU itself was not, as has often been observed, really a political party, but a number of parties, and also because society at large responded in unanticipated ways to the reforms.

4. The Impact of *Glasnost*

Between 1986 and 1989, Soviet society was exposed for the first time to a flood of hitherto suppressed information about the failures, inefficiencies and inequities of the Soviet system, about its crimes against its own citizens and the corruption of its rulers. Ordinary citizens were confronted with uncomfortable truths and questions, which obliged at least some of them to reassess their attitudes to the regime. A leading role in this process was played by the anti-Stalinist intellectuals of the elite, who had formed their views under the Thaw and were enthusiastic about Gorbachev's extension of the parameters of public debate and his broached reforms.

Until 1988, *perestroika*'s main effect was on cultural life, rather than on the economic or political system. The gradual opening of Soviet society involved the recovery of Russian identity – the discovery of the past, the true lineaments of which began to be revealed to the Soviet public only in 1987, and the assimilation of Russia's cultural inheritance, particularly of the modern Russian experience. Under Stalin the CPSU had effectively destroyed the traditional basis of society. The integration of Russia's intellectual elite into the culture of Europe had been ended: links with the outside world, and with Western Europe in particular, had been severed and many of the assumptions and values associated with European high culture of the nineteenth century (the primacy of individual moral inquiry, the autonomy of culture), which the *intelligenty* of the nineteenth century had generally embodied (if not always professed) were challenged and condemned. Just as most of the churches and monasteries were ruined, so too the spiritual heritage of Orthodoxy had been, as far as possible, obliterated. It was all but impossible, until recently, to buy religious literature in Russia and it was a crime to impart one's religious beliefs to one's children.

In these circumstances, the publication of the banned poetry of

Akhmatova, Gumilev and Mandelstam, of Grossman's *Life and Fate* and Pasternak's *Doctor Zhivago*; the unveiling of the magnificent collections of Russian modernism (including the work of Kandinsky, Lentulov, Popova, Udalstova, Malevich and Filonov); the revelation of the truth about present shortcomings and past tragedies – all this amounted to a recovery of consciousness. The years 1986-89 were marked by the reawakening of the Russian thinking public and a partial rediscovery of its traditional role by the Westernizing intelligentsia. These changes contributed to a development of real importance – the rebirth of Russian public opinion and public life.

This recovery was achieved through the exploration of three main themes: the shortcomings of the present (which led to the problem of the CPSU's policies and its responsibility for the current predicament); Stalinism and its legacy (which raised the question of whether Stalinism was a distortion or a natural outgrowth of Leninism); and the recovery of national identity, through the rediscovery of the country's cultural and historical heritage.

Initially, the exploration of the first theme was encouraged by Gorbachev and his supporters, as it helped to legitimate their new policies. In 1986 and until mid-1987, *glasnost* tended to concentrate on instances of corruption and inefficiency, rather than on the exploration of 'slippery' cultural themes, but as Alexander Yakovlev's position was consolidated, so too the subjects covered by *glasnost* multiplied. First among the previously taboo topics to be explored was the legacy of Stalin.

STALINISM

In 1987, the exploration of Stalinism and its significance began in the Soviet press.[1] Speaking in February 1987, Gorbachev pronounced that there should be no more 'blank spots' in Soviet history – a change from his attitude the previous year, when he had told the French Communist paper *l'Humanité* that Stalinism was an invention of opponents of communism, who wished to discredit it.[2] Once this

---

1 For an account see S. White, *Gorbachev* (1990), pp. 60-66; A. Nove, *Glasnost in Action* (Boston, MA, 1989), pp. 15-36, 73-102.
2 Gorbachev, *Rechi* (1987), III, p. 162; IV, p. 373.

statement of policy had been made, journals began to fill with articles, stories and novels in which Stalinism was analysed. There were three aspects to this examination. The first involved the revelation of the truth about those who had been defamed, executed or exiled: this gradually broadened into a wider reassessment of Stalinist policies (on industrialization and collectivization). The second entailed an indictment of the political and legal system which allowed Stalin to exercise his tyranny. Finally, as a consequence of the growing rejection of Stalinism, Russians were brought to the point of examining their own complicity in, and hence responsibility and guilt for, what had happened.

Initially, the reassessment of the past, in official statements, proceeded cautiously. By the end of 1987, the Terror of 1937 was deplored and *Ogonek* was allowed to publish Bukharin's testament as recalled by his widow. Bukharin himself was not finally rehabilitated until the start of the following year, however. Expectations of Gorbachev's speech on the seventieth anniversary of the revolution, in October 1987, were high, but he stopped short of condemning Stalinism - referring instead to certain excesses and deformations in policy - and skirted around the question of collectivization, which, it had been hoped, he would criticize. However, he did announce that a Party Commission had been established (chaired initially by Mikhail Solomontsev and subsequently by Alexander Yakovlev) to re-examine the legal judgments and records of the period; while a new history of the Party was to be issued.[3] The Commission's work resulted in the posthumous rehabilitation not only of Bukharin, but ultimately of hundreds and thousands of others too - from Kamenev and Zinoviev, to those implicated in the Leningrad affairs and the 'doctors' plot' of the late 1940s and early 1950s, and then on to thousands of more obscure cases.

The revelation of the extent of Stalin's crimes inevitably raised other questions, with more immediate political consequences. Initially, Soviet intellectuals were obsessed with the question once asked by Alec Nove: was Stalin really necessary? The past, observed Andrei Fadin, of the *Perestroika* Club, still hung over them, preventing them from discussing the material problems and difficulties of the present.

---

3 Gorbachev, ibid., V, pp. 397-402. For tentative moves to rehabilitate Bukharin, see *Ogonek*, 1987, no. 48; *MN*, 1987, no. 49.

People felt impelled to conduct an agonized examination of the past, to see whether or not Stalinism had been inevitable.[4] Numerous polemical historical articles were published on this theme. Among the most famous of these was Igor Klyamkin's 'Which street leads to the Church?', which concluded that the weight of tradition, the array of problems faced by the Soviet Union in the late 1920s, made the Stalinist option the most effective at the time.[5] Others – such as Andrei Nuikin and Nikolai Selunin – disagreed, while economists such as Gavriil Popov and Nikolai Shmelov argued that the Stalinist system, based on a tyranny, was no longer effective and should be abolished.[6] Having concluded that Stalin's rule had not only been bloodthirsty but had also failed to create an effective economic system, Soviet intellectuals and society at large went on to condemn the political and legal system he had established and which had survived, only slightly modified, until the present.

The lesson that the Stalinist experiment had been misguided and that the Soviet peoples had, to some extent, been responsible for allowing it to happen was difficult to digest. There was a widespread reluctance to admit that Stalin had been a tyrant: photographs of the former leader could still be seen routinely stuck in the cabs of lorries and taxis. People still liked to repeat myths about the widespread availability of caviar in the shops under Stalin; prices, under the dictator, had gone down – not up, as under Gorbachev; there had been no crime; people had been idealistic and honest, not cynical and corrupt, as today. And even if a few innocent people had been condemned, what about Stalin's great achievements – industrialization, collectivization and winning the War? These sentiments – which chose to overlook the misery and poverty of the country under Stalin, the great famines, before and after the War – were exploited by Party *apparatchiki*, nationalists and *literaty* who resisted change. Writers and publicists such as Ales Adamovich, Yuri Chernichenko, Yuri Afanasiev and Yevgeny Yevtushenko frequently intervened to point out Stalin's disastrous effects on the country in the past and his continued impact on it in the present.

4 A. Fadin, *Vek XX i mir*, 1988, no. 6, p. 34.
5 I. Klyamkin, *MN*, 1987, no. 11, pp. 150–88; Nove, *Glasnost* (1989), Ch.1 for a sustained discussion of this debate.
6 See G. Popov, *Nauka i zhizn*, 1987, no. 4, pp. 54–65; N. Shmelev, *NM*, 1987, no. 6, pp. 142–64; Popov and Shmelev, *Znamya*, 1988, no. 5, pp. 158–83.

Adamovich compared the Soviet Union to a plane hijacked by a terrorist, who kills the pilot and crew and some of the passengers and is then forced to take the controls himself: when he lands the plane, does he expect to be praised and congratulated for the next forty years or to be killed? What, asked Adamovich, is the normal reaction?[7] Yuri Chernichenko reminded voters in 1989 that food supplies were poor because of the ruin of agriculture by Stalin: 'Nearly sixty years have passed since the Stalinist "Great Change", yet the people – as one whole – has not eaten its fill ever since. Stalinism today means empty food stores and "sausage" trains to Moscow.'[8] Stalinism had resulted, Yuri Afanasiev pointed out, in the destruction of public opinion and civil society. The social disintegration caused by the Terror had deprived people of political power and influence. Afanasiev went on to plead for the importance of overcoming Stalinism in the present and urged people to join the anti-Stalinist public movement Memorial.[9] By 1988, open warfare between opponents and supporters of Stalinism had been declared and everyone understood that what was at issue was the kind of government which would henceforth prevail in the country.[10] The labels Stalinist and anti-Stalinist were shorthand for authoritarian and conservative or liberal and democratic.

Apart from the intellectual debate, Stalinism remained to be exorcised from the nation's conscience and consciousness and this was an even more painful process than reassessing Stalin's historical role and drawing conclusions from it for the political and economic system. 'The journey into Stalinism [...] involves looking into ourselves,' observed Ales Adamovich. For a long time people had preferred not to acknowledge the truth and horror of what was happening and had happened around them:

> We could have asked ourselves what happened to all the millions of prisoners who were driven into exile throughout the thirties. Yet we did everything we possibly could not to ask, and we couldn't even admit it when people came back from there and talked about

7 Cited in 'Plenum', *Sov. ekran*, 1988, no. 4, p. 4.
8 Yu. Chernichenko, *MN*, 1989, no. 6, p. 9; the 'sausage' trains refer to the common practice of taking the train to Moscow, which was relatively well supplied, to buy food unavailable in the provinces.
9 Yu. Afanasiev, *MN*, 1989, no. 6, p. 4.
10 See Popov, in *SK*, 7 April 1988, p. 6; A. Gelman, *SK*, 9 April 1989, p. 5.

it. [...] We clutched at our illusions and were unable to admit the truth, either to ourselves or to others.

However, it was no longer possible to continue evading the issue: 'The time has come to remember.' The process was difficult. 'Grief and pain attend our every step, our every breath and memory. This is the legacy of the Stalin cult.' But it was a necessary catharsis, without which Soviet society could never advance towards democratic norms: 'If we do not understand our own history, we cannot hope to advance towards a new, legal, democratic society.'[11]

The poet Yevgeny Yevtushenko also commented on people's reluctance, at the time, to admit, or inability to absorb, the arrests and terror. Stalinism had existed alongside anti-Stalinism in people's hearts and minds, he suggested. The dangers of deviation had been too great to allow oneself to indulge in conscious criticisms of the leader and yet instinctively it was impossible to condone what was happening. Even children, Yevtushenko commented, were influenced by the fear of the age: 'The instinct of fear penetrated into children, forcing them not to think of all the crimes which were committed around them. But the instinct of truth was stronger than the instinct of fear. Stalin's death freed the instinct of truth.'[12] But the exorcism conducted by the Thaw had been suspended, so that now, a generation later, none of the old problems – psychological and political – had been solved.

The past, he observed at Memorial's founding conference, could never be recovered: its horrors could not be wiped out, nor its mistakes righted, nor its crimes punished. The long toll of murders – of Party and army leaders, of writers and artists – the persecution of the innocent, the invasion of Czechoslovakia and Afghanistan belonged to the cruel past.

> But if we cannot save anyone or anything in the past, then we can at least save the present from a repetition of the tragic mistakes and crimes, which have brought our country to the brink of spiritual and economic catastrophe. And a repetition remains possible [...]

11 A. Adamovich, 'Look about You' in V. Korotich and C. Porter (eds.), *The Best of Ogonek* (1990), pp. 7–14 (originally published in *Ogonek*, 1988, no. 39).
12 Ye. Yevtushenko, *Politika–privilegiya vsekh* (1990), pp. 10–11.

The only hope for the future and for fundamental reform lay in renunciation of this legacy and in repentance:

> Let our young people, born after Stalin's death, assume the historical guilt for Stalinism, for which they are not personally responsible. But a self-satisfied, indifferent sense of one's guiltlessness is beside the point - it is even a grave fault before the Fatherland. Citizenship starts with a feeling of historical guilt, with the feeling of responsibility for all that happened in our country and in all the globe. Saving the present by remembering the past, we will also save our own future and the future of our children [...] This in my opinion is the Memorial society's main task and the task of our whole society.[13]

Many intellectuals shared Yevtushenko and Adamovich's conviction that Soviet society needed to repent, to experience that 'zero hour' in which it would confront its past, the crimes for which it had been collectively responsible.[14] An open letter in *Pravda* in February 1988 commented: 'It would be very desirable if Stalin were to leave not only the stage, but also our lives, that his methods should go, his "mentality", his ways of resolving arguments, *inter alia*, in the arts.'[15]

The year 1987 was remarkable for the publication of a number of previously banned works, which helped society to come to terms with Stalinism, its moral and psychological impact.[16] Among these works, some were outstanding. These included Anna Akhmatova's *Requiem*, written in 1940 on the prompting of a woman, who had stood beside the poet in the queue of wives and mothers at the prison in Leningrad, waiting to see whether they could obtain news of their arrested relatives and send them food parcels. At the end of this sequence of poems, Akhmatova - like Pushkin, claiming to speak for the thousands of simple people who had been murdered or whose relatives had been killed - requested that if a memorial should ever be erected to her, it

---

13 Yevtushenko, Speech to the founding Congress of Memorial, January 1988, in ibid., pp. 17-18.
14 See the comments of Dudintsev, *SK*, 17 February 1987, p. 6.
15 'Open Letter', *Pravda*, 29 February 1988.
16 Among them were Anatoly Rybakov, *Children of the Arbat*; A. Pristavkin, *A Golden Cloud*; V. Shalamov, *Kolyma Tales*; Yu. Trifonov, *Disappearance*; M. Bulgakov, *A Dog's Heart*; A. Tvardovsky, *By Right of Memory*; A. Platonov, *Foundation Pit*; and M. Shatrov, *Brest Peace*: published respectively in *Druzhba narodov*, 1987, nos 4-6; *Neva*, 1987, nos 1-4; *Znamya*, 1987, nos 3-4; *Sovetskaya molodezh'*, 1987, no. 7; *Druzhba narodov*, 1987, no. 1; *Znamya*, 1987, no. 6; *Novy mir*, 1987, no. 3; *Novy mir*, 1987, no. 6; *Novy mir*, 1987, no. 4.

should be placed not where she had been happy, but at the red walls of the main prison in Leningrad:

> [...] Here, where I stood for 300 hours
> And where the bolts were not opened for me.
> Since I'm afraid that in blissful death
> I'll forget the creaking of the Black Marias.
> Forget how hatefully the door slammed shut
> And the old woman wailed like a wounded animal.
> And from my unmoving bronze eyelids
> May the melting snow stream like tears,
> And may the jail dove coo in the distance
> And the boats glide quietly by on the Neva.[17]

The film of Georgian director Tengiz Abuladze, entitled *Repentance*, was also harrowing and as an almost contemporary work (completed in 1984 and then banned) perhaps more accessible. It posed the problem of Stalinism so that its relevance for each viewer could not be evaded. Abuladze adopted a metaphor to explore the tenacity of Stalin's legacy in contemporary society: the film turns on a trial, in which Katya, the daughter of an artist persecuted thirty years earlier and then arrested and banished to a camp, is arraigned for digging up the body of her father's tormentor, the old dictator, Varlam Aravidze. This character is presented in the film as a black-shirted fascist, with a strong physical resemblance to Beria. Katya's father was arrested for his alleged involvement in a plot to dig a tunnel from London to Bombay. The director makes no attempt to embrace realism: on the contrary, by presenting the story as a grotesque fantasy, he makes a point about reality in Stalin's time. For the viewer is left in little doubt that this film is an allegory about Stalin and Stalinism. Pursuing Katya in the courts is the now respectable family of the dead dictator. Why, wonders the dictator's son, Abel, can she not leave his father and his memory in peace? He did nothing wrong: he lived in difficult times and was surrounded by enemies. Katya disagrees: 'Burying him means forgiving him, closing our eyes to all his crimes. Aravidze is not dead as long as you go on defending him.'[18] Abuladze goes on to suggest that Abel's refusal to admit the truth can bring nothing but further tragedy.

17 Akhmatova, 'Requiem' in *Stikhi* (Moscow, 1988), p. 240.
18 Quoted in Roxburgh, *Revolution* (1991), p. 61.

Lest Soviet viewers miss the point about Katya's obsession, part of the film is devoted to a debate between Abel and his son about Varlam's role: the grandson demands to know the truth, while the father prevaricates, using just the terminology of official ideologists and, indeed, of Stalin's contemporaries and silent collaborators – they were difficult times, great results were achieved despite the obstacles, some sacrifices and mistakes were inevitable. The grandson shoots himself and only then can Abel admit the truth. The last scene shows him digging up Varlam's body and throwing it down a mountainside. This film – initially shown only to a limited audience – was eventually seen all over the Soviet Union in 1987 and administered one of the first shocks to society's self-consciousness, forcing people to reassess their behaviour in and attitude to the past.

The other great storm in 1987 was Rybakov's novel about the generation that came of age during the Great Terror of 1937. *Children of the Arbat*, first of a trilogy, was a *succès de scandale*: in it, Rybakov (who belonged to the generation in question) tried to make sense of his experiences and of the entire Stalin episode. The novel hit a chord. The magazine in which it was published was eagerly passed from hand to hand, as readers devoured the latest chapters. Rybakov got dozens of letters each day, mostly from young people. 'The readers understood my book,' he commented. 'They write that the truth about their country's history enriches them spiritually and morally. The young readers' response shows their yearning for knowledge and hatred of lies and semi-truths.' Ultimately, *glasnost* for Rybakov, meant 'being brought up on the truth', and this was a precondition of private and public morality.[19]

In 1988 and 1989, further classics were published,[20] and the truth finally dawned: the entire experiment had been flawed and had taken an enormous toll in human suffering and death. Films like *Solovki Power* (*Vlast' Solovetskaya*, 1988) (on Lenin's camps in the Solovki islands) were greeted as horrifying but necessary. Some believed that the feeling of shame they provoked was ultimately purifying.[21] Others began to call for a public trial of those responsible for the horror and crimes of the

19 Rybakov, interview with I. Okunev in *Soviet Literature and Art* (1989), pp. 83–4.
20 These included Pasternak's *Doctor Zhivago*, Grossman's *Life and Fate* and *Forever Flowing*, Solzhenitsyn's *Gulag Archipelago*, Lidia Chukovskaya's *Sofia Petrovna*, Platonov's *Chevengur* and Dombrovsky's *Faculty of Unnecessary Things*.
21 N. Izyumova, *MN*, 1989, no. 7, p. 4.

past. Writing in *Moscow News*, S.P. Zinchenko commented that the Stalin era was 'shameful because we accepted the atmosphere of suspicion and the defamatory letters, the mass rallies demanding capital punishment for "people's enemies" who were often just neighbours, colleagues, friends and relatives the day before. It is shameful now, because Stalinism still has its advocates today.'[22] But it was not practical to put thousands, even more, perhaps, on trial. Nor was there any widespread support for this kind of public recognition of the evils of Stalinism. Too many people had been compromised.

Many in the CPSU believed that the Party's tolerance of criticism of Stalin was misguided and that it led to a fatal erosion of the Party's power and authority. One of the chief authors of the policy, Alexander Yakovlev, had no such reservations. Speaking at the Twenty-Eighth Party Congress in July 1990, he defended his efforts to eradicate Stalinism – which he considered essential if the Soviet State were to evolve into a democratic, law-based State. Nor did he shrink from asking painful questions:

> By whom and how was the mechanism of repression founded and started, how did it work, how did its organizers subordinate to themselves the Party, the organs of State, society? Why did no one stand in its way? To what extent and in what ways was our development distorted, as a result? Why was an attempt made to reanimate the bloody face of Stalinism later?
>
> These are not unnecessary questions. But there is only one answer: the truth about Stalinism is a condemnation of the system it created.[23]

However, for all Yakovlev's hopes and those of the liberal intelligentsia he had encouraged, the great renewal of public morality did not take place. History was increasingly seen as irrelevant and, partly as a result of this, the great democratic reorientation of society was flawed. The anti-Stalinist campaign was to sink out of public view in 1990 and the whole question of responsibility for the crimes of the past and of the need to renew the sources of public morality all too quickly faded from view.

Stalinism was one of the most divisive and formative issues in the late 1980s. As the reformers in the intelligentsia became increasingly explicit and sweeping in their condemnations of its impact and insistent on the necessity of renewing the values on which Soviet

22 S. Zinchenko, *MN*, 1989, no. 6, p. 4.
23 A. Yakovlev, *Muki, prochiteniya* (Moscow, 1991), pp. 189–92.

society was founded, the nationalists reacted by rejecting what they saw as an attempt to foist Western models on Russia and to jettison Russia's political traditions. Most of the reformers in the intellectual elite started out not as subversives but as loyal Soviet citizens, committed to Soviet socialism; but they were anxious to humanize the system – believing in the 1960s' dream of socialism with a human face. Rejecting the Stalinist model, some looked back to the origins of the Revolution, the reign of Lenin and an idealized 1920s, when, they thought, socialism had been popular and had not precluded pluralism, when citizens enjoyed rights of association, expression and enterprise of which Stalin later deprived them. Gradually, however, anti-Stalinism carried part of the intelligentsia towards liberalism: concern for human dignity, for respect for the individual and his rights and freedoms gradually led them to look for inspiration beyond Soviet experience and particularly to West European social democratic traditions. At first, in 1987, they emphasized the importance of legality and of an end to the arbitrary rule inaugurated by Stalin. In 1989, they drew the logical implications from this and called for the introduction of full political pluralism and representative government. The exploration of Stalinism in the press from 1987 on was thus of signal importance in forming a body of opinion in favour of democratic reform.

RECOVERY OF IDENTITY

The *glasnost* years – from 1987 to 1989 – were marked by the Russians' recovery of their national heritage in more than its purely tragic aspects. Russia's artistic and philosophical legacy and the Orthodox religion were gradually rehabilitated. In history, this was signalled not only by the gradual straightening of the record on Stalin and on the Soviet regime as a whole, but nineteenth-century historiography, starting with Karamzin, began to be republished from 1988 on. Intellectual history began to be rewritten in a less partisan spirit, with thinkers other than the revolutionary socialists receiving attention. In 1989 this process extended to the great religious writers of the late nineteenth and early twentieth centuries. Journals such as *Novy mir* and *Voprosy filosofii* published excerpts from their writings, while a special commission was established with a view to bringing out a new edition of their works. For the first time since the 1920s, it became possible to acquire the works of Solov'ev, Rozanov, Fedotov, Berdyaev and others. Thus, a more complex picture of the past and of men's responses to the world began to emerge for a reading public, many of whom had been allowed access to nothing other than conventional and often bowlderized Marxist-Leninist accounts of everything from history to aesthetic theory.

In 1988, another great change took place: the introduction of a degree of religious tolerance. On 29 April 1988, the Patriarch of the Orthodox Church met the Soviet leader, for the first time since the wartime meeting between Stalin and Patriarch Sergii in September 1943. Some of the desecrated and forcibly closed churches and monasteries were returned to the Church, chief among which were: Optina Pustina, the famous monastery in the Orel district, whose elders led the spiritual revival of Orthodoxy in the nineteenth century; the Danilov monastery in Moscow; and the Pechorskaya Lavra monastery in Kiev. Restrictions on religious life were eased, making it less difficult to register new parishes and to obtain religious literature. In 1988, for the first time under Soviet rule, the Bible was printed in a small edition in Russian and a reprint of a pre-revolutionary annoted exegetical edition of the Bible was also issued. In February 1988, a draft law on freedom of conscience was introduced, which - although criticized by dissident and church leaders for its limitations - nonetheless represented significant progress on what had gone before. Now parents were to be allowed to give their children a religious education and believers were granted rights hitherto denied them (such as that of conscientious objection). Finally, the Millennium of the coming of Christianity to Russia (in 988) was celebrated with great pomp and ceremony and the participation of dignitaries of State and the diplomatic corps, in Kiev and Moscow. A great exhibition of Russian religious art was mounted in Moscow and it seemed that the Russian religious heritage was gradually being readmitted to national life (though not, it is true, without encountering the staunch opposition of some Party conservatives, led, on this issue, by KGB chief Viktor Chebrikov). The net result of these changes was a renaissance of religious life. By April

1989, 1600 new Orthodox congregations had been registered, while almost 1000 churches opened in 1989 alone.[24]

The arts saw not only the publication of banned classics of the Soviet period, but also the restoration to the literary and artistic pantheons of entire schools of work hitherto ignored, because of their deviation from the canon of socialist realism. Thus, the poets of the Silver Age and the first half of the twentieth century – among them Ahkmatova, Gumiliev, Mandelshtam, Tsvetaeva and Khodasevich – were finally republished, and separate editions of their work appeared, albeit initially in limited numbers. Memoirs of intellectual and artistic life of the first half of the century (by Nadezhda Mandelshtam, Nina Berberova and Vladimir Nabokov) concerning the experiences of emigration and repression were published in the literary journals.

The existence of modernism in the visual arts, to which Russians had made such a significant contribution, began to be admitted and examples of it to be displayed. A new note of scepticism accompanied these departures from the established aesthetic canon: the exhibition in honour of the Twenty-Seventh Party Congress, in the centre of Moscow, included among some canvases from the Costakis collection, a painting provocatively entitled 'Cogito ergo sum': intellectuals would have recognized this quotation from Descartes, whose analysis of reason included the capacity for doubt.[25] Thereafter, the Russian public began to see the work of artists previously banned because of their stylistic deviations or because they had emigrated. Exhibitions were devoted to the idiosyncratic Leningrad painter Pavel Filonov (1988), to Chagall (1987), Malevich (1988), Popova (1990), Kandinsky (1989) and Lissitsky (1990). The Soviet Cultural Fund, chaired by Dmitri Likhachev, organized the first exhibition devoted to the World of Art and related schools from the turn of the century –

---

24 Sakwa, *Gorbachev* (1990), p. 220. The literature on this subject is considerable: see M. Bourdeaux, *Gorbachev, Glasnost and the Gospel* (London, 1990), pp. 43–86; *Pravda*, 30 April 1988, for the Gorbachev–Pimen meeting; *Izvestiya*, 8 April 1988, for interview with Pimen. Interviews with other members of the Church hierarchy were also published: see *New Times*, 1988, no. 20, pp. 30–31; *NT*, 1988, no. 22, pp. 31–2; *NT*, 1988, no. 23, p. 25–6; *NT*, 1988, no. 40, pp. 24–6; 'Religiya v SSSR', *Russkaya mysl'*, 20 May 1988, p.5.

25 I am indebted to Professor R.J. Hill for this observation: see his 'Gorbachov's Politics: Results and Prospects', *Irish Slavonic Studies*, no. 7 (1986), pp. 22–2.

giving Russians their first chance to see privately-owned works by Somov, Sudeikin, Bakst, Benois, Lentulov, Kandinsky, Goncharova, Shterenberg and Larionov. The Fund was also responsible for the 1988 exhibition of theatrical design, which covered much of the same ground. The Russian Museum in Leningrad, in the same year, organized a large exhibition of art of the 1920s and 1930s. This trend continued after the August 1991 *coup* in the exhibition devoted to the Russian *art nouveau* in 1992.

Initially, many of these works caused confusion (catalogues being in chronically short supply and the idiom of anything after impressionism being unfamiliar) and reactions were guarded and suspicious (was this not a hoax or fraud, perpetrated by dubious characters, rightly condemned by the authorities?) but these attitudes gradually changed. Russians recovered a sense of their rich artistic heritage, with its emphasis on elaborate design and colour. No one viewing the works of these artists, dating from approximately 1880 to 1930, could doubt that they emanated from a rich civilization and from a society which contrasted favourably with the present. Tolerance towards contemporary art also increased and, although condemned to more marginal venues, exhibitions of experimental and amateur art were a popular feature of the late 1980s.

Finally, the works of the Russian *émigrés* also began to appear in the late 1980s. The first step in this direction (the publication of an obituary of Viktor Nekrasov in *Moscow News* in Autumn 1987) nearly led to the dismissal of the paper's editor, Yegor Yakovlev.[26] In 1988, however, short excerpts from Sinyavsky (the writer whose imprisonment in 1966 had marked the end of the Thaw), Galich, Aksionov and Voinovich appeared in the 'thick journals' – a trend which became much more marked the following year.[27] By the early 1990s, separate editions of the *émigrés*, of all three waves (that is those who had left after the Revolution, after the Second World War and in the 1970s) were to become available for the first time in Russia. A different, usually rather caustic perspective on Soviet life thus percolated through to the Russian reading public, enabling them to situate the entire period since 1917 in a new, critical context. The

26 Interview with N. Ivanova, 29 November 1990.
27 For detailed references see J. Graffy, 'The Literary Press' in Graffy and Hosking (eds.), *Culture* (1989), pp. 117-20.

émigrés were generally far from enthusiastic about Western life, which they did not propose as a model for Russia to follow. Their testimony in relation to the Soviet past therefore seemed to Russians all the more reliable, as it became evident that they were not agents of capitalist imperialism and writing from an anti-Russian standpoint.

For the first time in the history of the regime, Russia abroad was integrated into the mainstream culture of the Motherland. As exiles and dissidents (such as Timofeev) began to be published, the classic 'split' in the consciousness of the Soviet intellectual began to disappear and an integral view of the Russian experience in the twentieth century began to emerge. This flow of information helped to change public attitudes to the regime and its pretensions and briefly, in 1989 and 1990, it helped to stimulate the desire for a new departure, for a reconnection with the civilization, shattered by war and revolution, whose diversity and riches now seemed enviable.

The anti-Stalinists in the cultural elite played a vital part in forming this new consciousness and, in doing so, they furnished the ideological leadership of the democratic revolution in the late 1980s. But they seemed more powerful than in reality they were. As Sergeev and Biryukov have pointed out, the disposition of forces in the mass media (where the liberal, Westernizing intelligentsia were preponderant) was not an accurate reflection of the alignment of political forces in the country – or even of the democratic movement itself.[28] Nor was it clear how far the public would be ready to go in exorcising Stalinism: it was one thing to opt for freedom, for greater personal liberties and for political accountability, but another to endorse the end of empire and the switch-over to capitalism. But these ambiguities and hesitations were not to become apparent until much later.

28 Sergeyev and Biryukov, *Russia's Road* (1993), pp. 88–9.

5. The Political Clubs

While the anti-Stalinist intellectuals of the establishment were gradually redefining the past, discussing the need for a civil society based on the rule of law and respect for civic freedoms, and debating how to reform the economic system, the lower reaches of the academic intelligentsia – Zinoviev's Moscovia – were trying to find a way of participating in the reforms. They established political clubs – which marked the tentative reemergence of a civil society and formed the nucleus of the broader democratic movement in the capitals.

The new political clubs emerged after the January 1987 Party Plenum, as the CPSU was preparing for the Nineteenth Party Conference, which was ostensibly to renew the Party's structures and give them a more democratic character. The next eighteen months saw the tentative growth of independent public life – manifested particularly in the rise of the conservation movement and in the emergence, in the capitals, of non-Party political discussion groups and clubs.

THE CONSERVATION MOVEMENT

The first embryonically politico-social movement, which found widespread support among the population and which was allowed to plead its cause, was ecological in inspiration. The ecological movement in Russia dates from the 1960s but was effectively emasculated under Brezhnev. The rebirth of the ecological movement as an autonomous popular movement dates from the mid-1980s: both the committee to preserve the unique ecology of Lake Baikal (initially founded in 1967) and the campaign against the diversion of Siberia's rivers, which also dated back to the 1960s, were revived in the Gorbachev years. Eminent writers, editors and scientists (including the editor of *Novy mir*, Sergei Zalygin, the academician Dmitri Likhachev, and the nationalist novelist, Valentin Rasputin) played a major role in these campaigns, which challenged the power of the planners in Moscow. They collected thousands of signatures protesting against the proposal to divert the rivers. How this campaign would have fared had not mischance intervened is impossible to predict. However, it is clear that the fire at the nuclear power plant in Chernobyl in April 1986 did much to legitimize the cause of ecology and conservation and to mobilize popular support behind the movement, while it made its case more difficult to resist.

The unanimity of independent scientific opinion on the issue of the Siberian rivers, combined with the Party's new reservations about the economic agencies' and ministries' expensive projects, all helped to give the ecologists their first significant victory: in August 1986, the Politburo halted work on the scheme.[1] It seemed that public opinion had triumphed over the bureaucracy. The virtue of *glasnost* in the case of the campaign over the rivers – and the concomitant ones about Lake Baikal, the sea of Aral and Tolstoy's home – was that the public was enlivened by hearing and seeing protests from eminent scholars and writers (non-Party figures, who enjoyed authority because of their erudition, ability and non-involvement in politics) and realizing that these protests were now tolerated, rather than bringing disaster to those who voiced them. Gradually, as a result of this new sense of what was possible, clubs devoted to good works, cultural restoration, conservation and sports began to form.

The ecological movement in Russia was, therefore, in the forefront of the development of public life. It began as a campaign on one or two major issues, led by distinguished members of the intelligentsia but in 1987 it rapidly spawned innumerable small groups (varying in size from groups of 10-15 to groups of around 100) all over the country.[2] In this, the ecological-conservation movement was unlike the more exclusively political clubs, which were initially almost exclusively confined to Moscow and Leningrad. The ecological

1 Gromov and Kuzin, *Neformaly* (1990), pp. 94-5; Laqueur, *The Long Road* (1989), p. 51.
2 Tolz, *The Multi-Party System* (1990), p. 10; Berezovsky and Krotov, *Rossiya* (1990), p. 55; Sudiniev, 'Nashchestvie' in Yushenkov (ed.), *Neformaly* (1990), p. 21, for a list of areas in which the movement was active and for the principal groups involved; Gromov and Kuzin, *Neformaly* (1990), pp. 96, 103-4; Alexandrova, *Informelle Gruppen* (1988), pp. 23-4.

movement took off (a) because of the official endorsement of its aims, indicated by the eminence of its leaders and its early successes and (b) because of the appalling state of the environment and the wanton destruction of historical monuments around the country.[3] It was, however, oppositional in character, as it pitted ordinary citizens against insensitive and ignorant officials.[4]

While Russian researchers usually distinguish between the green movement and the conservation movement (the latter being additionally concerned with the preservation of cultural monuments), a more fundamental distinction would seem to lie between the nationalist and the democratic wings of the movement. The nationalist wing was particularly strong in the provinces, especially in Siberia, where living standards and environmental conditions were worse than in the capitals of European Russia. The Siberian movement was led, at least in a spiritual sense, by the nationalist writers, Rasputin, Belov and Astafiev, who first came to the fore in the 1960s and 1970s, with their attacks on the spiritual and material devastation wrought by the Party's readiness to sacrifice the legacy of the past to its obsession with progress and its vast programmes of economic development. The romanticism of these writers, with their rejection of the modern, tended to veer into obscurantism – a narrow, unrealistic and at times vindictive nationalism, which struck a chord particularly with the elderly and the poor.

Many of the Siberian ecological groups were nationalist and opposed to the democratic movement. *Pamyat'* of Novosibirsk (many of whose members were scientists from the local branch of the Academy of Sciences) worked out an alternative energy plan for the conservation of Lake Baikal. The theories underpinning this plan were such that the group has been classified as 'eco-fascist'. According to this *Pamyat'* group, environmental pollution has been caused by an anti-Russian plot hatched by Jews; ecology was necessary not to save

---

3 Statistics show that at the current rate of restoration, one-third of existing cultural monuments will have been lost in twenty years and 50 per cent in forty years: Plasky, *Mol. gruppy* (1988), p. 21. In Kemerovo, pollution from the steelworks and power stations was such that drivers had to turn on their headlights at midday and smoke from the area reached Lake Baikal, 750 miles east: Sakwa, *Gorbachev* (1990), p. 211. For a brief survey of green issues in Gorbachev's USSR, see C. Ziegler, 'Environmental Politics' in J. Sedaitis and J. Butterfield (eds.), *Perestroika from Below* (Oxford, 1991), pp. 113–31.

4 Berezovsky and Krotov, *Rossiya* (1990), p. 57.

humanity, but to save Russia. Greenpeace of Krasnoyarsk allegedly shared this outlook, holding that Chernobyl was an attempt to kill the Slavic race.[5]

In Leningrad, however, the movement was more democratic in orientation, while in both Leningrad and Moscow there was a significant anarchist element in the ecological movement.[6] The Leningrad movement developed in 1987 around the issue of the proposed demolition of the Hôtel d'Angleterre: the hotel was a famous landmark, associated with many cultural figures (principally with the poet Sergei Yesenin, who committed suicide there in 1925). The proposal to demolish the building provoked a public outcry, led by the ecological pressure group, *Spasenie* (Salvation), which was formed the previous year under the auspices of the local Komsomol. *Spasenie* organized mass meetings to save the hotel and enlisted the support of Academician Likhachev. The group also whipped up support for the preservation of houses associated with Dostoevsky and the poet Delvig and went on to found the Council for the Ecology of Culture, with other conservation groups in the city, to coordinate the various campaigns being waged against the authorities and to raise the general level of awareness and interest in ecology and conservation.[7]

The green movement in the capitals appealed not only to those involved in old hippy subculture:[8] anarchists, Christian Democrats, nationalists and followers of Berdyaev and Vernadsky all found the vision of an alternative lifestyle, based on the renunciation of the military-technological society, engaging. The idea of a return to the land, to the village, with its natural rhythms of life and its respect for nature, and, in some quarters, the idea of the resurrection of the village commune (the *obshchina*), in which all things would be held in common and the individual could seek self-fulfilment, attracted people exhausted by noisy, dirty and ugly cities.[9]

5 Interview with Vadim Damie, 17 September 1991.
6 Ibid.
7 O. Petrichenko, *Ogonek*, 1987, no.20, pp. 30–31; *Obshchestvennye dvizheniya Leningrada* (Leningrad, 1989), pp. 114–16, for *Spasenie*'s own account of itself; Plasky, *Mol. gruppy* (1988), pp. 22–4; Gromov and Kuzin, *Neformaly* (1990), pp. 95–6, 103–4, for other groups active in Leningrad to promote rational planning and respect for the cultural heritage.
8 Nenashev, *S'affirmer* (1990), pp. 5, 10, on hippies in Leningrad.
9 Dobrynina *et al.* (eds.), *Samodeyatel'nye* (1990), pp. 40–41.

As a result of the diversity of views and inspiration which it encompassed, the ecological movement was prone to fragmentation – despite various attempts to unite it, not least by the Party, which hoped thereby to control it. Among numerous concessions made to ecologists' concerns, the Party endorsed the foundation in Moscow in June 1987 of Greenpeace as an official environmental agency, under the chairmanship of Sergei Zalygin.[10] All ecological initiatives were to take place under its aegis or with its collaboration. The intention was to direct the ecological movement into official channels and to represent the movement abroad. Only a few local green groups associated themselves with it, however. While Greenpeace was small, counting only 100–120 members, ten academicians worked in it on a voluntary basis. The organization was more practical than political in orientation, concentrating on scientific expeditions and research, rather than on demonstrations and protests, as a way of countering the more wayward or shocking excesses of the planning agencies and ministries.[11]

The ecological movement's autonomous attempts to organize itself on a broader basis were fraught with difficulty. Not until December 1988 was an all-Union structure for the green–ecological movement finally devised. Then, on 24–26 December 1988, the Social-Economic Union (SEU) was founded, uniting 150 groups from 90 cities. Just as the diversity of views within the movement had prevented the foundation at an early stage of a single organization for all of Russia, thus depriving the most popular of the early socio-political movements of any coherent political influence, so its centrifugal tendencies prevented the SEU from developing along political lines. Although the idea of founding a green party met with considerable support at the founding Congress of the SEU and further meetings were held in the Spring and early Summer 1990 with a view to realizing this idea, the attempt foundered on the internal divisions of the movement (and partly through the undemocratic manoeuvres of

10 Interview with S. Zalygin, 3 December 1990; Alexandrova, *Informelle Gruppen* (1988), p. 56; Gromov and Kuzin, *Neformaly* (1990), p. 99; Laqueur, *The Long Road* (1989), p. 213. Another attempt was made to control the green movement by founding a Party-sponsored organization in February 1989; this seems to have been less successful than Greenpeace: see Gromov and Kuzin, *Neformaly* (1990), pp. 99–101; interview with V. Damie, 17 September 1991.

11 Interview with S. Zalygin, 3 December 1990.

the anarchist minority in the movement).[12] The political significance of the ecology movement was, as a result, largely confined to the early years of democratization (1986–88), when it helped to encourage the expression and mobilization of public opinion.

EMERGENCE OF THE POLITICAL CLUBS

More significant for the future political life of Russia was the emergence, principally in Moscow and Leningrad, of political debating clubs and societies.[13] Most of their members were researchers, engineers and economists – members of the underprivileged intelligentsia. Few unskilled workers or women participated. Nor were its members particularly young: most were aged between twenty-five and forty. The absence of women and young students was a striking feature of the informal movement: it may be explained by the fact that women were too busy combining professional and arduous domestic duties, while students stood to lose their scholarships and university places.[14]

The clubs were among the earliest indications of the development of a new political consciousness among hitherto largely quiescent or apparently conformist groups in Russian society. At the same time, the first clubs – which date from the start of 1987 – testify to the quite rapid politicization of the informal movement.[15] The non-Party

---

12 Interview with V. Damie, 17 September 1991; V. Pribylovsky, *Slovar' politicheskikh partii* (Moscow, 1991), pp. 34, 89.

13 See I. Snezhkova, 'Natsional'nye aspekty', *Obshchestvennye nauki*, 1989, no. 6, p. 119; Sudiniev, 'Nashchestvie' in Yushenkov (ed.), *Neformaly* (1990), pp. 18, 20; Berezovsky and Krotov, *Rossiya* (1990), pp. 18–19, 21, 54; Malyutin, 'Vybor' in Yushenkov (ed.), *Neformaly* (1990), p. 75; *SK*, 30 December 1990, for interview with Gennadi Burbulis, who first came to notice as a leader of the political club Diskussionaya Tribuna in Sverdlovsk in the late 1980s.

14 Snezhkova, 'Natsional'nye', *Obshchestv. nauki*, 1989, no. 6, p. 122; Berezovsky and Krotov, *Rossiya* (1990), p. 25; Yushenkov in Yushenkov (ed.), *Neformaly* (1990), p. 53; Malyutin, 'Vybor' in ibid., p. 76; Kagarlitsky, *The Thinking Reed* (1989), p. 353.

15 By 1990, informal political groups and movements had spread to over 200 towns throughout the USSR. They were reckoned to have about 2–2.5 million members. In Sverdlovsk alone, there were 3000 informal groups with 120,000 members, according to the CPSU's estimates: Berezovsky and Krotov, *Rossiya* (1990), p. 32; Churbanov and Nelyubin, 'Neformal'nye' in Pechenev and Vyunsky (eds.), *Neformaly* (1990), p. 22; A. Gorenkov, 'Partiinye organizatsii', *Partiinaya zhizn'*, 1990, no. 2, p. 31.

public groups which suddenly began to multiply after 1985, and especially in 1986 and 1987, were not a new phenomenon, but a third and tidal wave of the alternative culture that had already existed more or less underground throughout the Brezhnev years. In a normal society, the existence of such groups would be unremarkable: their sudden efflorescence under Gorbachev was worthy of remark because they indicated the emergence of a civil society – i.e. of public life neither sponsored nor controlled by the CPSU. This was a highly significant development – as the concern and suspicion of the Party's reaction suggests – for it was clearly only a matter of time until this new-found social independence embraced political independence also.

There were three main tendencies among the early political clubs:

• the 'new left' or left socialist orientation;
• the social democratic tendency;
• the liberal democratic wing, which issued from and was inspired by the old dissident movement.

New Left Clubs

The first of the informal political clubs to appear on the scene were left-wing in orientation. They were also among the earliest to disappear, partly because they were small and fractious or utopian in character. These clubs were at their most influential in the early stages of the democratic movement – i.e. until Summer 1988 – when they were overtaken on the right by the social democrats and on the left by the neo-Bolsheviks and populist Stalinists. There were two main tendencies within this group of clubs:

• anarchism
• Leninism with a democratic gloss.

Unlike the social democratic clubs, which constituted the principal and most popular strain of the informal movement, the new left clubs were much more akin to the classic 'circles' of underground culture than were the mainline debating clubs. Most of them developed within the framework, or on the margins, of official structures, particularly the Komsomol.

Anarchism

One of the earliest of the left groups was the anarchist club *Obshchina* (Commune), which started life as a discussion club in the Lenin State Pedagogical Institute on 8 May 1987. The Institute had a tradition of radicalism among its students – in 1982, a political study circle had existed in the Institute illegally and had produced a paper.[16] This tendency resurfaced during the preparations for the Twentieth Komsomol Congress, which was to be held in Spring 1987. The Congress was preceded by a sharp debate about the Komsomol's rules, which were criticized as being too authoritarian and centralized and as stifling any independent initiatives among young people. As a result, it was argued, the Komsomol was moribund – a dull, official organization, which students joined out of necessity rather than enthusiasm, and which served only to allow ambitious young bureaucrats to develop a political career. In Autumn 1986, a group in the Institute drafted alternative rules, aimed at overcoming the Komsomol's centralization. These rules were ultimately rejected but during the wide-ranging discussion of the issues raised by the rules, a debating club developed, which, in May 1987, became known as *Obshchina*.

The club clarified its principles in a declaration which explained:

> The aim and means of the historical process is the liberation of the human individual. Societies and States, unions and groups have the right to exist only if they serve as a step on man's path to spiritual and material liberation. Everything which prevents or ceases to serve this goal is reactionary and should be abolished [...]

According to the declaration, 'socialism is not a cult and not a dogma, not a barracks of universal happiness, it is a construction which should secure for workers great freedom of thought and initiative, independence from the will of others.'[17] Needless to say, this emphasis on individual self-fulfilment and freedom was the antithesis of official Marxism–Leninism. *Obshchina*, in fact, was unabashed in drawing inspiration from Bakunin, Lavrov and the anarchist tendency in nineteenth-century populist thought. In

16 Berezovsky and Krotov, *Rossiya* (1990), p. 260.
17 A. Shubin, 'Obshchina' in Yushenkov (ed.), *Neformaly* (1990), p. 107.

accordance with this intellectual affiliation, they rejected the contemporary structures of the Soviet State – the centralized system of economic planning and the strict subordination of factories to ministries, the enormous power of the Party and State bureaucracy. It favoured giving the means of production to the workers of each collective, the abolition of the Party *nomenklatura*, the decentralization of political and economic life and the devolution of power to workers' soviets. They repeated Bakunin's aphorism: 'Freedom without socialism is privilege and injustice, socialism without freedom is slavery and brutality.'[18]

From September 1987 on, the club held regular lectures on historical themes, debates on socialism and democracy and on the economy. Among the questions they debated were: Why did the workers take part in the 1956 Hungarian uprising? How were Stalin's genocidal policies possible? Could he have been stopped? Was resistance possible? Could such horrors recur? What, if anything, could be retained from Russia's Soviet heritage?[19] Needless to say, all this was highly unorthodox – even heretical – and shows how far opinion, in some student circles, was ahead of the timid doubts and revelations on the official press at this time. Nonetheless, the fact that these delicate and very controversial subjects could be debated in public at all testifies to the radical change of atmosphere in both Moscow and in Party policy.

In 1987, *Obshchina* built up a following among school students in Moscow, visiting schools, organizing debates and discussions. Later the club began to develop an interest in *samizdat* publishing and concentrated on producing an eponymous newssheet and on running an information centre. The paper was produced regularly, with a print-run of about 150 copies.[20]

However, *Obshchina*'s attempts at collaboration and coexistence with other socialist clubs were fraught with tensions. The anarchists' insistence on independence and distaste for strict organization led them to break away from these confining structures, and ultimately to found the Confederation of Anarcho-Syndicalists (21–22 January

18 Ibid., pp. 102, 106–8; Dobrynina *et al.* (eds)., *Samodeyatel'nye* (1990), p. 36.
19 Shubin, 'Obshchina' in Yushenkov (ed.), *Neformaly* (1990), pp. 102, 107–9.
20 Ibid., p. 114; Dobrynina *et al.* (eds.), *Samodeyatel'nye* (1990), p. 36.

1989), which brought together anarchist groups from fifteen different cities, with a total membership of about three hundred.[21]

The heyday of anarchism was, however, at the very beginning of the informal movement, when the nature and scope of its activities broke new ground. There were about thirty or forty core members, who played a significant role in the early stages of the movement, when it required no little courage to come out in public and express non-conformist views. In a number of ways, *Obshchina* was unlike other informal groups: its membership was on the whole younger than that of the other political clubs; and its ideas were romantic rather than pragmatic. This lack of realism restricted its appeal to the young, idealistic and intellectual and resulted in the anarchists showing little taste or aptitude for real politics. While many of the other activists of the informal movement of this period went on to make careers in the new politics, journalism or business in the new Russia of the 1990s, the anarchists disappeared, almost to a man, into obscurity.

Leninist and new left clubs

The clubs on the Leninist wing of the informal movement were generally small – many were hardly distinguishable from the traditional underground circles of radical intellectuals.[22] The earliest and one of the largest of these clubs was the Social Political Correspondence Club, which developed under the auspices of *Komsomolskaya pravda* (hence, presumably, with the tacit approval of the Komsomol). In Autumn 1986, *Komsomolskaya pravda* published a letter from a reader from Orenburg about the problems of young people and the need to organize public opinion to support *perestroika* and oppose the conservative bureaucracy. This provoked a flood of letters of support to the paper and resulted in the creation of a social and political correspondence club.[23]

Despite the difficulties presented by distance and poor infrastructure, the club organized its first conference, attended by about forty

---

21 Berezovsky and Krotov, *Rossiya* (1990), pp. 260–61; V. Sirotkin, *Nedelya*, 16–21 January 1990, p. 9.

22 For the precursors of the new left (Soviet thinkers, with an interest in Eurocommunism, Latin-American left populism, social democracy and Trotskyism) see Malyutin, 'Sotsial-demokraty i sotsialisty', *Gorizont*, 1990, no. 8, pp. 17–18.

23 Malyutin, 'Neformaly v perestroike' in Yu. Afanasiev (ed.), *Inogo ne Dano* (Moscow, 1988), p. 222.

people, in May 1987. Gradually, three tendencies emerged in the club: a social-democratic wing, a centrist socialist position and an orthodox Marxist-Leninist trend. These differences led to the club's breakup in January 1988.[24] Despite its lack of positive achievements, the club was significant, however, by the mere fact of its existence, in enabling citizens to express their views publicly, to orientate themselves politically and even to organize public meetings of like-minded individuals from all over the country. With its emphasis on debate and public gatherings, organized without the overt involvement of the CPSU, it was characteristic of the early stages of the informal movement. It tested the waters and found them surprisingly warm. It was this experience which encouraged the informals to proceed, rather than suspend their activities.

One of the best-known and earliest of Leninist groups was the Club for Social Initiatives (KSI), which initially consisted of a handful of friends meeting in private flats. It became prominent thanks to its theoreticians (Mikhail Malyutin, Boris Kagarlitsky and subsequently, Vyacheslav Igrunov) and activities. Founded in September 1986, under the aegis, according to some, of *Komsomolskaya pravda*[25] (or, in other accounts, of the Soviet Sociological Association) its first task was the analysis of correspondence to the paper, with a view to dealing with some of the problems raised.[26] Malyutin, an academic specializing in Marxist theory, was interested in international communism, particularly its more radical manifestations. Kagarlitsky – a controversial figure in dissident circles – also had an interest in radical reinterpretations of communism – the so-called New Left, which in Russia owed an intellectual debt to Roy Medvedev, chief of the Leninist fundamentalists. According to Kagarlitsky, the Club for Social Initiatives had at most 20–25 members. It sought to encourage the emergence of a civil society through the development and coordination of the informal movement. The group did not organize

24 I. Sudiniev, 'Nashchestvie' in Yushenkov (ed.), *Neformaly* (1990), p. 19.
25 L. Semina, 'Po zakonam grazhdanskogo vremeni' in Pechenev and Vyunsky (eds.), *Neformaly* (1990), p. 164.
26 Berezovsky and Krotov, *Rossiya* (1990), p. 263. V. Igrunov says that the Soviet Sociological Association founded the club: Igrunov, 'KSI', *Vek XX i mir*, 1988, no. 6, p. 27; interview with M. Malyutin, 1 December 1990. Berezovsky and Krotov are indebted for their information on the clubs to Malyutin and Kagarlitsky, who were among the leaders of the club.

discussions and debates, but was more practical in orientation, trying to develop legal cover for initiatives.[27] The club also wanted to make contact with other groups, to organize an information network between them and to coordinate their activities.[28]

The KSI was therefore the earliest attempt to form some sort of coordinating and organizational framework for the informal movement – an enterprise which would, of course, have been of considerable interest to the authorities. The club was one of the main instigators of the August 1987 meeting of informals, when the first effort was made to establish an inter-club organization. In Autumn 1987, however, the political orientation of the club began to change, under the influence of Viktor Zolotarev, Grisha Pelman and Vyacheslav Igrunov. As liberalism rather than reform-Leninism began to guide its activities, the left-wingers, Malyutin and Kagarlitsky, moved away from it.[29] By 1989, the club had ceased functioning, having been overtaken by events.

In Autumn 1987, at the time of their defeat over the future orientation of the KSI, Kagarlitsky and Malyutin were not known to have any connections with the Party. They made no secret, however, of their commitment to reform socialism and now sought to promote this cause in other forums. Concerned about the amorphous nature of the informal movement, they were anxious to prevent it straying from the path of socialism. Hence, after the formation of the first umbrella organization for informal clubs in August 1987 (the Federation of Socialist Social Clubs or FSOK), Malyutin and Kagarlitsky founded another group to deal with ideological and organizational problems, called, confusingly, Socialist Initiative.

It saw its fundamental task in 'uniting Marxism with the new social movement'. Its programme sought to achieve this by preaching the restoration of socialist values, the development of democratic structures and human rights and the promotion of self-management in

27 Interview with Kagarlitsky, 26 November 1990.
28 Berezovsky and Krotov, *Rossiya* (1990), p. 263; Igrunov, 'KSI', pp. 27–8.
29 Berezovsky and Krotov, *Rossiya* (1990), p. 263. Semina, 'Po zakonam' in Pechenev and Vyunsky (eds.), *Neformaly* (1990), p. 165, observes that Kagarlitsky and Malyutin were members of KSI, then of Socialist Initiative, the Moscow Popular Front, and, in addition, Malyutin was a member of the *Perestroika* Club, the Inter-Party Club and the CPSU: interview with Malyutin of 1 December 1990; Berezovsky and Krotov, *Rossiya* (1990), p. 344–5; interview with V. Igrunov, 7 May 1992.

the workplace. Much of its work was done with regional groups, to which it sent theoretical and analytical material. Socialist Initiative's members were anxious to elaborate for the Federation of Socialist Clubs and, subsequently, for the Moscow Popular Front, a coherent social, economic and political programme, which 'could not be replaced with a collection of occasional demands'. This dogmatic orientation, with its resistance to popular opinion, was quite consistent with the traditions of the radical left in Russia but hardly represented a daring break with the attitudes enshrined over decades by the CPSU. After a brief flurry of activity in Summer 1988,[30] Socialist Initiative sank into obscurity, having been overshadowed by more radical and popular groups.

Its members now admit that it exerted little influence and held little appeal for the workers whom it hoped to mobilize.[31] The reason for this would seem to be twofold: Leninist socialism was becoming increasingly discredited among the radical intelligentsia, while those in the working class who still supported communism were attracted to a revitalized populist Stalinism. Nonetheless, some of those involved in Socialist Initiative (including Kagarlitsky) helped to found the Socialist Party in May 1989. This party's initial hesitations about parliamentary democracy and its rejection of the market economy were to deprive it of influence and popularity, even among the radical intelligentsia.[32]

Social Democrats

In general, anarchist and new-left groups exercised limited popular appeal, even among the intelligentsia or in the early stages of the informal movement, when few spirits were brave enough to deviate to the right. It was not the left socialists but the democratic socialists who represented the mainstream of the informal movement. The biggest and the most influential of the early political clubs, the *Perestroika* Club, was broadly social democratic in orientation, even

30 Berezovsky and Krotov, *Rossiya* (1990), pp. 327–8.
31 Interview with B. Kagarlitsky, 26 November 1990.
32 See Koval' (ed.), *Rossiya segodnya: politicheskii portret v dokumentakh* (Moscow, 1991), pp. 172–80, for its draft programme; interviews with Kagarlitsky, 26 November 1990, and M. Malyutin, 1 December 1990. See also I. Kudryavtsev, *Panorama*, 1990, no.7 (July), pp. 4–5.

though it attracted an eclectic audience. The club was founded in February 1987.[33] The idea of establishing a club emerged among a handful of young academics in Moscow and Leningrad. In Moscow, it was associated with the Central Economic-Mathematical Institute of the Academy of Sciences, where it held most of its meetings.

The young academics who founded the club believed that they could contribute their expertise to *perestroika* and even collaborate with Gorbachev and the reformers in the higher echelons in the Party. They felt that there was a need for a forum which would enable academics, especially those specializing in economics and law, and professional experts from the big factories to influence the *apparat* and public opinion and contribute to the formulation of the legal and economic reforms. This ambition was not perhaps as far-fetched as it sounds, as the institutes of the Academy routinely prepared reports and advice for the Central Committee. The club met with an uncertain response from the authorities. On one occasion, a television crew came to film the proceedings. On others, attempts were made to prevent its meetings – by pressurizing the Institute to withdraw the use of the conference room, on one pretext or another.

In February 1987, the first open meeting was held and soon the club's monthly gatherings were attracting 300–400 people.[34] That year, most active, ambitious supporters of reform, from the lower echelons of the academic world in Moscow, were attracted to the debates organized by the *Perestroika* Club. The influence of *glasnost* on the emerging civil society is seen in the issues the *Perestroika* Club considered. On 15 May 1987, they debated Gavriil Popov's review in *Nauka i zhizn'* of Alexander Bek's novel about the career of a Stalinist civil servant. On 2 June 1987, they discussed the *apparat*'s opposition to *perestroika*.[35]

Most of the club's members were academics and intellectuals in their thirties. Although not dissidents, they were poorly integrated into the system, languishing in badly paid jobs at the bottom of the academic ladder or in factories.[36] This made them more ready to take

33 Igor Chubais, interview of 20 November 1990; P. Kudiukin, interview of 5 December 1990.
34 Interviews with P. Kudiukin of 5 November 1990; I. Chubais of 20 November 1990; V. Kardailsky of 25 September 1991.
35 B. Bor, *Glasnost'*, 1987, no.1, p. 7.
36 Interview with A. Kalinin, 9 July 1990; A. Fadin (then a leading member of the club)

risks in getting involved in what was still a very innovative and daring departure. Not unnaturally, this initially obscure forum attracted few of *perestroika*'s famous names (although Igor Klyamkin, Yuri Afanasiev and Roy Medvedev were exceptions)[37] – a circumstance which led Oleg Rumyantsev, one of the club's leaders, to allege that the elite of the intelligentsia were afraid to get involved and left it to the young and daring to make the running in promoting reform.[38] This reproach seems hardly justified in that the political clubs – although a significant token of the new atmosphere of permissiveness and of a new public consciousness – remained on the margins of political life. The establishment intelligentsia could argue with some force that, in their collaboration with the reformers of the Party elite through the press, theatre and film, they did more to promote change in Soviet society at this time than did the obscure debating clubs.

In Leningrad, too, a pro-reform debating club opened (Leningrad *Perestroika*). It started meeting in May 1987 and also attemped to devise economic and legal reforms, arguing for more self-management and for wider involvement in the reform process. 'From the start,' the Leningraders proclaimed, 'the Club considered its task to consist not only in [...] criticizing the existing state of affairs, but also in elaborating proposals to change the situation'. No forum could better illustrate the disproportionate role played by the intelligentsia in the informal movement. The club's members were, overwhelmingly, middle-aged intellectuals, with an academic background. Excluded from the milieu of the intellectual elite, they took advantage of the new climate to create their own clubs, networks and reform caucuses.[39] Hence, the club was not the union of youthful radicals one

quoted in Yushenkov (ed.), *Neformaly* (1990), p. 61; Berezovsky and Krotov, *Rossiya* (1990) p. 247; MBIO: Informal Archive: Folder on *Perestroika 88* for information on its membership, aims and activities.

37 MBIO: Informal Archive: Folder on *Perestroika 88*. On 13 November 1988 Klyamkin, Afanasiev and Medvedev appeared at a club meeting on historic name-places.

38 Shlapentokh, *Soviet Intellectuals* (1990), p. 268, cites Rumyantsev as referring to 'liberal messers', 'foremen of *perestroika*' and 'rebels of the creative unions and the liberal democratic periodicals' who avoided participating in 'the real struggle of the democratic movement'. In view of some of Rumyantsev's own strategies and declarations, this judgement seems unduly harsh: see Malyutin, *Gorizont*, 1989, no.4, p. 11, who says that 'doktora nauk' (Doctors of Science) frequently spoke at the club.

39 By mid-1988, it had sixty-five members and a hundred candidate members, aged on average thirty-eight. Forty-six per cent of members were in their forties; 43 per cent

might have expected, but a gathering of modest, middle-aged and rather cautious reformers. The *Perestroika* Club in Leningrad as in Moscow was above all an institution of the lower intelligentsia - of able and well-educated, but frustrated individuals. In this, the *Perestroika* Club was typical of the early political informal groups. They were, to a significant extent, composed of struggling and no longer youthful intellectuals who had neither eschewed the bohemian habits of youth nor entirely renounced its aspirations.

Moscow *Perestroika*'s ideological platform was summed up in the formula: 'three noes and one yes':

No - to violence and the propaganda of violence;
No - to ideas of national and racial exclusiveness;
No - to claims to a monopoly on truth to the detriment of others' right to the independent search (for truth);
Yes - to socialism.

On the basis of this outlook, the club went to work and over the next two and a half years, organized forty or so public debates, produced two programmes (on political reform and the 'ecologization' of the economy), two revised laws (on cooperatives and state enterprises), three alternative draft laws (on public association, mass meetings and elections) and organized, with other groups, ten demonstrations. A consensus emerged in the club on the need to overcome the bureaucracy's opposition to reform and to erode the concentration of power in the hands of the Party, the KGB and the Interior Ministry.[40]

The club was important neither for the documents it produced nor for the ideas expressed during its meetings. It goes without saying that it had no known influence on the genesis of the economic reform programme and almost no impact on public opinion beyond that of the intelligentsia of the two capitals. Its importance lay in its contribution to the political culture of a key group in society - the articulate, the active and the ambitious, precisely the group which might be expected to participate most effectively in national politics.

belonged to the Communist Party. Moreover, they were well-educated: 46 per cent held doctorates; 21 per cent were economists, 22 per cent engineers and mathematicians, 10 per cent were sociologists or philosophers, with physicists (at 8 per cent) and writers (7 per cent) bringing up the rear, MBIO: Informal Archive: Folder on Leningrad *Perestroika*. See also *Obshchestvenye dvizheniya Leningrada* (1989), pp. 46–8.

40 S. Yushenkov, 'Neformal'noe dvizhenie' in Yushenkov (ed.), *Neformaly* (1990), p. 53; Berezovsky and Krotov, *Rossiya* (1990), pp. 246–8. Dobrynina *et al.* (eds.), *Samodeyatel'nye* (1990), p. 34.

The idea that people could meet in a public forum and express their ideas openly about political and social questions, without the Party interfering, was a radical novelty. It was the first opportunity of a long silent society to express itself, criticize policy and voice its opinion. It was important too as a forum in which many of the future leaders of the democratic movement first came forward.[41] It enabled the different tendencies of unorthodox thought to define themselves and stimulated new political initiatives and ideas.

During the Winter and Spring of 1987–88, the different political orientations within the informal movement began to emerge more clearly and, in advance of the Party Conference, to participate more actively in politics. This tendency was exemplified by developments in the Moscow *Perestroika* Club. The *Perestroika* clubs included both reform-minded ambitious young communists (about one-third of the overall membership in Moscow and 46 per cent in Leningrad were Party members)[42] and former dissidents, some of whom had been released from jail in the amnesty of February 1987. This disparate composition provoked a split in the Moscow club at the end of 1987. In January 1988, two separate groups were formed – Democratic *Perestroika* and *Perestroika 88*. The reform communists and socialists joined Democratic *Perestroika*, which emphasized discipline, organization and participation in Soviet politics, while those of dissident origin and liberal conviction mostly joined *Perestroika 88*. In other words, the original club divided into two naturally opposed political wings – the liberalism of *Perestroika 88* and the reform socialism of Democratic *Perestroika*.

Democratic *Perestroika* tried to gain influence and a place within official structures. In January 1988, Oleg Rumyantsev, one of the club's co-chairmen and founders, took part in a meeting on the political aspects of the informal movement organized by the

41 Among them were Igor Chubais, one of the leaders of the democratic wing of the CPSU in the late 1980s and a founder of the Republican Party; Pavel Kudiukin, a leading member of the Social Democratic Party and future Minister for Labour; Oleg Rumyantsev, one of the leaders of the Social Democratic Party, a member of the Russian parliament and secretary of the parliamentary commission on Russian constitutional reform; and Lev Ponomarev, a Russian Deputy and leader of the Democratic Russia movement.

42 Interviews with V. Kardailsky, secretary of the club, 25 September 1991; and with A. Kalinin, 9 July 1990.

Komsomol and Socialist Initiative. He advanced the view that as the *apparat* did not recognise the plurality of citizens' interests, the informal clubs organized and expressed those interests.[43] The clubs had therefore to work for the decentralization of power and direct democracy. His list of demands for the informal clubs was ambitious and included the right to participate in the legislative process and nominate candidates for election to parliament; an obligation on local authorities to consider and, on occasion, adopt, the informals' proposals; and civil liberties, including freedom of the press and association.[44] He had high expectations of what politics could achieve. *Perestroika*, he declared, should enable the 'political socialization of the popular masses' and the full realization of man. The informal movement had an important role to play in this: 'The social and moral formation of man is a task which is fully within the competence of the movement for social initiatives.' Thus the vocation of politics – in the new order, as in the old – was moral. The essence of the task at hand was 'the emancipation of man'. However, 'the socialist civil society, unlike the bourgeois one, should not emancipate him from politics.'[45]

At this stage, Rumyantsev, like other representatives of the social democratic wing of the informal movement, did not call for full political pluralism. He saw the future in terms of collaboration with a more tolerant CPSU:

> The overwhelming majority of independent public organizations do not have political programmes differing from the course, proclaimed by the Party, of fundamental reconstruction of all aspects of public life, or from the revolutionary principles of democratic socialism [...]

Hence, formal and informal structures should cooperate:

---

43 The emphasis on the representation of group or class interests, to which young reformers often reverted, may be ascribed to determinist political theory (to the effect that the motor of politics is class interest and political forces are necessarily based on class interest): see S. Stankevich, 'Tam gde nachinaetsya yedinstvo', *Yunost'*, 1989, no. 9, pp. 2–4.

44 Dobrynina *et al.* (eds), *Samodeyatel'nye* (1990), p. 35; O. Rumyantsev, *O samodeyatel'nom dvizhenii* (Moscow, 1988) (paper presented to this conference), pp. 21, 26–7, 40.

45 Ibid., pp. 23, 24, 44; Rumyantsev, 'Pereraspredelitel'naya model'' in Yushenkov (ed.), *Neformaly* (1990), pp. 210–11.

The organs of power should learn to be partners with the new elements in our political system - only equal relations with the independent organizations will serve as a real guarantee of keeping them within the sphere of socialist democracy.[46]

This line, favouring cooperation with the authorities, of working within the system to promote change, was revised only in Spring 1989, when the elections to the Congress of People's Deputies marked a new stage in the political life of the country. Not until May 1989 did Democratic *Perestroika* begin to move towards opposition to the CPSU.[47]

The *Perestroika* Club spawned a series of other groups and initiatives. One of the most important of these was the Inter-Club Party Group, which brought together many of the first supporters of democratic reform in the CPSU. It was the publication of Nina Andreeva's letter to *Sovetskaya Rossiya* in March 1988 which prompted the reform communists in Democratic *Perestroika* to found, in April 1988, a pressure group to prepare democratic reform proposals for the Nineteenth Party Conference. This group first called itself the Informal Party Group (*Neustavnaya partinnaya gruppa*). About a dozen people from Democratic *Perestroika* were involved (principally Igor Chubais, Mikhail Malyutin and Vladimir Kardailsky) but, as they were anxious for fresh ideas, they tried to attract reform communists from other clubs to join them and it was this expanded group which became the Inter-Club Party Group. Well-known members included Sergei Stankevich (then a junior researcher at the Institute of World History); Vladimir Lysenko (a teacher of scientific communism at the Moscow Aviation Institute and future Russian Deputy and Republican Party leader) and Igor Chubais (then a sociologist). The group hoped to see the Party rules changed to democratize the Party's structures and conduct.[48]

Liberal Groups

Considerably more radical in their outlook - less ready to compromise with the authorities and to believe in the likelihood of

46 Rumyantsev, *Dvizheniya* (1988), pp. 32-3.
47 See R. Sakwa, *Gorbachev* (1990), p. 205; Pribylovsky, *Slovar'* (1991), p. 84.
48 Interview with V. Kardailsky, 25 September 1991; see also Berezovsky and Krotov, *Rossiya* (1990), p. 278.

fundamental reform of the existing system – were groups on the right of the political spectrum. These clubs appeared on the scene a little later than the socialist clubs and, in character and outlook, were closer to the old dissident subculture (from which some of their members issued). Many of those who went on to found groups of liberal democratic orientation were involved in the *Perestroika* Club in 1987.

Doverie

One of the first of these groups was *Doverie*, or Trust, initially founded in 1982 to promote trust between the USSR and the USA and some of whose original eleven members had been imprisoned. In 1987, however, *Doverie* was able to resume its activities and on 6 June 1987 issued a Declaration of Principles, which outlined the group's main sphere of activities – pacifism, human rights and ecology – and its demands. These included the withdrawal of Soviet troops from Afghanistan, the demilitarization of public consciousness and the rejection of military–patriotic education. About twenty people were actively involved in *Doverie*; they organized meetings and demonstrations, distributed leaflets, published a monthly magazine (*Day by Day*) and held weekly gatherings of members in private flats. In December 1987, a number of those involved, more inclined to a positive view of the new Party leadership, broke away from the main group but within a few months no more was heard of them. The radical majority, which emphasized the importance of not conceding on principles, led by Ye. Debranskaya, went on to join the first independent political party in the USSR, Democratic Union.[49]

'Democracy and Humanism'

Another noteworthy group was the seminar 'Democracy and Humanism', which was founded in June 1987 by Asya Lashiver, Ye. Debranskaya and others involved in the *Doverie* group. Its main aim was declared to be 'the restoration of democracy in the USSR and counter-propaganda against the Bolsheviks' totalitarianism'. They organized demonstrations against human rights' abuses, held seminars on historical and social problems, read works by Solzhenitsyn and later helped to write Democratic Union's policy documents. A flavour

49 Interview with A. Lashiver, of Democratic Union, 22 September 1991; see also Berezovsky and Krotov, *Rossiya* (1990), pp. 255–6.

of their activities is given by their demonstration against the celebration of the seventieth anniversary of the Revolution in November 1987. 'We have nothing to celebrate on 7 November,' they explained. 'The establishment of a dictatorship, which brought with it the death of many millions of victims [...] cannot be a cause for national celebration.' Up to thirty or forty people took part in its seminars, which were held in private flats. The coordinator of the group was Valeriya Novodvorskaya, who became one of Democratic Union's founders and leaders.[50]

Civic Dignity

One of the most influential of the early liberal groups was Civic Dignity. It was founded on 10 September 1987 to uphold liberal democratic principles and to work for the defence of human rights and the establishment of a state of law. The group was led by Viktor Zolotarev, who had previously been involved in the Club for Social Initiatives and in the *Perestroika* debating club. Its membership consisted of a handful of young people of dissident style and outlook.[51] Civic Dignity's members, although not numerous, took an active part in the life of 'informal' Moscow in 1988 and 1989: they participated in *Perestroika 88*, helping to impel it towards adopting liberal democratic positions, and in the formation of the Moscow Popular Front – from which they quickly dissociated themselves because of its rigid socialism. Its leaders were subsequently coopted into the elite democratic club, Moscow Tribune, and the group backed every serious effort to found a united, democratic front, culminating in Democratic Russia.

Civic Dignity's members were among the first of the informals to attempt to give substance to the emerging political pluralism in Russia. In May 1989, just after the elections, they formed the Constitutional Democratic Union, which aspired to the role played at the start of the century by the Union of Liberation,[52] and which was subsequently instrumental in the reestablishment of the Kadet Party.

50 *Byulleten' soveta partii Demokraticheskii soyuz*, 1991, no. 6, p. 29; Berezovsky and Krotov, *Rossiya* (1990), p. 243; interview with A. Lashiver, 22 September 1991.
51 Interview with Yevgeni Ikhlov, 16 November 1990; Berezovsky and Krotov, *Rossiya* (1990), pp. 242-3.
52 A movement founded in 1903 by Peter Struve and others, and which was the forerunner of the Kadet Party.

However, Civic Dignity enjoyed more prestige than real influence. In the early stages of the democratic revival in Russia, opinion – both among those actively involved in official and unofficial politics and in society at large – appeared to be overwhelmingly in favour of the socialist option. Not until the rise of the new Russian nationalism, in 1991-92, was one wing of the Kadets to become a more serious political force and this was achieved by abandoning its liberalism.

These groups were, at least initially, less innovative in style than the socialist clubs; they were less popular than the big debating clubs and their style of work and atmosphere owed more to Russian tradition (both of dissidence in this century and of revolutionary politics in the last) than to the fashions and new possibilities of *perestroika*. However, they represented a corrective and an enriching addition to the narrow spectrum of political attitudes which dominated the informal movement. It took considerable courage to advance these views and the authorities were not alone in denouncing them. It was not uncommon in Moscow, at that time, to hear and read condemnations of the liberal right emanating not only from the official press but also from the informals themselves: it was feared that their extremism – in holding demonstrations and declaring their opposition to government policies – would provoke a wave of repressions and it was felt that their pronouncements were both unrealistic and irresponsible.[53]

Democratic Union

The most vocal and radical of the democratic groups was Democratic Union. Democratic Union was founded in April 1988 as an offshoot of Democracy and Humanism, *Doverie* and *Perestroika 88*. It was the first of the new political parties and the first outright opposition party. As such, it attracted a great deal of attention from the Party – despite the fact that its membership was always small and that it in no way posed a real political threat to the CPSU's prerogatives and popular authority. The idea of founding an opposition party emerged in the

53 See, for example, the August 1987 informal conference's failure to support Valeriya Novodvorskaya's calls, on behalf of Democracy and Humanism, for the de-ideologization of the Soviet Constitution and the recognition of the failure of socialism in Russia: Gubenko and Piskarev, *Komsomolskaya pravda*, 31 January 1988, p. 2; Zhavoronkov, *MN*, 13 September 1987, p. 12.

Democracy and Humanism seminar, which collaborated with *Doverie* and *Perestroika 88* in organizing the Democratic Union's first congress on 7-9 May 1988.

This Congress, attended by 150 delegates and guests from 27 towns, defined the new party's main aims: a multiparty system, a mixed economy, including private property, and national self-determination. The most striking aspect of the new party was its overt rejection of the 1917 Revolution and its consequences. According to documents adopted at its second Congress, October 1917 was a 'counter-revolutionary coup'; the system of government which emerged from it was condemned in the new party's documents, which went on to '[reject] not only Stalinism, but also the cult of Lenin and the ideology of Leninism, as the basis of the State ideology of the totalitarian system'. It declared its opposition to the existing social system. Democratic Union saw its main aim as being 'the non-violent replacement of the totalitarian State structures with a fully democratic system' and with 'a society founded on the principles of political, economic and spiritual pluralism'. Other aims included the abolition of the KGB, of the internal passport system and of censorship. The new party believed that the best way of achieving this was to hold meetings and demonstrations and to distribute leaflets – in short, to educate public opinion.[54]

The party was, however, beset by a number of difficulties, both internal and external. Its radical anti-Party line and gestures deprived it of popular support: people were frightened by its actions and rhetoric, which were indistinguishable from those which had for generations been condemned as subversive and which still encountered official hostility. Fear of being taken for a dissident prevented

---

54 Declaration, Programme Principles and Basic Political Principles of Democratic Union, adopted at the second Congress, documents courtesy of A. Lashiver. See also 'Vyderzhki iz stenogrammy pervogo s"yezda', *Byulleten' soveta partii Demokraticheskii soyuz*, 1991, no. 6, pp. 22-8, for proceedings of the first Congress; and 'Predistoriya DS' in ibid., pp. 29-33; Sudiniev, 'Nashchestvie' in Yushenkov (ed.), *Neformaly* (1990), p. 39; M. Sheshma, 'Dialog ili konfrontatsiya' in ibid., p. 154; Berezovsky and Krotov, *Rossiya* (1990), pp. 250-52; interview with A. Lashiver, 22 September 1991; Tolz, *Multi-Party System* (1990), pp. 56-9; Dobrynina *et al.* (eds), *Samodeyatel'nye* (1990), pp. 36-7; I. Sidorov, *Leningradskaya pravda*, 5 August 1988, pp. 2-3, for interview with Democratic Union leaders from Leningrad about the party's aims; G. Ovcharenko, *Pravda*, 24 August 1988, p. 6; V. Tolz, 'Creation of the Democratic Union', *RL* 189/88; Yu. Shabanov, writing in *Moskovskaya pravda*, 14 May 1988, for a hostile account of the first Congress.

people from listening to and absorbing the message. The party's decision to hold a protest rally in May 1988 over the projected decree on associations was sharply criticized within the democratic movement as ill-timed and likely to give the CPSU's conservatives ammunition against the liberal wing of the Party.

Then, Democratic Union itself was not cohesive: it represented a coalition between groups united in their opposition to the CPSU but divided in their political preferences. Russian analysts distinguish between four or five different currents within Democratic Union: Christian or constitutional democratic, liberal democratic, social democratic and democratic communist. Estimates of the strength of these tendencies differ: according to one source, liberal democrats represented 26 per cent, Christian democrats 10 per cent, social democrats 8 per cent and democratic communists 8 per cent of members, while a further 48 per cent of the party membership had aligned themselves with no particular group.[55] According to one of Democratic Union's leaders, even though it claimed to be a political party, it was really a more amorphous organization or movement. Even in its first year – when it attracted most attention and its membership peaked (at around 2000, at the time of its second Congress in January 1989) – it was divided on tactics. The fundamental difference was between those who rejected any form of collaboration with the existing state system and those who believed, after the Nineteenth CPSU Party Conference and the promulgation of constitutional reforms in November–December 1988, that new possibilities now existed and that change could now be promoted within the system.

This difference of view led to the secession of the 'constitutionalists' and the radicalization of Democratic Union's policies and declarations. Even during its first eight months, Democratic Union held 45 meetings and 2000 public debates and discussions, and organized 160 leaflet distribution campaigns.[56] However, as the pace of political change intensified, after March 1989, as the republics began to move towards independence and political pluralism became

---

55 Sheshma, 'Dialog' in Yushenkov (ed.), *Neformaly* (1990), p. 153; I. Zaitsev, 'Chelovecheskoe izmerenie' in Levichev (ed.), *Neformal'naya vol'na* (1990), p. 68.
56 From documents of the second Congress, cited by M. Sheshma, 'Dialog' in Yushenkov (ed.), *Neformaly* (1990), p. 153.

a real possibility in Russia itself, support for Democratic Union fell off and it really died as an effective political organization by 1990.[57] Democratic Union was nonetheless important in that it helped to activate the informal movement, to bring it on to the streets and out of the narrow intellectual and professional circles to which it had previously been confined.

Memorial Initiative Group

The liberal caucus which arguably did most to mobilize public opinion in favour of liberal and democratic reform was Memorial. The idea of a memorial to the victims of Stalinism had been raised at the Twenty-Second Party Congress in 1961 but had never been followed up. It was revived at the August 1987 meeting of informal clubs by anti-Stalinist intellectuals (including Dmitri Leonov, Pavel Kudyukin and Vladimir Lysenko) and, in Autumn 1987, the Memorial Initiative Group was formed. At this time, it was becoming clearer that a fight was developing in the Party leadership over whether or not to reject the Stalinist model of government and administration and that the fate of the reform was in the balance. For some of the early activists of Memorial, the significance of the proposed monument to the 'repressed' was not merely historical: it was intended to symbolize the rejection of the country's Stalinist legacy and the defeat of the Stalinists within the Party leadership.

In November 1987, a number of enthusiasts began to try to collect signatures in support of this demand for a monument. The campaign, launched on the streets of central Moscow and then pursued in Moscow's liberal theatres, ran up against public fear and official harassment. None the less, initiative groups and signature campaigns were formed in Leningrad and other Soviet cities. In January 1988, a separate drive was launched to collect the signatures of eminent liberal intellectuals in support of the demand. The singer Bulat Okudzhava, novelist Anatoly Pristavkin (who had grown up in an orphanage as a child of an 'enemy of the people') and the poet Yevgeny Yevtushenko were among the first of the 110 who signed the petition. Despite the official disfavour which greeted the

---

57 Interview with A. Lashiver, 22 September 1991; see also Sudiniev, 'Nashchestvie' in Yushenkov (ed.), *Neformaly* (1990), pp. 39–40, on the radicalization of the movement.

campaign, 50 000 signatures were collected by the early Summer and the petition was handed over by Yuri Afanasiev to Gorbachev at the Nineteenth Party Conference. In consequence, the idea of a memorial was adopted by the Party and a competition was subsequently held to choose a suitable design. That no monument was erected subsequently was due to the failure of the ensuing competition to elicit a suitable project.[58] Instead, camp survivors and their relatives carried a rock from the *gulag* through the streets of Moscow on a bleak evening in October 1990 and deposited it near the Lyubyanka – hidden from the sight of Dzerzhinski (then still on his pedestal in the middle of the square) by the ragged shrubbery of a decrepit little park. Unlike other early informal groups, Memorial was a campaign with a practical goal, rather than a relatively amorphous and theoretical semi-private club. Furthermore, the thrust of its activities was controversial: it raised a politically sensitive issue and sought to act as an independent public pressure group. This represented a significant step forward in the political development of the informals.

Public life had begun to develop also in more visible ways in 1987. The streets of the capital, previously crowded during the day with harassed shoppers and eerily empty at other times, began to come to life. In Summer 1987, Yeltsin ordered Moscow City Council to issue a directive permitting demonstrations in Moscow, if prior notice of the venue and the expected number of participants were given. The city began to show signs of unwonted vitality: gangs of young people – hippies, rockers, followers of hari-krishna – appeared on the streets, scandalizing older inhabitants; it became interesting to wander down the Arbat and survey the *chansonniers*, artists and orators who congregated there; unofficial art shows and markets sprang up on the outskirts of the city. These innovations testified to a new atmosphere: instead of isolated individuals darting furtively into gloomy courtyards or dragging wearily about on errands, a citizenry began to emerge, curious and bemused by the novel manifestations of variety and individuality on the streets. Timidly, a public if not yet a political life developed in the capital. Viktor Zolotarev, the leader of Civic

58 Interview with N. Braginskaya, 13 November 1990; Sudiniev, 'Nashchestvie' in Yushenkov (ed.), *Neformaly* (1990), pp. 24–5; Pribilovsky, *Slovar'* (1991), pp. 38–9; N. Braginskaya, 'Slava besslaviya', *Znanie–sila*, January 1991, pp. 12ff; *Obshchestvennye dvizheniya Leningrada* (1989), pp. 29–30.

Dignity, encapsulated this mood, in his speech to the August meeting of informals:

> The citizen's feeling of insignificance, oppression and timidity, when confronted with the lordly indifference of officials, is now, as we speak, being supplanted by the feeling of civic communion, the feeling of guilt for the worst within and around us and a completely new desire to participate directly and personally in the creation of society's well-being.[59]

DEVELOPMENT OF THE INDEPENDENT PRESS

Another token of the new confidence of the emerging civil society was the development of the independent press. The first step towards its creation in contemporary Russia was taken by Alexander Grigoryants, who, on his release from prison founded a new dissident paper entitled *Glasnost*.[60] The first number of *Glasnost*, edited by Grigoryants, was issued in July 1987 and was circulated illegally in Moscow. Foreigners were able to obtain copies, as the paper also appeared as a supplement to the Russian *émigré* publication, *Russkaya mysl'*. *Glasnost* published sharp criticism of the official reform process and of the regime's human rights record. The paper also functioned as a human rights agency, receiving complaints from those whose rights had been infringed by the authorities. Before long, Grigoryants was subjected to a campaign of harassment and intimidation by the KGB, which detained him and confiscated his press.

However, *Glasnost* was only one of a number of *samizdat feuilles volantes* devoted to controversial issues (including the environment, anarchism, radical literature and social criticism) and of which *Express-Khronika* was the earliest and most prestigious among informal circles in Moscow.[61] Although their circulation was minuscule, their symbolic importance was significant, not least as the proliferation of an underground press would have been impossible even two or three years earlier. *Express-Khronika* began to appear on

59 V. Yakovlev, *Ogonek*, 1987, no. 36, pp. 4–5.
60 For *Glasnost*'s principles, see *Glasnost*, 2–11 July 1987, p. 3.
61 B. Kagarlitsky, *The Thinking Reed* (1989), pp. 345–6, who makes rather inflated claims for these papers. See *Glasnost*, 1–4, July 1987, p. 13, for summary information about a number of independent papers.

1 August 1987: it was devoted principally to following the development of the informal movement throughout the country. In 1988, its circulation was still very low (100-200 copies) but by Summer 1989, the paper, which appeared weekly, had a print run of 10,000 copies. It had developed a network of correspondents in over 100 towns and was distributed throughout the country. Weekly meetings were also conducted with readers in Moscow.

These developments encouraged the editors of the independent press to establish contact with each other and to try to organize themselves. The first such meeting took place in Leningrad on 24-25 October 1987, when representatives from seventeen *samizdat* papers met. This was followed up by a second meeting in Moscow, on 7-8 May 1988, when the Independent Press Club was founded by 18 of the 27 participating publications. The meeting recognized the need to establish a *samizdat* library and an information network - given the partiality of the information available in the official press and libraries. The publication of the *Bulletin of the Independent Press Club* in 1988 was the response to the second of these aims, while the first was met with the foundation on 15 November 1988 of the Independent Public Library by, among others, the papers *Express-Khronika*, *Glasnost* and *Free Word* (the organ of Democratic Union).

At first, the library contained about 400 books and papers but by August 1989 - despite harassment by the authorities - it held five thousand photocopies of about five hundred books and dozens of papers and had established branches in fifteen provincial towns. Its declared aim was to assure the right to information, to promote free research in culture and the humanities and on the theme of democracy in particular. The Independent Press Club's third conference in Moscow on 19-20 November 1988 drew editors from 56 publications.[62]

By 1988, the Soviet Sociological Association knew of 48 *samizdat* papers of which twenty were liberal democratic in orientation, nineteen Marxist and six Christian. By 1990, over 300 *samizdat* journals existed, of which about sixty were published in Moscow and forty in Leningrad and around ten in most provincial cities. Over 150 of these publications were liberal-democratic, about sixty were Marxist or socialist and a little over thirty were Christian. Most (some

62 Berezovsky and Krotov, *Rossiya* (1990), pp. 234-5, 262.

150) were devoted to social and political issues, while approximately fifty concentrated on cultural questions. Print runs varied enormously – from 4–5 to tens of thousands of copies – but average print runs were in the hundreds.[63] By 1989, official journalists such as Selunin began to write for the unofficial press, which began to supply information also to *Novosti* and *Gosteleradio*.[64]

Samizdat became an increasingly important feature of public life after 1988. The embryonic political parties and movements of socialist and social democratic orientation began to establish contact with it – even though the papers grouped around the Independent Press Club were essentially preoccupied with human rights and hence stood on the more revolutionary or radical wing of the political spectrum. The role played by *samizdat* in this period (1987–89) was, therefore, both symbolic and substantive: in a society which was still subject to censorship, it was important as a source of factual information and of divergent opinion; and by its very existence, it testified to the possibility and viability of alternative and critical thought. It therefore served to encourage those who, working on the limits of the tolerated, required both courage and imagination to create new norms for public and political activity.

CONCLUSION

It was no accident that independent clubs were able to develop in 1987 in Moscow, a year before they emerged in provincial Russian cities. Boris Yeltsin was in charge of the Moscow Party machine and at an early stage encountered fierce opposition to his populist line from the local *apparat*. His tolerance of the informal groups that emerged in the city at this time may, therefore, have been connected with this desire to establish a degree of popular legitimacy for his rule, in the absence of support from his subordinates in the Party.

An early signal of his attitude was given in May 1987. About 400 members of *Pamyat'* (Memory) – an obscure nationalist conservation

---

63 Ibid., pp. 47–9; Dobrynina *et al.* (eds), *Samodeyatel'nye* (1990), p. 33; Tolz, *Multi-Party System* (1990), pp. 29–33.

64 *Gosteleradio* established the news agency *Interfax* in 1989, to sell this unofficial information to foreign correspondents in Moscow, as it often covered areas with which the official press was unfamiliar.

movement, which became one of the most popular informal move-ments in Moscow, despite its extreme anti-Semitic orientation – staged a demonstration in Red Square early in May 1987 to protest against the planned monument to the victory in the Second World War. They also demanded a meeting with Gorbachev or Yeltsin and the removal of Alexander Yakovlev and his protégé, the editor Vitaly Korotich. This was the biggest unofficial demonstration in Moscow since the time of Stalin and, extraordinarily, it resulted not in the arrest or imprisonment of the participants but in their being invited to a meeting with the Party First Secretary for Moscow, Boris Yeltsin.[65] This was a sign of exceptional favour (and suggests that *Pamyat'* was not without influential friends in the Party) and was understood (possibly misunderstood) at the time to herald a new era of liberation.[66]

This meeting signalled the start of a brief period of tentative collaboration between the informals (or part of the informal movement) and the Party, which was to last until the Autumn and Yeltsin's removal. It was because of Yeltsin's limited support for the informal movement that unofficial opinion in Moscow was able to take the initiative in organizing the first conference of informal clubs in August 1987. Although this meeting yielded few practical results, it inspired the participants, gave them confidence and enabled contact to be established among many different groups.[67] A wide range of

65 The most detailed account of this meeting – which reveals Yeltsin as an authoritarian nationalist rather than as a liberal democrat – is given in 'Chto takoe [...] Pamyat'?', *Russkaya mysl'*, 31 July 1987, p. 6.
66 A. Kiselev and A. Mostovshchikov, *MN*, 17 May 1987, p. 4; B. Yeltsin, *Against the Grain* (1990), pp. 99-100, refers to its slogans as having been 'of an entirely proper kind something about *perestroika*, Russia, freedom, the rottenness of the *apparat* [...]'. He urged them to continue their cultural and conservation work, deal with their extremists, get official registration and promote *perestroika*. See also Roy Medvedev's comparison of Yeltsin's treatment of this group with that of other demonstrators in G. Chiesa, *Time of Change* (London and New York, 1991), pp. 141-2.
67 For information on this meeting see Alexandrova, *Informelle Gruppen* (1988), pp. 33-4, 36-7; G. Ivantsov, 'Upryamye voprosy' in Yushenkov (ed.), *Neformaly* (1990), p. 217. The premises for the meeting were made available by the CPSU: Rumyantsev, *Dvizheniya* (1988), p. 9; Igrunov, 'KSI' (1988), p. 28; G. Zhavoronkov, *MN*, 13 September 1987, p. 12. Various estimates of the attendance are given ranging between 47 and 63 groups: Sudiniev, 'Nashchestvie' in Yushenkov (ed.), *Neformaly* (1990), p. 28; Tolz, *Multi-Party System* (1990), p. 26; Rumyantsev, *Dvizheniya* (1988), p. 9; Igrunov, 'KSI' (1988), p. 28. See also Churbanov and Nelyubin, 'Neformal'nye' in Kuptsov (ed.), *Demokratizatsiya* (1989), p. 244.

sometimes controversial issues was discussed at the meeting, ranging from relatively innocuous proposals on self-management and voluntary charity to human rights violations and the erection of a monument to the victims of Stalin's repressions. The group Democracy and Humanism even argued in favour of abolishing the CPSU's monopoly on political life and the 'de-ideologization' of the Constitution.[68]

Two views emerged as to how the clubs should organize their future work: Democracy and Humanism wanted it to be based on democratic pluralist principles, while the majority insisted on a strictly socialist orientation. This division, which split the informal movement throughout its existence, largely corresponds to its twin origins in the dissident movement and the lower reaches of the CPSU itself. The socialist majority founded the largely moribund Federation of Socialist Social Clubs (FSOK) and adopted a declaration which proclaimed:

> We support and are ready to take an active part in the process of *perestroika*, implemented by the Communist Party in all spheres of our life [...] We support every constructive initiative, draft and proposal, which will further *perestroika* and strengthen socialist principles in our country.

Not surprisingly, Party officials attending the meeting declared themselves satisfied with its results.[69] The conference testified, therefore, both to the tentative emergence of a civic society and to the constraints on both its independence of spirit and its room for manoeuvre.

The vulnerability of the informal movement was seen, however, in the Winter of 1987-88. These months were marked by sharp infighting in the CPSU leadership and by a conservative backlash. The most famous victim of these manoeuvres was Boris Yeltsin, who was summarily dismissed from his post as Moscow Party chief. This was thus a fallow period for the informal movement, which became

68 Yakovlev, *Ogonek*, 1987, no. 36 (September), p. 4; Gubenko and Piskarev, *Kom. pravda*, 31 January 1988, p. 2. for a hostile account; Alexandrova, *Informelle Gruppen* (1988), pp. 35-6. Rumyantsev, *Dvizheniya* (1988), p. 10, suggests that the emphasis was placed on cooperation on conservation, ecology, worker self-management and coordination of the informal movement.

69 Yakovlev, *Ogonek*, 1987, no. 36 (September), p. 5; Zhavoronkov, *MN*, 1987, 13 September 1987, p. 12.

the target of denunciations by the Party's deputy leader Yegor Ligachev and his ally, the KGB chief, Viktor Chebrikov.[70] Not until April 1988 did Gorbachev reestablish his authority and set the Party back on a course towards reform and were the clubs able to resume their activities in a more benevolent climate.

While important as an indication of the rebirth of civil society, the informal movement was, however, neither popular nor representative: it was supported and animated by a few hundred middle-aged, obscure intellectuals, who were neither by temperament nor by conviction committed to revolution. Many were members of the CPSU and most supported socialism in one form or another. What they most wanted to change was not so much the system itself as its decision-making process – they wanted not to overthrow the regime but to open it up to include them. Their political ambitions grew, however, when, with the Party Conference, they realized that the reform leadership of the Party looked to them for support. Thus encouraged, they sensed that it was now both possible and important to form a popular front, which would mobilize the public behind the Party leadership's reforms.

70 Chebrikov, Speech on Dzerzhinsky anniversary, *Pravda*, 11 September 1987; Ligachev, *Rechi* (1989), pp. 174, 200-201, 210, 246.

6. The Rise of the Popular Fronts

A vital role in the development of the democratic movement in modern Russia was played by the Nineteenth Party Conference in June 1988, which approved a semi-democratic reform of the Soviet Constitution. While the need for a measure of democratic reform had been acknowledged by the Central Committee Plenum of January 1987, it was a highly controversial policy within the Party, meeting with stiff resistance both within the Politburo and in the *apparat*. The reform leadership and their advisers were thus inclined to encourage popular support for their policies, to circumvent this opposition.

The intellectuals – both in the establishment and in the capitals' research institutes – were eager to respond. Within the elite, a whole generation, disappointed in its hopes of the Thaw and humiliated by its own compromises with the authorities during the Brezhnev years, was determined that this time the Party reformers should triumph and the Stalinist model be abandoned definitively, in favour of reform socialism. The lower intelligentsia hoped that the system would open up to enable them to play a greater role in the organization and direction of society. The intellectuals' first response to the Party Conference, with its vigorous debates and decision to introduce a reformed legislature, was to attempt to organize a broad democratic caucus in the Russian Federation, as the Party reformers seemed to want. Then, as the elections approached, they attempted to secure the endorsement of democratic candidates in the election campaign.

THE SEARCH FOR A POPULAR FRONT

Shortly before the Party Conference, two of Gorbachev's advisers, Boris Kurashvili and Tatyana Zaslavskaya, called for the creation of a Popular Front 'in support of *perestroika*', to unite the disparate political clubs and movements that had sprung up the previous year behind the Party's reformers. Neither envisaged the creation of an opposition or anti-Party movement.[1] The People's Front in Support of *Perestroika*, mooted by Boris Kurashvili, was 'not intended as a new party, "a party of non-Party people"'. There was no need for this, Kurashvili argued, as there were no opposed classes, only temporary discrepancies between supporters and hidden opponents of *perestroika*. 'Naturally, the new union would function under the general guidance of the Party', but it would also have to be 'an autonomous socio-political organization', with the right 'to criticize Party committees, soviets [...] and management machinery for [their record on] the implementation of the Party's decisions and legislation'. In short, the Front would mobilize public opinion in support of the Party line as defined by Gorbachev.[2] The possibility of opposition to the regime organizing and gaining strength was considered unlikely by Party reformers.

Moscow Popular Front

The Moscow Popular Front (MPF) was clearly an attempt to respond to these calls. On 5 June 1988, a meeting of informal clubs was held to debate the Central Committee's Theses for discussion at the Party Conference. Representatives of forty clubs attended and drafted an 'instruction' to the Conference, which demanded freedom of the press and free elections to the soviets and broached the idea of launching a Popular Front, in apposition rather than opposition to the Party.[3] A

---

1 T. Zaslavskaya, 'O strategii sotsial'nogo upravleniya perestroiki' in Yu. Afanasiev (ed.), *Inogo ne dano* (1988), p. 43; Zaslavskaya, *Izvestiya*, 4 June 1988; B. Kurashvili, 'Demokraticheski soyuz', *Sovetskaya molodezh*, 27 April 1988, pp. 1, 3: Kurashvili saw a popular or democratic union as a way of involving newly active sections of the population and non-Party members in the running of the country. He felt that their criticisms and ideas should be used to ensure that the institutions of state implemented the Party's policies. The front should have access to the mass media, participate in election campaigns, influence the nomination of candidates to the soviets and have the right to initiate legislation in the soviets. See also S. Yushenkov, 'Neformal'noe dvizhenie' in Yushenkov (ed.), *Neformaly* (1990), p. 54.

2 Kurashvili, *MN*, 1988, no. 10, p. 8.

3 Kagarlitsky, *Farewell* (1990), p. 7; Berezovsky and Krotov, *Rossiya* (1990), p. 289; see also Malyutin, *Gorizont*, 1989, no. 4, p. 9: 'None of the Popular Front organizations aspires to the role of a new party, they share the goals formulated by the CPSU after April 1985 [...] The Popular Front supports dialogue and cooperation with the higher

second meeting was called on 12 June and at this, eighteen clubs decided to found a Popular Front in Moscow and elected an organizing committee, which led to the official formation of the Front on 29 July 1988.[4]

However, even before its formal inception, the movement split. The division reflected the fundamental divergence of views within the informal movement: a majority of clubs favoured retaining a specific commitment to socialism in the Front's programme documents, while a minority (an alliance of anarchist and liberal-democratic groups)[5] wanted a more whole-hearted endorsement of democratic pluralism, which the socialists refused to concede.[6] As a result, the democratically inclined clubs withdrew their support for the proposed organization and the Popular Front which emerged in Moscow was not representative of the broad spectrum of views within the informal movement[7] and failed either to unite the informal movement or to attract wider popular support.[8]

The Spring 1989 elections infused new life into the divided organization and enhanced its support for democracy: the Front campaigned for independent candidates and helped to secure the election of a number of radical deputies.[9] None the less, it did not

authorities and, at the same time, it supports the self-organization of the popular masses and *perestroika* from below, hoping to forge a union between the progressive forces in the CPSU and the broad public movement.'

4 Sudiniev, 'Nashchestvie' in Yushenkov (ed.), *Neformaly* (1990), p. 32.

5 Commune, KSI, Civic Dignity, Memorial and *Perestroika 88.*

6 Interviews with Professor I. Surikov 13 October 1990; M. Malyutin, 1 December 1990. Berezovsky and Krotov, *Rossiya* (1990), p. 289, give a rather tendentious account (supplied by representatives of the predominant view); Kagarlitsky, *Farewell* (1990), pp. 9-12.

7 Gleb Pavlovsky affirmed that the MPF manipulated meetings, preventing non-socialist groups from attending and refusing to admit delegates of whom the leadership did not approve. He also criticized its centralization and the subordination of the provincial groups to the leadership at the centre: Pavlovsky, *MN*, no. 40, 1988, p. 9; Malyutin, 'Problemy formirovaniya N.F.', MSS. paper, 1988, p. 13, agrees that the central problem concerned interpretations of democratic socialism. (Document by courtesy of M. Malyutin). See Pribylovsky, *Panorama*, 28, July 1991, p. 6, for a good summary history of the Moscow Popular Front.

8 See Malyutin on the isolation of the Moscow Front and its lack of wide public backing, in 'Vybor' in Yushenkov (ed.), *Neformaly* (1990), pp. 77-8, and quoted in A. Trusov (ed.), 'Neformaly' in Pechenev and Vyunsky (eds.), *Neformaly* (1990), pp. 245-6.

9 Berezovsky and Krotov, *Rossiya* (1990), p. 36, estimate that 20 MPF candidates were elected and that several dozen more succeeded thanks to its efforts. Malyutin claims that the MPF managed to get several of its leaders nominated at the first stage of the

initially propose a view of democracy at odds with that of the reform leadership of the Party. It declared its aim to be 'cooperation with the democratic initiatives of the masses in the struggle for socialist renewal of society and for democratic socialism'. It supported the transfer of power to democratically elected soviets, freedom of the press and of association and demanded a 'democratically planned' economy and the introduction of worker self-management.[10] This newspeak reflected the Front's desire to cooperate with the Party. One of its documents, dating from August 1989, *50 Answers to 50 Questions about the Moscow Popular Front*, explained that the Moscow Popular Front was not a political party in its own right; unlike the CPSU, whose new democratic line it supported, the Front did not aspire to power – only to influence over it.[11] This careful approach is explained partly by the fact that the Front's coordinating council (a nine-member team elected in November 1988) included several Party members and left socialists,[12] who had not yet opted for opposition to the Party but sought to promote change from within it. Only later did the Front unequivocally embrace fully democratic principles.[13]

In practice, the occasionally turgid and ambivalent declarations of the Front translated into a form of populist socialism – a ticket that won the democrats most of their seats in 1989 and 1990, but which

campaign: Stankevich in Cheremushkin; Goncharenko in Medvedkov; Malyutin in Sevastopol; Druganov in Krasnogvareisk. Korotich's name was put forward in Dzerzhinski-Sverdlovsk district and that of Andrei Nuikin in Krasnopresenko-Fruzenski district with the MPF's help. Malyutin, *Gorizont*, 4, 1989, p. 12. (Most of these candidates did not survive the Party's careful weeding out of its critics.)

10 Berezovsky and Krotov, *Rossiya* (1990), p. 288.

11 L. Semina, 'Po zakonam' in Pechenev and Vyunsky (eds.), *Neformaly* (1990), pp. 177–8. The Front's charter, however, revealed its evolution towards more democratic positions, demanding political pluralism, parliamentary democracy, the rule of law and a constitution enshrining fundamental civic liberties (including freedom of association and speech and legal protection of the individual *vis-à-vis* the State and secret police). 'Khartiya Moskovskogo narodnogo fronta', *Trezvost' i kul'tura*, 1990, no. 6, pp. 30–34, for an abbreviated version.

12 Among them were three prominent activists of the informal movement, who also worked for Moscow Party district organizations in an advisory capacity, helping these to follow and analyse developments in the informal movement: Sergei Stankevich (subsequently an adviser to Yeltsin and deputy mayor of Moscow), Mikhail Malyutin (subsequently an adviser to one of the fractions in the Russian parliament) and Boris Kagarlitsky.

13 'Khartiya', 1990, pp. 30–34.

they were unable to sustain once in power. The Front criticized 'bureaucratic conservatism' particularly sharply. It attacked centralization and called for the devolution of power to workers in the factory and to their representatives in the soviets. While it argued for a measure of economic rationalization (notably, the reduction of subsidies to inefficient enterprises and farms) it insisted that this should not be achieved at the expense of the workers. 'The Popular Front movement holds that economic reform should not be conducted at the expense of workers', it declared. 'Hence, we shall vigorously oppose attempts to remove or limit social security. This security consists today of cheap housing and transport, free medicine and education and full employment.' Furthermore 'we oppose price rises for food and essential goods'. The remedy for inflation was not increased prices but the reduction of losses. Other measures supported by the Front, which corresponded to popular disenchantment with corruption and declining living standards, included limiting the number of cooperatives using hired labour and profiting from the shortages; banning the commercialization of medicine, education, transport and housing; strengthening the right to a minimum wage and annual reviews of pensions and scholarships.[14] Little about these demands was revolutionary: what was new, however, was the fact that a public body, other than the CPSU, should issue political statements and demands of any sort – apparently with some degree of official tolerance and even connivance. Despite this indulgence, the Front failed to win popular support and its cautious line was soon overtaken. By late 1989, the Front was already irrelevant and moribund.

Leningrad Popular Front

The Leningrad Popular Front was also founded under the indirect patronage of the Party reformers – with Boris Kurashvili and other academics present at the meetings of the Leningrad *Perestroika* Club in Spring 1988, when the decision to establish the Front was taken. The Leningraders were, however, subject to different influences from the Muscovites: on the one hand, the traditions of Leningrad were arguably more open and European than those of Moscow and the

14 Gromov and Kuzin, *Neformaly* (1990), pp. 188, 191–2, citing the draft programme.

academic intelligentsia were influenced by events in nearby Estonia, where the rapidly developing Popular Front was mobilizing popular opinion behind a radical political agenda. On the other hand, the Leningrad Party authorities were firmly on the side of the conservatives and there was no local counterweight to them (unlike Moscow).

The Popular Front movement in Leningrad was initially socialist in orientation. Its earliest declarations did not envisage an autonomous political role for the future organization: instead, it was 'to unite supporters of democratic *perestroika*, so as, through new elections at extraordinary Party, union and Komsomol gatherings and conferences [...] to rid the Party and economic *apparat* of conservatives and reactionaries'.[15] By the Autumn, however, the emphasis had moved away from socialism to democracy: the term 'socialist' was appended less frequently to projects for reform and interest was concentrated on how to use the forthcoming election campaign both to improve formal democratic practice and to develop public consciousness of the need for democratic change.[16]

This movement to the left (in Soviet terms) was accentuated by the election campaign, so that when the founding conference finally took place, on 17–19 June 1989, the Front – despite the multiplicity of views within it – was clearly in the democratic camp. Its manifesto declared the Front to be 'a movement for democracy, civil freedom and radical economic reform'. It rejected totalitarianism and demanded that society control the government and civil service. It called for the creation of independent trade unions and for respect for the rights of individuals and minorities. All power should be handed to the soviets, factories to workers, land to the peasants. The importance of a mixed economy, with social security guarantees, was stressed. Thus the Front aligned itself firmly behind the Inter-Regional Group of Deputies, which had just been formed in the newly elected parliament (the Congress of People's Deputies).[17] This identification with the radical deputies of the newly elected parliament reflected the degree to which the democratic movement in Leningrad had been radicalised by the election campaign and by the euphoria of unexpected victory.

15 Ibid., p. 199. The document was adopted on 15 March 1988 at the *Perestroika* Club.
16 *Obshchestvennye dvizheniya Leningrada* (1989), p. 21.
17 Gromov and Kuzin, *Neformaly* (1990), pp. 201–4.

Whereas, until the Spring, the democrats in the Front had talked of the need and their readiness to cooperate with the CPSU, their position was now one of virtual opposition:

> As a political movement, the LPF has, as one of its aims, wide debate and criticism of the CPSU [...] The LPF condemns the violent and bloody tactics of Bolshevism in our country. The LPF condemns the political course taken [...] in 1903, concerning the violent seizure of power. The LPF condemns all the theoretical bases of the political terror [...] in [...] the documents of the CPSU.

The current leadership of the Party was responsible not only for the appalling state of the country's economy, of its culture and spiritual condition, but was also to be held to account for the bloody political past of our country.[18] Although the LPF had not openly declared itself to be an opposition movement (a declaration which would have jeopardised its existence, given the illegality of such pretensions at the time), by aligning itself so unambiguously behind the radical delegates of the Congress, it had helped to create a *de facto* democratic opposition to the CPSU in Leningrad.

Provincial Popular Fronts

The Popular Front movement in the Russian provinces developed in response to different pressures. The dynamic which informed the first wave of the movement in Summer 1988 was unique. It represented an attempt to mobilize the spontaneous protest movement and euphoria which developed around the Nineteenth Party Conference in June 1988. The second-wave popular fronts (which emerged between Autumn 1988 and Summer 1989) started from a much less promising base and consisted mainly of nuclei of local activists and intellectuals emboldened by the new permissiveness of the centre. They acted essentially as ginger groups and were significant mainly in helping radical and democratic candidates during the election campaigns of 1989 and 1990. Few of these groups ever enjoyed the degree of popular support which was briefly experienced during the 'hot summer' of 1988 by the first fronts.

It came as a surprise to everyone – both to local Party *apparatchiki* and to radicals in Moscow – when popular protest demonstrations

18 Ibid., pp. 205–7.

erupted in the towns and cities of central Russia in May and June 1988. The importance of the moment consisted not in the novelty of popular discontent or in the abuses which provoked it, but in the fact that people dared to express their dissatisfaction. The key factor here was the new policies promulgated by the Party leadership in Moscow. Following the reversals suffered by the reformers in November 1987 (at the time of Yeltsin's dismissal from the Politburo) and in March 1988 (with the publication of Nina Andreeva's apologia for the values and norms of Stalinism), the reforming wing of the Party renewed its attacks on those in the Party who were resisting democratic innovations. Criticism of the *apparat*, of its insensitive and authoritarian methods of administration and of its corruption were now sanctioned from on high. A battle for power was conducted in advance of the Party Conference, with much of the provincial *apparat* entrenched in its resistance to the proposed changes and determined to pack the Conference with delegates opposed to significant reform. The reform leadership in Moscow was therefore interested in sanctioning criticism and protest against these manoeuvres, which threatened to derail the Conference. As a result, local criticism in the press and on the streets could now be assured of support from the centre of power.[19] This was of cardinal importance in inducing people in the provinces to protest against the local Party leadership: they knew that, for once, the local Party *apparat*'s discretionary control over potential critics and troublemakers was limited.

Many of the initial demonstrations were, therefore, directed against abuses in the election of delegates to the Conference and, in particular, against the election of local Party magnates.[20] These meetings drew several hundred, and in some cases several thousand, demonstrators on to the streets. In Yaroslavl, 5000 people turned out, initially to demand the removal of the local Party First Secretary as delegate to the Party Conference. In Kuibyshev, 25 000 demonstrated on 22 June and 30-40 000 on 21 July, in response to the calls of a

19 One of the clearest indications of this was the fact that the central press reported incidents of local unrest and discontent, rather than suppressing this information - a departure from established practice which points to a directive to this effect from the top of the Central Committee. Gorbachev himself openly endorsed these demonstrations at the start of June: see Roxburgh, *Revolution* (1991), pp. 92-3.
20 See A. Kolobayev, 'Demokratiya', *Yunost'*, 1989, no. 4, pp. 40-44, for a stenographic account of events in Kuibyshev; Kagarlitsky, *Farewell* (1990), pp. 8, 22-3.

newly-formed political club, *Perspektiva*, to protest against the local
Party First Secretary, Ye. F. Muraviev, and to demand his removal. In
many areas, the local Party secretaries were obliged to withdraw.
Protest meetings continued, even after the problematic delegates
had been replaced. Moscow discovered that once criticism of the local
Party's abuses of power had been unleashed, it was not easy to
confine that criticism to the few issues where the interests of the
reformers at the centre and those of the local population coincided.
Initially concerned with fraudulent elections, popular demonstrations
began, in several cities, to focus on other instances of irresponsible
and authoritarian rule: notably, social inequality, corruption – in the
allocation of housing, in the provision of child-care and medical
facilities – and ecology. The wave of protests spread throughout June
and July to many different parts of the country.[21]

It was on the back of this groundswell of popular protest that the
first significant attempts were made in the provinces to organize
critical public opinion and bring together its different strands in some
unifying or coordinating structure. Popular Fronts or initiative groups
were established in eleven cities and regions.[22] Only in 1988,
however, were large popular meetings such a feature of the
movement. Thereafter, the Popular Fronts were the creation of
activists of the local informal movement – from rock groups,
anarcho-syndicalist clubs and local branches of Memorial to various
ecological and nationalist groups – and represented little more than an
attempt to form umbrella organizations for quite disparate non-Party
clubs.

Some themes recur in the programmes of these organizations: the
commitment to a civil society, to democratic politics (initially not
always equated with political pluralism or parliamentary democracy
but meaning simply plurality of opinions within the one-Party state),

21 Berezovsky and Krotov, *Rossiya* (1990), pp. 87, 93, 111, 133, 138-9, 142, 148, 157-8,
   161, 195, 198, 201, 205, 211-2, 221-6; Malyutin, 'Vybor' in Yushenkov (ed.),
   Neformaly (1990), p. 92; Sudiniev, 'Nashchestvie' in ibid., p. 32; A. Mineev, 'Evolution
   of Social Awareness', *MN*, 15 January 1989, p. 8
22 In Novosibirsk, Pskov, Kazan, Kostroma, Chelyabinsk, Omsk, Yaroslavl, Kuibyshev,
   Yuzhnosakhalinsk, the Irkutsk region, Sverdlovsk, Ulan Ude, Leningrad, Stavropol,
   Khabarovsk, Karelia and Gorki: Berezovsky and Krotov, *Rossiya* (1990); Krotov *et al.*,
   Rossiya (1991) I, 1-2, for several articles on the Popular Fronts, their membership and
   activities.

to social justice and ecological renewal.[23] However, different interpretations might be put on the practical meaning of many of these terms and ideals. In Siberia, where Russian nationalism was a relatively strong tendency in the informal movement, the tension between different visions of the democratic future led to dissension and even splits within the local Popular Fronts, as in the Baikal (Irkutsk) and Ural (Sverdlovsk) Fronts.[24] The disparate composition of the Popular Fronts helps to explain why they failed to develop into a single, united opposition force, as in the Baltics, Moldavia and the Caucasus.[25]

A final question remains about the provincial Fronts: why, given such a promising start, did they peter out, at least as mass movements? A number of reasons for their failure to develop may be adduced. Firstly, the peculiar conditions that had prevailed up to and during the Party Conference ceased to obtain after its conclusion: once the Conference had done its work, the Party reformers no longer needed to encourage the popular protest movement and, on the contrary, became anxious to ensure that it did not exceed certain limits (that is, those fixed by the reformist centre). Local Party machines, initially caught offguard, became more adept at responding to popular opinion. Where confronted with a strong movement, as in Yaroslavl, the Party, rather than providing the stimulus of harassment, played along with it, affording it venues and establishing links with its leaders.

23 Berezovsky and Krotov, *Rossiya* (1990), and Krotov *et al.*, *Rossiya* (1991), I, 1-2, provide summaries of and extracts from many of the programmes.

24 Krotov *et al.*, *Rossiya* (1991), I, 1, pp. 128-9, 147-9.

25 Two organizations aspired to the role of Russian Popular Front: the first (*Rossiiski narodny front*) was founded by Valery Skurlatov in Moscow in December 1988. It amounted to little more than a circle of right-wing nationalists. Skurlatov had first come to public notice in the 1960s for anti-Semitic and neo-fascist proposals. His front rapidly split into a number of rival groups: that which he headed was associated with a number of dubious attempts to discredit the democratic movement in 1990 and, at the end of the year, rallied to the support of the Pavlov government. The Popular Front of the RSFSR was established in Yaroslavl in October 1989, when 116 delegates attended its founding conference; despite its disparate composition (including socialist, nationalist and democratic groups), it supported the Inter-Regional Group of Deputies; it ceased functioning in 1990: Pribylovsky, *Slovar'* (1991), p. 73; V. Orlov, *MN*, 1991, no. 12, p. 11; Kagarlitsky, *Farewell* (1990), pp. 102-3; Krotov *et al.*, *Rossiya* (1991), I, 1, p. 96; *MN*, 1989, no. 44, p. 2; Sakwa, *Gorbachev* (1990), p. 208.

Ultimately, however, the structures of Soviet society and Soviet power reasserted themselves. The atomization of Soviet society – the absence of a civil, plural society – was nowhere more complete than in the Russian provinces. The dependence of the town or city on a central Ministry made it easier to control: employment, housing and well-being were dispensed by few as opposed to several sources. This may help to explain why the provinces were much more effectively controlled by the conservative Party *apparat* than the metropolitan cities of Moscow and Leningrad and why they tended to be politically quiescent.[26] Hence, although the forces mobilized by the Popular Front movement were significant, they did not develop their full potential.

A number of factors prevented the formation of a united All-Union or even All-Russian Popular Front, which might have played a role analogous to that of *Sajudis* in Lithuania or the National Front in Estonia. Firstly, the protest movement was diverse in both inspiration and organization. The impressive geographical spread of the Popular Front movement, while testifying to the new vitality of public life, posed – under conditions where alternative political activity was illegal and where communications were problematic – serious logistic difficulties to aspiring organizers and coordinators. It was, moreover, fraught with centrifugal tendencies. The scope for political rivalries and jealousies increased as isolation and autonomy created local reputations and heroes unwilling to abdicate to an alien centre which was generally associated with privilege and pretension.

To the difficulties posed by distance, rivalry and the authorities' hostility was added another complicating factor: the fact that the Popular Fronts of different cities were animated by quite diverse preoccupations and ideals. These ideological differences coincided with geographical boundaries. Mikhail Malyutin sees the key distinctions as being between the Fronts of:

- the capitals (Moscow and Leningrad);
- the provinces of Russia; and

26 See Kerblay, *Society* (1983), pp. 60–73; H. Morton, 'The Contemporry Soviet City' in H. Morton and R. Stuart (eds.), *The Contemporary Soviet City* (London, 1984), pp. 3–22; Urban, *Soviets* (1990), p. 147, who points to the political consequences of these structures; V. Zaslavsky, *The Neo-Stalinist State* (New York, 1982), pp. 32–7, on the effect of closed enterprises and regions on reinforcing social and political conservatism.

- the Union Republics (the Baltics, Belorussia, the Ukraine and Moldavia).[27]

Underlying these regional distinctions, however, were more fundamental divergences of outlook and constitution. The Popular Fronts of the two capitals were inspired by formal political ideology to a far greater extent than was the first wave of provincial Popular Fronts; while in the Union Republics, the Fronts, which drew on resurgent popular nationalism, were not only more precocious but also incomparably stronger than their Russian counterparts. The ideological spectrum of the Fronts may therefore be broadly distinguished as left or democratic socialist (Moscow and Leningrad); populist, protesting against corruption, deprivation and pollution (Russian provinces) and nationalist (Union Republics).

In addition to these differences of inspiration, the Fronts were divided by their composition and character. Some of the Fronts were composed largely of intellectuals – as was the case in Moscow and Leningrad – while others enjoyed wider popular support but were politically ambivalent (as in Yaroslavl and Chelyabinsk). The Republican Fronts, on the other hand, were mass movements, whose development anticipated that of the democratic movement in Russia and was determined by a political and cultural dynamic largely independent of that of Russia as a whole.

Hence, differences of orientation, culture and support militated against the consolidation of the various regional and city Fronts into a unified movement. In some cases, the inspiration of the Fronts diverged significantly, or even fundamentally. Quite apart from all these factors, the movement was under pressure because it had to operate in a hostile environment. The authorities' attentions varied from open malevolence to attempts at subversion or cooption: the Fronts' reaction to these policies varied, with some becoming embroiled in intra-Party politics and collaboration with the Party, while others moved into open opposition.[28]

Finally, there was no legal framework for the opposition to work in. This deficiency had been less inhibiting when only perfunctory

7 Quoted by Trusov (ed.), 'Neformaly' in Pechenev and Vyunsky (eds.), *Neformaly* (1990), p. 247.
8 See *Gorizont*, 10, 1989, pp. 8–11; V. Lantratov in *Gorizont*, 11, pp. 10–11; A. Gorenkov, 'Kommunisty', *Partiinaya zhizn'*, 2 January 1990, pp. 31–6, for examples.

organization was involved – as was the case with the political clubs of the first phase of the reform. Now, when the tasks were more elaborate, the restrictions were more significant. Potential leaders of the democratic movement were still isolated individuals, expressing themselves at best occasionally through the mass media. It required unusual courage and energy even to attempt to create structures which might organize and unite a largely spontaneous and still limited popular protest movement.

However important the role of the Popular Fronts, their influence was only local and episodic. They neither developed as the Party reformers had hoped – as they failed to mobilize broad popular support for the Party's reform leadership and escaped the reformers' control – nor were they satisfactory as vehicles of the democratic movement. The organization which came closest to fulfilling this function in Russia was Memorial.

Memorial

After the Party Conference, Memorial was taken up by liberal intellectuals in the establishment, with the tacit support of reformers in the Party leadership. It thus began to act as an anti-Stalinist lobby, in an attempt to strengthen the reformers in their struggle with conservative elements in the *apparat*. The idea of forming an officially registered society had first been put forward in Spring 1988 by Lev Ponomarev. This was now followed up with an enthusiasm inspired not so much by the ostensible aims of the movement (which were largely focused on historical issues) as by the nature of the power struggle then being conducted inside the CPSU. In the absence of any legal cover for political activity outside the Communist Party, no public organization could profess openly political aims; while, at the same time, given the difficulty of marshalling support for reform within the Party, the liberal leadership had a vested interest in seeing the emergence of an articulate and influential body of support for them among the public.

However, the launching of Memorial as a public body marked its transformation into a sort of pre-political party, embracing opinion far more radical than that of the Party reformers. A governing Council of fifteen famous intellectuals was formed on 25 August 1988.[29] The fact that those elected should have been exclusively drawn from the intelligentsia was due both to the peculiar course of liberalization in Russia and to the unique prestige enjoyed by intellectuals in Russian society. This prestige was enhanced by *glasnost*, which restored and confirmed many reputations and enabled frustrated intellectuals at long last both to say something of what they really thought and to express and even lead public opinion between 1987 and 1989. The relative liberalization of the press in the late 1980s created, therefore, a moral leadership which was ready to assume the mantle of political leadership of the reform movement as soon as the Party relaxed its control of society.

A number of public bodies had agreed to sponsor Memorial, in accordance with the law, so that it could apply for official registration. A key role was played by the creative unions, led by Klimov's Film-Makers' Union (which worked in close association with Politburo member Alexander Yakovlev).[30] The sponsorship provided by these unions, as well as by the publications *Ogonek* and *Literaturnaya gazeta*, points to the fact that Memorial's cause enjoyed a degree of official support – if not of unalloyed enthusiasm: Memorial continued to operate on the confines of the permissible and it seems that some elements in the Party made every effort to curtail its influence and activities.[31]

Differences of opinion between the more radical original members of Memorial (Dmitri Leonov, Yuri Samodurov, Viktor Kuzin, Lev Ponomarev) and some of the new members, and particularly the chairman, V. Glazychev of the Architects' Union, soon became apparent. Two issues proved particularly difficult: the first was the pressure exerted on the committee in a conservative sense by the

---

29 The full Council included: Ales Adamovich, Yuri Afanasiev, Vasil Bykov, Daniil Granin, Yevgeny Yevtushenko, Yuri Karyakin, Dmitri Likhachev, Roy Medvedev, Bulat Okudzhava, Lev Razgon, Anatoly Rybakov, Mikhail Shatrov, Mikhail Ulyanov and Vitaly Korotich. Alexander Solzhenitsyn, who was also elected to the Council, declined to participate.

30 The Artists', Designers', Architects' and Theatre Workers' Unions also sponsored Memorial: Berezovsky and Krotov, *Rossiya* (1990), p. 283; Pribylovsky, *Slovar'* (1991), p. 39

31 See Afanasiev interview in *MN*, 1989, no. 6, p. 4, for the opposition Memorial encountered from Party leaders in the Ukraine, Orel, Saratov, Minsk and Alma-Ata.

sponsoring organizations and the chairman and the second was the question of the original members' participation in political meetings and gatherings on behalf of Memorial. In essence, the sponsors were afraid that Memorial, while exploiting the degree of official tolerance it enjoyed to the limits, was becoming an autonomous political force. Under pressure from the Party, the sponsors were anxious to control the movement and, as far as possible, to inhibit its radical political tendencies. Until there was some likelihood that the new organization would be innocuous – dealing with the arcana of past crimes and acting strictly within the limits set by the Party – conservatives in the Party were reluctant to grant it official recognition and a legal status. This opposition was conducted successfully over the next year and a half and Memorial – despite its large membership and the support it enjoyed among the Party reformers – was not registered as an official all-Union society until January 1990.

Memorial's first conference was held on 29–30 October 1988. The key question concerned the scope of the society's activities: was it to confine itself to the 'repressions' of Stalinism or should its investigations go further back and start with Lenin's rule? And where should its inquiries end? Behind this problem, ostensibly of historical periodization, lay a more fundamental question: was Memorial to be an organization concerned chiefly with history – however tragic that history might be – or was it to be an essentially political organization, whose vocation was to investigate illegalities committed by the State towards its own citizens up to the present, to attempt to develop a new public consciousness of the nature of political legitimacy and new expectations and standards of government?

Two views emerged: the radicals argued that it was neither logical nor principled to condemn only past abuses of power;[32] the moderates believed that widening the scope of Memorial's activities was impolitic and would result in the organization being banned – that the only practical course was to expose the shortcomings of Stalinism as a model of government and only when this argument was won, to contemplate applying these lessons to the present. The writer

---

32 The Party's attitude to this debate may be inferred from the introduction to an article on Memorial's conference in *Lit.Gaz.*, 2 November 1988, which condemned Democratic Union's alleged attempts to 'use the sacred business of Memorial for their ill-intentioned aims'.

A.N. Rybakov, author of the anti-Stalinist novel *Children of the Arbat* (1987), advanced the second viewpoint. The society should concentrate on practical aims, he argued:

> There is a concrete evil - for thirty years a tyrant ruled the country. He inculcated the organizational, psychological and other methods and [is responsible for their] consequences, from which we have been unable to rid ourselves [...] Hence, I think that, at the present time, our society, Memorial, is a society which should confine itself (I repeat, at this stage) to the period of Stalinism.

The opposite view was expressed by the dissident, Larisa Bogoraz:

> The society should not be limited by temporal boundaries. To fight against a dead tyrant and not to speak out about the roots of the tyranny and its consequences would mean to confine ourselves to what was done in Khrushchev's time.[33]

The point was put most succinctly of all by Sakharov:

> We recognize with bitterness [...] that Stalinism, lawlessness and terror are not limited by this or that date coinciding with Stalin's time at the summit of power, but that they throw their shadow over many events both in the earlier and future life of the country.[34]

These differences were to be exacerbated by the influx in 1989 into the rank and file membership of former political prisoners, most of whom wanted the society to concentrate on the historical phenomenon of the Terror and its practical consequences - their own often acute difficulties in eking out a living.

Initially, the radicals prevailed, as the founding conference, on 28–29 January 1989, made clear.[35] Speaking at this meeting, the poet Andrei Voznesensky saw Memorial as having a dual role: not only to do justice to those who had suffered in the past but also to overcome the legacy of the past in the contemporary Soviet Union:

> Now, for the first time in our country, the thousands and thousands of opponents of Stalinism have united forces. This numerous popular movement has no precedent in our history. Behind hundreds of thousands of people stand 30 million victims. 30 million shades: and the best memorial for them will be not monuments of stone, not monuments of bronze, but the complete democratization of the country, the impossibility of a repetition of the shame, the emergence of a new Stalinism.

33 MBIO: Informal Archive: Folder on Memorial, pp. 43–5.
34 Ibid., p. 10.
35 Berezovsky and Krotov, *Rossiya* (1990), pp. 284–5; Pribylovsky, *Slovar'* (1991), p. 49.

The political implications of Memorial were spelled out even more clearly by one of the newly-elected co-chairmen, Yuri Afanasiev:

> The most important task of Memorial is to give our country back its past. However, the past is living in the present. Therefore, Memorial is a political movement. [...] Speaking of terror and lawlessness, we are at the same time forming in the public consciousness an appreciation of lawfulness. Hence, Memorial is also a movement for legality and rights [*pravovoe*].[36]

The meeting demanded that Stalin's 'repressions' be recognized as crimes against humanity and that Stalin and those responsible for the bloodletting of the 1930s and 1940s be put on trial. Resolutions called for collectivization to be recognized as illegal; for the rehabilitation of victims of the regime to be extended beyond the period of Stalin's rule; for the creation of a commission to restore civil rights to deported peoples and to return them to their homelands. Calls were also made to have all political prisoners released.[37]

These demands far outdistanced the Party's new orthodoxy and were close in inspiration to dissident positions. The extension of Memorial's concerns beyond the past into the present, the exposure of the links between the two, of the derivation of much contemporary Soviet legal and political practice from that of Stalinism was precisely what the conservatives in the Party were anxious to avoid.[38] It implied that Memorial would become a critic of the Party and State in their present form and, furthermore, a critic whose observations, far from being offered in a spirit of cooperation and sympathy, were based on moral principles fundamentally at odds with those of the Party. In essence, Memorial had become a large public organization ideologically opposed to the regime. The Party therefore maintained its refusal to register the organization.[39]

Memorial therefore developed as a democratic political forum. Memorial enabled anti-Stalinist intellectuals to rally in a semi-

---

36 Gromov and Kuzin, *Neformaly* (1990), pp. 107–8; Afanasiev, *MN*, 1989, no. 6, p. 4.
37 Gromov and Kuzin, *Neformaly* (1990), pp. 108–9; S. Yanovsky, *Ogonek*, 1989, no. 6, p. 1, who comments on the censorship applied to the reporting of this event; *Lit.Gaz.*, 1 February 1989, p. 2.
38 Yanovsky, *Ogonek*, 1989, no. 6, p. 1, says that the authorities insisted on referring to Memorial as a 'historical-educational movement', overlooking its contemporary democratic, political vocation.
39 Gromov and Kuzin, *Neformaly* (1990), p. 109, say that Memorial was not registered; activists from Democratic Union played a significant role in it and tried to get elected to its leading organs.

political organization, which helped to identify them in the political debates of 1989. It became what the Moscow Popular Front had aspired but failed to be: the standard-bearer in Russia of democratic reform, at a point when no formal political opposition was tolerated. Its platform was broad enough to accommodate individuals with quite divergent political preferences ranging from socialism to liberalism. All that was initially required was a rejection of Stalinism; however, rejection of Stalin's peculiar form of despotism implied rejection of autocracy in general and support for political and a measure of economic pluralism. It was all the easier to adopt these positions because at least initially it was believed that both Gorbachev[40] and Alexander Yakovlev[41] supported them too. From the start, however, Memorial promised to raise many issues that many in the Party and in society at large wished to remain buried in oblivion. The problems it raised were fundamental to the Soviet regime: at issue was a complete political, economic and social renewal of the country. The logic of supporting Memorial was therefore to bring anti-Stalinist intellectuals into conflict with the mainstream Party's fundamental interests.

Although deprived of official registration and hence of the right to nominate candidates for election to the new semi-democratic parliament, several members of Memorial's Council were elected to the parliament.[42] The election campaign transformed Memorial from a potential into a *de facto* centre of opposition. The Party *apparat* did its utmost to frustrate the use of such democratic procedures as it had built into the revised electoral system and above all, to prevent the names of independent candidates from appearing on the ballot sheets. Its frequently unscrupulous tactics did much to define the battlelines and to precipitate radical intellectuals – and, preeminently, members of Memorial – into open hostility towards the Party.

40 In a telephone conversation with Ales Adamovich, according to Sakharov: recorded in MBIO: Informal Archive: Folder on Memorial.
41 For example, the commissions on repressions and rehabilitations, chaired by Yakovlev, and the release of the anti-Stalinist film *Pokayanie*, in which Yakovlev played a key role: interview with E. Klimov, 6 May 1992.
42 These included Academician Sakharov, Yuri Karyakin (from the Academy of Sciences), Yevgeny Yevtushenko (Kharkov), Ales Adamovich (Film-Makers' Union), Yuri Afanasiev (Noginsk), Boris Yeltsin (Moscow), Vasil Bykov (Writers' Unions), Roy Medvedev (Moscow), Vitaly Korotich (Kharkov), Dmitri Likhachev (Cultural Fund), Mikhail Ulyanov and Daniil Granin (CPSU): Pribylovsky, *Slovar'* (1991), p. 40. Ya. Etinger, *Novoe vremya*, 1989, no. 46. pp. 26–7; *Narodnye deputaty SSSR: spravochnik* (Moscow, 1990).

By 1990, Memorial had over 170 branches[43] and its membership had reached tens of thousands, making it the most significant both morally and numerically of the Russian informals. It collaborated closely with other democratic pressure groups as they emerged – *inter alia*, the writers' society *Aprel'* (April) – and with many of the new national committees and Fronts in the republics and autonomous regions of Russia. It allowed fledgling democratic societies outside the capital to shelter under its auspices – furnishing much-needed support for democratic forces in the provinces – and it helped a popular democratic movement to develop in 1989 and Spring 1990.[44] The worst fears of the Party *apparatchiki* had been realized: Memorial had brought its fight against Stalinism to its logical conclusion and had won wide popular support for it.

After Spring 1990, Memorial's political significance declined – largely because of the development of political pluralism and a more normal political life – and its philanthropic and educational role became more important. Human rights became a major focus of its activity.[45] Many of its anti-Stalinist leaders believed that Memorial also had a significant moral role to play and that unless society's collective memory acknowledged the horrors of Stalinism, unless people remembered and repented of the past, neither social values nor political culture could be renewed on a humanitarian basis. Writing on 25 July 1989 to *Izvestiya* to complain about the failure to register Memorial, a number of Stalin's distinguished victims, including the writer Lev Razgon, observed:

> The unmasking of Stalinism and compassion for its victims requires the awakening of people's conscience and charity. And it can enable the moral, spiritual cleansing of the people.[46]

Not surprisingly, not everyone rallied to this battle cry. Not only those with immediate material interests at stake, but the sons and daughters of those who saw themselves as having prospered under Stalin, bolstered by decades of propaganda and misinformation, by family

43 Etinger, *AiF*, 1990, no. 11, p. 8, claims that 180 branches existed.
44 Pribylovsky, *Slovar'* (1991), p. 40; Krotov *et al.*, *Rossiya* (1991), I, 1, p. 62.
45 Krotov *et al.*, *Rossiya* (1991), I, 1, p. 62; Pribylovsky, *Slovar'* (1991), p. 40; interview with N. Okhotin, Moscow, 21 November 1990; Etinger, *AiF*, 1990, no. 11, p. 8, insists on the charitable and human rights aspects of its work.
46 Gromov and Kuzin, *Neformaly* (1990), pp. 109–10.

loyalty and human vanity were repelled by these calls to repentance. Soviet society was not ready for a *Stunde null*.

In November 1988, under the joint sponsorship of *Ogonek* and *Moscow News*, the Society organized a Week of Conscience, enabling victims of the repression to meet for the first time publicly and organizing public discussion of the evidence for Stalin's crimes.[47] A map at the entrance showed the position of 162 camps: an exhibition upstairs displayed rare photographs of these desolate sites, still resplendent with edifying slogans. More poignant still was a wall dedicated to the memory of the camp inmates: here, hundreds of letters and old photographs of fathers, brothers, mothers and relatives were affixed, with brief notes about the date and circumstances of their arrest or disappearance and pleas for information about their fate. Distraught relatives hovered anxiously nearby. Accompanying the exhibitions were daily lectures and discussions about the sources and consequences of Stalinism and the need for guarantees for freedom and socialist democracy; the performance of camp songs and readings of prison literature and, on one night, a showing of the film *Solovki Power*, on the notorious island camps established under Lenin. The drift of this message was unambiguous: Stalin's tyranny was based on the earlier tyranny of Lenin.

Memorial gradually sank from public view and consciousness – especially after the defeat of the coup in August 1991 – but its role in the vital period between Summer 1989 and Spring 1990 was of great significance. Until the elections of Spring 1989, Memorial was the main voice of anti-Stalinist opinion in Russia and, for the next year, remained one of the chief centres of radical opposition to the conservatives of the Party and State *apparat* and one of the main agencies capable of mobilizing extra-parliamentary anti-Stalinist public opinion. Memorial became the training ground and focal point for democratic forces in the country and may therefore be said to have been the first broadly-based democratic political grouping to emerge in modern Russia.

It furnished Russia's emerging democrats with both an organization and a vision, which insisted on human dignity and freedom, the rule of law and the accountability of the authorities. Although Memorial

47 See *Izvestiya*, 24 November 1988; *Ogonek*, 1988, no. 41, p. 25; *MN*, 1987, no. 48 (issue devoted to Memorial).

was a broad house, including many Party members, and even old Bolsheviks and Stalinists from the camps, as well as opponents of the regime, the leadership furnished by the anti-Stalinist intelligentsia ensured that the organization represented essentially liberal humanist values. These were to carry many of Memorial's supporters further than they had expected to travel – ultimately into opposition to the Party, which refused to coopt them and reform. Memorial represented an important step for these intellectuals: through it they passed from the formation to the active leadership of opinion. Early in 1989, the liberal intelligentsia were at the summit of their fame and political influence.

1989 ELECTIONS

The most dramatic sign of this was the triumphant election of many eminent intellectuals to the Congress of People's Deputies in Spring 1989. Already distinguished in their profession, the intellectuals' prestige had been enhanced during *glasnost*, when they had been widely seen as taking risks in exploring controversial themes and advancing critical opinions. They alone enjoyed the fame and reputation to stand against the Party's endorsed candidates. The *apparat*'s ineptitude in trying to prevent their election cast them in a heroic light and they benefited both from a sympathy and from a protest vote. The euphoria of success blinded them to the exceptional circumstances of their election: if the reform were carried through and the *apparat* were defeated, the protest vote, the halo of martyrdom, the preeminence of the word over political procedure – and hence, their unique position and role – would all be eclipsed, and with them, the intellectuals' political prestige and power would vanish.

Not only the intellectuals but independent candidates in general (there was a large degree of coincidence between the two groups) were ultimately assisted by the *apparat*'s attempts to block their election. Independent candidates ran both in the constituencies and in the public bodies (for which one-third of the seats had been reserved). The elections were predictably liveliest in the intellectuals' organizations. Nominations from below were whittled down to a minimum by their conservative, Party-dominated management. In some cases – as in the Journalists' Union, where pro-reform candidates like Vitaly Korotich and Yegor Yakovlev (the editors of *Ogonek* and *Moscow News*) were excluded – the elections were successfully manipulated. However, the Film-Makers' Union led the way in rebelling against attempts to block nominations from below, as did the *Znanie* Society. Both in the Writers' and in the Theatre Workers' Union, proceedings were protracted and hotly debated even if the outcome was a list of generally cautious delegates and the defeat, in both forums, of many leading liberals.[48] There was a scandal when Gorbachev's foreign policy adviser Georgi Arbatov was rejected as a candidate by a joint Plenum of the Peace Committeee and UN Association.[49]

Most notorious of all was the scandal which surrounded the rejection, by the Plenum of the Academy of Sciences, of many of the country's most distinguished scientists, scholars and controversialists, who enjoyed wide support within the Academy's institutes, in favour of leading figures in its bureaucratic and political establishment. Those not elected included Andrei Sakharov, who had the support of over 60 institutes; Roald Sagdeev, Gavriil Popov, Nikolai Shmelev (with approximately 30 institutes each); the medievalist Dmitri Likhachev; Gorbachev's economic adviser Abel Aganbegyan; the architect of the 1960s economic reforms, Gennadi Lisichkin; the sociologist Ivan Bestuzhev-Lada; and the political scientist, Yuri Karyakin. The Central Electoral Commission received over 50 letters and telegrams of protest over the Academy's election procedures. An unprecedented protest demonstration, attended by about 3000 researchers, including representatives of the most prestigious institutes, was staged outside the Academy, demanding new elections. Eventually, in late April, after three months of controversy, additional elections were held, resulting in the inclusion in the Academy's list of delegates of several well-known, reformist intellectuals – among them, Andrei Sakharov.[50]

48 Ye. Gesheva, *Lit.Gaz.*, 15 March 1989, p. 2; G. Ivanov, *Lit.Gaz.*, 25 January 1989, p. 2; A. Rubinov, *Lit.Gaz.*, 1 February 1989, p. 13; *Lit.Gaz.*, 29 March 1989, p. 1; V. Astafiev, *Lit.Gaz.*, 1 February 1989, p. 1; V. Malukhin, *Izvestiya*, 2 January 1989, p. 2; *Lit.Gaz.*, 25 January 1989, p. 1; *Lit.Gaz.*, 22 March 1989; V. Dolganov, *Izvestiya*, 12 January 1989, p. 1; Urban, *Soviets* (1990), pp. 95–6.

49 R. Sagdeev *et al.*, *MN*, 15, 1989, p. 10; G. Apresyan, *Lit.Gaz.*, 29 March 1989, p. 1.

50 Sergei Averintsev, Georgi Arbatov, Pavel Bunich, Yuri Karyakin, Gennadi Lisichkin, Nikolai Petrakov, Nikolai Shmelev and Roald Sagdeev were among these additional delegates: V. Beletskaya, *Ogonek*, 1989, no. 7, p. 3; Sagdeev, *MN*, 1989, no. 18, p. 12;

None the less, the outcome of voting in the public organizations was to ensure that a large bloc of conservative *apparatchiki* and their supporters entered the Congress either *ex-officio* or thanks to patronage rather than through popular approval. The liberals who managed to gain admittance did so, typically, after a struggle. The public organizations, therefore, sent a polarized body of delegates to the Congress: the majority consisted of bureaucrats, officials or former officials and their supporters; the minority was composed of articulate intellectuals of liberal or even radical views.

In the constituencies, there were even more abuses and independent candidates found it even more difficult to overcome the obstacles placed in their way. Over a thousand complaints about the conduct of these meetings were lodged with the Central Electoral Commission.[51] A round table of experts at *Moscow News* concluded that extensive abuses had taken place and that the selection meetings, in particular, had been used to eliminate popular candidates and advance *apparatchiki*.[52] None the less, the packed audiences occasionally rebelled, refusing to vote for the approved candidate. In this, the seventy-four-year-old pensioner who objected to the attempted manipulation of a selection meeting he attended was representative of the new mood when he shouted: 'We've waited 70 years for this and now they want to shut us up.' Whatever the outcome, the turmoil of political debate was experienced by an estimated 400 000 electors, who participated in the pre-electoral selection meetings.[53]

While the spectacle of this stage of the elections hardly presented an inspiring example of democracy to the foreigner, for the Russians it was an exhilarating experience. For the first time in living memory, the voter – previously so despised by the authorities that the ballot-paper listed the name of a single approved candidate and a favourable vote was cast simply by dropping it into the box – now had a choice. The election campaign transformed *glasnost*'s limited criticisms of the system and the Party's self-criticism into free public and popular criticism. Citizens began to take over the Party's critical discourse: as

A. Borodenkov, *MN*, 1989, no. 7, p. 14; A. Kuteinov, *MN*, 1989, no. 11, p. 9; Shchepotkin and Kuteinov, *Proryv* (1990), pp. 19–21.

51 Urban, *Soviets* (1990), pp. 101–2.

52 *MN*, 1989, no. 11, p. 9.

53 Cited by Smith, *Soviet Politics* (1992), p. 148; Shchepotkin and Kuteinov, *Proryv* (1990), p. 57.

a result, *glasnost* ran out of control and became real freedom of speech. What only the Party had been allowed to say, what had been heretical when ordinary citizens had said it, now became the basis of a systematic attack on the Party's record in government. For the first time, it became possible to challenge the Party openly and both the new political activists and the general public began to take part in this assault. As soon as this process started, it was clear that the days of the one-Party state were numbered. The elections therefore generated a new consciousness, both of citizens' rights and of the Party's past infringements of them.

No clearer example of the counterproductive effect of the Party's approach exists than the election of Boris Yeltsin in Moscow. He had managed to secure his nomination through a combination of ruse and daring, despite fierce Party opposition. He was aided, however, by his opponents' ineptitude: their attempts to discredit him, by spreading slanderous allegations about him, were exposed; the Party Plenum, held on 16 March, by announcing the establishment of a commission to examine his heresies, confirmed him as a martyr and provoked the first large popular protest demonstrations in Moscow; finally, they fielded a podgy, prosperous and colourless *apparatchik* to run against him. The result was an overwhelming victory for Yeltsin, who got 89 per cent of the 5.7 million votes cast.[54] In Leningrad, the results were no less disastrous: the First and Second Provincial Secretaries, the First City Secretary, the Mayor, the Deputy Mayor and the President of the Regional Soviet were defeated. The Party suffered dramatic and widespread defeats in the Ukraine, Belorussia, the Far East and the Baltics. Thirty-three of the 166 regional first secretaries (about 20 per cent) were defeated, including all the Party leaders in the mining regions of the Urals and Western Siberia – this despite the fact that many of them ran unopposed.[55] These defeats were as dramatic as they were unexpected, and they provoked both the ire of the conservative *apparat* and popular delight.

What was the role of the informals and the radical intelligentsia in the election campaign? Were they able to exert a significant influence

54 V. Tretyakov, *MN*, 1989, no. 12, p. 4; Yeltsin, *Against the Grain*, (1990), pp. 31-3, 46, 108-10; Kagarlitsky, *Farewell* (1990), pp. 114-29; Roxburgh, *Revolution* (1991), pp. 128-30; J. Morrison, *Yeltsin* (London, 1991), pp. 88-93; Urban, *Soviets* (1990), pp. 106-7.
55 Ibid., pp. 11-13; *MN*, 2 April 1989, p. 8; A. Romanov, *MN*, 1989, no. 15, p. 10.

on it? The political clubs were important mainly in helping to organize support for independent candidates.[56] Many of the country's leading intellectuals ran for election and despite the *apparat*'s opposition to them, the ensuing Congress included more noted intellectuals than any previous parliament in Soviet history. Relatively large numbers of people, previously unconnected with the informal movement, became involved in the campaign to nominate and elect a number of popular heroes – above all, Boris Yeltsin. They were bound less by agreement on a detailed political programme than by hostility to the CPSU *apparat*. As a result, electoral clubs – based mainly on groups of local residents – were formed in many districts of the city. Yeltsin's campaign, in particular, was organized by such teams (notably, the Committee of the 19, which got its name from the electors of the nineteen Moscow factories that had nominated Yeltsin in Moscow). Telman Gdlyan – the public prosecutor, whose rough and ready investigations into corruption among the elite led to his suspension – was supported in his campaign by the Committee for the Defence of Gdlyan and Ivanov and by an electoral club known as 'Democratic Elections'.[57]

The voters' clubs were thus an important feature of the 1989 election campaign, but, as Vladimir Pribylovsky observes, they were quite various in inspiration and composition. The affinity between the Academy of Sciences' electoral club or that of Memorial with the Committee for the Defence of Gdlyan and Ivanov – which was based on the popular hostility to the *apparat* and the taste for heroes and martyrs rather than on a coherent set of political priorities and concern for legality – was not, at heart, deep. The electoral clubs, which supported Yeltsin and Gdlyan, were ideologically less developed and coherent than the intelligentsia's clubs, being inspired more by concern for social justice than by a theoretical interest in political and economic reform. The old informal clubs and movements were on the whole dominated by the intelligentsia and reflected its preoccupation with political theory. Typically, they hoped to provide the nascent democratic movement with ideological

56 Urban, *Soviets* (1990), p. 145; Kagarlitsky, *Farewell* (1990), p. 94.
57 Other independent candidates who benefited from this kind of support structure were Sergei Stankevich, Arkady Murashev, Ilya Zaslavsky, the economist Oleg Bogomolov and the writer Yuri Chernichenko: Yeltsin, *Against the Grain* (1990), p. 87; Pribylovsky, *Slovar'* (1991), p. 43.

leadership.[58] The Moscow Popular Front took the lead, forming the large electoral club which ran Sergei Stankevich's campaign in the Cheremushkin district of Moscow and coopting the club behind Yuri Ryzhov's campaign in the Leningradsky district.[59] The nature of the electoral clubs made it comparatively easy for the ambitious leaders of the informal movement to occupy key positions in the electoral clubs and thus mobilize the popular protest vote in favour of radical reform – and, within a few months, of democratic reform.

What were the radicals asking the electorate to endorse? There was, in fact, no coordinated alternative programme, no agreed opposition platform. However, those who ran against the Party's official candidates tended to agree on a number of general principles: anti-Stalinism, the need to enshrine the civil liberties granted by Gorbachev in law and, if possible, to enlarge on them; and economic reform (although there was no consensus on what form this should take). Many of the radical candidates were well-known intellectuals, writers and artists who had established their liberal credentials in the press, in the previous two years or under Khrushchev. However, their radicalism was still tempered by the power of the old regime and shaped by the anti-Stalinism of the Thaw. Few challenged the political parameters set by the Party. The most radical was Andrei Sakharov, who called for a market economy and political and personal freedoms. Leonid Gordon and his running mate A. Nazimova referred to the need for a parliament which would control the State budget and exercise 'a [...] kind of opposition [...] in relation to the executive authority.' Most candidates preferred more vague or general statements. Some, like Vasil Bykov, referred to the need for the further democratization of society, without specifying what they meant, or, like Viktor Astafiev, called for a more effective parliament. Roy Medvedev wanted a 'democratic, socialist, law-based State', without indicating how those who rejected socialism were to be accommodated.

Others steered clear of political demands altogether and confined themselves to economic reforms. Some were radical, like Yuri

---

58 See Ivanitsky who, contrasting the electoral clubs' campaign with that of the Party, thinks that while the latter was disorganized, the former owed their success to their coherent platform: V. Ivanitsky, *Dialog*, 1990, no. 3, p. 48.

59 Pribylovsky, *Slovar'* (1991), p. 43; V. Boxer, *AiF*, 1989, no. 50, p. 8.

Chernichenko's calls for profound agricultural reform, embracing long-term leases to free farmers (private farming by another name). Arkady Murashev wanted price reform, a restructured State budget and more decentralization. Roald Sagdeev, however, envisaged a Thirteenth Five-Year Plan, with the key elements of central planning (State orders for defence, space exploration, raw materials and medical research) being maintained. Gavriil Popov combined moves towards capitalism at a rate that would have made even Margaret Thatcher blanch (an 80–90 per cent reduction of managerial staff at all levels) with a variety of appealing and unrealistic demands: no price rises on essential goods; annual adjustments of wages and social security payments, in line with inflation; women with children under ten to be paid a monthly wage by the State; agricultural land near Moscow to be made available for leasing to Muscovites who wanted dachas; 'efficiency, but not at the people's expense'. This sort of programme sounded revolutionary, by placing the 'little man' at the centre of attention, but avoided fundamental issues of economic and political reform. Calls for improved supplies of consumer goods, welfare payments and transport, attacks on the Party bureaucracy, its privileges and corruption were common and popular but contrived to ignore the question of the Party's political monopoly and political pluralism.[60]

If at the outset, however, the intellectuals were relatively cautious in challenging the Party's political prerogatives, by the end of the election campaign and especially once the parliament met, they were much more forthright and some were even ready to argue the case for political pluralism and a formal opposition. The election campaign and its abuses thus radicalized the intelligentsia, as it did the public at large. The intellectual elite seemed poised to lead the democratic opposition, while their moral ascendancy had been confirmed by their election in disproportionate numbers to the new parliament.

60 *MN*, 1989, no. 4, p. 13, for platforms of Popov, Sagdeev, Gordon and Nazimova; Chernichenko, *MN*, 1989, no. 6, p. 9; G. Zhavoronkov, *MN*, 1989, no. 6, pp. 8–9; A. Flerovsky, *MN*, 1989, no. 11, p. 8; *MN*, 1989, no. 12, p. 6; V. Bykov, *Lit.Gaz.*, 15 February 1989, p. 1.

7. The Demand for Democracy

The unexpected defeat of many Party leaders in the elections generated a wave of unprecedented euphoria in the country, raising unrealistic expectations of reform and of improved living standards, while obscuring the nature of the changes that were taking place. This mood was reflected in the rhetoric of the radical intellectuals. V. Shchepotkin wrote in *Izvestiya*:

> Sunday 26 March is for me personally not just the Day of the First Elections, when each of us decided independently whom to delegate to the highest organ of power and, indeed, whether to delegate them at all, but also the Day of Resurrection of the People's Rights. One had only to visit a few polling stations to get this sense of participating in an awakening.[1]

Indicative of the new atmosphere and of the hopes of the period were the great popular pro-democracy demonstrations which swept Moscow between March and June 1989. Despite the Party's attempts to impose restrictions on mass meetings, both the prelude to the Congress and the Congress itself were punctuated by enormous gatherings in the Luzhniki sports stadium, near the Moscow river. On the first Sunday before the Congress, on 21 May, tens of thousands of demonstrators attended a rally at Luzhniki, organized by the informals (including the Moscow Popular Front, Memorial, Moscow Tribune, Democratic Union and the Anarchists). It called for independent trade unions, a free press and a fully democratic parliamentary system. The meeting was addressed by leading members of the liberal intelligentsia – Ales Adamovich, Leonid Batkin, Andrei Sakharov, Yuri Karyakin, Yuri Chernichenko – as well as by Yeltsin and the popular prosecutor Telman Gdlyan.[2]

1 Shchepotkin and Karpenko, *Proryv* (1990), p. 72.
2 N. Davidova, *MN*, 1989, no. 22, p. 2; Kagarlitsky, *Farewell* (1990), pp. 145–6.

133

This was a triumphant celebration of liberty and identity recovered, especially for the leaders of the intelligentsia, which saw itself retrieving its historical radical vocation and redeeming its debt to the people. After generations of fear, caution, compromise and isolation, Soviet citizens were able to speak out and organize openly. These meetings were the culmination of a process that had begun two years earlier, but they were still a heady novelty. Those who participated in the early democratic demonstrations can testify to the feelings of hope and elation they generated. The new atmosphere made sense of the French Revolution's celebration of fraternity as a revolutionary principle, akin to those of liberty and equality: it recognized that the feeling of fellowship, based on an avowed unity of purpose, was fundamental to free political activity, and particularly to the heroic politics of revolution. The mass meetings showed that it was now possible to discover this identity of purpose, after long years when such affinities were discovered only incidentally and confined to the realm of private life.

RISE OF THE PARLIAMENTARY OPPOSITION

It was in this atmosphere that the first plenary session of the Congress was held. The new parliament (or Congress of People's Deputies) was by no means without shortcomings but it gave a vital impulsion to political life and created institutions which – while doing little to resolve the problem of power in the country – enabled the anti-Stalinists to express their opposition to the *apparat* and demand changes in the way the country was ruled.

The radicals hoped that it would be possible to collaborate with the Party leadership in promoting further reforms.[3] To this end, the leaders of the anti-Stalinist intelligentsia and newly-elected and hitherto largely unknown young informal activists, like Arkady Murashev, Sergei Stankevich and Ilya Zaslavsky, joined forces with Boris Yeltsin to prepare an alternative reform programme to present

---

3 Roxburgh, *Revolution* (1991), p. 141; N. Zhelnorova and L. Novikova, *AiF*, 10 June 1989; G. Popov in *Pervy s"yezd narodnykh deputatov: Stenograficheskii otchet* (Moscow, 1989), I, p. 225.

to the Congress. The radicalization of the intelligentsia was not instantaneous: still less was their opposition to Gorbachev. At the Luzhniki meeting of 21 May 1989, Leonid Batkin still believed that cooperation with the reform leadership of the Party was possible and necessary: 'While maintaining independence of opinion with regard to Gorbachev himself,' he is reported to have told the meeting, 'we must support him against the Right. At this political moment, we cannot do without him. But neither can he do without us.'[4] The radicals' expectation that the Congress would act as a vehicle for promoting the necessary reforms, which had hitherto been blocked by the Party *apparat*, was soon to be disappointed, however.

The Congress opened on 26 May 1989, amid considerable confusion: there were headphones for each deputy but no microphones and no system for recording votes. It was clear that the bureaucrats who had made the practical arrangements for the assembly had overlooked the possibility that deputies might wish to intervene in debates or vote independently. The Congress itself was an amorphous body, not only by virtue of its impractical size, but also because of its lack of parliamentary structures and procedures.[5] Deputies were organized not according to political party (in theory, ideological unanimity still obtained) or persuasion, but geographically, with each province, region and ethnic group having its bloc of deputies. Not only did this make for disorganized debate – with individuals intervening at length and at random[6] – but it also distorted the alignment and weight of the forces in the Congress. In practice, it meant that the liberals, who were in an overall minority, often found themselves isolated in a bloc of provincial deputies, commanded by a conservative provincial Party secretary. As a result, the liberals' influence in the Congress was undermined and dispersed, as voting on the first substantive issue showed.

Although the radicals were consistently outnumbered in the Congress, its first session galvanized the public: throughout the USSR, the overwhelming majority of the population followed the

4 Cited in Kagarlitsky, *Farewell* (1990), p. 146.
5 See Urban, *Soviets* (1990), pp. 130–31; V. Tretyakov, *MN*, 1989, no. 24, p. 7.
6 See criticisms by L. Batkin, *MN*, 1989, no. 24, p. 9; Stankevich, *Yunost*, 1989, no. 9, p. 2; Stankevich, 'Trudnosti' in Yushenkov (ed.), *Neformaly* (1990), pp. 141–2, 144. Both pointed to the need for factions (or, as Batkin put it, a constructive opposition).

proceedings on television.[7] The psychological impact was enormous. The Chairman of the KGB and other high officials and ministers were subjected to hostile parliamentary interrogation, before being confirmed in office. The KGB's abuse of power and its 'underground empire' were criticized. Yuri Karyakin suggested that Lenin should be removed from his mausoleum and buried. Thereafter, criticism of Lenin became possible. Some relatively liberal legislation was passed. Although these achievements were modest, Yeltsin believed that the impact of the Congress, in terms of political education, was deep and that people's outlook was changed by it.[8]

Fundamentally, however, the Congress was not fully democratic. An unwieldy body of 2250 deputies, it was meant to elect from its ranks a chairman and a Supreme Soviet of 542 deputies, which would act as a permanent legislature. The election of the chairman (Gorbachev) was a formality – surprisingly ruffled, when an obscure deputy, Alexander Obolensky, offered himself as an alternative candidate. On the second day, the Supreme Soviet was elected. Each region or nationality was allocated a certain number of seats in the Supreme Soviet: each regional delegation proposed a list of deputies, on which the whole Congress voted. Most delegations chose to propose no more delegates than there were seats allocated to the region in the upper chamber, with the result that the Congress simply ratified their choice. The Moscow delegation was unique in the country in having a large democratic contingent. They decided to set a democratic example to the Congress, by proposing 55 deputies for Moscow's 29 seats in the Supreme Soviet. The result was that the conservative majority in the Congress voted against all the best-known radicals on the list – including Boris Yeltsin – and allowed only neutral or unknown deputies into the upper chamber.

Inter-Regional Group of Deputies

The results, when announced the next day, caused uproar. The non-election of Yeltsin, in particular, seemed outrageous, in the light

---

7 Urban, *Soviets* (1990), p. 134; 95 per cent of the adult population watched all or some of the proceedings.
8 Roxburgh, *Revolution* (1991), pp. 139–40; Shchepotkin and Karpenko, *Proryv* (1990), pp. 248–333; Yeltsin, *Against the Grain* (1990), p. 190.

of the overwhelming popular mandate he had received. A huge protest demonstration was held in Luzhniki, in which speakers intervened in a much more critical vein than previously. It was on the third day, in response to what was felt to be the manipulation of the Congress by the *apparat*, that Yuri Afanasiev and Gavriil Popov made their famous speeches, condemning the conservative majority in the Congress. 'We have formed a Stalinist-Brezhnevite Supreme Soviet', Afanasiev complained, to hoots of protest in the Chamber. '[...] And it's you in particular that I'm addressing, what I would call the aggressively obedient majority, who yesterday obstructed all the decisions the people expect of us.'[9] Gavriil Popov went further. Democratic deputies had faced a choice before the Congress, either to form some sort of opposition or to collaborate constructively in the work of the Congress. They had come prepared with drafts and documents on the reforms they thought necessary. Far from being welcomed, however, they were ignored, distrusted and even treated with contempt. Basic facilities, such as photocopying, paper and offices, were denied them. The final straw was the election of the Supreme Soviet:

It's becoming obvious [...] that the *apparat* is openly trying to avenge itself [...]

[...] Hence, we have to think about changing our position. Firstly, a group of Moscow deputies from research organizations and the creative unions considers it essential to leave the Moscow delegation. We propose that we should think about forming an inter-regional independent group of deputies [known as the IRG] and we invite all the comrade deputies to join this group.[10]

The change of position was clear: from an initial desire to cooperate in the work of the Congress, the democratic intellectuals were moving towards the alternative position of opposition. They enjoyed considerable popular support for this move. A public opinion poll in mid-June revealed that almost 50 per cent of respondents supported the IRG. Boris Yeltsin, in July, claimed that they had been inundated with telegrams of support.[11]

By the end of the first session of the Congress, 256 deputies had rallied to Popov's call and joined the IRG. This meant that deputies, instead of voting with their regional delegation, acted – or tried to

9 *Pervy s"yezd* (1989), I, pp. 223-4.
10 Ibid., p. 226.
11 *AiF*, 26, 1989; Yeltsin, *MN*, 1989, no. 32, p. 10.

act – in conjunction with other deputies, whose general political orientation they shared. An attempt was thus made to replace geographic with ideological distinctions. The IRG thereby became a virtual faction within the CPSU. It held its first meeting on 7 June 1989 to coordinate its position and tactics in Congress and subsequently scored a number of successes during the session – including the establishment of a number of parliamentary commissions (on the Tbilisi affair, the Molotov-Ribbentropp pact, on Party privileges and the Gdlyan affair). It also succeeded in having the second session of the full Congress brought forward from June 1990 to Autumn 1989, thereby increasing the role and significance of the Congress.

These tactical victories did not disguise the need for a more formal organization and coherent programme. The first steps in this direction were taken on 29–30 July 1989, when the first conference of the IRG was held in Moscow. Over 300 deputies attended.[12] Although agreement was reached on specific points of policy,[13] there were divergent views about the Group's purpose and character. The economist, Oleg Bogomolov, claimed that there was a need for organized dissent. Yevgeny Primakov, a Gorbachev adviser, expressed a different viewpoint – suggesting that the Group should act as a forum for discussion but as not a closed club which set itself up in 'antithesis' to the Supreme Soviet. The meeting split almost evenly on the issue.[14]

Five co-chairmen were elected at the first conference in July 1989. These were Andrei Sakharov, Yuri Afanasiev, Gavriil Popov, Boris Yeltsin and Victor Palm of Estonia. Even the list of co-chairmen indicates the diversity of views embraced by the IRG: from the country's leading and unrepentant ex-dissident to a former member of the Politburo, who had still not renounced his Party membership. Of

---

12 A. Romanov and V. Shevelev, *MN*, 1989, no. 32, p. 10, suggest that 393 deputies attended and 260 formally accepted the platform. Pribylovsky affirms that 316 deputies were present, of whom 268 were IRG members; others, unable to attend, wrote to pledge their support – bringing support for the group to 388 deputies: Pribylovsky, *Slovar'* (1991), p. 37. Grafova and Domnisheva give similar figures (269 deputies present and 388 members in total), *Lit.Gaz.*, 2 August 1989, p. 2.

13 A. Romanov, *MN*, 1989, no. 32, p. 10; Pribylovsky, *Slovar'* (1991), p. 37; L. Grafova and Domnisheva, *Lit.Gaz.*, 2 August 1989, pp. ; Tolz, *Multi-Party System* (1990), p. 73, for attendance figures and policy decisions.

14 Romanov, *MN*, 1989, no. 32, p. 10; Yeltsin, *MN*, 1989, no. 32, p. 10.

the five co-chairmen, only Sakharov was not a CPSU member: in the elections to this position, he received fewest votes (69), while Yeltsin received widest support, with 144 votes.[15] The IRG conformed to a by now familiar pattern: its members included a high proportion of Party-card-carrying Russian intellectuals. Yet again, in composition and culture, it was representative less of society at large as of the reformist intelligentsia.[16] Nonetheless, the IRG spanned a wide range of views within this constituency and initially it adopted a cautious approach. It did not immediately demand political pluralism, despite the considerable support for pluralism among its members.

The tension between the radicals, who favoured opposition in principle, and those who were more interested in the tactical uses of the Group became sharper in Autumn 1989. The more cautious view was put by Anatoly Sobchak, of Leningrad, and Sergei Stankevich, the former Moscow Popular Front activist. 'From the very first minutes,' Sobchak claimed in October, 'I spoke against the Group becoming a faction, an opposition force and suggested that it remain a sort of deputies' club, open to all, where it would be possible to exchange opinions, elaborate alternative draft laws.' He continued:

> I think it is too early for the concept of a faction, or an opposition [...] With only a nascent parliament, unity of views and a definite platform are more important. If [the IRG] matures, it could help *perestroika* and become a counterweight to conservative forces in the Party, the government and the Supreme Soviet itself. But some people think it could become an association of not very responsible people, if it starts proposing only ultimatums [sic], instead of giving the majority in the Supreme Soviet the most professional models for dealing with complex problems.[17]

This view was broadly shared by Sergei Stankevich, who wanted to see the work of the Congress rationalized and the division of opinion

---

15 Pribylovsky, *Slovar'* (1991), p. 37.

16 An information bulletin, published in mid-September, confirmed that a majority of the IRG's members were Communists. Some members were involved in the informal movement and had risen to prominence through it. Among these were Sergei Stankevich, of the Moscow Popular Front, Igor Shamshev, of the Yaroslavl Popular Front; Alexander Obolensky, from an academic community in the Murmansk area, and Sergei Belozertsev, of the Karelian Popular Front. Many IRG deputies were drawn from the intelligentsia (133 of the 388 members claimed by the Group in September 1989); most were Russian (286) and had been elected from Moscow: Pribylovsky, *Slovar'* (1991), p. 37; Tolz, *Multi-Party System* (1990), p. 75.

17 Sobchak in *MN*,1 October 1989, p. 2.

within it formalized in different factions, but who rejected the possibility of formal political pluralism on the grounds that it would be premature and unrealistic, in the absence of any social basis for alternative parties.[18]

A different approach was favoured by Yuri Afanasiev and Andrei Sakharov. At the IRG's second conference, on 23 September 1989, Afanasiev argued that the IRG should support Gorbachev but only as an ally with independent views, capable of offering criticism where appropriate:

> We must not be afraid to call ourselves a constructive opposition. [...] Our group has a political character and this should not be concealed. [...] We [...] united not around separate interests, but around a universal platform – around *perestroika* as a whole [...] We are the only political group and this should be said openly. If we have our own political programme, which does not coincide with others, including with the official one – then we are a legal, constitutional opposition.[19]

The Inter-Regional Group, according to Afanasiev, needed to concentrate on real change in the system of government. Hitherto, *perestroika* had been confined to an attempt to mend the system inaugurated by the October revolution. That system, however, could not be reformed. It was based on three unacceptable principles: those of the imperial, unitary and strictly centralized State; State socialism with a non-market economy and the CPSU's monopoly of political power. These elements of the system should be abolished, without bloodshed or violence and on the basis of agreement.[20]

In this, Afanasiev was following the lead of Andrei Sakharov, who as early as 9 June 1989 had called for the abolition of Article 6 of the Soviet Constitution and the creation of a fully democratic, federal State. Sakharov believed constitutional change to be of fundamental importance, as a precondition of effective economic, political and social reform. Sakharov elaborated a draft constitution, which envisaged decentralization, further democratization, full civil rights and social security guarantees. Sakharov even looked forward to the day when capitalism and socialism would fuse to form a single government for the world.[21] In the last speech of his life, which he

18 Stankevich, *Yunost*, 1989, no. 9, p. 2–4.
19 Yu. Afanasiev, *Ya dolzhen eto skazat'* (Moscow, 1991), pp. 234, 241.
20 Ibid., pp. 239–40, 242.
21 Decree on Power, 9 June 1989; Draft Constitution of the Union of Soviet Republics of

made at a meeting of the IRG, Sakharov again urged his colleagues to opt for opposition: 'I want to give a definition of opposition', he said.

What is opposition? We cannot assume responsibility for what the leadership is now doing. It is leading the country into a crisis, by drawing the reform process out over many years. [...] The only way, the only possibility of evolutionary development, lies in radical change. [...] By calling ourselves an opposition, we assume responsibility for the decisions we advocate [...].[22]

The day after delivering this speech, Sakharov died. His vision was, of course, too radical for the majority of the new politicians of the USSR.

The second conference of the IRG came close to endorsing Sakharov's vision. A platform was adopted, calling for the abolition of Article 6 of the Constitution (in essence, for the introduction of a multiparty system) and the introduction of fully democratic elections.[23] However, there was still a reluctance to challenge the CPSU openly and coherently in the way Afanasiev advocated and only some of the IRG's members opted for outright opposition to the CPSU, in December 1989.

The debate was overtaken by events. The third session of the Congress, held in March 1990, voted to end the Party's monopoly on politics. At this time, the IRG's influence in the Congress began to diminish: it lost seats in key parliamentary commissions; the number of deputies proclaiming allegiance to the Group began to fall.[24] What were the reasons for this? The IRG was politically amorphous, embracing quite a wide range of views.

In so far as the IRG offered opposition to the Party, it was an opposition of a peculiar kind: it took the shape of a challenge not to the Party as a whole but to the conservative *apparat*, to the elements in the Party which had already, before the Congress opened, openly declared their rejection of *perestroika* and of the Party leadership's reform policies. It was thus possible for members of the new group of deputies to see themselves as a caucus supporting the reform leadership against the entrenched conservatives in the Party. Clearly, this view was held by many deputies who joined the IRG, for they

Europe and Asia: both in Sakharov, *Trevoga i nadezhda* (Moscow, 1991), pp. 260-78.
22 Sakharov, *Trevoga i nadezhda* (1991), pp. 277-8.
23 Pribylovsky, *Slovar'* (1991), p. 37.
24 Ibid.

did not resign their membership of the CPSU. A year would pass before the leading members of the IRG would leave the Party. Hence, it would be erroneous to see the Inter-Regional Group of Deputies as from the first an unequivocal opposition, although a group of radical deputies within the IRG held that this should be its role.

While the IRG resulted in a partial realignment of the Congress along more conventional lines (dividing it into two opposed groups), it partly obscured the real range of forces in play in the Congress. The dramatic clash between the small articulate group of radicals and the conservative majority overshadowed other developments and tended to encourage analysts to see the new political life of the country in terms of a clash between the right and left, the *apparat* and the intelligentsia. But the struggle between David and Goliath did not subsume – nor was it even a faithful reflection of – the transformation of political life that was taking place. The opposition offered by the IRG was rhetorical, not merely because it found itself in a small minority but because it embraced a wide range of different views, ambitions and assessments of the room for political manoeuvre. As a result, neither as an opposition to the *apparat* nor as a source of support for the reform leaders was the IRG particularly effective.[25] Nonetheless, it helped to change the climate of opinion in the country and move the political agenda forward in a radical way. Until Autumn 1989, calls for political pluralism were considered almost treacherous. The IRG's sharp battles with and attacks on the *apparat*, in the first session of Congress in June 1989, gave the arguments in favour of radical political change a degree of political legitimacy and authority which they had until then lacked.

CRISIS IN THE PARTY

The IRG on its own could not have impelled the CPSU to abolish one-Party rule. It was the gradual disintegration of the CPSU which hastened the advent of political pluralism in Russia. Dissension within the leadership and at the top of the Party – although in theory

25 See Leonid Batkin's criticisms of its record, structures and programme at the Moscow Tribune meeting of May 1990 in MBIO, *Byulleten' Moskovskaya Tribuna*, 1990, no. 5, pp. 2-3.

non-existent – had been a constant and well-known feature of Soviet politics. The effect of Gorbachev's reforms since 1987 had been to increase the number of participants in the debate about policy, a process which culminated in the 1989 elections and the creation of a semi-democratic parliament. The elections not only revealed the wide divergences of view within the Party but also the variety of interest groups competing for influence within it – from the high *apparat*, to middle managers and the intelligentsia – and by pitting these groups openly against each other, increased dissension within the Party. The challenges of 1989 – from the unparalleled assault on the Party and its prerogatives in the Congress of People's Deputies to the fall of the Communist regimes in Eastern Europe and the calls at home for the end of the one-party system – far from helping the CPSU to overcome these difficulties, exacerbated its internal divisions.

Declining Authority

The growing crisis in the Party was indicated by its declining membership and waning public authority.[26] Profound scepticism prevailed about the Party's pretensions: as early as 1989, polls showed that far from the official ideology's claims being popularly acclaimed, only 2.3 per cent of Soviet citizens and 4.8 per cent of Party members connected the future of humanity with communism.[27] A poll the following year indicated that only 1 per cent of Muscovites believed the Party expressed the interests of the working class, while 43.5 per cent believed it represented the interests of the 'directing layers' in society.[28] By July 1990, the public was openly disenchanted with the Party: only 18 per cent thought the CPSU capable of extricating the country from the crisis, while 74 per cent felt the Party should be held responsible for its seventy-year rule and 31 per cent felt the CPSU should be disbanded (although 41 per cent disagreed). Only 6 per cent believed the Party's influence would grow.[29]

From 1989, Party membership began to decline. Whereas, in the

26 Shchepotkin and Karpenko, *Proryv* (1990), p. 86.
27 *Pravda*, 3 March 1990, p. 3.
28 V. Shostakovsky, *Moskovskaya pravda*, 17 June 1990.
29 V. Nikitina, *MN*, 27 July 1990, p. 7.

past, Party membership had been valued as a ticket to advancement in one's career, power and privilege, now fewer people deemed it necessary to acquire.[30] Many members began to resign either through disenchantment or to signal their disagreement with the policies pursued by the leadership. Loss of faith in the Party grew in 1989, as attacks on its record of incompetent government and corruption multiplied, following the election campaign and the first session of Congress. The lack of success and half-heartedness of the reforms also prompted people to leave the Party. These pressures grew with the fall of the communist regimes in Eastern Europe in Autumn and early Winter 1989.

The corruption and incompetence of Party officials sparked off a wave of popular protests throughout the country from Siberia to Ukraine.[31] In Volgograd, Tyumen, Bashkiria, the Siberian Far East and Chernigov, unpopular Party leaders of provincial Party committees were forced to resign. The resignation of Party committees was demanded in about ten other towns, with meetings and demonstrations even being organized by dissident Party members.[32] In the context of events in Eastern Europe, this was a threatening development, which the Party could not ignore. It was now faced with the prospect of an open challenge to its power and rule and was confronted with insistent calls from within for reform. The more the leadership resisted or hesitated on reform, the more its internal critics were impelled to leave the Party and mount the challenge to its prerogatives from without. In the first five months of 1990 approximately 130 000 people left the CPSU (as many as left in the previous year).[33]

Divisions Within the Party

The Party was also deeply and increasingly divided. The CPSU was never a single Party but a sort of common house, in which many different views co-existed. In 1989 these differences grew deeper and spilled over far beyond the conventional parameters of manoeuvre

30 *Izvestiya TsK KPSS*, 1989, no. 2, p. 138. Recruitment began to fall significantly in 1988.
31 V. Radzievsky, *MN*, 4 March 1990.
32 B. Keller, *IHT*, 5 February 1990, pp. 1, 5; *MN*, 8 September 1990, pp. 7, 9.
33 *AiF*, 1990, no. 24, p. 8.

and discussion. The centrifugal forces at work in the Party in 1989 propelled both the right and left wings of the Party further and further apart and the gamut of intermediate views also multiplied. By 1990, it was commonplace to observe that the CPSU was not one but several parties and that at least three or four trends might be identified within it.[34] Mikhail Malyutin distinguished eight strands of thought, ranging from the liberal democrats, who supported the market and political pluralism, to the greater Russian nationalists and neo-Stalinists.[35] The principal conflict at the heart of the Party, however, pitted conservatives, who wished to retain the centralized authoritarian power structures devised by Stalin, against those who wanted the Stalinist heritage to be dismantled and replaced by a system based on democratic principles and the rule of law.

From 1989 on, it was not clear how far Gorbachev was ultimately ready to go in pursuit of reform: whether he thought it necessary to temporize to try to carry the bulk of the Party with him or whether his commitment to reform was eclipsed by his fidelity to the Soviet system. His hesitations probably contributed to prolonging and embittering the debate, as they encouraged its various protagonists to hope that they might win the argument and thus control over the Party's direction.

Democratic Reform of the Party

Gorbachev and the reform leadership of the Party had arguably precipitated these difficulties by launching the idea of democratization of the Party in 1987 and by condemning the principle of democratic centralism and calling for more openness and accountability in the Party's affairs at the Party Conference in June 1988.[36] The initial idea seems to have been to diminish resistance to broader reform, by

34 B. Kurashvili, 'Kriticheskaya faza' in Vyshinsky (ed.), *Pravo i vlast'* (1990), p. 40; V. Parol, 'Mnogopartinost'' in *Obshchestvennye nauki*, 1990, no. 1, pp. 118–19; 'Ot politicheskogo monizma' in Yushenkov (ed.), *Neformaly* (1990), pp. 58–61; 'Partiya i novye obshchestvennye dvizheniya' in Pechenev and Vyunsky (eds), *Neformaly* (1990), pp. 316, 320–21; V. Vyunitsky, 'Ot dikii', *Dialog*, 1990, no. 17, pp. 34–5; V. Ivashko, *Lit.Gaz.*, 24 July 1991, p. 2; Gorbachev speech in *Sovetskaya Rossiya*, 26 July 1991.

35 Trusov (ed.), 'Neformaly' in Pechenev and Vyunsky (eds.), *Neformaly* (1990), pp. 260–61.

36 For summary of the changes approved by the Conference and the debate which preceded it, see S. White, *Gorbachev* (1990), pp. 33–6.

making the Party secretaries more responsive to public opinion and to create a more powerful constituency supporting reform within the Party.

Initially, elections for Party office were introduced on a limited basis: by 1989, 1117 district and city secretaries had been elected to office: however, this represented only 8.6 per cent of the total number of secretaries in the Party and only 6 per cent (or 269) of those involved were first secretaries. In addition, real power was wielded not at city and district level, but by provincial Party leaders and the centre. The principle of elections could hardly be said to have extended here: only 1 per cent of provincial secretaries appointed since 1986 had been elected to office. In any event, the elections were largely artificial, as the *apparat*, rather than rank-and-file Party members, controlled nominations. Having introduced the idea of limited competitive elections, Gorbachev none the less appears to have favoured old techniques in attempting to construct his power-base. He presided over two rounds of sweeping personnel changes (in 1985–86 and 1988–89) but these confined themselves to advancing not fresh, new personnel, but those who were already well ensconced in the system.[37]

After the Nineteenth Party Conference, there was a considerable gap between the Party's rhetoric and its internal practices. Little was done to give effect to the Conference resolutions on internal Party democracy and these prevarications generated a reform caucus in the lower echelons of the Party. It was this pressure group – rather than the reform leadership – which attempted to advance the cause of democratic reform in the Party from 1989 on.

On 30 October 1989, the first conference of democratically inclined Party clubs met in Moscow and announced the creation of a Movement of Reform Communists for a Democratic Platform in the CPSU. A declaration was adopted which proclaimed its support for 'a radical transformation of the Party into a fully democratic, self-governing organization [...] working in a multiparty, parliamentary democracy.' Among its leading demands were the abolition of the Party's monopoly on politics, the replacement of the *nomenklatura* (or

37 Nazimova and Sheinis, 'Vybory' in *SSSR* (1990), pp. 673–4.

appointment) system with elections and competition, the right to form factions within the Party and an end to the privileges accorded to the Party hierarchy.[38]

Vladimir Lysenko, one of the founders of the Moscow Party Club, explained Democratic Platform's ideas in an article published in January 1990. Lysenko did not mince his words. It was essential to recognize that the Party's official ideology had led the country – and the states of Eastern Europe – into a cul-de-sac. Among the notions which should be jettisoned were the historical mission of the working class, the dictatorship of the proletariat and the inevitability of revolution. Lysenko argued that the Party should abandon its messianic vision in favour of a more pragmatic approach to politics. He pointed out that Lenin's values and significance had been largely obscured by the myth surrounding him and the Party's opportunistic exploitation of it. 'I am proposing not a return to the Leninist conception of a new type of Party, as modern official propaganda proposes, [...] but the elaboration of a new conception of political parliamentary parties, operating in a context of democratic social-ism.'[39] In future, the Party should not have an official ideology but should instead draw inspiration from all the world's great thinkers, including non-Marxists. Lysenko affirmed that the neo-Stalinist model of the Party should be rejected. The CPSU should be democratized and turned into an ordinary political party, competing with other parties for power. It should be characterized by internal pluralism, wide local autonomy, horizontal as well as vertical structures, relaxed discipline and elective office.[40]

This programme was rejected by the Party's neo-Stalinist conserva-tives and also by its neo-Leninists, those who – with Gorbachev – dreamed of reviving the supposedly democratic political standards and Party of the 1920s. Even among supporters of reform, there were differences of view about how best to proceed. Lysenko and a majority of the Party Club supported immediate measures to separate the State from the Party (particularly, the transfer of power to the Soviets) and to allow intra-Party pluralism. This path, it was believed,

38 Krotov *et al.*, *Rossiya* (1991), I, 2, p. 243.
39 V. Lysenko, 'Krizis', *Politika*, 1990, no. 1, p. 37.
40 Ibid., p. 39.

would lead to the Communist Party becoming a democratic party in a democratic State.[41]

This argument furnished the basis of the programme adopted by Democratic Platform at its inaugural conference on 21–22 January 1990. Representatives of 162 Party clubs attended, as did many luminaries on the democratic camp (most of whom were Party members). The debate immediately centred on tactics and on the question of whether a new social democratic Party should be founded. The social democratic radicals, who favoured leaving the CPSU, were in a minority. The majority – which included the rector of the Higher Party School, Vyacheslav Shostakovsky, and Vladimir Lysenko – still believed that the CPSU might change, committing itself unequivocally to political pluralism and democracy and that it was thus premature to break away from the Party. They argued that Democratic Platform should work within the Party to promote reform and saw their opportunity in the forthcoming Twenty-Eighth Party Congress, then due to be held in Autumn 1990. The Congress was the only body with the authority to adopt a new programme and rules and, hence, to redefine the Party's aims, ideals and procedures.[42]

The moderates were encouraged in their hopes for reform on two counts. Firstly, political pluralism was about to be conceded, with the amendment of Article 6 of the Constitution. It is unlikely that highly placed Party figures such as Shostakovsky – who was reported to have close links with Alexander Yakovlev – would have been unaware that the leadership planned to concede this. They also believed that they might be well represented at the Twenty-Eighth Party Congress and be able to influence its key decisions. The founding conference was, then, divided more on tactics than on goals. Their platform was quite popular. The Central Committee estimated that by April 1990, Democratic Platform had the support of about 30 per cent of Party members.[43] However, the conservatives' successful

41 Ibid., pp. 33–41; Shostakovsky, 'Vozmozhen', *Dialog*, 1990, no. 8, pp. 29–31 for a similar statement of Democratic Platform's aims; see also Shostakovsky, *SK*, 7 December 1989, p. 3; Shostakovsky, *Moskovskaya Pravda*, 17 June 1990.

42 Interviews with V. Shostakovsky, 20 November 1990, and I. Chubais, 20 November 1990; *Pravda*, 3 March 1990; Shostakosvky, *SK*, 7 December 1989; also interview with S.P. Zinchenko, 20 November 1990.

43 Sakwa, *Gorbachev* (1990), p. 182; Shostakovsky, interview, 20 November 1990; see also Zh. Toshchenko *et al.*, *AiF*, 1990, no. 25, p. 2.

resistance to these demands before and during the Party Congress in July 1990 ultimately led to the CPSU splitting and the democrats departing to found a separate political party.[44]

THE ADVENT OF DEMOCRACY

While the case for constitutional reform – notably the need for the introduction of a multiparty system and the abolition of the Party's monopoly on political life – was advanced by a growing body of opinion within and outside the Party, the key factor in explaining the success of the campaign to amend Article 6 of the Constitution (which enshrined the Party's leading role and its monopoly on political power) was the revolution in Eastern Europe and the fall of the Iron Curtain.

Public opinion had been galvanized by events in the 'brother socialist' countries, which were now fully reported in the media and provoked wide discussion.[45] A poll, conducted by the Institute of Sociology of the Academy of Sciences early in 1990, concluded that opinion in Moscow had been radicalized by these events and that immediate and decisive reforms were now demanded by the public.[46] Anti-Party demonstrations broke out in a number of Russian cities in January and February 1990. On 4 February 1990, the biggest demonstration since the Revolution brought 200 000 on to the streets of Moscow, to demand an end to one-Party rule. Placards proclaimed: 'Party bureaucrats, remember Romania' and 'Freedom Now'. Yuri Afanasiev, Gavriil Popov and Boris Yeltsin were among the speakers calling for constitutional changes. All over Russia, the Ukraine and the Union, large democratic meetings were held in an unprecedented atmosphere.[47] On 25 February 1990, a second mass rally demanding constitutional reform was held in Moscow. These giant rallies, attended by almost a quarter of a million citizens, demonstrated the

44 *AiF*, 1990, no. 13, p. 8; Popov and Sobchak, *AiF*, 1990, no. 29, p. 2.
45 See *MN*, 1989, no. 46, p.12; *MN*, 1989, no. 47, p. 6, on fall of the Berlin Wall and German unity; *MN*, 1989, no. 49, pp. 8–9; *MN*, 1989, no. 50, pp. 89 for interviews with Dubček and Mlynář; *MN*, 1989, no. 51, pp. 6–7.
46 See T. Colton, 'Moscow Elections' in Hewett and Winston (eds), *Milestones* (1991), p. 362.
47 See Morrison, *Yeltsin* (1991), p. 117; D. Remnick, *IHT*, 5 February 1990.

disrepute into which the Party had fallen. They showed the democrats' organizational ability, built up in the previous year,[48] and were a tangible indicator of the new political culture and environment that had developed since the 1989 elections.[49]

Another development which heartened the reformers was the secession of the Lithuanian and subsequently the Estonian Communist Parties from the all-Union Party. This move was inspired by the local reform leadership in the republics, in the face of elections in which they stood to suffer serious defeats, unless they could demonstrate their commitment to democratic reform and national interest. The most effective way of doing this was by cutting the link with Moscow. The Lithuanians broke away on 19 December 1989, provoking another crisis at the centre, which summoned the Lithuanian Party leader Brazauskas to Moscow for a Central Committee hearing on 25–26 December 1989. Despite heavy pressure from Gorbachev and hostile questioning and attacks from the body of the Plenum, Brazauskas did not capitulate[50] and the New Year of 1990 opened with the unitary structure of the Party breached and the question of democratic reform firmly on the agenda.

Until November 1989, Gorbachev's declarations on the subject were reserved and he argued the case for the retention of the Party's leading role and the one-Party system. However, the events in Eastern Europe impelled him towards admitting the principle of pluralism, and by 9 December 1989 he was warning the Party of the dangers of delay. This provoked uproar at the Central Committee Plenum, on the

48 MOI claimed to have organized the February demonstrations: see MBIO: Informal Archive: 'Novosti partiinogo stroitelstva', 6 June 1990. I. Yakovenko, *MN*, 4 March 1990, p. 5, gives the findings of a poll of participants in the 25 February demonstration, which revealed that 72 per cent of them intended to vote for Democratic Russia candidates in the regional and local elections the following month, and that they were broadly sympathetic to and interested in the consolidation of democratic forces (69 per cent) and Democratic Platform (71 per cent).

49 The Interior Ministry estimated that in ten months of 1989, over three and a half thousand demonstrations had been held in the USSR, with the participation of about 10 million people. In Moscow, in this period, 324 demonstrations were held (209 without permission) and lowest estimates calculated that over half a million people took part in them: M. Topalov, '"Formal'naya"' in Levichev (ed.), *Neformal'naya volna* (1990), pp. 157–8.

50 See Roxburgh, *Revolution* (1991), pp. 162–6, for an account; for the proceedings, see *Izvestiya TsK KPSS*, 1990, no. 6.

eve of the second session of the Congress.[51] Nonetheless, Gorbachev pressed ahead with the elaboration of a reform-communist programme for presentation to the Party Congress, which had been brought forward to Autumn 1990, to enable sweeping reforms of policy and personnel be effected. What Gorbachev was to put to the Party early in 1990 was the need to convert the CPSU into a democratic party competing for power at the ballot box and committed to democratic socialism. However, he resisted the IRG's attempts to raise the issue of Article 6 of the Constitution at the second session of the Congress in December 1989, ensuring the defeat of the relevant amendment to the agenda. When Sakharov, on 12 December, two days before his death, attempted to hand Gorbachev a petition demanding the abolition of Article 6, Gorbachev dismissed him abruptly.

However, the great anti-Party demonstrations throughout the country forced the conservatives in the Party to capitulate. The extended Central Committee Plenum, which opened on 5 February 1990, discussed Gorbachev's draft Party programme. Entitled 'For a Humane, Democratic Socialism', it envisaged *de facto* political pluralism, including dialogue among proponents of different visions of reform socialism and an end to democratic centralism. It appears to have been a compromise document, however, for some of the key reform demands – such as the right to form factions (in effect, parties within the Party) – were withheld. The document implied, however, that at some unspecified future date a multiparty system might develop. The Party, it suggested, would ultimately have to be prepared to fight its way to power, in competitive elections. This vision of the future provoked the fierce opposition of Party conservatives, but did not go far enough to elicit the radicals' enthusiasm. Nonetheless, Yeltsin was alone in voting against the proposals, at the end of the Plenum.[52] Consideration of the precise wording of a revised Article 6 was deferred for a month, until 11–16 March, when another Central Committee Plenum again deliberated on the concession. With great reluctance, bowing to popular demand and with the example of their East European allies before them, the

51 *Pravda*, 26 November 1989; *Pravda*, 10 December 1989.
52 See *Materialy plenuma TsK KPSS* (1990), pp. 67–9, for Yeltsin's speech; *AiF*, 1990, no. 6, p. 1.

Central Committee amended Article 6, eliminating the reference to the Party's leading role. On 13 March 1990, the amendment to the Constitution was confirmed by the Congress of People's Deputies.[53]

A new era had thus been inaugurated. With the abolition of the provision enabling the CPSU to monopolize political and public life and the introduction of new legislation, it now became possible to form rival political parties, and they lost no time in emerging. Now the Party existed on the same legal basis as other political organizations and this heralded the end of its monolithic rule. By the late 1980s, the Party's unity had been based not on any real coincidence of its members' political views, but on their opportunism and on its internal discipline. The difficulty of taking part in public life outside the Party and the benefits and opportunities Party membership conferred had transformed the CPSU from a political party, in the sense of an association founded on political preferences, into an organization encompassing quite divergent views and fulfilling quite diverse functions. The depth and extent of these disagreements had been exposed by the 1989 election campaign, which, in addition to underscoring the disagreements on policy that divided the Party leadership, also pitted lower-level Party membership against the *apparat*. The logic of this dynamic, hitherto inhibited by legal constraints, was to have an immediate impact on the Party, which began to split up.

1990 ELECTIONS

The campaign for democracy coincided with the election, on 4 March 1990, of new republican parliaments and city councils. Just as the abolition of the Party's leading role in society signalled the end of its monopoly on political life, so too the centralized Soviet government was undermined by the new parliamentary institutions. Their creation inaugurated the final crisis of Soviet power: they challenged the legitimacy of central rule from Moscow and heralded the end of the Soviet empire. The political heritage of Stalin was thus fundamentally weakened in Spring 1990. Indeed, the Spring election campaign –

53 *Izvestiya TsK KPSS*, 1990, no. 5, pp. 32–59.

marked by the campaign against Article 6 of the Constitution and significant democratic victories at the polls – may be seen as the high-point of the democratic debate, until the attempted *putsch* in August 1991 once again rallied the public behind anti-Stalinism.

The election campaign for the republican parliaments and city councils started at the end of 1989. The rules under which the elections were conducted had been amended by the Congress of People's Deputies, in its December 1989 session, so as to eliminate most of the artificial barriers to direct democratic elections: pre-electoral meetings to weed out candidates were abolished and public organizations lost their right to nominate deputies.[54] The electoral system was thus more democratic than it had been the previous year. The campaign was also distinguished from its predecessor by its more clearly defined battlelines. Both the right (the nationalist and neo-Stalinist critics of the Party leadership) and the left (the liberals and democrats) were organized in electoral blocs.

Moscow Union of Voters

In 1990, the radicals were – by contrast with 1989 – organized around a relatively coherent platform and by a tactically shrewd campaign. The credit for this must go largely to the Moscow Union of Voters (MOI). The origins of this influential organization, which was to leave its imprint on the democratic movement in Moscow, go back to the election campaign of 1989 and the voters' clubs which were then established. The First Congress of People's Deputies and the mass meetings in Luzhniki helped to swell the ranks of the voters' clubs in Moscow and in other cities, where they had also appeared.[55] In Moscow, each evening, parliamentary deputies went to their local voters' clubs to report on the day's proceedings in the Congress; long debates and discussions followed. As a result, the number of clubs kept growing,[56] and by June there were 35 clubs (for 30 constituencies) in the capital.[57] It was clear that some effort should be

54 Krotov *et al.*, *Rossiya* (1991), I, 1, p. 95.
55 Sverdlovsk, Khabarovsk, Irkutsk, Novosibirsk, Tomsk and Vologda also saw the formation of Voters' Club: Tolz, *Multi-Party System* (1990), p. 38.
56 Belyakov, *AiF*, 10–16 June 1989, p. 3; Belyaeva, *MN*, 1989, no. 49, p. 3.
57 Krotov *et al.*, *Rossiya* (1991), I, 1, p. 95.

made to build on this popular political movement and to mobilize it in favour of reform.

The founding conference of the Moscow Union of Voters (MOI) was held on 27 July 1989. The new organization's goals were defined: the exchange of information between voters' clubs; coordination of meetings and demonstrations; assistance to deputies in elaborating alternative draft legislation and the popularization of these proposals. For tactical reasons, the club confined itself to following the general line of the Inter-Regional Group of Deputies.[58]

The principal preoccupation of the Moscow Union of Voters after its foundation was the preparation of the 1990 elections to the Russian parliament (the Congress of People's Deputies of RSFSR) and to the city councils. Its first major task was to ensure that democratic candidates were fielded and got adequate support in the campaign. The informal clubs (Memorial, Moscow Tribune, Democratic *Perestroika*, Moscow Popular Front, Moscow Party Club, etc.) therefore communicated the names of those who wished to run to the Moscow Union of Voters, which distributed them, as best it could, around the different constituencies, which might then adopt them as candidates.[59] The Moscow Union of Voters was thus more practical and better organized than most democratic groups hitherto.

Democratic Russia Electoral Bloc

It also attempted to inject greater ideological coherence into the campaign. On its initiative and with the help of the Moscow informals, a conference of democratic candidates from twelve regions of Russia (including Moscow, Leningrad, the Urals, Yaroslavl, Tver, Vladimir, Vladivostok, Gorky and Kaliningrad) was held on 20–21 January 1990. At this meeting, the Democratic Russia electoral bloc was founded. It called for political pluralism, limits of the power of the KGB, a democratic press law, freedom of conscience, the

---

58 Ibid., p. 95.
59 Ibid., p. 44; V. Bokser, *AiF*, 1989, no. 50, p. 8. The Moscow Union of Voters also collaborated with another democratic election organization – 'Elections-90'. This body was founded in September 1989, by the usual array of informal clubs: it attempted to mobilize support for democratic candidates and ultimately fused with the Democratic Russia election bloc, which was formed at the end of January 1990: Krotov *et al.*, *Rossiya* (1991), I, 1, p. 93.

introduction of the market economy, private property and Russian sovereignty.[60] Russian sovereignty was emphasized because the USSR Congress of People's Deputies was widely seen as having been captured by the Party *apparat*. The only hope, in the democrats' view, was to promote reform in a new, genuinely democratic body, and the Russian parliament now seemed the only forum in which this could be achieved. While hesitating to reject socialism or to declare themselves in open opposition to Gorbachev and the reformers in the Party leadership, Democratic Russia's supporters made no bones about expressing their hostility to the Party *apparat* and its greater Russian allies.[61]

Democratic Russia made every attempt to ensure that its message reached the electorate. Campaigners were instructed in the art of listening sympathetically to criticisms and complaints and of eliciting support by focusing on local issues and concerns. Stankevich's instructions to candidates in the Moscow elections advised that they should stress reforms that would make Moscow a more pleasant place to live in, for example, by regulating transport, construction, street clearing and supplies more effectively.[62] This carefully adapted campaign contrasted with the CPSU's vague generalities, which differed little from its past hortatory rhetoric, with which voters were all too familiar.[63]

Results

The voters were therefore presented with a clear choice in the 1990 elections. The democratic bloc scored significant successes in the elections, winning majorities in the city councils of Moscow, Leningrad and a number of other cities,[64] as well as approximately one-third of the seats in the Russian parliament (or Congress).[65] Boris

60 Pribylovsky, *Slovar'* (1991), p. 15; *Ogonek*, 1990, no. 6, p. 17.
61 Pribylovsky, *Slovar'* (1991), p. 44; V. Bokser, *AiF*, 1989, no. 50, p. 8.
62 Cited in T. Colton, 'Moscow Elections' in Hewett and Winston (eds), *Milestones* (1991), pp. 347-8.
63 V. Ivanitsky, 'Izbiratel'nye', *Dialog*, 1990, no. 3, p. 48.
64 Including Ryazan, Sverdlovsk and Yuzhno-Sakhalinsk.
65 Candidates from the Democratic Russia bloc won 370 out of 1026 seats in the Russian parliament, including 59 out of 66 seats in Moscow. In Moscow City Council, they won 292 out of 465 seats and in Leningrad 355 out of 400 seats: Sakwa, *Gorbachev* (1990), p. 141. Democratic Russia was able to count on more support than the formal

Yeltsin again won an overwhelming majority, capturing approximately 80 per cent of the vote in his home constituency of Sverdlovsk.[66] Most of those elected under Democratic Russia's banner went on to form the eponymous group of deputies in the Russian Congress[67] and helped to convert that body into a more effective parliamentary forum than the USSR Congress of People's Deputies.

In a little over a year (since January 1989) the political life of the country had been transformed. New representative institutions had been created and while these exacerbated rather than resolved the problem of power in the Soviet Union, they were significant in bringing forward a new generation of politicians and in stimulating the birth of a *de facto* democratic opposition to the CPSU's hardliners. This opposition was as yet amorphous: its organization was relatively undeveloped, it covered a wide spectrum of views and its popular appeal was grounded more in rejection of the corruption and inefficiency of the Party *apparat*'s rule than in an ideological commitment to capitalism and political liberalism. But just as the democrats were a diverse group, so were the new parliamentarians of the centre and centre-right. Their evolution was slower and more ambiguous but no less significant than that of their more articulate and vocal democratic colleagues. Like the democrats, they had an interest in wresting power from the centre and were hence to prove ready to support the cause of republican sovereignty. Hence, in the pitched battle that ensued between June 1990 and August 1991, the republican forces were not all equally committed to democratic and economic reform. Not until 1992 were the consequences of this to become evident.

membership of the parliamentary group suggested: Nazimova and Sheinis, *AiF*, 1990, no. 17, p. 1.

66 Morrison, *Yeltsin* (1991), p. 115.
67 Pribylovsky, *Slovar'* (1991), p. 15.

8. The New Politics: Actors and Issues

The anti-Stalinist intellectuals of the elite were at the height of their prestige in Spring 1989 but their political impact was to be short lived and the character of the democratic movement was to change. There were a number of reasons for this.

The Russian parliament, in which the old anti-Stalinist intellectual elite occupied a less significant place than they did in the All-Union Congress, was to become the focus of the democrats' political activity after March 1990. The All-Union Congress was controlled by the Party *apparat*, while the Russian parliament (like the other republican parliaments) had been elected on a fully democratic basis and the democrats were well represented in it. It therefore seemed that reform could be advanced only within the Russian parliament and, hence, the democrats' principal preoccupation, until August 1991, was to secure the transfer of power from the centre to the republics and an end to the Soviet empire in the form that Stalin had given it. For this reason, the Russian democrats (despite their hostility towards Russian nationalists, who generally opposed reform and made common cause with Party hardliners) were ready to support the calls of Baltic, Armenian and Ukrainian nationalists for greater independence.

Once this battle was engaged, the character of democratic politics changed. The focus of political activity switched away from debate, polemical journalism and politically engaged art to conventional politics. The intellectual and cultural elite found this new political era less congenial than that which had preceded it and they occupied a more marginal place within it. Instead, Russia's parliamentary deputies were to play a major political role in the next eighteen months. The parliamentary majority which backed the demand for Russian sovereignty – rather than the radical journalists and playwrights – were seen as the Stalinists' principal antagonists.

ECLIPSE OF THE ANTI-STALINIST INTELLIGENTSIA

Even in 1989, the political impracticality and social isolation of the cultural and intellectual elite, which contributed to their subsequent political marginalization, were evident. These characteristics were exemplified by the main political caucus they formed, Moscow Tribune. It illustrated the shortcomings of their style and outlook and their lack of popular touch. A debating club and pressure group of the higher intelligentsia of Moscow, Moscow Tribune was the brainchild of Leonid Batkin and Yuri Afanasiev. They approached Andrei Sakharov with the idea of forming a club, composed of the leading members of the Moscow intelligentsia, to act as a pressure group for reform. Sakharov lent his support and Moscow Tribune quickly became an authoritative voice in the democratic movement. The conception of a forum, where informed and tolerant debate might take place,[1] faithfully reflects the outlook which had long distinguished Leonid Batkin among his contemporaries. But it was ultimately to prevent Moscow Tribune from playing an effective role in the new politics of Russia. The gentlemanly spirit and Olympian tone of the club's proceedings cut it off not only from the style but also from the essence of national political life: Moscow Tribune was ultimately unwilling to depart from its liberal oligarchic conception of politics and embrace the vulgar realities of political life.

At Tribune's first meeting in October 1988, the club demanded economic and constitutional reform and respect for fundamental human liberties (including the release of political prisoners).[2] By mid-October, around 150 of the capital's leading intellectuals had pledged their support for the club. The physicist Roald Sagdeev, writers and political analysts Yuri Karyakin, Len Karpinsky, Ales Adamovich and Yuri Burtin were elected, along with the founders, to lead Tribune. Although counting no more than about 200 members, Tribune's membership was impressive and read like a who's who of Russia's intellectual world. It came to include not only most distinguished scientists, academics, artists and writers but also editors

1 N. Belyaeva, *MN*, 12 February 1989, p. 2.
2 See Sakwa, *Gorbachev* (1990), pp. 201–2.

of the reform press (*Moscow News, Ogonek, Twentieth Century and Peace*), leaders of the nascent political parties (Democratic Platform, the Kadets, social democrats, anarchists, the Christian democratic movement) and of the informals (Memorial, Civic Dignity, the paper *Panorama*), but also over ten deputies of the All-Union Congress of People's Deputies, 18 members of the Russian parliament and 65 members of Moscow City Council.[3]

Moscow Tribune was an organization not accidentally but consciously confined to members of the elite intelligentsia. Those who wished to join not only had to be proposed and vouched for by three current members of the organization, but also they had to be recognized intellectuals, with an established reputation.[4] This was because the founders believed that the intelligentsia had a duty to the country and people and that this lay in offering their authoritative advice to society and the government.[5] The tone of proceedings reflected these high-minded aspirations. Even when Tribune's membership was expanded, in Autumn 1989, to include leaders of the first-wave informal movement, this only resulted in representatives of the lower echelons of the academic intelligentsia joining Tribune's ranks.[6] In short, Moscow Tribune was more akin to a club of friends and colleagues than to a public organization.

In this, Moscow Tribune illustrated a characteristic feature of Russian social life, which was to influence the development of democratic politics in this period. This was the Russian taste for clubs and small cohesive groups of friends in which to engage in passionate discussion, a tendency to social exclusiveness and endless talk.

---

3 MBIO: Informal Archive: Bulleten' Moskovskaya Tribuna, 1990, no. 5.

4 Pribylovsky, *Slovar'* (1991), p. 41; Krotov *et al.*, *Rossiya* (1991), I, 2, p. 189; interview with L. Batkin, 6 December 1990.

5 Interview with L. Batkin, 6 December 1990, and with Y. Burtin, 7 May 1992. Tribune members believed that they might contribute to the resolution of the Nagorny Karabakh crisis but their offer of assistance was ignored by Gorbachev. The hostility of the authorities was seen in the refusal of *Izvestiya, Ogonek* or *Moscow News* to publish the group's material on a regular basis.

6 Among those coopted at this point were the leaders of the Union of Constitutional Democrats, or Kadets (Victor Zolotarev, Mikhail Astafiev, Sergei Chernyak, Igor Surikov); Memorial (Dmitri Leonov, Nina Braginskaya, Yakov Etinger); the Social Democratic Association (Oleg Rumyantsev, Leonid Volkov); the Moscow Union of Voters (Vladimir Bokser, Lev Ponomarev); the Confederation of Anarcho-Syndicalists; April (Valentin Oskotsky); the Church and *Perestroika* Initiative Group (Gleb Yakunin): Pribylovsky, *Slovar'* (1991), p. 41.

Despite the official ideology, Soviet society was surprisingly caste-ridden, with different social groups isolated by ethos and lifestyle: a gulf separated the manual worker or farmer from the intellectual of Moscow or Leningrad. It was therefore difficult for Russians to build broadly-based open organizations, not only because of the hostility of the Party and the virtual absence of civic life until the mid-1980s, but also because of the country's social structures and traditions.

Moscow Tribune illustrates this. It reflected both the self-consciousness of Russia's leading intellectuals – their rather old-fashioned sense of mission – and their snobbishness. Comparison of Tribune's membership with that of other democratic bodies at or around this time shows what an important role was played by Russia's intellectuals in generating pressure for democratic reform. Members of Tribune were also active in Memorial and, as time went on, in other democratic forums – in the writers' democratic group April, in the Inter-Regional Group of Deputies in the All-Union Congress and later in the democratic front, Democratic Russia. Rather than as a chain of interlocking links, the democratic movement in this period may be represented as a number of more or less concentric circles. The same relatively small group of people were responsible for most initiatives and led the most effective assaults on the Party's political prerogatives.

The ferment in public life did not bring forward a widely diverse or indeed even unknown generation of politicians: in 1989, the leaders of the democratic movement were drawn largely from intellectuals whose reputations and authority were already established, while in 1990 the democrats elected to the Russian parliament were those intellectuals and junior academics who had furnished the leadership of the early political clubs and the general staff of the more broadly-based movements which emerged after the Party Conference. The democratic movement in the capitals – for all the multiplicity of societies, clubs and organizations which grew up at this time – was not broadly based but drew on the same relatively narrow circle of people, most of whom were known to each other and came from similar backgrounds. Overwhelmingly, they were drawn from the intelligentsia – artistic, academic or journalistic – with the difference that the first-wave clubs were animated mainly by representatives of the lower intelligentsia, while after the Party Conference the intellectual elite played the leading role.

Over ten of Tribune's members were elected to the All-Union parliament or Congress.[7] The links between Moscow Tribune and the newly elected core of radical deputies remained close. In Autumn 1989, it was proposed to turn Moscow Tribune into a think-tank for the pro-reform Inter-Regional Group of Deputies. The idea was that Tribune, drawing on its unusual concentration of expertise, would elaborate new proposals and alternative draft laws from which the IRG could draw inspiration in contributing to the work of the Congress. The informal organizations, which were now associated with Tribune, would help to spread these ideas.[8] This represented the first of Tribune's several attempts to make a more effective contribution to public life. Little came of this project, however: other informal clubs had concerns of their own to promote and showed little inclination to play second fiddle to the lofty intellectuals in Tribune. These, in turn, had neither the time nor the inclination to fling themselves into a series of nebulous and undirected projects that would more appropriately have been undertaken by paid young researchers.

Lack of interest in organization was to bedevil Moscow Tribune all along: its composition, by definition, excluded the 'Indians' who might have enabled some of their ideas to bear practical fruit. The society's main activity had consisted, since its inception, in monthly debates on current affairs. However, its proceedings were not given wide publicity and, in view of Tribune's exclusive composition, amounted to little more than preaching to the converted. Its leaders – Batkin, in particular – believed that unlike other informal groups it should not attempt to evolve into a political party but should remain a club, in which different points of view could be aired.[9] As a result,

---

7 Its sister organization in Leningrad, founded in Spring 1989, put forward a number of candidates in the 1990 republican elections and published a programme; it was unable to match the success of Moscow Tribune, however: Krotov *et al.*, *Rossiya* (1991), I, 2, pp. 172, 189.

8 Krotov *et al.*, *Rossiya* (1991), I, 2, p. 190.

9 See MBIO: Informal Archive: Byulleten' Moskovskaya Tribuna, 1990, no. 5; interview with L. Batkin, 6 December 1990.

they rarely got beyond their regular debates, which – although more substantial and interesting than those of other forums – amounted to little in practical terms.

Tribune members were not unaware of the social imbalances in the reform forces and, in particular, of the need to attract broader public participation in the democratic movement. It was a constant theme at the society's monthly meetings, no matter whether the ostensible topic of discussion was presidential rule, economic reform, the elections or the nascent workers' movement.[10] As the club's bulletin pointed out in Spring 1990, the election campaign had shown that ordinary people were on the whole sceptical about those in power, no matter what their political orientation. In the factories, people could not understand why the democrats chose to remain so aloof, why they did not 'go to the people'.

The question of 'going to the people' is not a new one in Russian history but has belaboured the consciences of Russian intellectuals since the nineteenth century. Their late twentieth-century counterparts have, on the whole, devoted less thought to this problem than their predecessors and have certainly not shared the feelings of guilt which overwhelmed their aristocratic and revolutionary forebears. This change of attitude may be ascribed to the peculiar position occupied in Soviet society by the intelligentsia: distinguished, in official ideology, from the triumphant working class and, at least in theory, deprived of the same rights and prerogatives, the Soviet Union's intellectuals have always been the object of the Party's hostile attentions and, despite the privileges granted to conformists, have resented their real or threatened persecution by the regime. Under Brezhnev, the intelligentsia saw the erosion of the wage differentials, which protected it from the privations suffered by labourers and compensated, to an extent, for the regime's attitude towards them. Combined with the rise of a reinvigorated philistinism, this served to alienate both those who saw their standard of living eroded and the younger generation, which had experienced neither the Terror nor the

10 MBIO: Informal Archive: Byulleten' *Moskovskaya Tribuna*, 1990, no. 3. The April 1990 session of Moscow Tribune was devoted to economic reform: speakers pointed out that radical economic reform was perilous because there was no force in Russia which enjoyed the kind of popular authority that Solidarity had in Poland and that would enable a democratic government to implement the kind of painful measures which were necessary.

euphoria of the Thaw and which was to come to public attention as the informal movement gathered force. Partly because the old regime had harried the intelligentsia in the name of the workers and the people, the intellectuals, in helping to make the new revolution, were not initially inclined to make such gestures or concessions to the *narod* (or 'common people') as might have secured their active involvement in the democratic movement.

In all the talk of liberty, political and economic reform, little attention was spared for the problems of the large industrial proletariat – those whose interest in politics and culture was marginal and whose already miserable lifestyle was threatened by the reforms. The reserved or sometimes patronising attitude of the intelligentsia towards the working class is illustrated by Tribune's discussion of the independent labour movement in May 1990. On this occasion, an account of the first Congress of the Confederation of Labour, which was held from 30 April to 2 May 1990, was given by a leading expert in this field, Professor Leonid Gordon. Despite his exposition of the radical democratic orientation of the Confederation, most Tribune members appear to have been unready to support the Confederation, until more was known about it and its aims. One more liberal spirit suggested that Tribune (with scarcely 200 members) should join the Confederation and turn it into a joint movement of workers and the intelligentsia, on the assumption that the Confederation would welcome such a proposal.[11]

Among the intelligentsia, only the nationalists – with their increasing hostility towards democratic reform – dwelt on the plight of the common people. The theme of the 'people' became increasingly the preserve of the right, to the point where references to the term *narod* became shorthand for an obscurantist and nostalgic *mélange* of populism and Stalinism. Making this point during a discussion of Russian fascism at a Moscow Tribune meeting in Spring 1990, the Kadet, Mikhail Astafiev warned that 'We must defend the Russian people or else, God forbid, others will defend them.' Astafiev, whose gravitation towards the 'patriotic' end of the political spectrum was already becoming apparent at this early stage, accused Tribune of adopting an 'anti-popular' stance .[12]

11 MBIO: Informal Archive: Byulleten' Moskovskaya Tribuna, 1990, no. 5.
12 Ibid..

Underestimating the practical implications of their programme for ordinary people and hence for the future of the democratic movement itself, however, the liberalizing intellectuals tried instead to create an organization which would mobilize the citizenry. In Moscow, the formula proposed was that of a forum to become known as Civic Action. It was founded at a Tribune meeting on 27 January 1990, with the specific aim of inducing citizens to overcome their passivity and join the organization. Moscow Tribune was to be its intellectual power-house, formulating policy and initiatives.[13] An address to citizens was drafted, which explained that the democratic movement – despite its growing strength – was threatened by its lack of broadly-based popular support: 'Today, democratic forces are scattered among informal organizations and there is no basis, like Solidarity or *Sajudis*, for mass support for them.' Civic Action was proclaimed in response to this dilemma. It 'could become an organization along the lines of the Baltic Popular Fronts'. Civic Action's Declaration called on democratically-minded citizens to unite behind the organization and support a new Union Treaty of free sovereign states, the market economy, with mixed forms of property and social security provision, political and cultural pluralism and an end to the KGB's secret police role.[14]

The intellectuals who signed the declaration hoped to construct a broad democratic front, on the lines of those of Eastern Europe, which would hold round-table talks with the government to achieve a peaceful transition to democratic rule.[15] Its rather disparate tasks reflected the genesis of the idea among a group of intellectuals, better informed than most of their compatriots about developments elsewhere (and particularly Eastern Europe) but not unduly gifted with a sense of political realities or a flair for organization.

Civic Action immediately ran into difficulties. Two concepts of the kind of organization needed emerged: the first saw Civic Action as a broadly-based movement; the second as a round table, and, more

13 MBIO: Informal Archive: Byulleten' Moskovskaya Tribuna, 1990, no. 3.
14 The declaration was signed by Afanasiev, Batkin, Sagdeev, Bogoraz, Averintsev, Yakunin, Stankevich, Sobchak, Okudzhava and Selunin: *Ogonek*, 1990, no. 8, p. 5.
15 MBIO: Informal Archive: Byulleten' Moskovskaya Tribuna, 1990, no. 2.

importantly, as the centre of a shadow cabinet for the opposition. Two rival organizing committees were founded, one of which was led by Yuri Afanasiev. Not surprisingly, nothing was achieved under these circumstances and, after a month or two of disagreement, most of those involved were diverted into other ventures – principally into the Spring election campaign.[16]

The model which inspired these efforts was the East European experience, in particular Czechoslovakia's Civic Forum and the GDR's New Forum. However, what Tribune's intellectuals failed to realize was the fact that in Eastern Europe, these forums were cemented together by nationalism. Anti-Communism in Eastern Europe, as in the Baltics, was fuelled not just by democratic ideas but, above all, by the sense that Communism was an alien regime, imposed and maintained by force by an imperial power, whose values and traditions were diametrically opposed to those of the occupied countries. In Russia, no dynamic of this sort could exist. The demise of Communism entailed the collapse of the empire and of Russian might, the loss of the prestige and prerogatives of great power status, in which ordinary Russians took great pride and from which they derived marginal benefits. The liberal and democratic intellectuals were to address the problem of a broadly-based democratic organization again, more successfully, later in 1990, but the creation of a mass movement – briefly in sight between 1990 and 1991 – proved elusive.

Despite its eminent membership, therefore, and despite its conscientious attempts to break out of the confinement of its restricted circle, Moscow Tribune ultimately failed to influence the government and public opinion.[17] In Batkin's view, there were two reasons for this: it was accorded little internal publicity in the USSR, initially, and secondly, it was overtaken by events. The function to which it aspired was akin to that played by the *Perestroika* Club in 1987: but the time was now not so much with the formation of opinion as with action and organization.

16 MBIO: Informal Archive: Byulleten' Moskovskaya Tribuna, 1990, nos 2 and 3; Pribylovsky, *Slovar'* (1991), pp. 41–2.
17 Interview with L. Batkin, 6 December 1990.

THE NEW POLITICAL CLASS

A more fundamental reason for the intellectual elite's eclipse was the fact that they were outnumbered in the new political institutions. Both the All-Union and the Russian parliaments introduced economic managers and officials from the middle and lower ranges of the provincial Party and State administration to high politics and they were to form the backbone of the new political class and to play a key role in the political struggles of the following year.

The emergence of the managers, technocrats and administrators was first observed after the 1989 elections. Although the Party hierarchy remained powerful and was well represented in the All-Union Congress,[18] a great shift took place in the social composition of the corps of deputies. A closer breakdown of the figures indicates that the representation of middle management – meaning principally the directors and chief technicians of leading enterprises, directors of scientific and research institutions – more than doubled and that of lower management (*kolkhoz* and *sovkhoz* directors, industrial and research managers) more than quadrupled. The former now accounted for 21.5 per cent of deputies and the latter for 27.8 per cent.[19] These gains were achieved at the expense both of the highest level of administration (which lost out to the middle layer) and of workers and peasants, whose representation declined significantly (from 45.9 per cent to 22 per cent).[20] The latter were replaced by lower-level management: local *sovkhoz* and *kolkhoz* directors, in particular, tended to replace the model milkmaids and simple farmers, previously favoured for symbolic purposes.[21] Middle and lower managers had hitherto been underrepresented in the soviets. Now, the middle layer of society made its appearance on the political stage, principally in the form of industrial and economic managers and

18 Nazimova and Sheinis, 'Vybory' in *SSSR* (1990), pp. 657–9, 687; Romanov, *MN*, 1989, no. 24, p. 8.

19 Nazimova and Sheinis, 'Vybory' in *SSSR* (1990), pp. 660–61, 688; Romanov, *MN*, 1989, no. 24, p. 8. These two sources give slightly different definitions of the categories involved and hence give varying statistics, but they concur in the overall pattern and its significance. I have used Nazimova's estimates, as they result from a more sustained analysis.

20 The number of women who ran and were elected also declined: see Romanov, *MN*, 1989, no. 7, p. 14; Shchepotkin and Karpenko, *Proryv* (1990), p. 57.

21 Nazimova and Sheinis, 'Vybory' in *SSSR* (1990), pp. 661–2, 688.

technicians. There were also more *intelligenty* in the Congress than in any previous Soviet parliament: their representation increased from 6 per cent to 9.8 per cent and even, in some calculations (which included academic administrators and journalists) over 26 per cent of deputies.[22] Hence, the Congress witnessed a new phenomenon in Soviet political life – the emergence of a new political class.[23]

This new class was not, however, cohesive, but was composed of two quite distinct elements of largely divergent outlook, inspiration and education. The first of these was the category formally described by Soviet sociologists as the creative intelligentsia – meaning people with a higher education, academics, writers, artists and journalists. The intelligentsia, both of the cultural elite and of the institutes, was, in the old Soviet Union, a quite specific social and cultural milieu, relatively small and intimate and intellectually sophisticated. Its members' intellectual and cultural horizons were generally much broader than those of other Soviet citizens, on account of their privileged access to foreign travel, forbidden information and *samizdat*. As a result, they were more open to foreign and unfamiliar ideas, which they generally understood better than many of their compatriots, and it is no accident that it was from this group that the pro-reform Inter-Regional Group of Deputies (IRG) was to draw both its principal spokesmen and its main support.

The other element in the new generation of politicians were the economic and industrial managers – a quite different milieu. In intellectual profile – level of education, in particular – they constituted a kind of middle class, while in social and economic terms they enjoyed privileges not generally extended to ordinary workers, which ensured for them a modest level of prosperity. This group was largely overlooked, however, when decisions about strategic economic planning were taken, although their experience and expertise and the vested interests they represented made their views relevant and their cooperation necessary. This newly promoted category of politicians was not on the whole radical or non-conformist in outlook: their education was typically technical; most were Party

22 Ibid., pp. 662–3.
23 The Supreme Soviet was thought by Nazimova to be a more or less proportionate reflection of the Congress itself: Nazimova and Sheinis, 'Vybory' in *SSSR* (1990), p. 664.

members; few were prone to the ideological questioning characteristic of the intelligentsia. This group took longer to orientate itself in the new parliament than did the intellectuals. But for all that they appeared to be amorphous and subservient, they were a significant group.

At first they conformed, submitting to the leadership of their regional delegation. But were they really to be assimilated to the Stalinist–Brezhnevite majority, as Yuri Afanasiev seemed to think? Most observers recognized that the majority in the Congress was more complex than the applause with which it greeted General Rodionov, the commander in charge of the Tbilisi massacre, suggested. The middle managers' attitude to divisive political issues was, Leonid Batkin pointed out, more complex than Afanasiev allowed. For a variety of reasons – caution, disorientation, inexperience and habit – they were for the moment in the conservative camp, continuing to play by the old rules and observing Party discipline; gradually, however, they began to adjust to their new role and display more independence than the radicals had expected.[24] As Andrei Sakharov noted, the majority was not monolithic. In his view, it included centrists, who were ready to move – quite early on – towards reformist positions. The right-wing majority, he believed, reflected the will of the bureaucrats of the command-administrative economic system. Many of its representatives had not been elected but simply appointed. However, those in the majority who had fought for their seats in contested elections in constituencies, while now divided between the right and left, would gradually move towards the democrats.[25] Sakharov's analysis predicted with some accuracy the evolution of the new politicians in the Congress and Russian parliament, over the next two years.

Nazimova and Sheinis argue that the majority included many deputies whose inexperience inhibited their participation in the Congress. Many had as yet no clear political views and, hence, followed those who exercised authority and power. The *apparat* was also able to exploit the chauvinism of many Russian deputies. This

24 See ibid., p. 665. The authors point out that the Supreme Soviet adopted independent positions on many issues and that, in policy and composition, it was not Brezhnevite-Stalinist; they cite the hearings on the nomination of ministers as an example.

25 Sakharov, *Trevoga i nadezhda* (1991), pp. 285–6.

enabled the conservative *apparat* to exercise disproportionate influence in the Congress;[26] however, this group is estimated to have accounted for only about 20 per cent of deputies.[27] In Leonid Batkin's view, the majority which had applauded General Rodionov included firstly, the *apparat*, which well understood the aggressive conservatism he represented; secondly, those who, under the eye of the regional Party First Secretary, lacked the courage of their convictions; and thirdly, a group of deputies who, outside their own narrow area of competence, were at sea. It was the second and third groups, in Batkin's view, that the democrats needed to win over.[28]

Sakharov believed that some of these deputies would, with time, escape from the Party hierarchy's dominance. Batkin, Nazimova and Sheinis pointed to the fact that, in certain votes, the radicals were able to increase their support from 400 to 600 and even 800 deputies.[29] These votes came from those deputies who usually voted conventionally, for the reasons outlined by Batkin. As Sakharov had observed, the experience which may have predisposed them to a degree of political independence was the fact that a substantial number of them had fought for their seats. This independence manifested itself in the scrutiny to which the new Council of Ministers was subjected and in various legislative acts of the new Supreme Soviet.[30]

The elections to the Russian parliament in March 1990, although by no means unequivocal, again suggested that a new political class was emerging. At first, it seemed that little had changed and that the old *nomenklatura* was still in place: 79 per cent of deputies to the Russian Congress occupied official positions in the *apparat*, while Party members still accounted for more than 49 per cent of deputies.[31]

26 Nazimova and Sheinis, 'Vybory' in *SSSR* (1990), pp. 678–9.
27 Ibid., p. 679.
28 Batkin, *MN*, 1989, no. 24, p. 9.
29 Ibid.; Nazimova and Sheinis, 'Vybory' in *SSSR* (1990), p. 676.
30 This legislative record included a law on pensions, a law on holidays, and measures to reduce defence expenditure by 6.4 billion rubles; the establishment of a State ecological programme and of a Commission on economic reform; laws on labour disputes, land tenure and land leasing; a draft law on the press; a law on entering and leaving the USSR; reviews on the decrees governing public meetings and criminal law procedure: see Romanov, *MN*, 1989, no. 50, p. 10.
31 Sakwa, *Gorbachev* (1990), p. 141; Ostalsky, *MN*, 22 April 1990, p. 4, gives a much higher figure, which seems to apply to deputies elected from the autonomous republics; 'Rasstanovka sil', *NG*, 1 April 1992, p. 2.

However, many of the trends evident in the All-Union Congress, elected the previous year, were confirmed in the balance of forces in the Russian Congress. The number of workers and collective farmers dropped dramatically, from just over 21 per cent in 1989 to 5.9 per cent in 1990. The highly qualified intelligentsia's representation increased to over 13 per cent in 1990. Lower management[32] maintained their presence in the Russian Congress (21.2 per cent in 1989 and 21.7 per cent in 1990); middle management[33] increased their representation (from 31.7 per cent in 1989 to 37.9 per cent in 1990) although upper management[34] succeeded in recapturing lost ground (with their representation increasing from 14.4 per cent in 1989 to 18.7 per cent in 1990).[35]

In short, the elections of 1990 confirmed the trends visible in 1989. The Party's formal presence had declined but it still exercised significant influence: the relatively high level of representation of the Soviet executive committees (12.7 per cent) may be read as a reflection of the weight of the old *apparat* – as many Party workers switched from the Party to the State *apparat* in 1989–90, to protect their careers and livelihood. Nonetheless, these deputies had shown resourcefulness and adaptability in their readiness to switch career and, above all, to stand for election – not hitherto the hallmark of the *apparatchik*. In 1989, Russia (strictly speaking, the Russian Federation) had elected 147 deputies (23 per cent of the total) in uncontested elections. In 1990, this was the case in only 23 constituencies (3.1 per cent). The *apparatchiki* in the Russian Congress were, to some extent, a new breed: keen to defend their interests but pragmatic in outlook.

The 1990 elections marked the entry on to the political stage of middle- and lower-level managers and of what might be called the middle layers of society in general, at the expense above all of manual workers and of the senior officials, in whose hands power had

---

32 Local Party and State officials; junior officers; heads of workshops; technicians; heads of department in farms; heads of technical schools.

33 District small city Party first secretaries; executive committee secretaries; factory and farm directors; directors of scientific institutes.

34 Defined by Nazimova as Ministers, provincial and large city Party secretaries, chairmen of Soviet executive committees at provincial and city level, senior officers in the security forces: *AiF*, 1990, no. 17.

35 Nazimova and Sheinis, *AiF*, 1990, no. 17, p. 2, for these figures.

hitherto been largely concentrated. These new politicians had a mainly technical and administrative background and little in it disposed them to revolutionary change or theoretical argument.[36] They were to show more interest in economic modernization, in the rationalization of economic management (undermining the role of ministries and State agencies, for example) than did the conservatives. They were less constrained by ideology in the social sphere (having fewer objections to the call of '*enrichissez-vous*') and in culture. But these attitudes represented not so much an ideological commitment to democracy as a pragmatic concern for their own interests. This pragmatism led them, initially, to work within the system; it made them reluctant to embark on dramatic reversals of policy or to envisage ditching the system entirely, until it became clear that their interests would be best preserved by a different order. Hence, the spectrum of conservative views expressed in the Russian parliament was quite broad, enabling the Democratic Russia bloc to draw on quite wide support on certain issues.

The intelligentsia was strongly represented in the Russian parliament, as in the All-Union Congress. However, it was not the anti-Stalinist cultural elite but the informal activists – the technocrats, experts and less eminent journalists – who represented it there. Whereas the intellectual establishment (Korotich, Klimov, Popov, Ulyanov, Shatrov and others) were elected in large numbers to the quickly discredited and largely impotent All-Union parliament, the lower intelligentsia was elected to the more democratic republican parliament. The junior researchers moved in a different cultural and social milieu from the cultural and intellectual elite and they differed subtly from them in outlook and instinct. Their sense of exclusion from the real centres of power and privilege fuelled their ambition and their readiness to replace the cultural elite in leading the democratic movement. In outlook and vision, however, they were hardly more imaginative and daring than the elite. This is understandable. Theirs was a more technocratic background: experts

36 The RSFSR Soviet of Nationalities (one chamber in the Russian Supreme Soviet) was a particularly conservative body, with an estimated 61.5 per cent of officials of the State and Party *apparat* in its ranks – a disproportionate number of whom (26.4 per cent) lived in Moscow (an indicator of an entrenched privilege): V. Vorontsov, *AiF*, 1990, no. 21, p. 4.

and researchers in technical disciplines or in such politicized, often bowlderized subjects as sociology, Marxism–Leninism, philosophy, economics and history; there were few writers or artists in their midst. As junior, though largely conformist academics, they had better than average access to information and foreign data but in general less experience and knowledge of the outside world than the elite. Their intellectual horizons were therefore rather confined.

The Democratic Russia parliamentary bloc, while dominated by intellectuals, was thus not composed solely of ardent radicals. While over 30 per cent of its candidates in Moscow were researchers or faculty members, and over 64 per cent had a higher education and were employed in science, arts, the media, engineering or education, more than 50 per cent were Party members.[37] This reflected non-Party members' difficulty in being admitted to research but it also pointed to the essentially conformist aspirations of many of the radical *intelligenty* who provided the general staff of the democratic movement.

The managers, technocrats and experts predominated therefore in the Russian parliament. This gave them significant influence over the formulation and thrust of the democratic campaign for the next eighteen months – even though many of them were neither elected on the democratic ticket nor supporters of the general democratic platform. The importance of this development was initially obscured, however, by the impression created by anti-Stalinists' earlier clashes with the *apparat* and the formal ideological terms in which this struggle had been expressed. The contest between the centre and the republics in 1990–91 thus appeared, at first, to be a natural continuation of the earlier campaign for democracy and legality but – despite being couched in terms of an ideological battle between opponents and supporters of democracy – it concerned not so much the renewal of political inspiration and institutions as a redistribution of power. This contest before long overshadowed the largely rhetorical battles between the anti-Stalinist elite and their opponents in the Party and cultural world and necessarily diminished the elite intelligentsia's political role.

Until Spring 1990, two forces drove the democratic movement in

37 Colton, 'Moscow Elections' in Hewett and Winston (eds), *Milestones* (1991), pp. 339–40, 350.

Russia: firstly, the intelligentsia's criticism of the authorities and the political culture they represented, and secondly, spontaneous popular protest against inefficient and corrupt government. The case for reform was advanced principally by the anti-Stalinist intelligentsia. Alexander Yakovlev, the Party's ideological commissar, summarized the spirit of this first period of the reform at the Twenty-Eighth Party Congress in July 1990:

> Yes, I actively helped [...] the living waters of *glasnost*, as a most important aspect of democracy, to break through to the surface, to wash our countenance, to quench our spiritual and moral thirst [...].
>
> And I count myself [...] fortunate to have lived through and played an active part in the great renewal of our great country, in its historical entry into the world of freedom.[38]

In 1990, the perspective changed. The legitimacy of the old regime had been challenged and a new generation aspired to leadership of the country. Where the emphasis of the early reformers – the generation of the Thaw – had been on historical truth, cultural freedom and reform socialism, the questions which now absorbed leading democrats were exclusively practical and mainly political – the problems of power, of the economic and constitutional order. After March 1990, the democratic movement changed imperceptibly in its inspiration, leadership and focus. Some of its early idealism was lost. The euphoric period of heroic rhetoric had been replaced by prosaic problems of government in an as yet unfinished State structure. The mood changed, difficulties multiplied and tension grew. It was in this atmosphere that the democratic movement was born and had to struggle for survival.

NEW ISSUES

The change in the character and orientation of the democratic movement was prompted not only by the creation of new institutions and the rise of a new generation of politicians through them but also by the political problems with which they were confronted.

38 Yakovlev, Speech to Twenty-Eighth Party Congress of 2 July 1990 in *Muki* (1991), pp. 190–92.

Gorbachev's constitutional reforms precipitated institutional dead-lock and a new political crisis. The election of the Russian and other republican parliaments in 1990 now exposed the fiction on which the Soviet Union had reposed: the USSR, which passed itself off as a free federation of sovereign States, was in fact an empire, created by force by Stalin and his predecessors. The coming of democracy meant that the subject nations began to demand greater freedom. Starting with Estonia in 1988, the movement quickly embraced the Baltic republics and then extended to Western Ukraine and Moldavia, while, from 1988 on, ethnic conflicts engulfed the Caucasus and, to a lesser extent, Central Asia. Those parts of the USSR incorporated by Stalin after the Second World War or whose native populations he had deported were the areas principally affected by unrest.

There were two broad approaches to these difficulties: the first, advanced principally by Andrei Sakharov and supported by most Russian democrats, proposed redrafting the Union Treaty to give the republics and the ethnic minorities fundamental, democratic rights and restore their sovereignty. The effect would be to renew the USSR as a voluntary federation of democratic States which would delegate powers – on defence, foreign affairs, communications – to the centre.[39] The second approach was to resist change to the last: espoused by the army high command, the Party hardliners, by Russian nationalist opinion and the State *apparat*, this view suggested that any change to the existing system would result in anarchy and, ultimately, in the collapse of the State. Gorbachev attempted to placate both sides of this argument – granting a measure of economic sovereignty to the Baltic republics – but moving so reluctantly and slowly as to alienate both camps.

The election of the republican parliament was to transform this debate. Within weeks of the reformed Russian parliament's convocation, it became clear that a constitutional crisis had been precipitated. Hitherto, demands for national sovereignty had been advanced by small, peripheral states of the Union. Now, however, the Russian parliament asserted Russian sovereignty, demanding that the fictitious constitutional theory of Russian statehood be turned into a reality. This crisis was made more acute by the deep personal antagonism

39 Sakharov, 'Dekret o vlasti' and Draft Constitution in *Trevoga i nadezhda* (1991), pp. 262–76.

between Gorbachev, as Union President, and Yeltsin, soon to be installed in office as Russia's leader, and by the ideological differences between the centre (with its insistence in retaining the old State structures) and the republics, claiming the right to national self-determination in the name of democracy. This deadlock between Yeltsin and Gorbachev, the Union Congress and the Russian parliament – sometimes called 'dual power' – paralysed Russian politics between May 1990 and August 1991.

These competing claims to legitimacy resulted not so much in the duplication of power structures as in a power vacuum, which prevented any of the country's fundamental problems being resolved. The country remained suspended between strict centralization and voluntary federation, while Gorbachev hesitated between the market (an option he favoured in Summer 1990) and an adjusted or revamped command economy (the approach he supported between Autumn 1990 and April 1991). As a result, production levels declined steeply, the distribution system disintegrated and, hence, the black market flourished, inflation increased and living standards fell. Economic collapse does not provide a propitious environment for the development of democratic politics. Public confidence in the competing governmental structures declined.

The Fight for Russian Sovereignty

In their response to these issues, Yeltsin and Gorbachev were constrained by their power-bases. The relations between the two men were strained not only by the different interest groups they represented and by their ideological differences but also by their personal rivalry. Yet it would be inaccurate to see Yeltsin merely as a radical champion of democratic reform or Gorbachev as indissolubly wedded to the economic and constitutional *status quo*. Both were Party politicians, fundamentally interested in gaining and retaining power. Yeltsin had ended up as the leader of Russia's democratic forces as much by accident as by design. His autobiography *Against the Grain* (1990) makes it clear that he was an ambitious provincial Party *apparatchik*, who had been out of his depth in the labyrinthine intrigues and formal manoeuvrings of Moscow. Promoted by Gorbachev, he was necessarily on the side of reform. A convert to change, from the time of his promotion to the position of Party First Secretary for Moscow in January 1986, Yeltsin found that he no longer enjoyed the complete discretion that he had possessed as First Secretary of a large industrial Siberian province. His conflicts with the conservatives in the Politburo, notably Ligachev, had led to his famous explosion at the October 1987 Plenum, when he had suddenly resigned, leaving Gorbachev and other reformers in the leadership vulnerable to attack. Not for nothing did Gorbachev remark at the time that Yeltsin had been politically naive.

The result, for Yeltsin, was catastrophic: a dramatic fall from power and grace – painfully enacted in a Stalinist indictment by his Party enemies in front of the Moscow Party organization, at a meeting to which he was dragged from his hospital bed. Ironically, the very circumstances of his removal from power were to ensure his popularity and his future career. In 1987, Yeltsin had courted public opinion, eschewing his *Zil* limousine – at least on occasion – to travel by bus and occasionally appearing in the city's empty shops, like any other citizen, instead of appearing to rely on the special shops and deliveries reserved for the Party leadership. These gestures endeared him to the Muscovites, who believed that he was attempting to improve their standard of living by combating corruption. When he challenged the conservatives in the leadership and was punished for doing so, he was popularly seen as a heroic martyr and the basis of his future political career was laid. Yeltsin had nothing more to hope for from the system, although he made a bid to return to favour at the Nineteenth Party Conference in June 1998 and it took him another two and a half years to leave the CPSU.

His fall from grace was definitive. Yet Yeltsin remained in Moscow, occupying a junior ministerial post and was thus not so far removed from the centre of power as to be unable to take advantage of the new opportunities opened up by Gorbachev's democratic reform. Having nothing to lose and everything to gain, Yeltsin, the popular hero, stood for election to the new institutions. His overwhelming victory, despite the Party's unscrupulous attempts to obstruct his campaign, turned him into a leader of the democratic movement just as it was breaking on to the political stage. But Yeltsin was no daring theoretician or publicist, nor had he been actively involved in any of the pre-election informal movements until these seemed to be a force worth reckoning with. Yeltsin joined the intellectuals and leaders of the informal clubs on the radical fringes of Soviet political life because there was no room for him elsewhere, since his career as a Party official was over. This is not to say that Yeltsin was simply an opportunist. Circumstances, rather than ratiocination, impelled him into the radical democratic camp.

Yeltsin was not, therefore, a natural candidate for the role of leader of the motley collection of intellectuals, researchers, controversialists, idealistic and hungry haunters of political clubs who constituted the officer corps of the democratic camp. Indeed, his strength and appeal lay elsewhere. His popularity was founded not on intellectual argument but on emotion and instinct. Yeltsin was the all-Russian man, with whom the electorate found it easy to identify. His background as a tough engineer in Siberia's bleak building sites as a provincial economic manager won him the support of sections of the electorate that did not always feel instinctive sympathy for the cosseted and often patronizing intellectual elite of Moscow and Leningrad. Similarly, when it came to constructing a power-base in the Russian parliament, after the March 1990 elections, Yeltsin was better placed to succeed than other figures in the democratic movement (for example Sobchak, a suave Leningrad law professor). After the elections, the democrats accounted for about 30 to 35 per cent of the deputies in the parliament. It was therefore essential to win the support of deputies in the centre of the spectrum who accounted for approximately another 30 per cent (while the Party hardliners accounted for another third).[40] The parliament was therefore fairly evenly split into pro- and anti-democratic forces, with a floating centre separating these camps. An indication of the range of political opinion in the parliament may be gauged from the variety of 'factions' (or groupings) formed within it.

Approximately thirty 'factions' were formed in the first months of the Russian parliament's existence: most of these were professional or regional, while others reflected the deputies' political orientation.[41] Many deputies belonged to several factions at once, a rather bizarre

40 See Morrison, *Yeltsin* (1991), p. 161.
41 G. Satarov, *Partiinaya Zhizn'* (1991), p. 5; 'Kommunisty', *AiF*, 1990, no. 23, p. 2; Bychkova, *MN*, 1991, no. 9, p. 8. The number of factions oscillated, until measures were adopted, after the coup, to limit their number: see Steele, *Eternal Russia* (1994), pp. 278–82; Buckley, *Redefining Russian Society* (1993), pp. 235–6.

configuration that may be explained by the fact that political pluralism was still at an embryonic stage of development. The new political parties were only just beginning to organize; they had not been able to participate in the electoral campaign. The provinces generally lagged behind the capitals, in terms of their political development. Hence, while the radical deputies of Moscow, Leningrad and some other big cities were already politically prepared for the parliament and while higher Party and State officials were clear where their affiliation lay, there was a large group in the middle which was still fairly indeterminate. These were the middle and lower *nomenklatura*, the provincial economic and agricultural managers, who had not hitherto been noted for their radicalism or political activism. In the absence of clear political guidelines, they formed sectoral groups and regional factions (in the latter instance, imitating the structures in the Union Congress). These included the Food and Health faction composed mainly of directors of collective farms and medical institutions[42] with 215 members, the Organizers of the National Economy with 67 members, and the Agrarian Union bloc. All of these groups generally tended to support the communist rump in the parliament.

The principal communist faction was the Communists of Russia, led by Igor Bratishchev, which included 216 deputies. Although the hardline leader of the Russian Communist Party, Ivan Polozkov, was not a member of this faction, it usually followed the Polozkov line – despite spanning a range of views from the centre to the extreme right. Bratishchev's group provided the anti-democratic pole of the parliament's activities, leading the opposition to Yeltsin and the Democratic Russia bloc. The Communists of Russia, however, by no means included all the communists in the parliament: only 216 of the 917 CPSU deputies elected to the parliament joined it (many favouring more moderate or even democratic positions). Bratishchev's faction was composed principally of senior Party secretaries and officials of the State *apparat* and economic management system.[43] Another hardline faction (founded in May 1991) was *Otchizna* (Fatherland) with up to 150 members (51 of whom were simultaneously members of the Communists of Russia bloc). It was

---

42 Doctors, like teachers, were found by sociologists to be generally conservative.
43 'Kommunisty', *AiF*, 1990, no. 23, p. 2.

composed principally of members of the army high command and higher *nomenklatura* favoured a return to militaristic patriotic values and the promotion of Russian power and greatness. The Russia group – led by Siberian Sergei Baburin – claimed to occupy a more centrist position but in fact generally supported nationalist communist positions. Baburin's faction was particularly concerned with preserving State unity and the Union structures (and were at one with the communists in this), although they were ready to envisage a degree of economic reform. Support for this nationalist faction grew from 87 deputies in June 1990 to 160 in March 1991.[44]

At the other end of the spectrum, the Democratic Russia bloc counted about 205 deputies. The democrats had prepared carefully for the parliament, holding a conference on 31 March–1 April to agree their tactics and elaborate a programme which might attract deputies from the centre who were, as yet, uncommitted to either side. They professed to believe that the transition to the market economy, which they advocated, could be effected at the expense of the corrupt bureaucracy (in the event, the only group that managed to survive the upheaval of the next two years more or less unscathed).

The key to power in the parliament for the democrats therefore lay in attracting some of the economic factions to their side, such as the Organizers of the National Economy (17 of whose 67 members also belonged to the communist faction) or the agricultural lobby. Contemporary Soviet analyses suggest that they succeeded in this. Whereas the Communists were supported by the overwhelming majority of the higher *nomenklatura* of the Party, State and army, the democrats were reckoned to have attracted three-quarters of the lower management of the country and 73 per cent of the lower army officer corps, and a little over 63 per cent of the middle-ranking officers. Just as the communists monopolized the support of the governing structures, so too the democrats had the overwhelming majority of the intelligentsia (87 per cent) with them, but vitally they succeeded in attracting the support of many middle managers of the old Soviet system.[45]

44 MBIO: Folder on Otchizna; B. Tarasov in *SR*, 10 July 1991, for Otchizna; S. Baburin, *Rossiya*, 18–24 March 1992, p. 4; Pribylovsky, *Slovar'* (1991), pp. 56, 75; Satarov, *Partiinaya Zhizn'* (1991), pp. 6–7. The membership of these groups fluctuated.
45 E. Yefimova, *AiF*, 1990, no. 29, p. 2.

The democrats achieved this by their shrewd choice of issues and tactics. The first task facing Yeltsin on the opening of the parliament was to capture the chairmanship of the Supreme Soviet – a vote which *de facto* conferred the office of President of the Republic on its occupant. In the context of the growing demand for greater republican independence, the office of Russian President promised Yeltsin a prominence and a power-base far greater than that which he had hitherto achieved. It would also ensure that he emerged as the undisputed leader of democratic forces in the country and place him, alone among the democrats, on a level with Gorbachev and in a position to challenge his preeminence. In backing the demand for republican sovereignty, therefore, Yeltsin and the democrats were hoping to create a counterweight to the central Soviet structures, which were controlled by the conservatives, and to wrest executive and legislative control from them, in order to implement political and economic reform.

However, in standing against the hardline Party candidates (Alexander Vlasov and then Ivan Polozkov), Yeltsin stressed not confrontation but compromise. He promised to try to reach an accommodation with Gorbachev, to enable the gradual introduction of market reforms, alongside (rather than instead of) the old system. The suggestion was that the transition to the market would be a painless and prolonged process and that the old structures were not in imminent danger of being replaced. Similarly, on the Constitution, Yeltsin offered a fudge: the republics should no longer be bound by laws they themselves deemed contrary to their interests and the republican parliaments (rather than the central ministries) should control the economy. (In May 1990, the Russian government controlled only 10 per cent of Russian industry.) Yet, this transfer of power would not undermine the central Soviet government and the USSR should be retained. Hence, deputies were offered a combination of old structures and new powers. This proved enough to allow Yeltsin to be elected to the chairmanship of the Supreme Soviet (or standing parliament) on 29 May 1990, on the third ballot, despite Gorbachev's sharp opposition.

Following this vote, the parliament went on to adopt a series of decrees – proclaiming Russian sovereignty (12 June) and the separation of State and communist ideology – which were passed by a substantial majority (with the democrats commanding 530 and 540 votes).[46] Yeltsin had thus succeeded in winning centrist deputies over to the cause of political and constitutional reform. These deputies – the middle and lower levels of the *nomenklatura*, who are estimated to have accounted for 36 per cent and 21 per cent of the parliament – were, as we have seen, new to the political stage. Their support for republican sovereignty and economic reforms, which devolved more power to the factory director, was motivated by the frustrations they had experienced in the old, highly centralized system. In essence, the democrats were proposing the transfer of power to these representatives of the new *nomenklatura* who had hitherto been excluded from the decision-making process; and, so long as it was not a question of introducing reforms that would sweep away the entire economic edifice (that is, of introducing measures which would result in the rationalization and breakup of industry and agriculture), they were ready to envisage a measure of reform. However, the alliance was necessarily a temporary one, which broke down after the coup, when sweeping reforms were put on the agenda.[47] Even in 1990 and 1991, it was uncertain.

The battle between the Union and the Russian parliament was conducted with vigour and venom throughout the Autumn and Winter of 1990 to 1991. Under heavy pressure from the resurgent right wing of the Party, hardliners in the parliament proposed in February 1991 putting the question of Yeltsin's tenure of the post of chairman of the parliament to an extraordinary session of the full Russian parliament in March 1991. Enormous crowds demonstrated in the major Russian cities in support of Yeltsin, in the critical confrontation that ensued. Yeltsin was seen to have a political legitimacy denied to his opponents, especially when the referendum of 17 March 1991 endorsed Yeltsin's proposal to create a new, directly elected executive Russian Presidency. As against this, the increasingly repressive actions of the central government were not merely unpopular and incompetent, but they were also plunging the country into chaos. The coal industry was paralysed by an all-out, anti-government strike, prompted by the promulgation of yet more price rises. The final straw

46 'Kto', *AiF*, 1990, no. 26, p. 4; *AiF*, 1990, no. 24, p. 1; *AiF*, 1990, no. 25, p. 2; Bychkova, *MN*, 1991, no.9, p. 8.
47 See analysis of 'RF-Politika' Centre, 'O rasstanovke sil', *NG*, 1 April 1992, p. 2.

was the deployment by Party hardliners of thousands of troops in central Moscow, as the Russian parliament gathered to debate Yeltsin's fate. Yeltsin, by again adopting a conciliatory tone – calling for collaboration between the centre and the republics, compromise, a coalition government and the signing of a new Union Treaty – won waverers to his side. He reminded the parliament that Russian sovereignty remained purely a rhetorical concept, that it had still to be realized. In this manner, Yeltsin re-created the alliance of the previous Summer between the left and the centre in parliament and even managed to split the Communists of Russia bloc (from which a large self-proclaimed pro-democracy – in fact, pro-republican – group, under Colonel Alexander Rutskoi, broke away). The upshot was that, far from losing control of the parliament and its chairmanship, Yeltsin won backing on 4 April 1990 for his proposal to create an elective Presidency, by 607 votes to 228.

The formalities for the election of the new President were elaborated remarkably quickly and election day was settled as 12 June 1990. Yeltsin found himself running against principally discredited or extremist figures. His chief opponent was Nikolai Ryzhkov, the Union Prime Minister until his resignation on the grounds of illness the previous December. Vadim Bakatin, a liberal *apparatchik*, dismissed as Interior Minister by conservatives the previous Autumn, occupied the centre ground. And on the extreme right were two authoritarian imperialists, General Albert Makashov and Vladimir Zhirinovsky. The army was well represented in this array of candidates: Ryzhkov chose as his running mate the right-wing 'Afghan' General, Boris Gromov, while Yeltsin – in a shrewd stroke – chose Alexander Rutskoi, the nationalist communist and Afghan war hero who had ensured his victory in the parliament's confidence vote, by splitting the communist bloc. None of his rivals was able to mount a serious challenge to Yeltsin who won around 57 per cent of the vote (with former Prime Minister Ryzhkov trailing with 17 per cent and Vladimir Zhirinovsky winning almost 8 per cent). Last of all was the compromise figure of Vadim Bakatin, with 3.5 per cent of the vote, who suffered from being neither sufficiently to the right nor to the left to suit anyone.

Yeltsin's power-base was now greatly strengthened. He had received his mandate directly from the people and, therefore, there could be no repetition of the attempt, the previous February and March, to unseat him. He was thus freed from his dependence on the parliament and from the need to conciliate so many different forces within it. The President's powers were to include the right to appoint ministers and issue decrees but he did not have the right to dissolve the parliament or to veto its laws. However, relations between the parliament and the President were not fixed in any fundamental legal act, so that, after the coup in August 1991, a new constitutional problem was to arise: namely, the relation of the presidency to the parliament. In April 1991, however, Yeltsin had emerged triumphant from the trials of the Winter, with his power and authority greatly increased.

Gorbachev's Decline

Gorbachev, by contrast, found his power-base eroding. Always a supreme tactician, he had advanced his reform policies more through the skill with which he manoeuvred than by being able to rely on a solid body of support for change within the Party. On the other hand, a General Secretary could rely on the inertia and conventions of the system to retain his position, so long as he was ready to compromise on policy and did not 'rock the boat'. However, the democratic reforms, approved by the Nineteenth Party Conference and inspired by Gorbachev, appeared to a large section of the Party and State *apparat* as an appalling error, revealing the regime's lack of political legitimacy and short-circuiting their hitherto well-ensconced opposition to the General Secretary's policies. Removal of the culprit (Gorbachev) clearly seemed desirable to many of the participants in the Party plenums held between April 1989 and March 1990 but the rules of the game had been changed and removal of the General Secretary seemed likely to create more problems than it would solve: the Party without Gorbachev was likely to lose ground more quickly than if he at least appeared to head it. The abolition of the new political institutions was fraught with international consequences that even the hardliners were reluctant to contemplate. The preferable option was therefore to retain Gorbachev and the new institutions for cosmetic purposes, but to control their activities.

From late 1989 on, and especially after the lamentable election results of March 1990, the Party hardliners began to regroup – creating, in June 1990, the Russian Communist Party (RKP), as a republican party on the same footing as that of the Estonian, Ukrainian and Georgian Communist Parties within the All-Union Party. In this way, it was hoped to abstract from Gorbachev's control much of the CPSU's large membership, income and property, and to achieve political and organizational autonomy from Gorbachev, leaving him stranded at the head of a non-existent army. Thus armed, the conservatives attending the Party's main policy forum, the Twenty-Eighth Party Congress in July 1990, were able to prevent democrats exercising decisive influence on the Party's rules and policies or from capturing key positions within it. This prompted the bulk of the democratic faction in the Party to leave the CPSU forthwith, thereby depriving the reformers in the Party leadership of a significant body of support within the Party. In fact, Gorbachev had shown little interest in or sympathy for their activities, principally, it would seem, because the focus of his interest had shifted from the Party to the State.

The sense of the proposals on democratization which he had put to the Party Conference in June 1988 had been to create an alternative power structure to that of the Party *nomenklatura*. It seems that Gorbachev initially believed that he would be able to control the new parliamentary bodies and use them to legitimate policies opposed by the Party's hardliners. But the elections had radicalized public opinion and debate and the new Soviet parliament was a clearly inadequate reflection of the popular will: its legitimacy was thus flawed from the outset and Gorbachev could derive little authority from presiding over it. The rejection of the Party *apparat* in the 1989 elections was followed, in the Autumn, by the collapse of the East European regimes, where communist rule was revealed to have been a tyranny. The question of the Party's right to rule was unavoidable and Gorbachev conceded its monopoly on power in February and March 1990.

It was at this point that he chose to create a new basis for his power, by persuading the Congress on 14 March 1990 to approve the institution of a new indirectly elected USSR Presidency, with wide powers including the right to declare war, to rule by decree, to impose direct presidential rule, to declare martial law (with the agreement of the Supreme Soviet) and to appoint the Prime Minister. The switch from the Party to the State as a power-base was confirmed by the reform of Party structures: the Central Committee Secretariat had been effectively abolished (on the authority of the Nineteenth Party Conference) in September 1988. In 1990, the Twenty-Eighth Party Congress approved a new extended Politburo consisting of 24 members, many of them obscure and insignificant figures: the Politburo had already been on the decline, however, meeting less frequently in the previous months. Gorbachev had thus established a position which left him a large measure of authority and to a considerable extent independent of the Party structures which had hitherto constrained him.

However, the formula was flawed on three counts: the new central presidency and Union Congress lacked democratic legitimacy; a complete reform of the remaining organs of State was not implemented, so that the government, army and security forces were not subject to effective democratic supervision and remained in the control of Party hardliners; and finally, Gorbachev underestimated the political impact of the new republican authorities. Gorbachev's majority in the Congress was founded on the conservative *apparat*, whose presence in the parliament was due to the rigging of the electoral law and to the Party's traditions of discipline, subservience and loyalty to the leader. Both of these elements were being eroded by his reforms. Although this constituency was under threat and its continued loyalty could not be guaranteed, Gorbachev made no attempt to secure his authority by seeking a public mandate. Sensing that his lack of popularity made victory at the polls uncertain, Gorbachev resisted proposals to create a directly elected Presidency. This was to undermine him in his relations with Yeltsin, whose popular authority was not in doubt.

Gorbachev was therefore outflanked on his left by the radicals, who had rallied around Yeltsin, and on his right by Party hardliners, who controlled key positions in State and government. The amorphous centre of the Party lacked decisive power and its democratic and reform wings rapidly lost in both size and influence, from the Autumn of 1990 on. Reluctant to rally to the democrats with their demands for republican sovereignty and their support for Yeltsin, who was rapidly emerging as a rival in the battle for power, Gorbachev had no for manoeuvre left and no base to fall back to other than the Party's right wing. The period 1990 to 1991 was to reveal Gorbachev's vulnerability to the right and the limitations on his conception of reform, just as it was to reveal the democrats' difficulties in building a secure power-base.

CONCLUSION

There was a tendency – especially after the August 1991 coup – to associate the pro-republican deputies in the parliament (only some of whom had been elected on a democratic ticket) with the broader democratic movement that supported them and with the anti-Stalinist intellectuals of the *glasnost* era – to see them as all equally committed to democratic renewal and united in a single democratic movement. But it is questionable if such unity of purpose really obtained. The pro-republican parliamentarians and their leaders appropriated, in some measure, the democrats' rhetoric. But they spoke less of legality, moral renewal, and respect for the individual and his rights, emphasizing instead republican rights. Republican power, although a legitimate and democratic demand, in view of the flawed central structures, was not necessarily backed on this account. Alexander Rutskoi and his followers, who, at a key juncture, supported Yeltsin's demand for Russian sovereignty, seem to have been attracted more by the nationalism and the new distribution of power it implied than by a clear vision of the legal, constitutional and economic reforms it might usher in.

In short, the majority of deputies in the Russian parliament, who formed the basis of the new political class, diverged in background and outlook from the cultural elite and, to a lesser extent, from the intelligentsia of the research institutes. Their lack of ideological commitment to democracy is suggested by the failure, after the August 1991 coup, to introduce constitutional reform, hold new elections or proceed with a coherent and consistent plan of political, legal and administrative reform. The ambiguity underlying the republican–democratic alliance in the Russian parliament is further illustrated by its rapid collapse after the coup, when disagreements in conceptions of government (parliamentary or presidential rule, monetarism or economic conservatism, decentralization or central rule) undermined it.

Finally, the fragmentation of the democratic movement after Spring 1990 is also significant. The backbone of the democratic movement – in the sense of a movement committed to ideological, constitutional and legal reform – was, until the 1991 coup, furnished by the intelligentsia. If the intellectual elite had led the campaign against Stalinism in the press and the arts, the intelligentsia of the research institutes had led the political clubs and, after the lifting of the ban on independent political activity, formed many of the first non-communist parties; they had been active in the many attempts to found a popular democratic front that ultimately resulted in the establishment of the Democratic Russia movement in October 1990; and many were elected to the Russian parliament. But this ideological movement never definitively attracted the support or adherence of the majority of Russian parliamentary deputies, while, after March 1990, the democrats' political leaders were cautious in their dealings with the popular movement. The democratic movement was thus not as securely based in the new institutions as appearances suggested.

One might almost say that, after March 1990, the democratic camp was composed of two distinct tendencies, superficially united by the call for republican sovereignty. One, inspired and led mainly by the intellectuals and enjoying a significant – if not overwhelming – measure of popular support, was committed to a rejection of Stalinism, in all its aspects – economic, political and legal – and emphasized the need to guarantee human rights and freedoms in legal form. The other was inspired less by ideology than by practical problems of power and administration, its republicanism was more pro-Russian than anti-imperial; its power was based at least as much on economic and political institutions as on popular sentiment. It was the latter of these tendencies which, after the 1991 coup, left its imprint on Russian politics, although representatives of the former were given high political office. Arguably, it was the failure of these two tendencies to coalesce into a single movement that undermined Russia's democratic revolution.

9. Problems of Organization: The Democratic Parties

The difficulty of their position was not entirely clear to the euphoric democrats in the Spring and early Summer of 1990. They initially hoped that new political parties would provide the new framework for politics after March 1990. However, this was not to prove the case and political life largely escaped the disciplines they implied. The reasons for this are numerous. General scepticism about politics and political parties in particular was one factor. Another was the difficulty of communicating effectively in a country the size of the Russian Federation, a state whose cultural and ethnic traditions were diverse and whose level of economic and social development varied widely from region to region. The political parties were strongest in the large cities of European Russia, where familiarity with the political culture of Western Europe and North America was more common and social structures were more developed than elsewhere; while they were weakest in the rural and non-Russian areas of the Federation. As a result, the new parties were superseded by broader public organizations, parliamentary factions and networks of personal alliances. Many of the new parties, or pseudo-parties, reflected the outlook and political instincts of the intelligentsia and suffered from this cultural isolation, while the parties whose impact was greatest grew out of the CPSU.

The new parties, while united in their anti-Stalinism, covered a wide spectrum of political opinion. Broadly at one on the need for a market economy, they were to diverge in 1991 in their response to Russian nationalism. Andrei Sakharov observed perceptively that the main fault-line between the new parties would prove to be their attitude to the Soviet Union's empire: centralization and Russian dominance or a free federation of independent States.[1]

However, at least as significant as their ideological divergences were the origins of the new parties, for these influenced not only their policy preferences but also their character and approach. There were two main sources for the parties which emerged in 1990 and 1991: the CPSU and the informal movement. Of these, the CPSU was to exert more influence. The parties which issued from it in this period were more pragmatic, powerful and better organized than their rivals. Typically, they adopted centrist positions. The parties to which the informal movement gave birth were both more various and colourful, ranging from the Greens and the Anarchists on the left and the ultra-nationalist and religious parties on the right. They were also more amateurish and few were to attract much support or interest. Most successful in these respects were the Social Democrats on the left and, to a lesser extent, the Christian Democrats on the right.

A key element in the emergence of Russia's new political forces was thus the disintegration of the CPSU, which began in earnest in Spring 1990, when the Party's democratic wing began to break away, leaving Gorbachev's centrists and the vocal and resurgent neo-Stalinists competing for power within the CPSU itself. The democratic rebels formed two new parties in 1990 – the Democratic Party of Russia, on the centre right of the political spectrum, and the Republicans, on the centre left. In March 1991, a further split in the Party resulted in another wave of more cautious anti-Stalinists, under Alexander Rutskoi, breaking away from the CPSU to form a separate party. Motivated above all by their commitment to the principle of Russian sovereignty, Rutskoi's supporters were also to endorse a measure of economic modernization and reform. These parties were to become the best organized and most numerous after 1991. It was these ex-CPSU members from the centre right and centre left of the Party who were to provide much of the general staff of the democratic movement, under the erratic leadership of the Kutuzov-like Yeltsin and to offer the country such new political values and policies as they deemed appropriate.

1 Cited in Morrison, *Yeltsin* (1991), p. 139.

DISINTEGRATION OF THE CPSU

The conflict between the Stalinists and the democrats in the CPSU reached its apogee in Spring 1990 during the republican elections of March 1990 and the selection of delegates to the Twenty-Eighth Party Congress of July 1990. The reformers from Democratic Platform campaigned in the 1990 elections on the democratic ticket; several of its supporters (including Vladimir Lysenko) were elected to the new Russian parliament under the banner of Democratic Russia.[2] In essence, two wings of the Party had openly campaigned against each other and if a formal split within the Party had not occurred it was largely because both sides were intent on capturing the organization, with its enormous resources and still significant authority, an intent all the more stubborn because the Party seemed to be the only effective public organization in the state.

A split became imminent, however, after March 1990, when the Central Committee, after reluctantly endorsing the principle of political pluralism, voted to allow regional Party committees to decide how the election of delegates was to be conducted. This in effect guaranteed the *apparat*'s continued control over the nomination of delegates to the Congress and meant that the democrats would be deprived of any significant influence in it. The radicals within Democratic Platform, on learning of these arrangements, pressed the case for a complete break with the Party. What was the point of attempting to persuade the Party to adopt reforms when it was already possible to predict that these attempts would fail? The breakaway forces were, however, no longer cohesive.

One strand represented democratic socialism, of which Igor Chubais was the main spokesman. The other wing, which emphasized the importance of introducing a market economy, was led by Nikolai Travkin, a former alumnus of the Moscow Higher Party School, leader of a construction brigade and member of the Moscow Party provincial committee (*obkom*). Travkin, a machine politician with a popular touch and a man of considerable personal ambition, was disappointed by his failure to be invited to attend the March Plenum and by its results. As a result, he and his associates began to incline to

2 For their reform programme, see *Pravda*, 3 March 1990, p. 3; Shostakovsky and Yakovenko, *Dialog*, 1990, no. 8, p. 31.

an early split with the Party. Travkin resigned from the Party on 22 March 1990. The moderates continued to argue that an early departure from the Party and failure to await the outcome of the July Congress would lose them support. However, they did not prevent the adoption of a resolution by Democratic Platform's Coordinating Council on 19 March calling for preparations for an independent party to be made, while Democratic Platform itself continued to work within the Party to promote reform and demanding that the Party turn over its property to State.[3]

This brought a swift reaction: the Central Committee published an open letter in *Pravda* on 10 April attacking Democratic Platform and forbidding membership of it. This letter condemned the democrats who, it claimed, 'attacked the ideological and organizational bases of the CPSU'. Democratic Platform was 'attempting to split the CPSU from within and to remove it from the political arena'. It called for the expulsion of its leaders and like-minded radicals from the Party.[4] A wave of expulsions from the Party confirmed that the conservatives were on the offensive. Igor Chubais was expelled on 10 April after having been summoned to a meeting in the local Party branch for 'a little chat'. This turned out to be an inquisitorial examination of the motives for his involvement in Democratic Platform.[5] Chubais's radicalism was well known and he had the reputation of being a hot-head, ever since he suggested storming the Lubyanka to the crowd at the pro-democracy mass meeting of 4 February. His expulsion was, therefore, not surprising. It was followed up by a wave of more obscure but no less significant expulsions in the provinces, where local Party committees, basing themselves on the Central Committee's *Pravda* letter, expelled supporters of Democratic Platform.[6] The *Pravda* letter provoked both great dissension among the supporters of Democratic Platform and a round of resignations from the Party, including, on 18 April, that of Yuri Afanasiev, who was now convinced that the Party was unreformable.[7]

3 V. Orlov and I. Yakimov in *MN*, 6 May 1990, p. 6.
4 *Pravda*, 10 April 1990.
5 Chubais in *MN*, 22 April 1990, p. 4.
6 Shostakovsky and Yakovenko, *Dialog*, 1990, no. 8, p. 30.
7 For examples of controversy see MBIO: Informal Archive: Byulleten' Moskovskaya Tribuna, 3, 1990, p. 4; Karpinsky in *MN*, 22 April 1990, p. 5; Popov *et al.*, *AiF*, 1990, no. 15, p. 3.

It was against this background that the Democratic Platform's second Conference was held on 16–17 June 1990 in Moscow, on the eve of the formation of the conservatively inspired Russian Communist Party. Most delegates agreed that a new party should be formed, should the Twenty-Eighth Party Congress reject their proposals.[8] On 19–20 June, representatives of Democratic Platform attended the Party Conference which resulted in the resurrection of the Russian Communist Party. The democrats objected ineffectually to the revanchist neo-Stalinist tone of the proceedings and to the election of the right-winger Ivan Polozkov as its First Secretary. The formation of the Russian Communist Party was a triumph for Party hardliners, who hoped to use it to undermine Gorbachev's control of the CPSU. It was therefore viewed with dismay by liberals in the Party and disheartened the democrats on the eve of the Party Congress.

On 2 July 1990, the Twenty-Eighth Party Congress opened. Democratic Platform succeeded in getting only 100 out of a total of 4700 delegates elected to the Congress.[9] As a result, it was unable to press reform proposals successfully. However, Vyacheslav Shosta-kovsky shocked the Congress with his frank speech. It was no longer enough to proclaim that the Party was committed to humane, democratic socialism, he observed. The immediate aim should be 'the formation of a civil society, where man will be legally guaranteed the free choice of his social, political and economic way of life, where the Universal Declaration of Human Rights will be really established, where no one ideology or outlook will hold a monopoly on ideas, where freedom of conscience will reign'. He demanded a mixed economy and the depoliticization of the army, KGB and State. 'For me, there is only one criterion of socialism', he said:

> The well-being and freedom of man. And the form of property [that predominates] is absolutely without importance. [...] Yes, the people went for the Bolsheviks' slogans in 1917. And for seventy-three years, we have repeated these slogans over and over again: land to the peasants, factories to the workers, power

8 Pribylovsky, *Slovar'* (1991), p. 67; Krotov *et al.*, *Rossiya* (1991) I, 2, p. 244, for a brief account of the proceedings from different perspectives; 'Vtoraya konferentsiya dem. platformy', *Rech'*, 1 July 1990, p. 3.
9 Karpinsky in *MN*, 20 July 1990, p. 7.

to the Soviets, peace to the peoples. We have not delivered on these slogans [...].[10]

Not surprisingly, the mostly conservative delegates were outraged. Democratic Platform's proposals were rejected but it is a measure of Gorbachev's liberalism that such a speech could now be delivered to the Party Congress. Although changes were made to the Party's structures – largely to free Gorbachev from the constraints imposed on him by his increasingly militant and conservative Party *apparat* – they did not address any of Democratic Platform's main concerns. No firm decision was taken on changing the organizational base of the Party, which remained, as before, founded on cells in the workplace – at factories, institutions, organizations and the state services (including the security services) – and strictly centralized. The Party took no steps towards reconstituting itself as a democratic, parliamentary party.[11]

As was pointed out by Boris Yeltsin – resplendent in his new-found authority as Chairman of the first democratic Russian parliament – the failure to address this fundamental issue was fraught with danger for the Party; it would at its peril forget the example of Eastern Europe, where Communist Party leaders were now standing trial for their past irresponsibility and incompetence. Yeltsin signalled that a split could not now long be postponed. 'It has not proved possible to neutralize the activity of the Party's conservative forces. On the contrary, we have spoken too much about us all being in the same boat', he warned. The Party Congress was deluding itself if it imagined that it was defining and setting the pace for *perestroika*: the pace and direction of the reform programme was being set not by the Party but by the parliaments. What the Party could and should decide was 'the fate of the CPSU itself.'[12]

It was clear that Yeltsin's departure would not be long delayed and on 12 July, just before the end of the Congress, as he was about to be re-elected to the Central Committee he announced his resignation, to

10 See *Pravda*, 8 July 1990, for Shostakovsky's hard-hitting speech.
11 For a short summary, see Sakwa, *Gorbachev* (1990), p. 387. Compare *Proekty ustava KPSS Moskovkogo i Leningradskogo partiinykh klubov* (Moscow, 1990), and 'Ustavy KPSS' in *Materialy XXVIII s"yezda KPSS* (Moscow, 1990), pp. 108–27.
12 *Pravda*, 8 July 1990, p. 4.

cries of 'shame' as he strode deliberately from the hall. He was motivated not so much by a desire to register a protest against the failure to reform, as by the realization that the Party no longer had anything to offer him. Its old monopoly on power was broken: new representative institutions which challenged the Party's power had been created, and it was in these institutions and in the democratic vote that Yeltsin's power-base now lay. None the less, the break with the Party did not come easily. In a subsequent interview, he claimed to have had 'colossal doubts' and to have agonized about the decision for some days, before acknowledging that resignation was inevitable. Although he had been a Party member for about thirty years and had joined it at a time of romantically high hopes, he now realized that the Party had taken a false route. Resignation for him 'was not a tragedy but rather a liberation from a false religion'.[13]

Yeltsin's resignation was followed almost immediately by that of several other leaders of the democratic wing of the Party. The newly elected mayors of Moscow and Leningrad, Gavriil Popov and Anatoly Sobchak, left the Party as soon as the Party Congress closed. In their letter of resignation, Popov and Sobchak alleged that the Congress had shown the Party to be incapable of leading the country out of the crisis. It had rejected fundamental ideological and political reforms, such as renouncing the idea of class hatred and accepting the priority of universal human values over class ones; the introduction of a market economy and private property; the abolition of the Party's monopoly on the mass media; the transfer of power to the soviets and of most State and Party property to ordinary citizens.[14]

Most of Democratic Platform's delegates at the Congress also resigned and at a meeting of 14–15 July announced their intention of forming a new political party.[15] Fifty-four CPSU members, who supported Democratic Platform and had been elected to the Russian parliament, announced their departure from the Party. They resigned because

The Twenty-Eighth Party Congress did not justify the hopes of democratic forces in the Party and society. The hope that the Party would transform itself into a

13 Morrison, *Yeltsin* (1991), pp. 122–3.
14 Popov and Sobchak in *AiF*, 1990, no. 29, p. 2.
15 See *Proekt zayavleniya o namereniyakh organizatsionnogo komiteta po podotovke uchreditel'nogo s"yezda novoi politicheskoi partii* (distributed at July meeting); also

parliamentary party proved illusory. The Party, which has brought the country to so cruel an economic, social and political crisis, is keeping its command structures in the organs of State and does not want to renounce its monopoly on political power [...] The leadership of the CPSU is holding on to the property which by rights should belong to the people.

Hence, they called on all democratically-minded people to unite in an independent democratic bloc under the auspices of Democratic Russia.[16]

PARTIES FROM THE CPSU

Republican Party of Russia

Within five months, the secessionists had formed a new party, committed to democracy and the principles enunciated by Democratic Platform. They demanded the 'dismantling of the totalitarian system and the transition to a parliamentary, multiparty, law-based state; the abolition of the CPSU's monopoly on power'. The social democratic orientation of the new party was clearly stated: 'The main aim of economic policy is the creation of dignified living conditions, the free development of the individual and social security for everyone, on the basis of an effective market economy, including all forms of property.' Respect for human rights – including the right of self-determination – and an end to the CPSU's repressive nationalities policy were also stressed. Finally, they held that national security should be based not on a military build-up but on 'integration with the rest of the world'.[17]

The Republican Party's founding congress was held on 17–18 November 1990 in Moscow. Unlike those of many other new parties, it was prepared and conducted with professional dispatch, which enabled rules, a programme and a public declaration of purposes to be adopted. Vladimir Lysenko and Vyacheslav Shostakovsky were among those elected to lead the party, which claimed the support of

Karpinsky (interview with Shostakovsky), *MN*, 20 July 1990, p. 7.
16 *AiF*, 1990, no. 29, p. 4; *Rech'*, 3, September–October 1990, p. 3; interview with V. Shostakovsky, 20 November 1990.
17 *Rech'*, 3, September–October 1990, p. 3.

over 20 000 former CPSU members.[18] The party emphasized its commitment to the restoration of Russian sovereignty, which held the key to reform:

> We support the real completion and defence of Russian sovereignty, the restoration of its State system in the form of a democratic republic, realizing the rights and freedoms of all citizens, in accordance with the UN Declaration of Human Rights; friendly cooperation with other sovereign States connected with Russia by a shared historical destiny.[19]

The Republicans therefore believed that the Soviet Union should be replaced by a federation of sovereign republics which would delegate powers on economic, military and security matters to the centre. They called for a Treaty, guaranteeing these arrangements, to be negotiated[20] and demanded the replacement of the USSR Congress and government by a new inter-republican government. The Republicans also favoured the introduction of a market economy, with the State intervening to control macroeconomic policy and assure an adequate level of social security and ecological controls.

The first Congress endorsed the proposal of union with the Social Democrats, whose inspiration was very similar. The first half of 1991 was devoted to this attempt, but it became clear that a considerable section of the Party and a majority of the leadership (notably Shostakovsky) opposed the deal, and at the Party's second Congress on 29-31 June 1991, this view prevailed.[21] Although the Social Democrats and Republicans cooperated in the Russian parliament (where the Republicans had eight deputies and could count on the support of about fifty more) they were drawn not so much to the old informal wing of the democratic movement as to the reform wing of the CPSU leadership. When the Movement for Democratic Reform was established by Yakovlev and Shevardnadze and other Party notables, in July 1991, the Republicans hastened to pledge their

18 Koval' (ed.), *Rossiya* (1991), p. 107; Krotov *et al.*, *Rossiya* (1991), I, 2, p. 244. Pribylovsky, *Slovar'* (1991), p. 68, gives a much lower estimates of 3000 members for mid-1991. The Congress was attended by ten USSR deputies and sixty Russian deputies and claimed to have branches in all provinces and regions of Russia except Kirovsk province: *Izvestiya*, 18 November 1990.
19 Koval' (ed.), *Rossiya* (1991), p. 105.
20 Declaration of the Republican Party, cited in Koval' (ed.), *Rossiya* (1991), pp. 105, 107–9.
21 Pribylovsky, *Slovar'* (1991), p. 68.

support and were before long represented in its leading councils. The new party also maintained close contact with Yeltsin: three of its leading members were appointed as Yeltsin's prefects after the August 1991 coup and the Republicans' support for the Russian president in the parliament was significant. The Republican Party did not take off in the way it had been hoped but its leaders were prominent in the political life of Russia after August 1991. Their presence in the new political elite and their importance in the democratic movement before the coup point to the limits of the political renewal initiated by the decline and fall of the CPSU. If the old leadership and elite were swept from the political stage after August 1991, the democrats' ranks were nonetheless drawn in large measure from the dissident rump and lower echelons of the old establishment, as the Republican Party shows.[22]

Democratic Party of Russia

The Democratic Party of Russia, founded in Spring 1990, illustrated the same phenomenon – the rise of the Party pragmatists and centrists. The idea of founding a powerful democratic party was first raised in December 1989 by radicals in the Leningrad Popular Front – principally by the RSFSR deputies, Marina Salie and Ilya Konstantinov. The proposal gathered support after March 1990, both among leaders of the Moscow Union of Voters (MOI), in particular Lev Ponomarev and Vera Krieger,[23] and among radical USSR deputies – including Arkady Murashev and Gennadi Burbulis (a former teacher of Marxist theory from Sverdlovsk)[24] – and supporters of Democratic Platform.[25] The founding conference of the new party, held in Moscow on 27–28 May 1990, was thus attended by supporters of the informal movement, former political prisoners, former (and current) CPSU members and officials, and a new generation of non-Party

22 This may also be seen in Telman Gdlyan's People's Party: see *Panorama* (28), July 1991, p. 7; Pribylovsky, *Slovar'* (1991), p. 45.
23 MBIO: 'Novosti partiinogo stroitel'stva', 6 June 1990, p. 2, in folder on Democratic Russia.
24 The champion chess player, Gary Kasparov, promised to support the party financially: Pribylovsky, *Slovar'* (1991), p. 31; Khatsenkov, *Dialog*, 1990, no. 12, p. 34.
25 MBIO: 'Novosti' in folder on Democratic Russia. Travkin, with the support of thirty others, at a Democratic Platform Coordinating Council Meeting on 21 April 1990, decided to establish an organizing committee for the new party.

politicians anxious to establish their careers. Not unnaturally, they had different visions of the party they were about to create. The Leningrad delegation was committed to the idea of a mass party 'based on the Universal Declaration of Human Rights, Academician Andrei Sakharov's draft constitution, the electoral programme of the "Democratic Russia" bloc'.[26] They, and many of the informal movement's supporters and old opponents of the regime, wanted to create a party unlike the CPSU not merely in ideology but also in organization, hoping to avoid excessive centralization and discipline. Rivalries between (and even within) the Leningrad and Moscow organizing committees had already developed.[27] In particular, those who had emerged from the informal movement distrusted those who had issued from the democratic wing of the CPSU. Above all, there was considerable resistance, led by the Leningrad delegation under Salie and Konstantinov and the Moscow Union of Voters (MOI) contingent led by Ponomarev and Krieger, to Nikolai Travkin's openly stated ambition to become the unchallenged leader of the new party.[28] These delegates favoured a collective leadership, which would enable them to influence the new party.

Travkin, on the other hand, was equally determined to avoid creating an ineffectual body given over to endless debate: 'I categorically oppose [the idea of a collective leadership]. [...] We have already gone through that stage [...] I will not get involved with [...] some amorphous affair and chatter.'[29] Travkin and his supporters conceived of a political party in much more business-like terms; not surprisingly, given that most of them were former CPSU members, the model they sought to emulate was the Communist Party itself. 'We need to create a party', Travkin explained to *Ogonek* shortly after the May conference. 'Because otherwise we will not be able to deal with this monolith [the CPSU *apparat*]. [We need neither] movements nor unions, but a strict party with strict structures [...] To have real influence, one has to be organized. A party is needed.'[30] His logic was simple: the CPSU was the rival and therefore it was

26 Quoted in Krotov *et al.*, *Rossiya* (1991), I, 1, p. 91.
27 V. Krylovsky and K. Zavoisky, *Express khronika*, 9 October 1990, p. 4.
28 Krotov *et al.*, *Rossiya* (1991), I, 1, p. 91.
29 V. Krylovsky and K. Zavoisky, *Express khronika*, 9 October 1990, p. 4.
30 Travkin and Glotov, *Ogonek*, 24, June 1990, p. 3.

necessary to build up structures capable of opposing it at every level in society.[31] As Arkady Murashev, Travkin's principal opponent in the new party, commented ruefully: 'He [...] wants the DPR to take the CPSU's place [...] to have the same structure as the CPSU.'[32] These divergences of view led to an immediate split, with most of the informal activists withdrawing from the party.[33]

Nonetheless, a largely successful effort was made to maintain the appearance of unity and the party was able to adopt definite policy positions. Among its aims was the adoption of a new Constitution consistent with the Universal Declaration of Human Rights and international legal acts which guaranteed basic human freedoms.[34] It also called for the development of free enterprise, private farming and market economy and social security guarantees.[35] Its demands also included the privatization of state property and anti-monopoly measures, cutbacks in the defence programme and a limit on the level of income tax.[36] It successfully attracted the support of elements in the emerging private sector and counted a representative of this interest group, Sergei Zimin, among its Deputy Chairmen. At the same time, Travkin was careful to suggest that this haste to embrace capitalism should not entail excessive sacrifices – supporting generous social security arrangements, while declaring for the early integration of the Russian economy into the world economy. He even professed to believe that this transition could be accomplished without too much difficulty. ('We are sure that it is possible to switch over to the market in Russia without causing people hardship, even during the transition.')[37] Even when not carried away by enthusiasm, Travkin was anxious to reassure the large numbers of people who were

---

31 Interview with S. Zimin, 30 November 1990; A. Davydov, *Izvestiya*, 3 December 1990; Koval' (ed.), *Rossiya* (1991), p. 198.

32 A. Murashev cited in Koval' (ed.), *Rossiya* (1991), p. 203.

33 Interviews with S. Zimin, 30 November 1990, S.P. Zinchenko, 20 November 1990, and Lev Ponomarov, 16 July 1990; Krylovsky and Zavoisky, *Soglasie*, 29 June 1990; Krotov *et al.*, *Rossiya* (1991), I, 1, p. 92.

34 Programme Theses, *Demokraticheskaya Rossiya*, 1990, no. 1, supplement, p. 2.

35 Organizational principles of the DPR in *Demokraticheskaya Rossiya*, 1990, no.1, supplement, p. 5. See also I. Zaramensky, *Dialog*, 1990, no. 15, p. 19, for a brief summary of its economic programme.

36 Programme theses of DPR in *Demokraticheskaya Rossiya*, 1990, no. 1, supplement pp. 3–4; Travkin in *AiF*, 1990, no. 20, p. 8.

37 Travkin and Glotov, *Ogonek*, 1990, no. 24 (June), p. 3.

reticent about opting for the democrats and their reform programme because they feared its effects on their standard of living.[38] They needed to believe that the introduction of capitalism would not plunge them into the kind of Dickensian poverty, which the Party had encouraged them to believe was prevalent in the West.

The most original element in the DPR's programme – and that which distinguished it from other parties of the centre and right – was the importance it attached to the realization of Russian statehood, conceived of not in religious or national terms, but within the framework of a pluralist, secular democracy. Its programme theses called for: 'the creation of an all-Russian [*rossiiskii*] state system, guaranteeing equal rights to all citizens, without reference to their social position, confession, nationality or party affiliation.'[39] The pragmatists of the DPR were not inclined to discursive reflections on the peculiarity of the Russian national soul and destiny or on the place of man in society. They were moved by a concern with securing their power-base and as the democratic camp was better placed to exert influence over the Russian rather than the Union parliament, the demand for Russian sovereignty made sense. The party's programme theses declared:

> The Russian Federation is to be an independent democratic state, a member with equal rights of a voluntary union of sovereign republics, which delegate some of their rights to the centre.[40]

Democrats of Travkin's cast of mind – despite their concern with strong government – were obliged to opt for a radically reformulated Union structure, not because they were necessarily unsympathetic to the imperial connection but because their political opponents in the CPSU held the centre, exercising an effective monopoly on State power and blocking all economic and political reforms.

The DPR became one of the largest of the early democratic parties, with almost 30 000 members by the end of 1990 (it claimed around 80 000 additional supporters). It could also boast of several Russian and Union deputies (including the eye surgeon Svyatoslav Fedorov) and around 170 lower-level deputies. These achievements were due

38 Ibid., p. 2.
39 Programme Theses, *Demokraticheskaya Rossiya*, 1990, no.1, supplement, p. 2.
40 Ibid., p. 3.

both to the organizational abilities of its members (many of whom were ex-CPSU members) and to the fact that the party was able to inherit (from one wing of the CPSU) an already organized body of reform opinion. This rather hybrid party, whose radicalism was tempered by the political origins and pragmatic outlook of many of its members, played a significant role in the democratic movement, despite its failure to meet Travkin's unrealistic expectations.

Free Russia People's Party

The other main party of ex-communists, the Free Russia People's Party, emerged after a split in the communist faction in the Russian parliament in April 1991. The latter half of 1990 had witnessed a concerted and partly successful attempt by the Party hardliners to restore their political influence. The first clear indication of this was the formation of the Russian Communist Party with its vocation of undermining the reformist leadership by capturing the Party's Russian organization and resources. The Russian Communist Party (RKP) was led by Ivan Polozkov, who inherited the leadership of the con-servative cause in the Party from Yegor Ligachev. At first, it was assumed that the Russian Communist Party would reflect faithfully the conservatism of its founders but these expectations were disappointed. Firstly, the leadership of the new party was not united. At a lower level, the Russian Communist Party mirrored the divisions in the all-Union party: there were two broad tendencies in the RPK – the conservative, orthodox wing, led by Polozkov, and a centrist position, to which it is thought a majority of party members subscribed; this view supported democratic political institutions within the framework of a socialist ideology and economy.[41]

These divergences of view were reflected in the Russian parliament, where members of the Russian Communist Party belonged to a wide variety of factions – from the Democratic Russia bloc (with 205 members) on the left of the spectrum, to the Communists of Russia (with 225 members under Igor Bratishchev) on the right.[42] The Communists of Russia articulated classical Party orthodoxies, oppos-ing both Yeltsin and economic and political reforms but it none the

41 Koval' (ed.), *Rossiya* (1991), pp. 23–4.
42 See Satarov, *Partiinaya zhizn'* (Moscow, 1991), pp. 6–7.

202 The Rise of the Russian Democrats

less included many who, while not ready to opt conclusively for the democratic platform – with its emphasis on market as well as political reforms – were equally uncomfortable with Polozkov's position.

The tension within the Communists of Russia bloc came to a head in February–March 1991, during the dramatic third plenary session of the Russian parliament, when Party hardliners attempted to eject Yeltsin from the office of Chairman of the Supreme Soviet of the Russian parliament (hence depriving him of the position of Russian President). Yeltsin's response to this was to call for Gorbachev's resignation and for the direct election of the presidency (an election which he knew he could win and which would free him from dependence on the parliament). The conservatives' attack on Yeltsin split the Communists of Russia: centrists in the bloc broke away under the leadership of Alexander Rutskoi to form a separate parliamentary faction, Communists for Democracy. Rutskoi, an Afghan war hero, had first entered public life in 1989 as president of the nationalist and neo-Stalinist body, *Otechestvo* (Fatherland).[43] He was thus a rather unlikely hero of the democratic movement and it seems that nationalism rather than liberalism was decisive in drawing him towards the democratic camp at that stage.

Rutskoi's group pronounced in favour of democracy, Yeltsin and Russian State sovereignty.[44] The new faction attracted the support of around 102 deputies including highly-placed communists.[45] Rutskoi, far from intending at that point to break away from the CPSU, quickly expressed his interest in developing a popular political organization within the CPSU:

> We do not intend to form some sort of new communist party. I have proposed founding a public political organization [...] 25 000 people have expressed interest in joining this organization, while remaining in the CPSU.

43 A flavour of Rutskoi's orientation is given by his election manifesto of Spring 1990: 'ENOUGH of turning our country into a raw materials' appendage and colony of the West! Shame on those who trade away their native land to the benefit of transnational monopolies, abandoning the people to a cabal of foreign capital. ENOUGH of electing representatives of the elite intelligentsia as representatives': *Panorama*, 1991, no.28, (July), p. 1.

44 See Rutskoi's speech to the Third RSFSR Congress of People's Deputies in Koval' (ed.), *Rossiya* (1991), pp. 70–71.

45 Letter of Latsis and others in *Izvestiya*, 10 April 1991; interview with P. Fedorov and V. Zharikin, 27 September 1991.

The organization was to be populist, not elitist in character:

> I support the democratic reorganization of the CPSU. In its current form, it is not
> a party of the people. It expresses the will of the top hierarchy. Democratic
> reforms are essential [...] There is a mass of honest, decent communists –
> workers, peasants, representatives of the intelligentsia – who don't occupy
> leading positions and aren't involved in politics. I support their position, I want to
> defend their interests [...][46]

This interest in attracting popular support was doubtless encouraged
by his new political eminence: in May 1991, Yeltsin chose him as his
running-mate in the presidential elections. Rutskoi's impeccable
military credentials seemed likely to attract votes from the right and it
was hoped he might split the communist vote.[47]

Meanwhile, the idea of forming another Russian Communist Party
to challenge Polozkov's RKP began to gather support. Polozkov's
party laid claim both to all CPSU members on Russian territory and
to Party property on Russian soil and was attempting to wrest a
certain degree of autonomy from the central CPSU to this end.
Rutskoi's supporters felt that these efforts to capture the CPSU's
resources and power in Russia could only be effectively countered by
a separate party organization, to challenge the prerogatives of
Polozkov's party. Hence, in July 1991, it was decided to proclaim the
formation of the Democratic Party of Russian Communists, in
opposition to Polozkov's RKP, but within the CPSU. The new party's
founding congress was held on 2–3 August 1991. Rutskoi was elected
leader. The party declared support for the principle of privatization for
the benefit of workers and the partial nationalization of the CPSU's
wealth – though the specifics of how these policies were to be
realized were left vague.[48] The Central Committee of the CPSU
immediately declared the new party incompatible with CPSU's rules
and refused to recognize it.[49] Rutskoi's party attempted to strengthen
its position by joining Yakovlev's and Shevardnadze's Movement for
Democratic Reform. The conflict was overtaken by the coup on 19
August, from which the party dissociated itself, breaking away from

46 A. Rutskoi cited in Koval' (ed.), *Rossiya* (1991), p. 72.

47 See Morrison, *Yeltsin* (1991), p. 262.

48 Interview with Fedorov and Zharikin, 27 September 1991.

49 Pribylovsky, *Slovar'* (1991), p. 46.

the CPSU and renaming itself the Free Russian People's Party some weeks later.[50]

Rutskoi's party, by virtue of its strong presence in the parliament and the prominence and background of its leader – who contrived to exploit all the advantages of his office of Vice-President, while dissociating himself from the failures of the government's policies – was destined to become one of the leading political parties in post-coup Russia. In May 1992, the White House's own analysts confirmed that Rutskoi's party enjoyed the widest popular support among the public. By Spring 1992 Rutskoi had formed an alliance with Volsky's industrialists and Travkin's Democratic Russia, which gave Yeltsin only qualified support and which urged a modification of the government's monetarist policies in favour of greater aid to industry (a programme which appealed not only to factory directors but also to workforces threatened with unemployment). That this was the most powerful of the political coalitions to emerge in 1992 indicated the extent to which politics remained the preserve of the old elite (albeit its lower echelons).

FORMALIZATION OF THE INFORMALS

What the events of 1990 and 1991 obscured – with the sharp polarization of opinion they witnessed – was the heterogeneity of the democratic movement before the coup. The terminology of contemporary debate counterposed democrats to the Party hardliners, overlooking the fact that behind the general slogans of the democratic movement – Russian statehood, popular sovereignty, economic reform – quite diverse forces were assembled: communists, anti-communists and ex-communists; Orthodox believers and agnostics; liberals and nationalists; democrats and authoritarian populists; supporters of the market economy and those who were unsure what it entailed. After the 1991 coup, power passed not to the most radical wing of the democratic movement – to the intellectuals who had furnished most of its ideas or to the most independent supporters of the informal movement (although many of the latter were by then well-ensconced in the new *nomenklatura*) – but to former, sometimes highly placed

50 Ibid., p. 46.

members of the CPSU, who, while content to rearrange political institutions, were less inclined to embrace the loss of power implicit in radical economic reform or the abolition of their newly acquired economic powers and prerogatives.

While the rebellious wings of the old CPSU may have exercised preponderant influence on the new democratic parties, the old political clubs were determined not to allow the Party or its offshoots to monopolize the new politics. They believed that they had played a key role in the advent of democracy in Russia and now wished to bring this work to fruition. In the euphoria of Spring and Summer 1990, they therefore founded a number of political parties (or pseudo-parties)[51] which attempted to offer a novel vision of Russia's future to the public. These parties were various and colourful but few succeeded in attracting a significant popular following or in developing into more than open political clubs.

Nationalists and Pseudo-Liberals

On the conservative wing of the spectrum were a number of liberal, religious and nationalist parties. Among the most prominent of these essentially right-wing groups was the Russian Christian Democratic Movement and Party, led by Viktor Aksyuchits and, initially, Father Gleb Yakunin. The Russian Christian Democratic Movement, which was founded on 8-9 April 1990, thus had its origins not only in the human rights movement but also in the non-conformist wing of the Orthodox Church. As such, it drew on a tradition of conservative nationalism. Some of its leaders were conversant with the ideas of the religious nationalists and imperialists of the nineteenth century and, before long, it was this heritage (of which Aksyuchits was the most articulate exponent) – rather than the liberal democratic ideals of the human rights movement – that predominated in the new party.[52]

Liberalism fared little better than Christian democratic principles in the new Russia. The idea of founding a liberal party, along the lines

---

51 See R. Sakwa, *Russian Politics* (1993), p. 171. He points to the parties' lack of support and suggests that they were not parties but pseudo-parties.

52 Declaration of the R.kh.d.d. in *Rossiiskoe khristiansko-demokraticheskoe dvizhenie: sbornik materialov* (Moscow, 1990), pp. 33-5. See *MN*, 1990, no. 21, p. 6, and ibid., 1990, no. 34, p. 8, for interviews with Aksyuchits.

of the pre-revolutionary Constitutional Democratic Party or Kadets, was first raised by Viktor Zolotarev in the Civic Dignity club in May 1989.[53] The party which was ultimately founded was never more than a club of enthusiasts. The spirit of the liberal intelligentsia reigned in it but failed to attract popular support or win a parliamentary seat.[54] In their oft-repeated desire to see Russia rejoin 'the civilized world', in their sense of sharing European political values, Zolotarev's Kadets may be seen as representing the Westernizing tradition; their nationalism, like that of religious activist Alexander Ogorodnikov, did not lead them towards the cultural isolationism of the patriots. The chief Constitutional Democratic Party, led by Mikhail Astafiev, however, soon abandoned liberalism for an increasingly authoritarian and strident nationalism. 'The Kadets', they declared, 'are united by democratic ideas [...] while recognizing the need for enlightened patriotism and strong institutions of state power'.[55] This preoccupation with state unity and strength led the Kadets to form an alliance with Aksyuchits's Christian Democrats in 1991, and by the following year they had drawn close to other vocal (mainly neo-Stalinist) imperialists. By virtue of Astafiev's parliamentary mandate, the right-wing Constitutional Democrats – despite their minimal support – managed to maintain a noticeable political presence throughout 1991 and 1992.

Centrist Parties

Many small centrist parties proclaimed their existence in 1990 but few succeeded in attracting any significant following. An interesting indication of the difficulties faced by the democrats in rural Russia is afforded by the fortunes of one of these parties – Yuri Chernichenko's Peasant Party. The party hoped to encourage private farming and defend the interests of country people and those engaged in agriculture. The founding meeting was held on 4 September 1990 and in the entire Soviet Union only 60 people attended. By the time the first Congress was held, on 16–17 March 1991, support for the project

53 Political programme in Koval' (ed.), *Rossiya* (1991), pp. 162–7; interview with Professor I. Surikov, 13 November 1990; Surikov in *AiF*, 10–16 February 1990, p .8.
54 Cited in Koval' (ed.), *Rossiya* (1991), p. 164.
55 Krotov *et al.*, *Rossiya* (1991), I , 2, p. 299.

had grown only modestly: 286 delegates (200 of whom were farmers) were present.[56]

On 4 September 1990, the party called for 'the abolition of the *sovkhoz* [state farm] and *kolkhoz* [collective farm] monopoly on agriculture [and] the restoration of land to the peasants'. They stressed the importance of 'the material spiritual rebirth of the villages', which meant putting 'the peasant family with its needs, concerns, health, supplies and social equality at the centre of attention'.[57] The party subsequently characterized collectivization as 'genocide' and demanded a public apology from the CPSU.[58]

The Peasant Party was unique in addressing itself to the problems of agriculture and to the difficulties faced by country people. While most *intelligenty* and political activists in the city lamented the politically backward state of the countryside, few paused to consider what could be done about it. References to the deplorable poverty of the Russian countryside and to the poor performance of agriculture were minimal in most of the new parties' programmes. There were a number of reasons for this: firstly, the majority of the population were city dwellers, whose concerns and needs were different from those of the farmer. Awareness of the countryside and its problems was underdeveloped, a heritage of the Soviet contempt for the peasantry. Soviet agriculture was notoriously backward not only under the Soviet but also under the Tsarist regimes: at first inhibited by serfdom and then, after 1862, by the terms of emancipation, which had lumbered an overtaxed peasantry with impossible redemption payments, agriculture had only just begun to develop thanks to Stolypin's land reforms before 1914 when war and revolution overtook the country. The problems these caused were exacerbated by the Bolsheviks' initial policies towards agriculture (principally consisting of forced deliveries and starving the countryside of resources and money). Despite the brief respite afforded by the NEP in the 1920s, the situation of farmers under the Soviets declined dramatically. The Bolsheviks regarded the peasantry as political enemies, whose

56 Pribylovsky, *Slovar'* (1991), p. 30; Krotov *et al.*, *Rossiya* (1991), I, 2, pp. 241, 327; *MN*, (1990), no. 37, p. 5.
57 'Appeal of the Peasant Party of Russia', *Ogonek*, 1990, no. 38, p. 3.
58 Peasant Party's Programme in Koval' (ed.), *Rossiya* (1991), p. 220.

interests were at odds with those of the industrial working class and whose political allegiances lay with capitalism and private property: they saw the overwhelming victory of the Socialist Revolutionaries (SRs) in the November 1917 elections to the Constitutional Assembly as confirmation of this – overlooking the fact that the SRs' commitment to revolutionary (though rural) socialism was no less ardent than their own.

Motivated by this hostility and by the need to feed his rapidly expanding army of industrial workers, Stalin proceeded to collectivize agriculture – despite fierce resistance – precipitating a famine in which seven million are estimated to have died, deporting up to twelve million resisters and *kulaks* (richer peasants) and destroying the economic and social basis of the Russian countryside. Incidentally, the peasants were again subjected to an essentially feudal regime in which their labour was scarcely paid, their access to education and health-care minimal, and their right to free movement restricted. Not until the mid-1970s was the peasant to be automatically entitled to an internal passport (an indispensable adjunct to any degree of mobility) and even then it took several years for this commitment to be realized in practice. Until then, the peasant could leave his collective farm only with the permission of its director, a situation which differed little from that which prevailed in much of Russia before emancipation. The poverty of the countryside after the Second World War may be gauged by the pay of the collective farmer, who could have bought a box of matches with his daily wage.

To the end of the Soviet era, the farmer was paid less than the industrial worker (about 25 per cent less, on average, in the late 1980s). Running hot water, bathrooms, consumer goods, food: all were in short supply. Country people were even obliged to come to town to buy food, which could not be found in the villages. Cars were a rarity (and in any case, for part of the year, unusable, as roads were poor and at times impassable). Most young people born in the country were anxious to escape and took advantage of military service to do so. Many villages, as a result, were (and are) inhabited only by elderly people. The lack of services made doctors, teachers and gifted engineers anxious to avoid a rural posting.

In these circumstances, the necessity of a party which drew public attention to the plight of the countryside was obvious. But

Chernichenko and his associates had great barriers to overcome: the long tradition of neglect, coupled with fear and inertia in the countryside itself, where an ageing population remained politically passive and where the influence of collective farm directors was decisive. Chernichenko made little headway against these obstacles, as the modest forces (500 to 600 party members in late 1991) at his command indicate. The problems of political proselytism in the countryside were unresolved by the democratic movement, as this isolated attempt to address its specific problems showed.

Social Democrats

The most successful of the parties with roots in the informal movement (including the Moscow *Perestroika* Club) was the Social Democratic Party of Russia, which was founded on 4 May 1990. The first step towards establishing the new party was taken on 13-14 February 1990 in Tallinn, when the Social Democratic Association was founded. Over a hundred representatives of Social Democratic clubs, parties and groups attended, as did several people's deputies, including Yuri Afanasiev and Alexander Obolensky.[59] Soon after the Russian elections, the Social Democratic Party of Russia was founded. It held its first conference in Moscow on 4 May 1990. Alexander Obolensky, Oleg Rumyantsev (of the *Perestroika* Club and newly elected to the Russian parliament) and Pavel Kudyukin (who had been imprisoned under Andropov for his interest in unorthodox varieties of socialism) were elected its leaders.[60] Leonid Volkov explained that the party wanted to advance new values, aims and 'create a new social-democratic ideology out of the ashes of real socialism'.[61] The party favoured moving to a regulated market economy with mixed forms of property and adequate state services in education, health and culture. The market, as Kudyukin pointed out, was not a utopia and had to be controlled.[62]

---

59 Declaration of Principles of the Social Democratic Association in *Otkrytaya zona*, (11), 1, 1990, pp. 29-30. See also *Respublika*, 1990, no. 3, pp. 10-13; Zaramensky, *Dialog*, 1990, no. 15, pp. 17-18; Pribylovsky, *Slovar'* (1991), p. 84; Krotov *et al.*, *Rossiya* (1991), I, 1, p. 77.
60 Pribylovsky, *Slovar'* (1991), p. 85; Krotov *et al.*, *Rossiya* (1991), I, 1, p. 113.
61 L. Volkov, *MN*, 1990, no. 19, p. 5.
62 Interview with P. Kudyukin, 5 December 1990.

The founding Congress's manifesto was somewhat more long-winded, reflecting the ideas and style of the party's main theoretician and leader, Oleg Rumyantsev:

> Our aim is a party of political, economic and social democracy, which we see as a society of popular self-government, based on the harmonious combination of developed productive forces with social relations, which secure for every member of society (citizen) a standard of living adequate for a dignified existence and which at the same time create conditions enabling the individual to realize his initiative and creative potential fully in the sphere of human activity.[63]

These imposing philosophical goals enthused mainly younger members of the intelligentsia, long bored and frustrated by the ideological straitjacket imposed by the CPSU.[64] The Social Democrats were to remain a party of the intelligentsia rather than of the labour movement. Over 80 per cent of the Social Democratic Party members at the first Congress had a higher education and 65 per cent were under the age of forty. This social profile did not change, as the party failed to draw the labour movement into its ranks. The second Congress in Sverdlovsk, in October 1990, was attended principally by members of the intelligentsia (between 70 and 90 per cent) while workers accounted for 10 per cent of those present.[65]

Nevertheless, the Social Democratic Party enjoyed the reputation of being one of the most significant parties to emerge in the new Russia. Its origins in the informal movement also accounted for the Social Democratic Party's innovative image. Its style seemed refreshing and attractive to the political scientists and journalists who followed its development; its ideas – combining emphasis on social security and equality of opportunity with support for political and economic reform – seemed likely to appeal to a public tired of communism but in which socialist values had been so insistently inculcated as to make their outright rejection unlikely. Indeed, the Social Democrats' success in the Russian parliament (they claimed about twenty-six

63 Cited in Koval' (ed.), *Rossiya* (1991), p. 123.
64 Interview with V. Lyzlov, 12 July 1990.
65 Krotov, *Rossiya* (1991), I, 1, pp. 113, and ibid., I, 2, p. 333. According to Pavel Kudyukin, 40 per cent of those present in Sverdlovsk belonged to the non-technical intelligentsia and 30 per cent to the technical and engineering intelligentsia: interview, 5 December 1990.

people's deputies at Union and republican level)[66] seemed to confirm these predictions.

But presence in the parliament was also fraught with temptation: it tended to draw the party leaders' attention away from the prosaic tasks of organization and development of popular support and into purely parliamentary activities. The Social Democratic Party's deputies in the Russian parliament were included in Yeltsin's team of advisers and some – notably Rumyantsev himself, who became chairman of the Committee charged with drafting the new Russian Constitution – were given heavy and time-consuming responsibilities. The failure of the party's second Congress to adopt a programme was a setback. The party was also impeded by the competition of the Republicans, who embraced essentially identical policies. At the third Congress, in Leningrad on 20 April–3 May 1991, it emerged that the Social Democrats had failed to attract as many members as had been expected or believed: only a little over 4000 people had joined the new party.[67]

CONCLUSION

The destiny of the new parties – if such indeed they can be called – was problematic. They were founded in a moment of euphoria, when democrats had won considerable electoral successes and Stalinism had met with a signal defeat. This tended to obscure the magnitude of the problems facing both the country and the democratic movement. The economic and constitutional crisis with which the democrats were confronted did not afford a propitious environment in which to establish a democratic political culture and new, liberal organizations.

It was inevitable that the new parties would take some time to establish their identity. However, support for the democratic movement as registered in the elections did not translate into support for

66 These included Gennadi Bogomolov, Oleg Rumyantsev, Leonid Volkov and Alexander Obolensky.

67 Pribylovsky, *Slovar'* (1991), p. 86. Around this time, Party leaders were claiming 5–10 000 members: see Koval' (ed.), *Rossiya* (1991) p. 122. Kudyukin estimates their membership at around 10 000 in December 1990, of whom 2–4000 were actively involved in the party: interview of 5 December 1990.

the new parties, as reflected in enrolment in their ranks. Few of the new parties exceeded two or three thousand members and those that did, or that claimed to do so, succeeded in large measure because they were able to build on CPSU structures and personnel. In the case of the smaller 'informal' parties, which were founded mainly by intellectuals, the notion of the political party as an ideological body – in the liberal nineteenth-century mould – was influential. Hence, more time was often devoted to the elaboration and discussion of programmes than to organization and when organization was the preoccupation (as with Travkin) the aim was to emulate the CPSU. Few saw the strength of the political party as lying in management of image, popular opinion and resources, rather than in mass membership or the quality of its ideas.

Thus the parties that emerged in 1990 were either parties of the intelligentsia – which relied mainly on intellectual debate to draw support and which remained very small and weak – or parties of politicians formed in a discredited political culture, which they were unable to jettison in its entirety. In neither case were the party leaders entirely aware of how to mobilize support in a modern democracy and, after the initial euphoria, the new parties led a tenuous existence, insecurely anchored in the country's political life and in public opinion.

A final question that arises is: how democratic were the new parties and how did they contribute to Russia's new political culture? While all these new parties initially proclaimed their commitment to democracy, they were not unanimous in their understanding of what it entailed. Their early agreement on the need to respect human rights and enshrine them in law, to protect the individual from the incursions of the State, to replace the old Soviet empire with a democratic federation and to dismantle the State's economic monopolies was eroded already in 1991 and broke down in 1992. The threat to Russian hegemony and its collapse after the August 1991 coup was the first problem to undermine the parties' early liberal consensus: the Kadets and the Christian Democrats were to gravitate towards the former neo-Stalinists as a result, while Rutskoi's followers and Travkin's Democratic Party were to move away from the early consensus, stressing the need to protect the power of the state and the rights and interests of the Russian people. In advocating economic reform, the new parties had all suggested that the transition to the market would be relatively painless and would enhance people's prosperity; the details of what reform meant and how it would be achieved were left vague: not surprisingly, when Yeltsin's government began to implement a programme of economic liberalization, albeit ineptly, the consensus on economic reform also began to collapse.

The significance of the new parties should not be entirely dismissed, for, if they failed to win wide popular support, they none the less revealed the political inclinations of many of the new politicians and of politically active people. While the CPSU's authoritarian rule and pseudo-populist rhetoric left its imprint on some of the new political leaders – Alexander Rutskoi and Viktor Aksyuchits are examples – most none the less looked to unequivocally democratic ideals for inspiration. However, the democratic ideology adopted by the new parties was an expression of rebellion against the *apparat* and its rule rather than a programme of government. It described an ideal city, but without giving directions about how to get there; as a map for politicians travelling towards a new democratic Russia, it omitted much of the information and guidance they required: that they got lost on the way is understandable.

10. Problems of Organization: The Democratic Movement

By Autumn 1990, the democratic leaders were more aware of the difficulties that faced them in marshalling their forces against the central Soviet Party and State machine. They knew that they did not have a secure and established constituency outside the big cities and that, even here, the reform vote was politically ambiguous, being prompted as much by protest as by enthusiasm. If they were to hold their position – or ultimately to win a decisive majority – they needed to create a firm political power base. The 30 per cent of the public who supported the democrats had to be anchored in some sort of organization that would confirm them in their views, mobilize them when necessary and inspire the uncommitted.

DEMOCRATIC RUSSIA

The first attempts to organize support were taken in Autumn 1989[1] but not until the following year were these efforts to yield results. On 20-21 October 1990, the founding conference of Democratic Russia – conceived as a popular movement as distinct from the parliamentary bloc – was held in the Rossiya cinema in Moscow. Around 1300 delegates attended. Every significant reform club, pressure group or

---

1 Among these was the Inter-Regional Association of Democratic Organizations and Movements (MADO), founded in Chelyabinsk on 28-29 October 1989. It called for a multiparty, parliamentary system; the introduction of a market economy, private farming (with rights of inheritance of landed property) and the transformation of the USSR into a free federation of sovereign states. However, the diversity and rivalry of MADO's members (it included both the Azeri and the Armenian national fronts) undermined its effectiveness and by June 1990, MADO had ceased to exist: Krotov *et al.*, *Rossiya* (1991), I, 1, pp. 60-61; Zhavoronkov in *MN*, 1989, no. 47, p. 13; V. Vyunitsky in *Dialog*, 1990, no. 17, p. 32.

movement was represented: apart from the new political parties, the writers' club April, Memorial, the army group Shield, the Social-Ecological Union, the Confederation of Labour and the Academy of Sciences' Union of Voters were all present – while the new left groups, anarchists and greens attended as observers.[2]

At the very outset, differences emerged over the nature and purpose of the new organization. The majority favoured a broadly-based, inclusive association of all democratic forces in Russia and hence supported loose organizational ties and rules. The partisans of this more liberal formula included, at this stage, Lev Ponomarev and most of the leaders of the Moscow Union of Voters (MOI) who had helped to organize the conference. A minority, headed by Nikolai Travkin, leader of the newly-founded Democratic Party, believed that the movement should be a strictly disciplined body, ideally a single political party under his leadership. It was therefore with annoyance that he first greeted the proposal to found Democratic Russia as a mass movement and loose federation of organizations and parties. He felt that these forces should really have rallied around his party and, at Democratic Russia's inaugural conference in October 1990, he expressed his belief that not a movement but a party was required. Travkin's view did not prevail, however. His intentions were viewed with some misgivings by other participants in the meeting; his ambition was feared and there was a general reluctance to envisage creating a movement in the image and likeness of the hated, but disciplined, CPSU.[3] As a result of this defeat, Travkin's party did not initially join Democratic Russia (although regional branches of the party joined *en masse* at an early stage and the party leadership and the central party followed suit in January 1991).

Travkin was never entirely happy with Democratic Russia, however, or with the influence within it of his old rival, Lev Ponomarev. His goal of founding a single, disciplined democratic party rather than a broader front was, however, over-ambitious, as the democratic movement was united more by the anti-Stalinism of its participants than by any agreement of the future constitution and character of Russia. The distrust and differences in outlook within the

---

2 Pribylovsky, *Slovar'* (1991), p. 16; Krotov *et al.*, *Rossiya* (1991), I, 1, p. 229.

3 Author's notes of meeting; Yu. Bychkov, *Karetny ryad*, 19, 25 October 1990; T. Menshikova in *MN*, 1990, no. 43, p. 2.

democratic movement – especially between former dissidents and former Party members – were too great to be overcome other than by a loose federation and even that, as Democratic Russia showed, was held together only with difficulty.

Despite these differences, the conference succeeded in defining the movement's general principles and aims. Economic and political reform – as embodied in the 500-Day plan for transition to the market, which both Gorbachev and Yeltsin had endorsed in the Summer – were now under threat, they declared. The Party bureaucracy was privatizing Party property, thereby establishing a new power-base for itself. Democratic forces were being discredited, the food situation was difficult and civil war seemed close:

> Salvation is possible only through the joint actions of all democratic forces in the context of a general civil movement.
> 'Democratic Russia' is [...] founded on the following principles:
> 1. Priority of the rights and interests of the individual over the rights and interests of the State, parties, social and ethnic groups.
> 2. Implementation of the right to self-determination, while observing the rights of the ethnic, religious and other minorities of the non-native population.
> 3. Creation of a social [sic] market economy through privatization.
> 4. Social security and charity as essential elements of the civil society.
> 5. Intellectual and confessional tolerance, while fighting totalitarian parties and structures which aspire to a political monopoly.

It called on citizens to unite behind the demand for the USSR government's resignation, for economic and political sovereignty for Russia and for the rejection of totalitarianism.[4]

Democratic Russia was therefore an overt opposition movement. 'The tasks of the movement consist in the coordination of democratic forces, which oppose the state-political monopoly of the CPSU, in the conduct of joint election campaigns, parliamentary activity and other concrete joint actions with the aim of founding a civil society', announced the rules.[5] But, as some commentators pointed out, the only element uniting the participants of the forum was their

---

4 Declaration of the Congress of Democratic Russia, Moscow, 21 October 1990.
5 'Rules of the Democratic Russia Movement' published in *Soobshchenie, 3, Orgkomiteta dvizheniya 'Demokraticheskaya Rossiya' (NDP)*, p. 1. An immediate aim of the movement as defined by Arkady Murashev was the preparation for the mayorial election campaign which would be fought the following year: I. Zaramensky in *Dialog*, 1990, no. 15, p. 21.

anti-communism.[6] This enabled the formation of a strategic alliance but did not sow the seeds of 'a coherent, constructive opposition'. Tatyana Menshikova of *Moscow News* observed that the intelligentsia lacked broad public support and a popular base and that this was a danger. 'While engaged in a wrangle on the political Olympus, the delegates have no reliable ties with the grassroots forces that voted them in. The edifice of democracy is threatened by cracks even before it has been completed. I mean rifts between its leaders and activists, parliamentarians and their electorate, parties and movements.'[7]

Despite these differences, however, a united forum was established which brought together most of the leaders and chief organizations of the democratic movement – although two of its 'stars' (Sobchak and to some degree Yeltsin) maintained some distance from it. By March 1991, Democratic Russia's leadership included several radical deputies,[8] many of whom were associated with newly-founded democratic parties. Its co-chairmen included Yuri Afanasiev, Father Gleb Yakunin, Lev Ponomarev, Gavriil Popov and Arkady Murashev. Initially, Democratic Russia was successful in building up popular support: in 1991, branches were established in over 300 towns and cities and the movement claimed between 200 000 and 300 000 members.[9] Its capacity to organize meetings of up to half a million people in support of democratic reform – which it demonstrated during the critical and tense weeks of February and March 1991, when Russia's sovereignty and Yeltsin's position were challenged by the Soviet hardliners[10] – gave Yeltsin moral and political authority and showed that Democratic Russia enjoyed considerable popular support.

Differences within the leadership of the movement, however, were to undermine its strength. The task of keeping groups of quite diverse inspiration and vocation within one organization – no matter how general its overall commitments – was difficult. Democratic Russia included not only literary and intellectual pressure groups – like April, the Anti-Fascist Centre and Memorial – but also political parties

6 Bychkov, *Karetny ryad*, 19, 25 October 1990; Menshikova in *MN*, 1990, no. 43, p. 2.
7 Menshikova in *MN*, 1990, no. 43, p. 2.
8 Yuri Chernichenko, Nikolai Travkin, Mikhail Astafiev, Viktor Aksyuchits, Arkady Murashev, Alexander Obolonsky, Gavriil Popov and Yuri Afanasiev.
9 Pribylovsky, *Slovar'* (1991), p. 16.
10 Krotov *et al.*, *Rossiya* (1991), pp. 326–7; Morrison, *Yeltsin* (1991), pp. 235, 238.

motivated not only by ideas but also by ambition. The Christian Democrats under Viktor Aksyuchits had little in common with the Republican Party and, like Travkin's Democratic Party and Astafiev's branch of the Kadets, had joined Democratic Russia reluctantly. Their overall orientation was right of centre, not only on issues like the economy and the place of the individual in society, but, more significantly, on law and order and greater Russian nationalism. In the conflict between the *apparat* and Yeltsin, in Spring 1991, over Russian sovereignty and the need to reform the Soviet Union, Democratic Russia had aligned itself unambiguously with Yeltsin and radical reform of the Soviet Union. The right of centre parties did not share the majority view in the democratic camp on this issue, believing the conservation of strong, centralised State structures, both at Union and at Russian federal level, to be essential. These divergences of view ultimately split the Moscow branch of Democratic Russia[11] and resulted in an open breach in the movement in October 1991, when Travkin, Astafiev and Aksyuchits withdrew from it.[12] This was the first step in the disintegration of the democratic alliance of the previous two years and it marked the beginning of the realignment of political forces in Russia after the August 1991 coup. Rivalries and divisions about how and when to engage Democratic Russia's authority continued to bedevil the organization, undermining its effectiveness and prestige, and by Spring 1992, many of its erstwhile leaders (including Yuri Afanasiev) had resigned from it.[13]

THE DEMOCRATIC LEADERS

The attitude of the leading democratic politicians to Democratic Russia on its inception is worth considering. The elections of March 1989 had transformed a number of intellectuals into prominent democratic politicians. Chief among them were the academics

11 Pribylovsky, *Slovar'* (1991), p. 12.
12 Ibid., p. 17; V.P., *Panorama*, no. 3, December 1991, p. 7.
13 Karpinsky in *MN*, 21 September 1990, p. 10; T. Malkina in *NG*, 17 March 1992, p. 2; Afanasiev in *MN*, 8 March 1992. See Afanasiev, Salie, Burtin *et al.*, 'Dem Rossiya: byt' ili ne byt'', *Dvizhenie 'Dem. Rossiya'*, no. 12, February 1992, p. 4; Burtin, ibid., no. 13, February 1992, pp. 2-3. Moscow Memorial also withdrew from Democratic Russia at that stage: ibid., p. 10.

Anatoly Sobchak of Leningrad, Yuri Afanasiev and Gavriil Popov of Moscow and, of course, Yeltsin. But the man who enjoyed greatest moral authority after the March 1989 elections was the Nobel prize-winning physicist and human rights defender, Andrei Sakharov, whose contributions to the first and second sessions of the All-Union Congress, in June and December 1989 – although not uncontested – defined the fundamentals of the democratic position. When Sakharov died in December 1989, the radicals had no-one of comparable stature to replace him. Closest to him in outlook among the new generation of politicians was Yuri Afanasiev, but he was soon to be overtaken – in terms of power and public eminence – by others. Yeltsin, elected by an overwhelming majority in March 1990 from Sverdlovsk to the Russian parliament and later to the Russian presidency, had become the leader of Democratic Russia's forces in parliament and in the country. The Spring 1990 elections had also resulted in the indirect election of Sobchak as Mayor of Leningrad and Popov as Mayor of Moscow. This triumvirate, invested with popular authority and public responsibility, led the democratic movement.

None of these stars of the democratic movement chose to join the new democratic parties. Yeltsin, in common with the others, believed that it was premature to do so. In his autobiographical essay, *Against the Grain*, he commented:

> Why have I always been one of those who have not responded to the call for the immediate adoption of a multi-party system? Because the mere existence of several parties does not in itself solve any problems [...] My view is that we still need to grow and mature towards a real, civilised, multi-party system.[14]

A year later, his views had not fundamentally changed. During the miners' strike, in March 1991, Yeltsin believed their demand for immediate multiparty elections to be premature, as the democrats 'have not yet got themselves together'. What Yeltsin seemed to favour was an enormous CPSU-style party:

> If the democratic movement were now to set up a really large-scale people's legislative party, with ten or fifteen million members, which could form an alternative to the CPSU, then of course it would be realistic to [...] move to such elections. But as long as there is one party with 15 million members while the other has 20,000 - well, the correlation of forces is too unequal.

14 Yeltsin, *Against the Grain* (1990), p. 194.

220   *The Rise of the Russian Democrats*

Besides the CPSU retained a *de facto* monopoly in power.[15] The logic
of this position was – given the artificiality of the CPSU's high
membership – that elections would be put off indefinitely. Yet
Sobchak and Popov seemed to have shared this assessment of the
democrats' real strength.[16]

When Democratic Russia was formed in October 1990, neither
Yeltsin, Popov nor Sobchak attended, although the first two sent
messages of support, with Popov already arguing for close links
between left of centre 'oppositional' politicians (whether or not in the
executive arm of government) and a well-organized mass movement.[17] Popov served as one of Democratic Russia's leaders until
April 1991 when, following his election as Mayor of Moscow, he
resigned. This move was apparently prompted by the punctilious
feeling that high office and membership of a political organization
were incompatible. It was on these grounds that Boris Yeltsin had
justified his resignation from the CPSU the previous July.[18] The
severing of the open connection between Popov and Democratic
Russia, which gave the former freedom of manoeuvre, did not in fact
undermine the close contacts maintained between the mayor's office
and the popular movement and the tactical alliance forged between
them continued to cause tension within Democratic Russia.

Yeltsin benefited from the support which Democratic Russia gave
him and his policies throughout 1990-91 but refrained from assuming
leadership of the movement, apparently preferring to maintain his
freedom of manoeuvre. In addition to his misgivings about the
organizational weaknesses of the democratic movement, Yeltsin was
almost certainly prompted by two considerations: his own constituency – the voters to whom he had appealed and who had
supported him in 1989 and 1990 – was larger than that of the democratic movement as a whole. In the 1989 elections, he had received
over 89 per cent of votes cast in Moscow's constituency No. 1; in
1990, in Sverdlovsk, he had again won an overwhelming victory; and
in the first direct election of a Russian president, in 1991, Yeltsin

15 Morrison, *Yeltsin* (1991), p. 250.
16 Sobchak in *MN*, 1991, no. 13, p. 7.
17 Notes of proceedings Moscow, 20 October 1990. The full text of his speech, which was
   read out by M. Schneider, was published in *Soobshchenie, 3, Orgkomiteta dvizheniya
   'Dem. Rossiya' (NDP)* later that Autumn.
18 Sobchak, *Khozhdenie vo vlast'* (1991), p. 266.

received over 57 per cent of the votes with higher proportions in Moscow (72 per cent) and Sverdlovsk (90 per cent).[19] These scores were far higher than the basic democratic vote, as measured in seats in the Russian parliament or in opinion polls – which oscillated between 30 and a maximum of 40 per cent of the electorate. Yeltsin therefore enjoyed a large personal vote, attracting voters who did not fully subscribe to democratic positions. In the Russian parliament, the support of deputies from the centre – who had not always aligned themselves with the Democratic Russia parliamentary faction – was crucial both to his election as Chairman of the parliament in 1990 and to his survival in the following Spring. Hence, for tactical reasons, Yeltsin kept a formal distance from the Democratic Russia movement.

Anatoly Sobchak seems to have shared Yeltsin's reservations, for not dissimilar reasons. In 1990 he was anxious to occupy the middle ground between the extremes of right and left, hoping that the rapid polarization of Russian political life in 1990 could be reversed. He thought that the intolerance and mutual hostility of the radical democrats and the conservative *apparat* threatened to plunge the country into civil war and had resulted in the growing paralysis of executive power. In 1990, Sobchak tried to support Gorbachev in what he took to be his efforts to mediate between the two extremes and to prop up the declining power of the government, realizing only belatedly that Gorbachev had become incapable of effecting the necessary sweeping reforms.[20] Gavriil Popov too, in the Summer and Autumn of 1990, hoped that a coalition between the democrats and Gorbachev with that part of the *apparat* that realized the inevitability of change would be possible, believing that this was the best hope for implementing fundamental reforms.[21]

Not only was the reserve of these politicians towards the wider democratic movement prompted by tactical considerations and different assessments of the political situation but it was also motivated by their peculiar predicament: neither Popov, Sobchak nor Yeltsin was actually backed by a political party nor did they enjoy a secure base in popular opinion, which seemed to be volatile. Throughout 1991, the rating of the new politicians declined – Popov

19 Morrison, *Yeltsin* (1991), pp. 93, 267.
20 Sobchak, *Khozhdenie vo vlast'* (1991), pp. 249–52, 256–7, 266–70.
21 Popov in *AiF*, 1991, no. 7, p. 5; Ye. Yakovlev and Popov in *MN*, 1990, no. 42, p. 7.

in particular suffering from allegations about his management of Moscow – as they failed to solve the pressing economic problems besetting their administrations and as the country continued to slide into chaos. The need for some sort of organized support was evident. All of them had previously been members of the CPSU: they were not used to life as 'exposed' politicians. Yet they were not ready to commit themselves to the newly-emerging parties, despite some initial overtures and hesitations in the Summer of 1990. This reluctance seems to be explained by two considerations: firstly, the new parties were weak and isolated, hardly more impressive in some cases than the informal political clubs that had preceded them; and secondly, the new chiefs were accustomed to thinking of political parties in monumental terms. As we have seen, Yeltsin was prepared to consider a party counting several million members as a serious force, but dismissed one with 20 000 members as entirely insignificant. Sobchak, like Travkin, also argued for the need for a united democratic front and alluded to the desirability of the democrats forming a single party.[22] Hence, ambitious politicians were unlikely to attach their careers to currently unknown and negligible organizations, which could offer them neither support networks nor a dependable popular constituency.

Another factor which disinclined this new generation of political leaders from anchoring themselves formally in the new political parties or movements was the widely-held belief in Russia that political parties are rooted in social classes – socialists in the working class, liberals and conservatives in the middle classes. This remnant of Marxist-Leninism survived the general collapse of the ideology. But while sociological theory was amended – abolishing the idea that Soviet society was composed of two classes (the proletariat and the peasantry) and a 'layer' (the intelligentsia) – many of the new politicians subscribed to the idea that there was no middle class in Russia and that this was likely to inhibit popular support for reform.[23]

---

22 Morrison, *Yeltsin* (1990), p. 250; Sobchak in *MN*, 1991, no. 13, p. 7.
23 This is one of the reasons why many of the new parties adopted a broadly social-democratic orientation: S. Kordonsky in *MN*, 1990, no. 28, p. 9; Stankevich, *Perestroika* (Moscow, 1990), pp. 17-18, on the prevalence and dangers of populism. See also Stankevich's comments in a round-table discussion in 1990 in Yushenkov (ed.), *Neformaly* (1990), pp. 65-6: a multiparty system had not emerged, he asserted, because new social interest groups, on which it could be based, had not yet developed. See also

As Afanasiev put it:

> A society consisting for the main part of employees, in conditions of the
> monopoly of state property, cannot be democratized, and, what is more, its sphere
> of development is totalitarian.[24]

Some of the new leaders seem, in consequence, to have believed that
not only did no significant reform parties or organizations exist, but
that they were also unlikely to develop in the immediate future. The
alternative, therefore, was to attempt to pitch their appeal so as to
draw as many people as possible to their standard, while not
constricting themselves within the narrow field of formalized,
structured politics. This helps to account for the populist preferences
with which they were sometimes taxed.

THE MOVEMENT FOR DEMOCRATIC REFORM

The democratic leaders were thus sceptical about both the new parties
and the consistency of the popular democratic vote and they therefore
hoped that it might still be possible to capture some of the CPSU's
massive organization and resources. Hence, when the reform
leadership of the Party, led by the former Foreign Minister, Eduard
Shevardnadze, and by Alexander Yakovlev, finally left the CPSU in
July 1991 and established another democratic front (the Movement
for Democratic Reform), both Popov and Sobchak hastened to
associate themselves with it. On 2 July 1991, as the conflict between
the Party hardliners and Yeltsin's Russian parliament became acute,
some of Gorbachev's former colleagues and advisers on the centre
left of the Party announced the foundation of a new democratic
organization, the Movement for Democratic Reform. The document
advising the public about this new body was signed by Yakovlev and
Shevardnadze – both of whom had lost office and influence the
previous year – and by Popov and Sobchak. Other signatories
included Nikolai Petrakov (director of the Academy's Institute for
Problems of the Market and a former member of the Presidential

Kurashvili's passing comment on the relationship of class to Party in *MN*, 1988, no. 10,
    p. 8.
24 Afanasiev in *MN*, 1992, no. 10.

Council); Stanislav Shatalin, a reform communist and author of the 500-Day Plan, which provided for a crash transition to the market economy and which Gorbachev had briefly endorsed in Summer 1990; Ivan Silaev, Yeltsin's centrist Russian Prime Minister; and Alexander Rutskoi.

In addition, Arkady Volsky, a Central Committee official and former Andropov aide, who now headed the USSR Scientific–Industrial Union, also backed the movement. Unlike most of the other signatories, Volsky had not fallen from grace or been forced into resignation. In the early years of *perestroika*, Volsky had been given particular responsibility for the machine-tool industry – a traditionally well-funded but increasingly inefficient sector of industry and one of particular significance to the army. This enabled Volsky to develop his contacts in one of the most advanced areas of the Soviet economy, which had benefited from large State investment. As the reform policies moved firstly towards granting enterprises greater independence and then towards introducing market mechanisms, it became clear that directors in this sector of the economy would be better placed than most to survive and prosper in the new order, so long as they could retain some control over the terms on which the change was effected. In consequence, they began to support the transition to the market and to organize themselves as a lobby of entrepreneurs: Volsky, with his impeccable contacts and skills in political manoeuvring, was a shrewd choice as leader of this interest group.

At the time of its foundation, a number of the new movement's leaders (including Shevardnadze and Yakovlev) were still members of the CPSU. The movement had been approved by Gorbachev, journalists were assured, and for the first month of its existence it carefully refrained from criticizing his policies – notably his insistence on the need to preserve the Union, albeit in a reformed version.[25] This reticence led some people to believe that the new movement was intended as an organization in which Gorbachev could find political refuge and support, in the event of his failing to effect radical change in the CPSU's programme and policies at the Party Congress which was due to be held in the Autumn.

25 Pribylovsky, *Slovar'* (1991), p.9; Peter Pringle in *The Independent,* 5 July 1991; A. Barsukov in *NG,* 2 July 1991, p. 4.

The impression of the Movement for Democratic Reform as a regrouping of the centre and centre-left forces of the CPSU was reinforced when, within a month of its inception, leaders of the Republican Party (formerly the Democratic Platform in the CPSU) – including Vyacheslav Shostakovsky and Vladimir Lysenko – joined the movement's councils. The two major breakaway parties of reform communists (the Republicans and Rutskoi's national democrats) had joined forces with the two former leaders of the democratic camp in the Politburo (Shevardnadze and Yakovlev) and with architects of reform policies (Shatalin and, to a lesser extent, Petrakov).

Why then did Sobchak and Popov, two leading democrats, join this movement of the reform wing of the old establishment? A number of reasons may be adduced. Firstly, as democrats in power, they had felt their isolation in two ways: in relation to the power structure and machinery of government, an isolation which resulted in their ineffectiveness in office; and in relation to the public and their constituency. The unreformed administrative and economic system prevented the democratic councils in Moscow and Leningrad from ruling effectively, just as they had been able to frustrate Gorbachev and his team at a higher level. This, in turn, had an impact on public opinion, eroding the democrats' support. Secondly, they did not have at their command an efficient political machine, in the shape either of a party or of an organization. As dissension split the ranks of Democratic Russia, and as their public support rating dropped, so the appeal of an organization capable of mobilizing a dependable vote grew. The Movement for Democratic Reform appeared to offer the chance of consolidating that centrist alliance which Sobchak had supported in 1990 and for which Popov had called after his election to office. Above all, it offered the hope of inheriting some of the CPSU's formidable resources.

On 23–24 September 1991 the Movement for Democratic Reform held its founding conference. It declared its support for a civil society, a law-based state – founded on political pluralism, parliamentary democracy, the market and social solidarity – and looked forward to playing an active part in political life.[26] Fewer delegates attended than

26 *Rules of the Movement for Democratic Reform*, 23 September 1991.

might have been expected[27] but the coup had undermined the authority and appeal of the movement's leading figures. The meeting revealed the motley nature of the allied forces. Shevardnadze and Yakovlev were openly committed to democratic change. In July, Shevardnadze had defined the aim of the movement as being 'to save *perestroika*, to save democracy, to develop democratic processes and provide guarantees that there is no going back to the past, to a totalitarian regime'.[28] In August, by which time both he and Yakovlev had left the CPSU, Shevardnadze outlined his views in a article for *The Independent* of London: 'We believe the Democratic Reform Movement can help to create a democratic law-based society. Its formation is an attempt to create a democratic opposition. Against whom? Against the old command structures and the *apparat* at the top of the Communist Party.'[29] Arkady Volsky, however, was reported as suggesting 'that it was a movement that was "for" not "anti". It was not against anything, including communists.'[30] At the September Congress, further differences of view emerged, this time between Gavriil Popov, who wanted the movement to develop clearly capitalist policies (a line backed by Volsky), and Alexander Yakovlev, who favoured a socialist orientation.[31] Shevardnadze and Popov were also divided on whether or not a new party should be founded – with Popov, under increasing pressure in Moscow, in favour and Shevardnadze believing that the move was premature. Alexander Rutskoi was also strongly opposed to the formation of a new party, on the basis of the movement,[32] seeing it as competition to his own fledgling party.

None the less, the formation of a new party – the Russian Party of Democratic Change – was announced. Proclaiming its commitment to the market, political pluralism and civil society, it stressed its commitment to the individual and claimed to represent the interests of the new middle class and of entrepreneurs. 'The Party is targeted

27 The Movement's own figures indicated that 780 persons had attended the Conference, 334 as delegates.
28 Pringle in *The Independent*, 5 July 1991.
29 Shevardnadze in *The Independent*, 12 August 1991, p. 17.
30 Pringle in *The Independent*, 5 July 1991.
31 Satarov in *Partiinaya zhizn'* (1991), p. 9.
32 Interview with Ye. Maksimov, 26 September 91. Popov was strongly backed by the meeting which passed a resolution supporting his performance in Moscow: see resolution adopted by Movement for Democratic Reform on 23 September 1991.

towards the support of the creative intelligentsia, scholars, entrepreneurs, highly qualified specialists and politically active young
people', it declared.[33] Thus, Democratic Reform's supporters realized
that the most active participants in political life came from the
technical and cultural intelligentsia, who were by education, and to
some extent economically, a middle class. In anticipation of a radical
and rapid programme of privatization (which did not in the event
materialize) they believed that they could attract many of those
previously ensconced in managerial positions in the old regime to the
new party, and the initial response to their calls confirmed this.[34]
Their calculations were to prove mistaken, however: neither the
movement nor the party flourished, just as the democratic movement
as a whole quickly lost support and a sense of direction after August
1991.

CONCLUSION

Why did the democratic movement prove so weak in the long term?
The reason is twofold: firstly, it was conceived as a broad,
anti-totalitarian front, not as a disciplined homogeneous organization;
and, secondly, its leadership was divided. Although the democrats
were able to command impressive support at key junctures, these
demonstrations were exceptional, for they were provoked by crises in
the battle against totalitarian rule and involved people not normally
engaged in politics. Both this popular support and the leaders'
cooperation depended on the conflict between opponents and
supporters of the Soviet regime. The democratic movement, as
exemplified by Democratic Russia, was held together less by shared
political beliefs than by the identification of a common enemy. In
general, the democrats objected less to the socialism the regime
proclaimed than to the specific form of rule Soviet socialism had
engendered: they were at one on the need to end Soviet totalitarianism
but not on what should replace it. As long as the democratic
movement could focus on the abolition of the old regime, its leaders

33 Declaration of the delegates of the founding conference of the Russian Party of
    Democratic Change, 24 September 1991.
34 Interview with Maksimov, 26 September 1991.

acted in concert and the movement survived; but, once the Soviet rule was overthrown and the question became what kind of regime and policies should be adopted instead, the leaders disagreed and were unable to propose a clear vision and aims to the wider public. Hence, although the democratic revolution was not fully carried through after the August 1991 coup, the democratic movement – as a united front of all those opposed to Soviet totalitarianism – fell apart, undermined by the political pluralism it had championed.

After March 1990, the democrats' prestige began to wane as they confronted intractable problems. In addition, opinion polls suggest that not all of those who voted for the democrats in fact supported fully democratic policies or understood their implications for the economy and for the Soviet empire.[35] While there was a significant degree of support for radical positions (not less than 25 to 30 per cent of the population), it was at times inhibited by fear of reprisals, unemployment and poverty. Hence, the democrats were confronted with the problem of maintaining a popular base that was neither adequately secured in an organized political framework nor evenly distributed throughout the country. Furthermore, a large section of the population was reserved or confused about its political preferences and had yet to be converted to the democratic cause. These considerations appear to have tempered the democratic leaders' revolutionary zeal and to have inclined them towards a political rhetoric and style distinguished by its pragmatism and occasional ambiguity.

---

35 A. Rubtsov in *MN*, 1992, no.4, p.7. An all-Russia poll showed that 47 per cent of respondents were unable or unwilling to define democracy; pollsters believed that 21 per cent had an accurate idea of what democracy was, while 79 per cent did not.

11. The Problem of Support

The euphoria of early 1990, when it seemed that Russia might make a smooth transition to democracy, evaporated in the Autumn and Winter of 1990. The rapid rise of the democratic movement, which had encouraged these hopes, was shown to have been a less ambiguous statement of political commitment than was at first believed. Changes in the country's political institutions and direction were still insecurely based on popular support. A profound and widespread change in public attitudes had begun but was not yet complete: the limits of this transformation inevitably affected the fortunes of the democratic movement in its struggle against the entrenched CPSU hardliners in the months leading up to the 1991 coup.

THE INDEPENDENT LABOUR MOVEMENT AND POLITICS: 1989–1991

Even the most encouraging early sign of independent popular support for radical economic and political reform – the emergence of the miners' movement in 1989–91 – was to prove disappointing. Shortly after the first session of the Congress of People's Deputies, which in May and June 1989 had riveted the country's attention, the Siberian and Ukrainian coalfields were swept by a wave of strikes. Both the political leadership and the public at large were taken by surprise. Soviet workers were supposed by everyone – from analysts to Party *apparatchiki* – to subscribe to socialism, as preached by the CPSU, to believe the official ideology about the USSR being a workers' state guaranteeing the privileged position of the working man.[1] The strikes

1 B. Koval' (ed.), *Rossiya* (1991), p. 322.

were all the more unexpected because the independent labour movement had been effectively stifled since the 1920s. The official trade union movement (of which the August coup leader, Gennadi Yanaev, was a boss) had, since its inception, been an arm of industrial management, effectively stifling rumblings of discontent and making – as the workers themselves were to point out – no effort to represent their members' interests.[2] The official unions were above all a bureaucracy, which offered its officials a comfortable career.

Summer 1989 Strikes

The strikes were precipitated by the failure of management and of the official union movement to attend to the miners' demands and concerns on pay and working conditions. What ignited the fire was a combination of acute local shortages with the general decline in living standards.[3] The strikes started in the Kuzbass coalfields, in central Siberia, on 10 July 1989 and quickly spread to the Vorkuta fields in the Arctic Circle and to the old coal-mining centres in the Donetsk region of the Ukraine. Over half a million miners were on strike between 10 and 22 July with over 150 000 other workers out in sympathy. The miners demanded improved pay and conditions and in the Kuzbass they also supported economic independence for the rich mines.

Once the strikes had started, the authorities' reaction was to panic. In Novokuznetsk, Donetsk and the other eight cities principally affected, life ground to a halt, as enormous demonstrations filled the city centres and the authorities abdicated control to the local strike committees. The strikes were so unusual and seemed so fraught with danger to the regime that the government almost immediately conceded the strikers' main demands. Initial concessions made by the government on 13 July were followed up by an investigatory commission, headed by Politburo member Nikolai Slyunkov, who negotiated a more detailed agreement with the miners. By 20 July, the

2 The Declaration of Basic Principles, adopted by the newly formed Independent Confederation of Labour on 1 May 1990, observed: 'For many decades, the official trade unions did not defend workers, and so far it is too early to say that the situation has changed.' Cited in Koval' (ed.), *Rossiya* (1991), p. 366.

3 See J. Aves, 'The Russian Labour Movement' in Hosking *et al.* (eds), *The Road to Post-Communism* (1992), p. 141.

Kuzbass miners had returned to work. In other regions, where the strikes had started later, a similar process of negotiation and agreement took place.[4] The government pledged £10 000 million to the acquisition of scarce supplies from abroad to buy the miners off.[5]

These generous deals were prompted not by guilty consciences but by fear. The strikes exposed the lie of the State's reigning ideology. The working classes, far from ruling the country, or benefiting from Soviet socialism, were ruthlessly exploited by it. The regime's lack of authority and legitimacy was reflected in the workers' alienation.[6] The strikes, with their unprecedented support, the economic dislocation they had caused, and the political crisis they had precipitated, appeared to pose a real threat to the regime. The miners represented a key sector of the economy: disruption in the energy industry threatened the entire economy and, hence, miners wielded power disproportionate to their numbers and seemed particularly well placed to lead a politically inspired independent workers' movement. It was this prospect, above all, that seems to have impressed the government. The example of Solidarity in Poland was one which they did not want to see emulated in Russia. There were grounds for this concern, not merely because of the sensitivity of the sector affected by the strikes. The miners had shown some inclination towards political radicalism, as well as considerable organizational ability.

Politicization of the Miners' Movement

One of the reasons for the politicization of the miners' movement was the government's failure to honour the accords signed in July 1989. Workers' committees had shown their readiness to work alongside the authorities to ensure the implementation of the accords[7] – in some cases losing their reputation for independence and integrity in the process. During the first wave of strikes, in July 1989, the miners' demands had been primarily economic. Only in Vorkuta had political

---

4 P. Rutland, 'Labour unrest' in Hewett and Winston (eds), *Milestones in Glasnost and Perestroyka* (1991), pp. 297–301.

5 Sakwa, *Gorbachev* (1990), p. 212.

6 This was also reflected in the strikers' wariness of the government's concessions: they were unwilling to accept them until formal agreements had been signed.

7 Rutland, 'Labour' in *Milestones* (1991), p. 308. Berezovsky *et al.*, in *Dialog*, 1990, no. 14, p. 55, makes the same point.

demands figured prominently: in addition to improvements in pay and conditions, the Vorkuta miners had called for the abolition of Article 6 of the Constitution, the direct election of the president and changes to the election law (the elimination of deputies nominated by public organizations).[8]

The failure of the government to honour its promises made cooperation with the authorities seem futile. In addition, the Supreme Soviet's law of 9 October 1989, banning strikes for fifteen months, was clearly intended to emasculate the labour movement before it had been able to establish itself. It provoked the most radical of the miners – from the Vorkuta fields – into proclaiming a strike, on 25 October 1989. Political demands (principally for political pluralism and the direct election of the presidency) now came at the top of the list of demands.[9] Later, these demands were extended to include an end to the 'anti-democratic' laws on meetings, demonstrations and strikes, a new democratic press law and freedom of political association.[10] The strike call did not win the enthusiastic support of all the Vorkuta miners and the response was tepid throughout.[11] The strike dragged on until 2 December when a compromise was reached, with the most radical pit being guaranteed economic independence.[12] Once again the Vorkuta miners had settled without any of their political demands being met. Although their strike effectively destroyed the 9 October anti-strike law, it also demonstrated the largely ineffectual nature of the political strike, principally because of the limited support it enjoyed.

Developments in the next two years were to confirm the inability of the radical labour leaders to mobilize widespread support behind their demands. Nor were they always able to count on the support of radical deputies and activists. Sakharov welcomed the strike as a sign of growing popular political consciousness and participation and had even hoped for a general strike in early December in support of the

---

8 Sakwa, *Gorbachev* (1990), p. 212.
9 Ibid., pp. 350–51.
10 Koval' (ed.), *Rossiya* (1991), pp. 353–4.
11 Rutland estimates that a core of about 3000 radicals from the Vorgashorskaya mine kept the strike going with 'only patchy support from the 20 000 other miners in Vortuka and still less from miners elsewhere in the country': Rutland, 'Labour' in *Milestones* (1991), p. 307.
12 Ibid., pp. 305–7 for a lucid summary of events.

demand to abolish the CPSU's political monopoly. 'The important thing', he said in the last speech of his life, 'is that the people [*narod*] has finally found a way of expressing its will and that it is ready to give [the Inter-Regional Group of Deputies] political support'.[13] Other members of the IRG had visited the strikers. But some of its leading members took a different view: Anatoly Sobchak criticized the Autumn strikes on the ground that they were illegal[14] – a view shared by the Leningrad Popular Front, which refused to support the strikers.[15]

The Vorkuta strike had one demonstrable effect, however: it helped to radicalize the powerful Kuzbass workers. The Union of Kuzbass Workers was founded on 18–19 November 1989 in the middle of the Vorkuta strike.[16] Its programme called for radical reform of the political system, freedom of association and free access to information. On the role of the CPSU, the union summoned the courage to recommend the removal of the CPSU's political monopoly.[17] The miners had an opportunity to press for the adoption of their ideas in the election campaign for the local and republican soviets. Five Kuzbass leaders were elected to the Russian parliament, while 30 candidates from the Kuzbass workers' ticket were elected to the 250-seat provincial Soviet in Kemerovo.[18] They thus constituted a significant minority in the provincial soviet – while winning outright majorities in the cities of Novokuznetsk and Kisilevsk.[19]

The Donetsk region was also convulsed by the Spring election campaign. Large – but inconclusive – demonstrations were held in Donetsk between 7 and 14 February 1990 in protest against poor living standards and the local Party committees. Over 100 000 Donbass miners held a two-hour strike in March to demand the abolition of Article 6 of the Constitution. In the elections, the miners won 49 of the 150 seats of the provincial soviet.[20] The elections

13 Sakharov, *Trevoga i nadezhda* (1991), p. 278.
14 R. Bova, 'Worker Activism' in Sedaitis and Butterfield (eds), *Perestroika from Below* (1991), p. 39.
15 Bova, 'Worker' in Sedaitis and Butterfield (eds), *Perestroika* (1991), p. 19.
16 Krotov *et al.*, *Rossiya* (1991), I, 1, pp. 124–5; Rutland, 'Labour' in Hewett and Winston (eds), *Milestones* (1991), p. 309; Berezovsky *et al.*, in *Dialog*, 1990, no. 14, p. 56.
17 Koval' (ed.), *Rossiya* (1991), pp. 358–63.
18 Pribylovsky, *Slovar'* (1991), p. 83.
19 Rutland, 'Labour' in Hewett and Winston (eds), *Milestones* (1991), pp. 309–10.
20 Ibid., p. 312.

marked the end of the uneasy collaboration between the miners and the authorities but the results were inconclusive – showing both the strengths and the limitations of the miners' support. Their real constituency remained concentrated in the coal-mining areas and their impact elsewhere was insignificant: they were therefore failing to win support from workers in other industries and sectors of the economy. Support for the miners was consistent with the general level of support in society at large for radical democratic and economic reform – at about 25–30 per cent of the popular vote.

The Confederation of Labour, formed at the start of May 1990, in the hope of creating an independent, coordinated trade union movement, confirmed the increasingly radical orientation of the labour movement.[21] The Confederation's Declaration of Basic Principles defined the 1989 strikes as a protest movement: strikers had wanted to say 'a decisive "no" to the past; "no" to the administrative command system and lack of political rights; "no" to arbitrariness and an extraordinarily contemptuous attitude to workers; "no" to empty counters, low pay, poverty'. It defined the Confederation's most urgent task as the 'abolition in fact of the *diktat* of the CPSU and its *apparat'*.[22] The Confederation was thus intended to play a political as well as an economic role[23] but the organization remained weak as workers from other industries failed to join it in significant numbers. What 1989 and 1990 had seen was the development of a radical miners' movement but this was not accompanied by the emergence of similar movements in other sectors of the economy – in engineering, in the oil, steel, metallurgical or chemical industries and among white-collar workers. Hence, the miners were relatively isolated and they were to find support for their increasingly radical demands hesitant.

The lack of broad support for the miners and the failure of other workers to develop analogous structures has not yet been thoroughly investigated. Among the factors which might be cited, however, are the very circumstances which might have been expected to radicalize the workers: declining living standards and growing instability.

21 See Krotov *et al.*, *Rossiya* (1991), I, 1, pp. 56–7.
22 Koval' (ed.), *Rossiya* (1991), pp. 364–8; see also V. Kuznetsova, *Moskovsky Komsomolets*, 1 May 1990, p. 2.
23 Rutland, 'Labour' in Hewett and Winston (eds), *Milestones* (1991), pp. 310–11; Koval' (ed.), *Rossiya* (1991), p. 321.

Opinion polls through 1990 and 1991 showed the public's increasing preoccupation with both of these problems.[24] Political instability – the breakup of the Union and the breakdown of the old command administrative system – threatened people's jobs and livelihood. Under the new economic policies that emphasized efficiency, few workers were unaware of the threat of redundancy. Fear of unemployment was particularly inhibiting in a society hitherto unfamiliar with the phenomenon and which had elaborated no means of dealing with or alleviating it. Disorder was unfamiliar and experienced as threatening. Hence the widespread reluctance to embark on its novel incarnation – the strike. In addition, Soviet workers were unprotected during the strike: independent unions hardly existed and strikers, forgoing their normal wage, could not expect to receive significant aid. People therefore did not have the resources to go on strike for long.

A further disincentive was the perception that strikes were futile. The miners, in a key and powerful sector of the economy, had managed to wring substantial concessions from the government (causing some resentment, as it was felt that deprived workers in less sensitive areas of the economy had paid for them) but these benefits – to the extent that they had materialized – had been eroded by inflation. The government had manifestly bought an agreement with the miners and then managed to avoid honouring it. If the miners – whose work actually had an important impact on the economy – were unable to extract binding concessions from the government, what could workers in strategically insignificant or economically inefficient enterprises hope to achieve? Hence, the passivity of workers in other sectors, their failure to develop independent union structures or to support the miners significantly, does not necessarily mean that there was no sympathy for the miners and their radical demands, but simply that where such sympathy existed, its expression was inhibited by poverty and insecurity.

However, there were other factors complicating the emergence of a united and independent labour movement. One was the fact that the working class was united neither in its interests nor in its composition. Levels of education, differences in professional and sectoral occupation and in geographical location created quite

24 See for example Yu. Levada in *MN*, 1991, no. 38, p. 5.

significant divergences in levels of pay, bonuses, privileges and lifestyle, which themselves led to divergent interests. Skilled workers and technicians were likely to have a different outlook from unskilled labourers and the very large numbers of migrant manual workers. Workers in the defence industries had a vested interest in maintaining the status quo, with its high military expenditure; those employed in the energy sector, who could appreciate the international market value of their product and its importance to the national economy, were likely to favour economic reform and to be in a position to express their views; workers in light industry, which had always been underfunded, might favour change but lacked industrial muscle. The 1990 election results suggest that there was support for as broad a range of political views among Russia's industrial workers as among society at large.[25] In these circumstances, the likelihood of being able to challenge the government successfully in a protracted political strike was slight.

The inherent difficulties of the independent labour movement were compounded by the vulnerability of the broad democratic movement from Autumn 1990 on, when the CPSU hardliners regained control of the USSR government and adopted repressive policies. The battle of the central and republican parliaments tended to isolate many leading democratic politicians in the theatre of high politics, drawing them into an elaborate, largely rhetorical battle, which they lacked the resources to win. As a result, the leaders of the independent unions were to find themselves dealing with politicians, absorbed in tactical manoeuvres, rather than with popular tribunes. Hence, the sort of alliance that took place in Poland with Solidarity failed to materialize in Russia.

The last great strike before the coup was to illustrate these problems. By January 1991, the concessions the miners had won in 1989 were worthless. Inflation had eroded the value of pay increases and the Pavlov government had announced its intention of introducing further price rises. Food supplies had not improved: in Vorkuta most staple foods were still rationed and shortages were the norm in the Donbass and Kuzbass. Although the price of coal had been trebled at the start of January 1991, wages had not been increased and miners, in common with everyone else in the country, found their standard of

25 See also Koval' (ed.), *Rossiya* (1991), p. 323.

living declining sharply. Finally, the miners had not been granted economic independence but worked to specifications set by the USSR Ministry of Coal.

At first, the reaction to this was to demand pay increases in the order of 100-150 per cent. The Kuzbass demanded improved food supplies.[26] The now more resolute authorities rejected these demands and the miners were forced to strike. The hardline attitude of Gorbachev and Prime Minister Pavlov's USSR government prompted the miners to look to Yeltsin and the Russian parliament for salvation. They called for the abolition of the USSR Congress of People's Deputies, for Gorbachev's resignation and for the transfer of power to the Russian parliament.[27] The central government sat back and waited. It knew that the miners' resources were limited and that the success of the strike depended on its spreading to other sectors. *Izvestiya* calculated that some 280-300 000 miners were out.[28] None the less, the miners were conscious of their vulnerability and attempted to forge alliances with workers in other sectors, at first without significant success. As the strike wore on, despite help with food from the Baltic region and financial contributions from the public, the miners felt isolated. 'Other regions and other industries have failed to give us their support', one Kuzbass strike committee member declared bitterly.[29] Expressions of sympathy from steel and engineering workers were not enough. 'This is our last strike', said a leader of the independent miners' union. 'If we fail to get support today, there will be no other chance to rise from our knees.'[30]

Support, at first so sparse, eventually began to be expressed as the strike dragged into April and as Pavlov introduced big price increases. West Siberian metal workers staged a five-day sympathy strike. Copper and nickel plants in Norilsk struck for a day, as did several mines in Severouralsk and Soligursk.[31] Major enterprises in Minsk came out to express solidarity with the labour and democratic movements in Russia and advanced political demands of their own.[32]

---

26 V. Radzievsky in *MN*, 1991, no. 12, p. 5; V. Kiselev in *MN*, 1991, no. 8, p. 6.
27 Radzievsky in *MN*, 1991, no. 12, p. 5.
28 Koval' (ed.), *Rossiya* (1991), p. 383; Kiselev in *MN*, 1991, no. 14, p. 7.
29 Radzievsky in *MN*, 1991, no. 12, p. 5.
30 Kiselev in *MN*, 1991, no. 14, p. 7.
31 Radzievsky in *MN*, 1990, no. 15, p. 6.
32 A. Adamovich in *MN*, 1991, no. 16, p. 13; V. Glod in *MN*, 1991, no. 16, p. 13.

Workers and students proclaimed a three-day strike in Kiev.[33] But it was now too late. The miners' resources were exhausted and they knew they had failed. They had hoped to provoke a general strike in support of their political demands but for six weeks nothing had happened. These brief gestures of token support did not change the balance of power. Furthermore, the miners were becoming inconvenient to Yeltsin, as Gorbachev began to move back towards a reformist course. On 24 April 1991, Yeltsin and Gorbachev signed the Novo-Ogarevo Agreement which, it was hoped, would put an end to the constitutional crisis and growing economic and political chaos, by negotiating a new set of relationships between the centre and the republics. With this as the prize, Yeltsin was ready to abandon the miners, whose support had been so timely just a month earlier. The Agreement therefore exhorted miners to return to work and condemned 'attempts to attain political goals by [...] strikes or by calls to overthrow the existing and legitimately elected organs of state power.' Yeltsin attempted to justify the agreement, pointing to his success in getting the mines transferred to Russian jurisdiction.[34] But this was not what the miners had fought for; they felt betrayed and the spirit went out of the strike movement. By mid-May, the strike was over.

Not only had the miners failed in their main demands, but they had been abandoned and condemned by their preferred leader and they had been shown to be isolated. Their attempts to develop a wider labour movement, with political influence, had also foundered. Even in 1990, the Union of Kuzbass Workers could count on only a few thousand activists[35] and there was a considerable gap between their level of politicization and that of ordinary miners. The glue which initially held the movement together and which helped to gather support for the increasingly anti-communist orientation of the independent miners was, in the view of the editor of *Rossiya segodnya*, a widespread anti-*apparat* feeling, which transcended political preferences.[36] By 1991, the miners had succeeded – thanks to the deepening crisis – in transforming this anti-*apparat* sentiment into

33 T. Menshikova in *MN*, 1991, no. 17, p. 5.
34 Cited in Morrison, *Yeltsin* (1991), pp. 254–6.
35 Pribylovsky, *Slovar'* (1991), p. 95.
36 Koval' (ed.), *Rossiya* (1991), p. 324.

active anti-communism, but because it was not strongly enough supported or shared with the same degree of conviction by other industrial workers, it was shown to be politically ineffective. The strikes of March–April 1991 revealed both the weaknesses of the new labour movement and the ambiguity or reticence of wider public opinion.

POPULAR SUPPORT FOR DEMOCRACY

The 1989 Vote

Before the Nineteenth Party Conference in June 1988, Soviet citizens were reluctant to commit themselves to democratic principles. A poll conducted early in 1988 revealed that the principle of competitive elections was rejected by a majority of respondents and that only a small minority (7.7 per cent) felt that the soviets (or old undemocratic parliaments) were in need of reform.[37] Given the results of subsequent polls endorsing democracy, should we conclude that a dramatic change in outlook took place in the next two years? The problem with opinion polls, at least until the Nineteenth Party Conference, was that people were reserved about expressing their real views, particularly on sensitive ideological issues. Few people would have been ready to anticipate the Party's own brave new policy departures. One of the effects of Stalinism was that revolution, in the Soviet Union, had come – at least initially – from above: experience counselled ordinary citizens to be cautious. The supposition that people did not respond entirely honestly to polls enables us to explain the sudden appearance of a majority in favour of democratic change in June 1988, in the changed atmosphere leading up to the Party Conference. A poll of 1927 persons throughout the USSR showed a majority (56 per cent) in favour of reform of the system of soviets while 72 per cent of electors believed that reforms guaranteeing full popular sovereignty should be introduced.[38]

The 1989 election results appeared to confirm that the country was moving away from its authoritarian past. The stunning defeats of

37 Cited in Urban, *Soviets* (1990), p. 43.
38 *Izvestiya*, 26 June 1988, p. 2.

higher Party officials in the 1989 elections were seen, at the time, as a vote for democracy and they inspired the democratic and liberal intelligentsia to press for further change. In retrospect, however, the meaning of the vote seems more ambiguous: what appeared to be an endorsement of democracy can also be seen as a protest vote – the rejection of the Party *apparat*, its incompetence and corruption – rather than an ideological vote (or rejection of Communist ideology). As we have seen, most candidates in the 1989 and 1990 elections were Party members: in 1989, they were not organized into blocs or factions and their programmes, while sometimes vague and parochial, were generally socialist and egalitarian in conception. Hence, the electorate in 1989 was not offered a choice between coherent alternative policies or even overtly divergent ideological orientations. As a result, the electorate voted for individuals and what they thought they represented, rather than for a clearly stated set of policies and ideas. As many as 40 per cent of the electorate voted on the basis of campaign speeches and platforms but more (54 per cent) voted for candidates on the basis of their earlier authority and achievements.[39] A substantial minority of Muscovites, according to a *Moscow News* poll of 25 March 1989, could remember nothing about the candidates (28 per cent) or about their programmes (26 per cent): again, 40 per cent of the electorate could name one or more candidates and were conversant with some of their proposals.[40] This suggests that a substantial proportion of the population remained alienated from political life and that formal political debate was not the key factor influencing the majority vote (the 60 per cent unfamiliar with candidates' platforms).

In these circumstances, the alternative facing the electorate was either to endorse or to reject the Party leaders who offered themselves for election. In many areas of the country – mainly in the large cities of European Russia and Western Siberia – voters chose to reject the Party *apparat*.[41] Indeed, in some cases, the Party's support proved to be positively unhelpful. When the Party *apparat* decided to back the liberal independent G.I. Filshin's campaign in Irkutsk, he almost lost the election.[42] Some poll analysts concluded that the population's 'no'

39　N. Popov in *Izvestiya*, 22 April 1989.
40　A. Romanov in *MN*, 1989, no. 20, p. 9.
41　V. Komarovsky and A. Usol'tser in *AiF*, 1989, no. 22, p. 5.
42　Yu. Golik, 'Deputat' in Vyshinsky (ed.), *Pravo i vlast'* (1990), p. 255.

vote was directed not so much against a single candidate as against the entire style of work of the local Party.[43] The deputy Yu. Golik was told by many Muscovites that they had voted not for Yeltsin but against the *apparat*'s *diktat*.[44]

Popular Concerns

If the population voted primarily against the Party *apparat*, rather than against the reigning ideology, this should be reflected in their priorities and concerns. Do the polls indicate that ideological principle was overshadowed by pragmatic considerations among the population at large? According to Michael Urban, readers' letters addressed to *Izvestiya* suggest that the main issues in the 1989 campaign were social justice and an end to the Party's special privileges.[45] A poll of 200 000 *Moscow News* readers indicated that people were more concerned with economic than with political reform: 71 per cent of those who replied wanted military expenditure to be reduced; 75 per cent were preoccupied by the need for adequate food and consumer goods' supplies; 67 per cent favoured the reintroduction of private farming; and 64.5 per cent an end to the 'bosses'' privileges. Basic political and social freedoms were accorded less importance: freedom of expression (demanded by 54 per cent), freedom to travel abroad (38 per cent), and the abolition of the internal passport system and residence rules (36 per cent), came lower in the list of priorities.[46] An earlier poll of 800 *Moscow News* readers – who may be taken to represent a relatively liberal constituency – confirmed this bias towards practical rather than ideological questions. While 81 per cent of those polled thought the pace of *perestroika* too slow, few seem to have felt inhibited by restrictions on their individual liberty and most were concerned primarily with economic reform. Only 18 per cent felt legally defenceless or deprived of full human rights; even fewer (5 per cent) felt *glasnost* to be inadequate or thought that Party interference, the lack of a formal opposition and the one-party state to be a problem (6 per cent). Whereas 41 per cent felt food supplies to

43 Komarosvky and Dugin in *Izvestiya*, 12 May 1989.
44 Golik, 'Deputat' in Vyshinsky (ed.), *Pravo* (1990), p. 255.
45 Urban, *Soviets* (1990), p. 121, n. 116.
46 Levada in *MN*, 1989, no. 13, p. 9.

be the most urgent problem, followed by consumer goods and housing shortages (39 per cent), prices and inflation (22 per cent), political problems figured less prominently on their list of urgent concerns. True, 39 per cent of those polled considered full democracy and the observance of human rights to be desirable; however, only 8 per cent listed constitutional and political reform, the introduction of political pluralism, support for *glasnost* and a press law and 5 per cent de-Stalinization as being among the most urgent problems facing the country.[47] In other words, while people considered problems of political constitution to be generally important, they appear not to have felt immediately affected by the lack of legal guarantees or to have accorded priority to the introduction and implementation of precise political reforms.

Subsequent polls were to confirm the growing importance accorded to practical, material problems, especially as the euphoria of the 1989 and 1990 elections wore off. A poll of country and town residents showed that, whereas people had always been concerned by the poor quality and supplies of food and consumer goods, by the late 1980s these, with inflation, became overwhelming concerns: 59 per cent of town dwellers and 52 per cent of country people were worried about food supplies in 1985–86, but in 1989 these problems worried 84 per cent of townspeople and 81 per cent of country people; inflation, which preoccupied only 37 per cent of urban inhabitants and 36 per cent of rural residents in 1985–86, concerned 80 per cent and 81 per cent respectively in 1989.[48] The slide into disorder and chaos witnessed in the early 1990s, however, made the concerns of the late 1980s look comparatively insignificant; instead of the personal calamities which had most worried people in 1989, crime, anarchy, civil war and unemployment figured high among the worries of Russians in Spring 1992.[49] By then, interest in political reform had almost completely disappeared from the list of popular concerns, being replaced by scepticism and weariness.[50] The constituency which favoured profound political reform rarely seems to have exceeded

47 V. Tretyakov in *MN*, 1989, no. 8, p. 10.
48 *AiF*, 1990, no. 20, p. 4.
49 *NG*, 26 March 1992, p. 2; similar finding by Levada in *MN*, 1992, no. 10, p. 16.
50 Trust in the political leadership had decreased, 70 per cent believed, while only 12 per cent of those polled were ready to pledge full support: Levada in *MN*, 1992, no. 10, p. 16.

about 40 per cent of the public. Several polls, over a period of months, suggest that the hard core of support for constitutional reform fluctuated around this figure.[51] Support for the introduction of a multiparty system seems to have peaked at around 50–56 per cent on the eve of the March 1990 elections.[52]

Social Background and Opinion

A substantial minority of the population, however, remained detached from political life. Passivity and caution were characteristic of a significant minority of the overall population. Thirty-four per cent of those who participated in election meetings in 1989 are thought to have voted according to the Party's instructions, not according to their convictions.[53] Young people, in particular, showed surprisingly little interest in democratic politics. In 1989 *Moscow News* conducted a poll of young people aged between 18 and 30. It discovered that, while 62 per cent of them intended to vote, only a small majority (40 per cent) approved of the new electoral system, while 31 per cent could see no difference in it, 16 per cent did not care about it and 10

51 See Komarovsky and Usol'tser in *AiF*, 1989, no. 22, p. 5. Forty per cent of the electorate believed the Party exercised undue influence and pressure on the campaign. In Moscow, 37 per cent of the electorate were most impressed by the informals' campaign (as opposed to 16 per cent in the country at large). Forty-five per cent of respondents of a poll published in *Izvestiya* in mid-1988 wanted the soviets turned into something like a parliament: *Izvestiya*, 16 June 1988, p. 2. Thirty-nine per cent of *MN* readers in 1989 attached primordial importance to full democratization and respect for human rights, while a slightly larger percentage favoured closer supervision of the security organs: Tretyakov in *MN*, 1989, no. 8, p. 10. This also corresponded to the level of political consciousness in society in general. Forty per cent of the electorate voted for candidates on the basis of their platforms and speeches: Popov in *Izvestiya*, 22 April 1989. Forty per cent also could name one or more candidates and remembered something about their platforms: Romanov in *MN*, 1989, no. 20, p. 9. Popov estimated that support for capitalism and multiparty system ranged, in September 1989, from 25 to 30 per cent; supporters of the reform Party leaders and of *perestroika* accounted for another 25–30 per cent; mild economic reform, in line with what had been proposed in the 1960s, won the support of 10–15 per cent; about 25 per cent of the population favoured the status quo or the policy of 'acceleration': see Popov, 'Narod' in Protashchik (ed.), *Cherez Ternii* (1990), p. 784.
52 Sakwa, *Gorbachev* (1990), p. 183, cites a poll conducted by Zaslavskaya's institute which put support for the abolition of Article 6 at almost 50 per cent of the population. Vera Tolz estimates supports for the IRG to have stood at about 56 per cent of the electorate on the eve of the 1990 elections: Tolz, *Multi-Party System* (1990), p. 43.
53 Levansky *et al.* in *AiF*, 1989, no. 10, p. 2.

per cent were undecided.[54] More conclusive evidence about young people's indifference to politics was adduced by sociologists. In 1989, a poll showed that while 17.5 per cent of young people had a keen interest in politics, 28.2 per cent had no interest at all. The sociologist Borovik concluded that young people were unengaged and uninterested in politics and did not generally discuss it with their friends. Such political convictions as they acquired at school soon disappeared, when they were freed of the constraints of that institution.[55] This lack of clear political preference was noted also by M. Topalov, who agreed that young people's level of political involvement and organization was minimal.[56] Even those who were active enough to become involved in the informal movement were chary of politics. According to a poll published in *Argumenty i fakty* in early 1988, the informal organizations of the young were concerned above all with the quality of available goods (66 per cent), accommodation (51 per cent) and living standards (50 per cent). Formal political problems interested them to a lesser extent: 28.2 per cent wanted to see more democracy – fewer than were concerned about founding a family (28.8 per cent).[57] One of the surprising features of the 'second Russian revolution', then, was the fact that young people played such an insignificant role in it, whether in inspiring, leading or supporting it. The Russian revolution was a revolution of the middle-aged.

The polls also revealed how far involvement and interest in the country's new political life extended in society, both professionally and geographically. According to a poll of March 1989, those most active in the election campaign were administrators and directors, while the least active were employed in less prestigious positions in commerce and education. Members of the CPSU were more involved than non-Party members,[58] while they furnished over 80 per cent of candidates and, ultimately, of deputies. A poll of 1990 suggested that the scientific and technical intelligentsia and entrepreneurs provided the backbone of support for liberal-democratic reforms. Manual workers in heavy industry – except those radicalized by the strikes of 1989 – had right-wing populist views, being attached to the

54 *MN*, 1989, no. 13.
55 V. Borovik, 'Sotsial'nye mekhanizmy' (1990), pp. 37, 40–46.
56 M. Topalov,'"Formal'naya"' in Levichev (ed.), *Neformal'naya volna* (1990), p. 159.
57 Cited in V. Kozbanenko, *Komsomol* (Rostov, 1989), p. 27.
58 Levansky in *AiF*, 1989, no. 10, p. 2.

maintenance of the social security system and price controls and hostile to the bureaucracy and the intelligentsia.[59] The intelligentsia, especially in the big cities of European Russia – although to a lesser extent in smaller provincial towns – held generally more liberal political views than manual workers (favouring the abolition of Article 6 of the Constitution and the introduction of a multiparty system) and the level of distrust between the two was significant.[60] In July 1989, Tatyana Zaslavskaya's institute found that support for the Soviet parliament (the All-Union Congress of People's Deputies) as a useful reform forum – an indicator of relative conservatism – was highest among older people (63 per cent in favour as opposed to 17 per cent critically disposed) and manual workers (51 per cent in favour and 25 per cent against) while more highly educated and qualified people were more critical of it.[61]

Geography of Radicalism

The degree of support for reform was not uniform throughout Russia and the Soviet Union. The Baltic republics, particularly Estonia, were in the vanguard of political reform, reflecting their imperfect and late assimilation into the Soviet empire and their traditional European and Hanseatic connections and outlook. In general, areas incorporated into the USSR only after the Second World War – the Baltics, the Western Ukraine and Moldavia – were quicker than the rest of the state to react to the new freedoms of the Gorbachev era, demanding greater economic autonomy and then political and national liberty. The memory of previous prosperity and of subsequent annexation and terror was sustained by Moscow's discriminatory colonial policies and provoked bitter resentment, which quickly was translated into political radicalism. In the Caucasus, both the legacy of bitterness caused by Stalin's deportations of entire ethnic groups that traditionally

---

59 Merridale, 'Pluralism' in Merridale and Ward (eds), *Perestroika* (1991), p. 22.
60 For divergences between the outlook of the intelligentsia and the working class, especially on political issues, and mutual distrust, see L. Semenova, 'Politicheskoe soznanie intelligentsii' in V. Mansurov *et al.* (eds), *Intelligentsiya i perestroika* (1991), pp. 17–20. See also Mansurov (ed.), *Intelligentsiya o sotsial'no-politicheskoi situatsii* (1990), pp. 29–56, for indications of the conservative instincts of the provincial intelligentsia especially schoolteachers and functionaries.
61 T. Zaslavskaya and Ya. Kapelyush in *AiF*, 1989, no. 26, p. 1.

inhabited the region, and the conflict between the Azeris and Armenians helped to alienate and radicalize whole nations. Both the relatively prosperous Georgians and the cosmopolitan, Western-orientated Armenians were on the left of the Soviet political spectrum in the late 1980s, supporting democratic reforms.[62]

The situation in Russia proper was more patchy. Moscow was the capital of the democratic movement, followed by Leningrad and Sverdlovsk. While the mining and industrial cities of Western Siberia generally supported the democrats, many of the smaller provincial towns of European Russia and of Eastern Siberia were more conservative in outlook[63] - reflecting their social composition, the Party's greater effective power in these areas and the provinces' resentment of the centre,[64] and their feeling of deprivation and humiliation which fuelled nascent Russian nationalism. Eighty per cent of the inhabitants of Gorky thought that the Congress was democratically minded; 50 per cent of those living in Siberian cities were pleased with the composition of the Supreme Soviet (so criticized by Afanasiev) while only 30 per cent of Muscovites and of the inhabitants of Riga were satisfied with it. Tallinn was the most radical city in the Union, according to this poll,[65] while the following week it was joined by Tbilisi, Moscow and Leningrad in leading democratic opinion.[66] The countryside - where the *apparat*'s control was largely undiminished - was more conservative than the towns. The Academy of Social Sciences polled 1100 town and country residents in June 1989 and found that support for the transfer of power from the Party to the new parliament was weakest in the countryside and strongest in the cities: while 66 per cent of city dwellers favoured the transfer of all power to the Congress, only 57 per cent of townspeople and 53 per cent of villages supported this proposal. Conversely, only 10 per cent of city residents wanted power to be vested in the Party and State machine, while 12 per cent of

---

62 V. Mansurov in *AiF*, 1989, no. 23, p. 1; Shchepotkin and Karpenko, *Proryv* (1990), pp. 120, 150–51; Yadov in *AiF*, 1989, no. 22, pp. 1–3.

63 See *Intelligentsiya o sotsial'no-politicheskoi situatsii* (1990), pp. 29–56.

64 See Sakharov, *Trevoga i nadezhda* (1991), p. 285, who points to the Moscow delegation's failure to reckon with provincial resentment of Moscow, in their attempts to attract support in the first session of the Congress.

65 Yadov in *AiF*, 1989, no. 22, pp. 1–3.

66 Mansurov in *AiF*, 1989, no. 23, p. 1. See also Shchepotkin and Karpenko, *Proryv* (1990), pp. 120, 150–51, for similar trends.

townspeople and 18 per cent of villagers were ready to accept this arrangement.[67] This pattern of political radicalism was evident again in a poll of mid-July 1989: only 45 per cent of townspeople approved of the composition of the Supreme Soviet, while 63 per cent of country people approved of it.[68]

This overall pattern had not changed significantly the following year. An attempt to gauge the political temperature of Russia, by analysing the voting patterns of deputies to the Russian parliament, revealed a similar picture. Moscow, Leningrad and, surprisingly, Magadan province were strongly democratic, followed by Western Siberia and the extreme Far East. Eastern Siberia (east of the coalfields and industrial centres of Krasnoyarsk and Norilsk) was broadly conservative, as was the Muslim south and east of European Russia and its borderlands; the north-west of Russia (where the military and industrial complex was strong) and the agricultural steppes of the south and north Caucasus were conservative, while the Volga and Don basins and North Central Russia were broadly democratic.[69]

While Russia's political geography was still in flux, certain characteristics and trends can be identified: the relative political conservatism of the countryside and of the smaller towns; the leading role in the democratic movement of the capitals of European Russia and of western Siberia; the relative conservatism of Muslim populations and the radicalism of the non-Russian European, Armenian and Georgian nationalities. It has been suggested that conventional chronology does not apply to Russia and that several different historical periods or stages of development coincide within contemporary Russia; in the Russian countryside and provinces, the historical clock was far behind Moscow time.

Hence, although 1989–90 witnessed an explosion of democratic feeling in Russia, it was neither consistent nor evenly spread. Large tracts of the country appeared to be largely untouched by the revolution taking place in the big cities of European Russia. Even within the cities, considerable numbers of people looked on events with detachment or even scepticism: it was the middle-aged

67 Ya. Kapelyush and Kinsbursky in *MN*, 29 July 1989, p. 10.
68 Zaslavskaya and Kapelyush in *AiF*, 1989, no. 26, p. 1.
69 D. Yuriev and A. Sobyanin in *AiF*, 1990, no. 37, p. 4.

intelligentsia, rather than the young or the poor, who made the revolution of the late 1980s. Many of those who supported democratic candidates were primarily concerned with the practical problems of everyday life, to which the democrats seemed more attentive than the *apparat*.

Fear of Reform

By mid-1990, faith in old verities and authorities was declining, while commitment to new values and new authorities was slow in developing. The prestige of the Communist Party among the public was disappearing. The Twenty-Eighth Party Congress competed for public attention with sessions of the Russian parliament and few believed that the Congress – once the principal event in the country's political life, determining Party and State policy for the following five years – would have a significant impact on the country.[70] Only 15 per cent of the population hoped their grandchildren would become Party members (while 54 per cent hoped they would not). Attitudes to the government and pillars of the old order were consistently negative: 64 per cent of those polled were critical of Gorbachev; 63 per cent had a critical attitude to both the army and the KGB; even more, 75 per cent, were critical of the government.[71] This rejection of the old leaders should have translated into support for the democrats. In Spring 1990, it seems that it did: in the local and republican elections of March 1990, the democrats won approximately one-third of the vote in all Russia and majorities in Moscow and Leningrad.[72]

However, sociologists distinguished a wide range of political views among the public. A survey of 900 Muscovites conducted early in 1990 identified six main trends:

- Westernizers (with 15 per cent support) who favoured the American model of political and economic freedoms;
- left populists (17 per cent) who wanted a modified and more humane form of

70 Twenty-four per cent of the population believed it would play an important role; only four years earlier no one would have disputed its significance.
71 Academy of Social Sciences' poll of 1486 citizens from 24 cities and 12 regions of the USSR: V. Nikitina in *MN*, 27 July 1990, p. 7. A similar trend was noted in a confidential poll prepared for the Party by the Academy of Social Sciences in late October and early November 1990: see 'Tri Dnya', *Postfaktum* (1991), pp. 68-9.
72 *MN*, 1990, no. 12, p. 4.

socialism but who had reservations about rigorous market reform of the economy;

- right populists (25 per cent) who courted the working class and were anti-bureaucratic, anti-intelligentsia and critical of the political elite for its corruption;
- imperialists (*gosudarstvenniki*) (27 per cent) who wanted to maintain a powerful military state, based on strict public order and discipline;
- ecologists and pacifists;
- national patriots (5 per cent) who were concerned with fighting off foreign and 'cosmopolitan' influences and with developing Russia's separate identity (*samobytnost*).[73]

This diversity testified to the growing sophistication and openness of society. At the same time, the sociologists found that right-wing views (those associated with the right populists and supporters of the strong state) predominated, with 57 per cent in support, as opposed to 32 per cent for radical democratic positions.

The democrats' appeal was undermined by two factors: firstly, by their premature promotion to political office and reponsibility, at a time when they were not effectively marshalled under ideological and organizational disciplines; and secondly, by the country's slow slide into chaos, which increased popular fear of change, and the conservatism of much of the Russian electorate. After March 1990, the democrats' victories and responsibilities soon began to work against them, as they found their attempts to resolve the intractable problems of supplies and structural reform running up against the traditional passive opposition of the old *apparat*. Increasingly, it seemed that their election victories of 1990 had given them responsibility without power. It was an unpropitious formula.

Under these circumstances a growing note of scepticism began to be heard about the new authorities in public opinion polls. Even before the full impact of the crisis had made itself felt the public was sceptical about its political representatives, while having high expectations about the qualities they should have. An Academy of Social Sciences' poll of March 1990 showed that people looked for honesty, independence of outlook, a sense of equity and a high level

---

73 Byzov and Gurevich in *AiF*, 1990, no. 7, p. 6. A *Postfaktum* poll revealed, on the eve of the Twenty-Eighth Party Congress, the same cross-section of views, but identified a seventh category – the apolitical majority of the population, which they saw as fertile ground for the right populists: Merridale, 'Pluralism', in Merridale and Ward (eds), *Perestroika* (1991), p. 27.

of culture and education in their prospective deputies. However, they expressed little enthusiasm for those actually in power: 52 per cent of those polled expressed a low level of trust in the Russian Congress of People's Deputies and 69 per cent had a low opinion of Moscow City Council (*Mossoviet*).[74] By the Autumn, stories of the alleged corruption of *Mossoviet* deputies and leaders were doing the rounds in Moscow, with ordinary citizens as well as Party conservatives retailing stories of trips abroad and electronic booty acquired. It was not so much the veracity of these tales that mattered but the fact that they were recounted and often believed. A confidential Academy of Sciences' poll, conducted in late October and early November 1990 for the Party, noted the same trend of disenchantment with the reforms and with the new authorities. It found that 52 per cent had lost faith in *perestroika*, while only 29 per cent still had some degree of belief in its prospects of success. Support for newly-elected deputies was also declining. Only 26 per cent of those polled said they would vote again for their current deputy if elections were held then; 42 per cent would vote against them, while 17 per cent would not participate.[75]

Before the worst upheavals began, polls were already revealing the innate conservatism of many Russian citizens. A poll conducted in Spring 1990 showed that while there was a majority in favour of modifying existing State structures to give Russia more power, opinion was hostile to private enterprise and capitalism. While 43 per cent wanted Russia to have full economic and political independence, 35 per cent wanted the centre (the Union) to have ultimate control and 18 per cent wanted no change. A small majority (48 per cent against 45 per cent) believed, however, that Russia's economic interests should no longer be sacrificed to the Union. The priority of the interests of the Russian Federation over those of the autonomous non-Russian ethnic groups within it was affirmed by a considerable majority (57 per cent against 20 per cent). Even more looked with

---

74 V. Shtukin, *Moskovskaya pravda*, 22 June 1990. Another poll of this general period showed a low level of trust in the new institutions and political actors: forty-five per cent believed that those newly elected to office quickly forgot their electors and their cares; 31 per cent viewed the leadership as a remote elite: Popov, 'Narod' in Protashchik (ed.), *Cherez ternii* (1990), p. 777.

75 Cited in 'Tri Dnya', *Postfaktum* (1991), pp. 68–9.

disfavour on the idea of the breakup of the RSFSR into several independent republics (68 per cent against 13 per cent).

On economic matters, opinion was firmly conservative. The Russian economy should be developed through strengthening the planned economy in all sectors, according to 31 per cent of those polled; a further 36 per cent favoured the retention of the planned economy in the main sectors and developing the market economy in the services and consumer sectors. Only 28 per cent saw the future for Russia in terms of moving to the market economy. Only 8 per cent of those polled favoured abolishing the old, unreformed State enterprises: 73 per cent favoured retaining them. Similarly, 81 per cent believed that State firms operating on a cost-accounting basis should be retained in their current form or constitute the main body of firms and only 3 per cent favoured their abolition. On the other hand, 28 per cent favoured abolishing the newly-established cooperatives (while 4 per cent wanted them to become the basis of the new economy) and 24 per cent favoured the abolition of the private companies, as opposed to 7 per cent who hoped private enterprise would become the dominant sector of the economy and 51 per cent wanted no change – which in Spring 1990 meant that there should be no private enterprise.[76]

Thus concern for Russia's interests – growing Russian nationalism, not support for the transition to capitalism – was the force fuelling radical opinion in 1990, according to this evidence. These priorities also seem to have motivated a key group of deputies in the Russian parliament (notably those led by Rutskoi), who supported both the demand for Russian sovereignty and Yeltsin against the neo-Stalinist centre, in 1990 and 1991. This points to the ambiguity of popular support for democracy after 1990. The demand for Russian sovereignty and for economic reform figured in the programmes of every democratic party and were fundamental to the democratic position after Spring 1990 – but support for the first of these aims did not entail unqualified enthusiasm for the second, especially where this was taken to mean the dismantling of the command economy. Once Russian sovereignty had been established in September 1991, therefore, it did not follow that the democrats would be able to

76 'Kakim', *AiF*, 1990, no. 21, p. 4.

maintain popular support for the rest of their programme, notably, the transition to the market economy.

As early as Autumn 1990, the Academy of Social Sciences' sociologists believed that people's fears and the resilience of old attitudes, combined with the rapidly tarnished image of the democrats, could work to the CPSU's advantage: 'The population's demand for a force capable of guaranteeing social stability is becoming stronger all the time [...] This data shows that the CPSU has a real chance of gaining political rehabilitation and the strategic initiative in the fight for the people's support.' The Party was supported by 34 per cent of the population, according to their information, and this was more than any other political party could claim. The most popular opposition party was Nikolai Travkin's Democratic Party of Russia, with 15 per cent support in the population. (The Academy's sociologists did not find it necessary to comment on this extraordinary rating for a party that had existed for barely six months and whose programme had not yet been adopted.) Anxious, no doubt, to please the Party managers for whom the report was written, the sociologists pointed not to the surprising success of the little-known and newly-formed opposition parties, but to the popularity of socialism (supported by 73 per cent of those polled) and the qualification of the October revolution as 'a progressive moment'.

More worrying was the tendency to search for social enemies. 'The image of the "enemy of the people", against whom the authorities are powerless, is forming in the popular consciousness', the report noted. Sixty-one per cent saw this enemy as the corrupt administrative *apparat*; 58 per cent as those in power; 23 per cent as nationalists; and 19 per cent as criminals. This readiness to believe in a conspiracy theory was accompanied by a growing fear of poverty, chaos and crime. Fifty-seven per cent of those polled felt threatened by the economic situation and declining living standards; 41 per cent were afraid of violence and crime; 38 per cent of chaos and danger; 31 per cent feared inter-ethnic conflict; and 44 per cent were afraid of unemployment.[77] These trends in public opinion were to be confirmed by developments the following year. In August 1991, five days before the coup, the Party bulletin *Glasnost* published an opinion poll which again pointed to the conservatism of public opinion. Seventy-nine per

77 'Tri Dnya', *Postfaktum* (1991), p. 68.

cent of those polled in Russia (and 86 per cent of those in the Ukraine) wanted State control of the majority of industrial enterprises to be maintained and were unenthusiastic about the introduction of the market economy. They also expressed their readiness to accept an authoritarian regime which would restore order.[78]

An all-Russia poll conducted on the eve of the coup, in July 1991, confirmed people's weariness and disenchantment with the reforms and their fear of poverty and disorder. Forty-eight per cent of those polled named fatigue and indifference as the predominant feelings of those around them in the previous year (as opposed to 25 per cent who thought hope set the tone). People were concerned primarily with inflation (69 per cent), shortages (56 per cent), crime (28 per cent) and weak State authority (20 per cent). The political and constitutional problems that had preoccupied democratic deputies figured low on their list of concerns: the disintegration of the USSR preoccupied only 8 per cent of those polled, while 5 per cent were worried about dictatorship. On the contrary, rather than being concerned by the rise of authoritarianism, there was significant feeling in favour of it: 70 per cent agreed with the proposition that Russian salvation would come from someone who would lead the people and restore order, while only 12 per cent disagreed. Support for *perestroika* and the reforms had dwindled. Asked if they would have supported the proposed changes in 1985 had they known where they would lead, only 23 per cent said they would, while 52 per cent claimed they would not, and 25 per cent did not know. Just as support for reform was declining, so support for Yeltsin was tepid: only 29 per cent fully agreed with Yeltsin and his policies; 11 per cent were ready to support him as long as he remained a democratic leader. For more (16 per cent), he held no special appeal, while 15 per cent supported him in the absence of any other worthy candidate. He might, however, have drawn comfort from the fact that only 8 per cent outrightly opposed him.[79]

Some political scientists believe that these polls encouraged Party

78 Cited in ibid., p. 72.
79 Levada in *MN*, 1991, no. 38, p. 5. In a poll conducted in Spring 1992, 28 per cent of Russians questioned supported liberal democracy, while 49 per cent stressed the importance of order; only 26 per cent would have supported the coup leaders (on the assumption they could have kept their promises) while 54 per cent would not: A. Rubtsov in *MN*, 1992, no. 4, p. 7.

conservatives to make their move against democratic reformers on 19 August 1991.[80] The desire to prevent the dismantling of the Soviet empire and preserve the political and economic power of the centre was paramount for the plotters, just as the desire to defend the prerogatives of republican sovereignty inspired the resistance of the Russian parliament. It may be argued that the outcome of the coup proves once again that polls are not always reliable indicators of public opinion. But the majority of the inhabitants of Moscow – the most democratic city in the country – did not initially protest against the hardliners' attempt to seize power in August 1991 and were ready to come on to the streets only when the coup had failed. Who, then, defended the White House? The answer should come as no surprise – the middle-aged intellectuals manned the barriers.[81] The evidence consistently suggests that, in 1989-91, support for democratic reform among the public was neither maintained at a consistent level nor evenly spread in society or within the country, and that support for the democrats was founded less on enthusiasm for their policies and persons than on fear and rejection of their opponents – a case of the child 'keeping hold of nurse, for fear of finding something worse'. Not surprisingly, this constituency was to prove volatile, as the State and economy began to slide towards chaos after the coup.

80 'Tri Dnya', *Postfaktum*, 1991, p. 72.
81 J. Steele, *Eternal Russia* (1994), p. 75, cites a poll which indicated that 55 per cent of the defenders of the Russian parliament were aged over thirty; 69 per cent had a higher education, while blue-collar workers accounted for 19 per cent. For evidence of the public's initially cautious response to the coup and their reluctance to condemn it, see ibid., p. 76.

12. Conclusion

The democratic coalition was more complex than it seemed. Its intellectual origins lay in the anti-Stalinism and reform socialism of the Thaw rather than in classical liberal theory of the eighteenth and nineteenth centuries. Its support was based on popular disenchantment with corrupt and inefficient government rather than on wholehearted enthusiasm for liberal economic reform and the breakup of the Soviet Union, which democratic reform necessarily entailed.

The parliamentary supporters and political leaders of the democratic movement were far from being at one in their political instincts. Some were anti-communist but not anti-authoritarian, others were inspired by Western economic and political models; some were anti-Soviet but sympathetic to Russian imperialism, others wanted the Soviet Union to be replaced by a voluntary federation of sovereign States; some were committed to modernization and efficiency, others hesitated at the prospect of sweeping reform. Many had little interest in, or commitment to, the intellectual or moral ramifications of liberal and democratic reform, being moved above all by the call for economic and political decentralization, which would devolve more power to the interest groups they represented. The democratic movement was therefore not united by liberal political ideals and theories but was a coalition of divergent interest groups and outlooks, welded together by opposition to the remnants of Stalinism.

The rejection of the tempered totalitarianism of late Soviet socialism was as much a reaction against the Soviet system's inefficiencies and inequities as a repudiation in principle of the old order. Amongst the democratic leadership, anti-communism was fuelled by three not always compatible concerns. The anti-Stalinist intellectuals rejected much of the Soviet legacy and tended to draw inspiration from the political norms of the West. Dissidents such as Sakharov, and those in the intelligentsia who, like Yuri Afanasiev and

Leonid Batkin, were influenced by European thought, objected in principle to the relation in the old order between the individual and the State. They believed that the State exists for the individual and not vice versa and that the power relations between the two in the Soviet regime needed to be reversed. Others, such as Viktor Aksyuchits and some of the Slavophile dissidents, objected in principle to the relationship between the Russian nation or the Orthodox religion (or both) and the State under the *ancien régime*. Not all of them agreed, however, on how these interests were best defended or defined, with some opting for democracy and others for authoritarian solutions. Most numerous, it seems, were those who were moved by pragmatic objections to the inefficiency, the human and material waste of the old order. Many were former CPSU members who came to see the need to eject the old ruling elite in order to effect reform and modernize the country. Others, such as Rutskoi, were principally concerned with the transfer of power away from the higher echelons of the bureaucracy to the Russian Federation and ultimately themselves, and therefore supported economic and political decentralization. For many converts from the CPSU, then, the objections to the old order were often not so much moral and intellectual as practical: the effects, rather than the essence, of the old regime were abhorrent.

The differences between these schools of thought emerged more clearly after the 1991 coup. The Westernizers quickly became a beleaguered minority in the new dispensation, riven by disagreements between the old anti-Stalinist intellectuals and the young technocrats in government. The nationalists, forging alliances with their old neo-Stalinist enemies, gathered alarming strength on the right of the spectrum, while the pragmatic modernizers split into pro- and anti-Yeltsin camps. Hence, the classic confrontation between the Slavophiles and the Westernizers – initially provoked by the problems posed by modernization in Russia in the nineteenth century – has recurred in Russia's latest attempt to effect a liberal modernization.

A number of reasons may be adduced to explain why the democratic revolution remained so superficial. Firstly, it remained a revolution from above, isolated both geographically and socially. It was concentrated in the big cities: Moscow and Leningrad played a disproportionate role in its development. Much of rural and provincial Russia was untouched by the development of civil society and the new politics. The democrats' efforts to remedy this were inadequate and hampered not only by internal rivalries and distance but also by lack of imagination: they did little to address either specifically provincial and rural concerns or the problems of regional development, devoting attention instead to the rights of republics and ethnic groups outside the Russian Federation.

Not only was the democratic movement geographically isolated, it was socially isolated as well. It was launched and led by the elite and developed into a power struggle within the elite – between the reform Party leadership and the *apparat*, lower Party officials and economic managers, the creative and lower academic intelligentsia. Middle-aged intellectuals played a disproportionate role in the popular democratic movement, while blue-collar workers, women, the young and country people were hardly involved. Thus, as it developed and broke away from the Party's tutelage, the democratic movement was unrepresentative of the population at large.

The effects of this were exacerbated by the divisive nature of the democratic agenda. Economically, the transition to a market economy, advocated by the democrats, threatened mass unemployment, impoverishment and upheaval. The public remained broadly unconvinced by assurances that the transition could be effected painlessly and were consistently reserved about the introduction of capitalism. Only Yeltsin overcame the difficulties inherent in the democratic agenda, and this was due to the fact that his vote was based largely on personal popularity and because he evaded difficult questions.

Politically, too, the democrats' reform programme was divisive: in insisting that Stalinism should be rejected and condemned, they threatened to expose past and recent crimes (which, given the complicity of much of the population, alienated a large constituency). In addition, dismantling the Stalinist system entailed destroying the Stalinist empire: this undermined Russian State power and prestige and threatened the livelihood and security of thousands of Russians living outside the Russian Federation. In short, the entire liberal democratic agenda – and not merely the parts of its programme which called for repentance – opened old wounds, reviving past traumas as well as inflicting new ones. Not only could this programme not hope to be widely popular (it is surprising that it attracted as much support as it did), it tended to divide public opinion, to exacerbate the effects of Stalinism's fragmentation of society, rather than to create the sense of common identity, shared purpose and solidarity which – initially at least – the democratic movements in the Baltic republics and Armenia achieved, and on which they based their success.

Popular support for the democrats was thus limited and ambiguous. It was inhibited not only by a divisive, often unappealing and sometimes irrelevant agenda, by the remoteness of the democratic leadership and by physical constraints, but by other factors too. Much early support for the democrats (notably in the 1989 and 1990 elections) was based not on enthusiasm for democratic policies but on hostility to the *apparat*: the democrats benefited from a protest vote against poor living and working conditions, corruption and the abuse of power. Where the democrats assumed office, they were associated with the rapidly developing economic crisis and the collapse of State power, so that disenchantment with their programme soon set in. A final factor undermining popular support for and involvement in the new political structures was the crisis itself; people were too busy coping with its impact on their daily lives to have time or energy (even had they cherished the desire) to expend on political activism.

The influence of liberal democracy failed to grow in Russia after the coup not because it was generally repudiated but because the new government's interpretation of it intensified, rather than remedied, the economic crisis, while threatening vested interests and thus provoking further political conflict. Throughout its history, the democratic movement was a coalition of interest groups and individuals, with different, sometimes divergent political preferences; classical political liberalism was only one strand of thought within it. When the democrats finally came to power in Autumn 1991, they no longer preached the humanitarian liberalism of the anti-Stalinist intelligentsia but a technocratic, economic liberalism, which had little to offer the Russian people in the short term. In formulation and implementation, it did little to strengthen democratic rule in Russia, especially as it was not part of a coherent plan of legal, administrative and political reform. The democrats' prestige was undermined not only by the narrow and controversial conception of reform but also by the isolation and weakness of the government: power lay not with ministers but with the president and his team, while the parliament was hostile to a government which was neither responsible to it nor pursuing policies it approved of.

The political character of the new Russia was ultimately determined neither by the liberal intelligentsia nor by their heirs in the Russian government after 1991, nor even by the resurgent people, but by the professional politicians: Yeltsin and his advisers and the managers and officials in the Russian parliament, who were mostly drawn from the lower echelons of the old *nomenklatura*. The strength of their representation in the political institutions and in the highest echelons of power meant that the political culture of the old Party elite (with its clans, intrigues, caution and corruption, secrecy and authoritarianism) survived in the political life of Russia after the 1991 coup. The very dilemmas of the Russian government exemplify this: its technocratic approach and political weakness fitted the concept of subservient, almost apolitical government (in which ministers had been high civil servants with technical expertise) with which Yeltsin and most high Party officials had been familiar from the Soviet system. The new departure was less radical than many expected when Dzerzhinsky's statue was toppled in August 1991.

It is not necessary, therefore, to postulate a unique Eurasian culture or collectivist authoritarian mentality to explain why popular democratic parties failed to develop and the first democratic administrations lost support. It is enough to point to Russia's practical historical circumstances and the policies, programmes and character of the democratic movement itself. All countries and cultures are unique: but such has been the emphasis on Russia's singularity that we too often forget the points of similarity with other countries. Before dismissing modern Russia's democratic experiment, we should remember that it took France one hundred and fifty years to digest its great revolution and the Napoleonic adventure and to emerge as a fully and unequivocally democratic State. Russia too needs time not merely to establish its economic and political forms, but also to develop a sense of shared identity, of the common purpose and values, if it is to overcome the tragedies of the Soviet period and the traumas attendant upon the advent of democracy.

Bibliography

In addition to the works cited below, I have also referred to material found in the archive of the Moscow Bureau for Information Exchange, directed by Vyacheslav Igrunov. It contains an invaluable collection of material relating to the informal movement in Moscow in the late 1980s and early 1990s.

A.P. (1989), 'Shield – Informals and the Army', *MN* (44), 29 October.

Adamovich, Ales (1987), 'Yesli ne my, to kto zhe?', *SK*, 10 December.

—— (1988), 'Vospominanie o budushchem' in Yu. Afanasiev (ed.), *Inogo ne dano*, pp. 270–74.

—— (1990), 'Look about you' in V. Korotich and C. Porter (eds), *The Best of Ogonek*, pp. 7–14.

—— (1991), 'Byelorussians have had enough', *MN* (16), 21 April.

—— (1991), *My shestidesyatniki*, Moscow.

Afanasiev, V. G. (1987), 'Na pul'se perestroiki: shestoi s"yezd soyuza zhurnalistov SSSR', *SK*, 17 March.

Afanasiev, Yuri (ed.) (1988), *Inogo ne dano*, Moscow: Progress.

—— (1989), 'Memorial adopts its charter', *MN* (6), 5 February.

—— (1990), 'O pervykh shagakh sotsial-demokratii v SSSR', *Respublika* (3).

—— (1991), *Ya dolzhen eto skazat'*, Moscow: PIK.

—— (1991), 'The Coming Dictatorship', *New York Review of Books*, 31 January, pp. 36–9.

—— (1992), 'Vlast' i obshchestvo', *MN* (10), 8 March.

——, Yu. Burtin, M. Salie *et al.* (1992), 'Demokraticheskaya Rossiya: byt' ili ne byt'', *Dvizhenie Demokraticheskaya Rossiya* (12), February.

Agursky, Mikhail (1980), *Ideologiya natsional-bolshevisma*, Paris: YCMA Press.

Aitmatov, Chingiz (1988), *The Time to Speak Out*, Moscow: Progress.

Aksyuchits, Viktor (1990), 'Russia's Christian Democrats', *MN* (21), 3 June.

Albats, E. (1989), 'The Independent Press', *MN* (38), 17 September.

Alekseev, A. (1989), 'Nesvoevremennye mysli' in A. Vyshinsky (ed.), *V chelo-vecheskom izmerenii*, pp. 16–27.

Alekseeva, Lyudmila (1984), *Istoriya inakomysliya v SSSR*, New York: Khronika.

—— (1990), 'Kak pisalas' "Istoriya inakomysliya v SSSR"', *Panorama* (10).

Alexandrova, Olga (1988), *Informelle Gruppen und Perestroika in der Sowjetunion: Eine Bestandsaufnahme*, Cologne.

Alishev, G. and Lynev, R. (1987), 'Kuda uvodit Pamyat'' *Izvestiya*, 2 June.

Ambartsumov, Ye. (1988), 'O putyakh sovershenstvovaniya politicheskoi sistemy sotsializma' in Yu. Afanasiev (ed.), *Inogo ne dano*, pp. 77–96.

—— (1989), 'True to Oneself', *MN* (33), 13 August.

Amelin, P. (1970), *Intelligentsiya i sotsializm*, Leningrad.

Amvrosov, A. (ed.) (1984), *Problemy nauchnogo kommunizma*, Moscow (18).

Anan'ev, A. (1988), 'Chelovek na zemle' in V. Kanunnikova (ed.), *Yesli po sovesti*, pp. 16-27.

Andryushchenko, Ye. (1989), 'Whom will the electorate follow', *MN* (3), 15 January.

Apenchenko, Yuri (1989), 'Kuzbass: zharkoe leto', *Znamya* (10), pp. 163-86.

Apresyan, G. (1989), 'Pyat' iz shesti', *Lit.Gaz.*, 29 March.

Arseniev, K. (1909), 'Prizyv k pokayaniyu' in *V zashchitu intelligentsii*, Moscow.

'Article 13 of press Law lacks Pith' (1989), *MN* (47), 19 November.

Åslund, Anders (1989), *Gorbachev's Struggle for Economic Reform*, London: Pinter.

Astafiev, Viktor (1989), 'Slovo kandidata', *Lit.Gaz.*, 1 February.

—— (1989), 'Ne znaem sertse serediny', *Pravda*, 30 June.

Aves, Jonathan (1992), 'The Russian Labour Movement' in G. Hosking, J. Aves and P. Duncan, *The Road to Post-Communism*, pp. 138-56.

Babagyan, N. (1992), 'Raskol v R.kh.d.d.', *Ekspress-Khronika* (13).

Babenyshev, A. (1981), *Sakharovsky sbornik*, New York: Khronika.

Baklanov, Grigorii (1989), *Vremya sobirat' kamni*, Moscow: Novosti.

Bandura, Yu. (1989), 'Resumption of the Sverdlovsk trial', *MN* (32), 6 August.

Barabashev, G. and V. Vasiliev (1990), 'Etapy reformy' in V. Bokarev and D. Polyakova (eds), *Demokratiya – vlast' vsekh i kazhdogo*, pp. 62-7.

Barbakova, K. and V. Mansurov (1991), *Intelligentsiya i vlast'*, Moscow: Akademiya nauk, Institut sotsiologii.

Batkin, Leonid (1988), 'Vozobnovlenie istorii' in Yu. Afanasiev (ed.), *Inogo ne dano*, pp. 154-91.

—— (1988), 'Ne boyas' svoego golosa', *Iskusstvo kino* (11), pp. 77-101.

—— (1989), 'Son razuma' in Kh. Kobo (ed.), *Osmyslit' kul't Stalina*, pp. 9-53.

—— (1989), 'Two worlds meet at the Congress of Deputies', *MN* (24), 11 June.

—— (1990), 'Tri tseny iz pervogo akta' in A. Protashchik (ed.), *Cherez ternii*, pp. 402-33.

Beeson, Trevor (1982), *Discretion and Valour: Religious Conditions in Russia and Eastern Europe*, rev. edn, London and Philadelphia: Collins and Fontana.

Beletskaya, V. (1989), 'Vremya vybora', *Ogonek* (7).

Belyaeva, N. (1989), 'Moscow Tribune', *MN* (7), 12 February.

—— (1989), 'Memorial: a Review of Strength', *MN* (43), 22 October.

—— (1989), 'A Review of Strength', *MN* (49), 3 December.

Belyakov, Yu. A. (1989), 'Goryachaya tochka Moskvy', *AiF* (23), 10-16 June.

Benda, J. (1927), *La Trahison des Clercs*, Paris: Bernard Grasset.

Berdyaev, Nikolai (1963), *Les Sources et le Sens du Communisme Russe*, rev. edn, Paris: Gallimard.

—— (1990), *Vekhi* (reprint of first 1909 edn), Moscow: Novosti.

Berezovsky, V. (1990), 'Neformal'naya prem'era v politike i perestroike' in V. Levichev (ed.), *Neformal'naya volna*, pp. 49-64.

—— and N. Krotov (1990), *Neformal'naya Rossiya*, Moscow: Molodaya gvardiya.

——, N. Krotov and V. Chervyakov (1990), 'Ot dvizheniya rabochikh k rabochemu dvizheniyu', *Dialog* (14), pp. 53-8.

Berlin, Isaiah (1981), *Personal Impressions*, Oxford: Oxford University Press.

Berseneva, V. (1990), 'Razvitie samodeyatel'nosti sovetskoi molodezhi v uslovii perestroiki', Moscow, Institut Molodezhi, doctoral thesis.

Bessmertny, A. (1989), 'Natsionalizm i universalizm v russkom religioznom soznanii' in T. Ryabikova (ed.), *Na puti k svobode sovesti*, pp. 122-71.

Bestuzhev-Lada, I. (1990), 'Moskva glazami sotsiologa', in *Vsya Moskva*, Moscow, pp. 38-43.

Bibler, V. (1989), 'Bytie na grani', *Vek XX i mir* (7), pp. 16-21.

—— (1990), 'O grazhdanskom obshchestve' in A. Protashchik (ed.), *Cherez ternii*, pp. 335-61.

Binev, A. (1991), 'Mitingi', *AiF* (9), February.

Black, Cyril E. (ed.) (1960), *The Transformation of Russian Society: Aspects of Social Change since 1861*, Cambridge, MA: Harvard University Press.

Bobkov, V. and A. Sergeev (eds) (1990), *Alternativa: vybor puti. Perestroika upravleniya i gorizonty rynka*, Moscow: Mysl'.

Bogomolov, G. (1989), 'Front bez flangov', *Leningradskaya pravda*, 25 July.

Bogoraz, L., V. Golitsyn and S. Kovalev (1991), 'Politicheskaya bor'ba ili zashchita prav?' in T. Notkina (ed.), *Pogruzhenie v tryasinu*, pp. 501-44.

Bokarev, V. and D. Polyakova (1990), *Demokatiya – vlast' vsekh i kazhdogo*, Moscow: Prosveshchenie.

Bokser, V. (1989), 'O MOI', *AiF* (50), 16 December.

Bolotin, A. and L. Sherstennikov (1989), 'Raskovannost', *Ogonek* (7).

Bonner, Yelena (1991), *Postskriptum: kniga o gor'kovskoi ssylke*, Moscow: Interbuk.

Bor, B. (1987), 'Diskussionye kluby, seminary, chteniya', *Glasnost'* (1) (published by *Russkaya mysl'*, 10 July 1987).

Borodenkov, Andrei (1989), 'Our opinion was ignored', *MN* (7), 12 February.

Borovik, V. (1990), 'Sotsial'nye mekhanizmy vzaimodestviya interesov i politicheskoi aktivnosti sovetskoi molodezhi', Moscow: Institut Molodezhi, doctoral thesis.

Borshchagovsky, A. (1988), 'Zapiski balovnya sud'by', *Teatr* (10), pp. 163-77, and (11), pp. 153-69.

Böss, Otto (1961), *Die Lehre der Eurasier*, Wiesbaden: Otto Harrossowitz.

Bourdeaux, Michael (1990), *Gorbachev, Glasnost and the Gospel*, London: Hodder & Stoughton.

Bova, Russell (1991), 'Worker Activism: The Role of the State' in J. Sedaitis and J. Butterfield (eds), *Perestroika from Below*, pp. 29-42.

Bovin, Alexander (1988), 'Perestroika: pravda o sotsializme' in Yu. Afanasiev (ed.), *Inogo ne dano*, pp. 519-49.

—— (1988), 'The Press and Perestroika', *MN* (19), 8 May.

Braginskaya, Nina (1991), 'Slava besslaviya', *Znanie-sila*, January.

Buckley, Mary (1993), *Redefining Russian Society and Polity*, Boulder, CO: Westview Press.

Burbulis, Gennadi (1990), 'Posmotret' na vse filosofski', *SK*, 30 December.

Burg, D. (1961), 'Observations on Soviet University Students' in R. Pipes (ed.), *The Russian Intelligentsia*, pp. 80-100.

Burlatsky, Fedor (1986), *Narod i vlast'*, Moscow.

—— (1987), 'Uchit'sya demokratii', *Pravda*, 18 July.

—— (1988), 'Kakoi sotsializm narodu nuzhen' in V. Kanunnikova (ed.), *Yesli po sovesti*, pp. 64-78.

264 *The Rise of the Russian Democrats*

—— (1988), *New Thinking: Dialogues and Judgements*, Moscow: Progress.
Burtin, Yuri (1988), 'Vozmozhnost' vozrazit'' in Yu. Afanasiev (ed.), *Inogo ne dano*, pp. 468-90.
—— (1990), 'Na zlobu dnya' in A. Protashchik (ed.), *Cherez ternii*, pp. 434-56.
—— (1992), 'Delo dlya "Demokraticheskoi Rossii"', *Dvizhenie Demokraticheskaya Rossiya* (13), February, pp. 2-3.
—— (1992), 'Vazhnye gosudarstvennye dela', *NG*, 21 April.
Butenko, A. (1990), 'Sovetskoe obshchestvo posle Stalina' in V. Bokarev and D. Polyakova (eds), *Demokratiya – vlast' vsekh i kazhdogo*, pp. 7-12.
Bychkov, Yu. (1990), 'Smogut li demokraty obustroit' Rossiyu?', *Karetny ryad*, October.
Bychkova, O. (1991), 'Battle over Legal Authority', *MN* (9), 3 March.
Bykov, Vasil (1987), 'Ne otluchaite sami sebya', *SK*, 10 December.
—— (1988), 'Yedinstvenny shans', *SK*, 11 June.
—— (1989), 'Put' demokratizatsii', *Lit.Gaz.*15 February.
—— (1989), 'Zhazhda peremen', *Pravda*, 24 November.
'Byt' tribuny grazhdanskoi pravdy' (1986), *SK*, 9 December.
Byzov, L. and G. Gurevich (1990), 'Peremeny politicheskoi soznanii', *AiF* (7), 17 February.
Carter, Stephen (1990), *Russian Nationalism*, London: Pinter.
Chalidze, V. (1990), *Zarya pravovoi reformy*, Moscow: Progress.
Chalikova, Viktoriya (1988), 'Arkhivny yunosha', *Neva* (10), pp. 152-62.
—— (1990), 'Position of Intellectuals', *MN* (21), 3 June.
Chernichenko, Yuri (1988), 'Dve tainy' in V. Kanunnikova (ed.), *Yesli po sovesti*, pp. 351-66.
—— (1988), 'Trava iz-pod stoga' in Yu. Afanasiev (ed.), *Inogo ne dano*, pp. 591-620.
—— (1989), 'Election Platform', *MN* (6), 5 February.
—— (1990), 'Zemlya i Volya' in A. Protashchik (ed.), *Cherez ternii*, pp. 151-203.
—— (1990), 'Ya obvinyayu', *Ogonek* (43).
—— (1991), 'Komu i zachem nuzhna krest'yanskaya partiya', *Lit.Gaz.*, 6 March.
—— (1992), 'The Land Situation', *MN* (4), 26 January.
Chernov, Andrei (1990) 'The Party which claims to be saving Marxism', *MN* (17), 6 May.
Chernov, V. (1989), 'Deti Sharikova', *Ogonek* (3).
Chiesa, G. and R. Medvedev (1991), *Time of Change*, London and New York: Tauris.
Christie, Ian (1989), 'The Cinema' in J. Graffy and G. Hosking (eds), *Culture and the Media in the USSR Today*.
Chubais, Igor (1990), 'How I was expelled from the Party', *MN* (16), 22 April.
Churbanov, V. and A. Nelyubin (1989), 'Neformal'nye ob''edineniya' in V. Kuptsov (ed.), *Demokratizatsiya sovetskogo obshchestva*, pp. 240-55.
—— (1990), 'Neformal'nye ob''edineniya i perestroika: nadezhdy i trevogi' in V.A. Pechenev (ed.), *Neformaly: kto oni? kuda zovut?*.
Churchward, L. (1973), *The Soviet Intelligentsia: An Essay on the Social Structure and Roles of Soviet Intellectuals during the 1960s*, London: Routledge & Kegan Paul.
—— (1987), *Soviet Socialism: Social and Political Essays*, London and New York:

Routledge & Kegan Paul.

Colton, T. (1986), *The Dilemma of Reform in the Soviet Union*, rev. edn, New York: Council on Foreign Relations.

—— (1991), 'The Moscow Elecctions of 1990' in A. Hewett and V. Winston (eds), *Milestones in Glasnost' and Perestroyka*, pp. 326-81.

Curtis, J. (1991), 'Literature under Gorbachev - A Second Thaw?' in C. Merridale and C. Ward (eds), *Perestroika: The Historical Perspective*, pp. 168-80.

Davidova, N. (1989), '100,000 strong Rally', *MN* (22), 28 May.

Davies, R. W. (1990), 'The Politics of Soviet History, 1985-8' in M. McCauley (ed.), *Gorbachev and Perestroika*.

Davydov, A. (1990), 'S"yezd demokraticheskoi partii Rossii', *Izvestiya*, 3 December.

Degtyarev, A. and D. Piskunov (1989), 'Raskryt' intellektual'ny potentsial partii', *Pravda*, 29 June.

'Deklaratsiya dvizheniya "Grazhdanskoe Deistvie"' (1990), *Ogonek* (8).

'Deklaratsiya printsipov sotsial-demokraticheskoi assotsiatsii' (1990), *Respublika* (3).

'Deklaratsiya sotsialistov-narodnikov' (1990), *Revolutsionnaya Rossiya* (6), May.

Denisenko, B. (1991), 'Dazhe yesli my proigraem', *Lit.Gaz.*, 20 March.

Denisovsky, G. (1990), 'Skol'ko iz nas antisemitov?', *Daidzhest* (14).

Devlin, K. (1988), 'Soviet Journalist describes Yeltsin's struggles against the Party "Mafia"', *RFE/RL Report* (206), 20 May.

Djilas, Milovan (1957), *The New Class*, London: Thames & Hudson.

Dobrynina, V., Ye. Suslova and M. Yuvkin (1990), *Samodeyatel'nye initsiativnye organizatsii: problemy i perspektivy razvitiya*, Moscow.

Dodolev, Ye. (1990), 'Pamyat' i KGB', *Moskovsky komsomolets*, 27 October.

Dolganov, V. (1989), 'Po raznym spiskam', *Izvestiya*, 12 January.

Doroshenko, N. (1990), 'Kto vinovat i chto delat'', *Moskovsky literator*, 19 January.

Dudintsev, V. (1987), 'Genetika sovesti', *SK*, 17 February.

Duncan, P. (1988), 'The Party and Russian Nationalism in the USSR: From Brezhnev to Gorbachev' in P. Potichnyj (ed.), *The Soviet Union: Party and Society*, pp. 229-44.

Dunlop, John B. (1983), *The Faces of Contemporary Russian Nationalism*, Princeton, NJ: Princeton University Press.

—— (1985), *The New Russian Nationalism*, New York: Praeger.

—— (1993), *The Rise of Russia and the Fall of the Soviet Empire*, Princeton, NJ: Princeton University Press.

Dupeux, Louis (1979), *National-Bolchévisme. Stratégie Communiste et Dynamique Conservatrice*, 2 vols, Paris: Champion.

'Dveri otkryty dlya vsekh: obrashcheniye k trudyaschikhsya Leningrada' (1989), *Leningradskaya pravda*, 8 June.

Dzubenko, G. and G. Kozlova (eds) (1987), *USSR: A Time of Change*, Moscow: Progress.

Eidelman, N. (1988), 'Revolutsiya sverkhu v Rossii', *Nauka i zhizn'* (10), pp. 97-105; (1989) (3), pp. 101-8.

'Election Platforms' (1989), *MN* (4), 22 January.

Engelhardt-Yurkov, S. (1990), 'Yest' li budyshchee u monarkhicheskoi idei?', *Dialog* (17), pp. 37-40.

—— (1990), 'O konstitutsionno-monarkhicheskoi partii', *AiF* (16), 21 April.

'Entretien des membres de l'Union des Ecrivains soviétiques avec Mikhail Gorbachev' (1987), *Cahiers du Samizdat* (125), February-March, pp. 2-5.

Etinger, Yakov (1989), 'Svechi na Lubyanke', *Novoe vremya* (46), 10 November.

—— (1990), 'O programme Memoriala', *AiF* (11), 17 March.

Fadeev, V. (1989), 'A chto yesli bez "vashikh" i "nashikh"?', *Sovetsky tsirk*, 16 November.

Fadin, Andrei (1988), '"Perestroika" v poiskakh neobratimosti', *Vek XX i mir* (6), pp. 31-7.

—— (1989), 'Vremya etakraticheskogo soznaniya' in A. Vyshnevsky (ed.), *V chelovecheskom izmerenii*, pp. 73-88.

—— (1991), 'Putch i nomenklatura: porazhenie - pochemu' in *Tri Dnya*, Moscow: Postfaktum.

Fedyukin, S. (1972), *Veliki oktyabr' i intelligentsiya*, Moscow.

—— (1983), *Partiya i intelligentsiya*, Moscow: Gospolitizdat.

Fischer, G. (1960), 'The Intelligentsia and Russia' in Cyril E. Black (ed.), *The Transformation of Russian Society*, pp. 253-74.

Flerovsky, Alexei (1989), 'Glasnost: No holds barred', *MN* (11), 12 March.

Fomicheva, I. (ed.) (1978), *Literaturnaya gazeta i yee auditoriya*, Moscow: Izdalel'stvo MGU.

Fomin, V. (1991), 'Estetika Goskino' in T. Notkina (ed.), *Pogruzhenie v tryasinu*, pp. 439-99.

Fomina, L. (1990), 'Poteri na pole brani', *Moskovskaya pravda*, 4 February.

Frank, V. (1967), 'Lenin and the Russian Intelligentsia' in L. Schapiro and P. Reddaway (eds), *Lenin: The Man. the Theorist. the Leader: A Reappraisal*, pp. 23-36.

Friedgut, Theodore H. (1979), *Political Participation in the USSR*, Princeton, NJ: Princeton University Press.

'From the Real Struggle to Real Elections' (1989), *MN* (11), 12 March.

Fukuyama, Francis (1992), *The End of History and the Last Man*, London and New York: Penguin.

Furman, D. (1988), 'Nash put' k normal'noi kul'ture' in Yu. Afanasiev (ed.), *Inogo ne dano*, pp. 569-80.

—— (1989), 'Stalin i my s religiovedcheskoi tochki zreniya' in Kh. Kobo (ed.), *Osmyslit' kul't Stalina*, pp. 402-26.

—— (1989), 'Religiya, ateizm i perestroika' in T. Ryabikova (ed.), *Na puti k svobode sovesti*, pp. 7-18.

Garrard, John and Carol Garrard (1990), *Inside the Soviet Writers' Union*, London and New York: Tauris.

Gefter, M. (1988), 'Stalin umer vchera' in Yu. Afanasiev (ed.), *Inogo ne dano*, pp. 297-323.

—— (1989), 'Ot anti-Stalina k ne-Stalinu: neproidenny put'' in Kh. Kobo (ed.), *Osmyslit' kul't Stalina*, pp. 497-545.

—— (1991), 'Nakanune' in T. Notkina (ed.), *Pogruzhenie v tryasinu*, pp. 607-28.

—— (1991), *Iz tekh i etikh let*, Moscow: Progress.

Gelman, A. (1987), 'First Things First' in G. Dzubenko and G. Kozlova (eds), *USSR: A Time of Change*, pp. 62-76.

—— (1988), 'Vremya sobraniya sil', *SK*, 9 April.

Gelman, H. (1990), 'Gorbachev's Struggle and the Soviet System' in U. Ra'anan and I. Lukes (eds), *Gorbachev's USSR*, pp. 41-67.

Gerber, A. and A. Andreev (1990), 'Sledsvie zakoncheno - zabud'te', *Moskovsky komsomolets*, 13 July.

Gesheva, Ye. (1989), 'Pervye deputaty', *Lit.Gaz.*, 15 March.

Glagolov, V. (1988), 'Khudozhestvennaya istoriya i istoricheskie sud'by', *Pravda*, 10 January.

Glazov, Yuri (1985), *The Russian Mind since Stalin's Death*, Boston and Dordrecht: Reidel.

Glazunov, Ilya (1985), 'Chto pomnit'? Chem gordit'sya?', *Pravda*, 11 June.

—— (1987), 'Poisk cherez traditsiyu', *Pravda*, 27 September.

—— (1991), 'Menya khotyat ubit'', *Den'* (5), March.

Glazychev, V. (1991), 'Agoniya kul'tury' in T. Notkina (ed.), *Pogruzhenie v tryasinu*, pp. 260-84.

Glenny, M. (1989), 'Soviet Theatre: Glasnost in Action' in J. Graffy and G. Hosking (eds), *Culture and the Media in the USSR Today*, pp. 78-87.

Glod, V. (1991), 'Byelorussia: anxious expectations', *MN* (16), 21 April.

Golik, Yu. (1990), 'Deputat, izbiratel', parlament' in M. Vyshinsky (ed.), *Pravo i vlast'*, pp. 253-65.

Goncharov, A. (1986), 'Naiti i otkryt' a ne ugadat' i ugodit'', *SK*, 16 January.

Gorbachev, M. (1985), *Izbrannye rechi i stat'i*, Moscow: Politizdat.

—— (1987-89), *Izbrannye rechi i stat'i*, 6 vols, Moscow: Politizdat.

—— (1987), *Perestroika i novoe myshlenie*, Moscow: Politizdat.

—— (1990), Speech to Central Committee Plenum, *Pravda*, 11 January.

—— (1990), 'Kakoi viditsya obnovlennaya KPSS', *AiF* (27), 7 July.

—— (1991), 'Preodolet' krizis', *Krasnaya zvezda*, 29 March.

—— (1991), 'O proekte novoi programmy KPSS', *Sovetskaya Rossiya*, 26 July.

—— (1991), *The August Coup: The Truth and the Lessons*, London: Harper Collins.

Gorbuntsov, D. (1988), 'Legko li stat' laureatom', *Pravda*, 26 March.

Gordon, Leonid (1989), 'Vozmozhen li plyuralizm v sovetskom obshchestve?' in A. Zav'yalova (ed.), *Postizhenie*, pp. 326-36.

—— (1991), 'The Soviet working class movement in the post-socialist perspective' in C. Merridale and J. Ward (eds), *Perestroika: The Historical Perspective*, pp. 81-95.

—— and Ye. Klopov (1990), 'Perestroika i novoe rabochee dvizhenie' in A. Protashchik (ed.), *Cherez ternii*, pp. 748-70.

Gorenkov, A. (1990), 'Partiinye organizatsii i samodeyatel'nye dvizheniya', *Partiinaya zhizn'* (3), pp. 29-33.

—— (1990), 'Kommunisty i samodeyatel'nye dvizheniya', *Partiinaya zhizn'* (2), 2 January, pp. 31-6.

Goryainov, Viktor (1988), 'Vozvrashchenie masterov', *SK*, 11 June.

'Goskomstat soobshchaet' (1989), *AiF* (10), 11 March.

Gozman, L. and A. Etkind (1989), 'Lyudi i vlast'' in A. Vyshinsky (ed.), *V chelovecheskom izmerenii*, pp. 378-92.

—— (1989), 'Kul't vlasti' in Kh. Kobo (ed.), *Osmyslit' kul't Stalina*, pp. 337-71.

Graffy, J. (1989), 'The Literary Press' in J. Graffy and G. Hosking (eds), *Culture and the Media in the USSR Today*, pp. 107-58.

268   *The Rise of the Russian Democrats*

—— and G. Hosking (eds) (1989), *Culture and the Media in the USSR Today*, London: Macmillan.

Grafova, L. and Domnisheva, Ye. (1989), 'My - ne oppozitsiya', *Lit.Gaz.*, 2 August.

Granin, Daniil (1986), 'Otvetstvennost' podlinnaya', *Lit.*Gaz., 12 February.

—— (1988), 'O miloserdii' in V. Kanunnikova (ed.), *Yesli po sovesti*, pp. 107-17.

—— (1988), 'Kogo my pryachem?' in Yu. Afanasiev (ed.), *Inogo ne dano*, pp. 343-53.

—— (1989), 'A letter to Prague', *MN* (48), 26 November.

—— (1990), 'Nash dorogoi Roman Andreevich' in A. Protashchik (ed.), *Cherez ternii*, pp. 106-31.

—— (1990), 'Doroga k zdravomu smyslu' in V. Bokarev and D. Polyakova (eds), *Demokratiya - vlast' vsekh i kazhdogo*, pp. 22-30.

Grigoriev, V. (1986), 'Na vystavke', *Pravda*, 21 July.

Grinevich, A. (1988), 'Artisty i pisateli', *SK*, 16 July.

Gromov, A. and O. Kuzin (1990), *Neformaly: kto yest' kto?*, Moscow: Mysl'.

Gubarev, V. (1992), 'An Interview with Arkady Volsky', *MN* (10), 8 March.

Gubenko, V. and D. Piskarev (1988), 'Samozvantsy i "samodeyatel'shchiki"', *Komsomolskaya pravda*, 31 January.

Gurkov, A. (1988), 'Shadows off the screen', *MN* (7), 14 February.

Gusev, K. (1985), 'Intelligentsiya Rossii i bor'ba politicheskikh partii', in K. Gusev (ed.), *Intelligentsiya i revolyutsiya*, pp. 34-43.

Haimson, Leopold (1961), 'The Solitary Hero and the Philistines: A Note on the Heritage of the Stalin Era' in Richard Pipes (ed.), *The Russian Intelligentsia*, pp. 101-10.

Herzen, Alexander (1978), *Ends and Beginnings*, rev. edn, Oxford: Oxford University Press.

'He who pays the parties calls the tune' (1992), *MN* (41), 11 October.

Hewett, A. and V. Winston (eds) (1991), *Milestones in Glasnost' and Perestroyka: Politics and People*.

Hill, Ronald J. (1980), *Soviet Politics, Political Science and Reform*, Oxford and White Plains, NY: Martin Robertson and M.E. Sharpe.

—— (1985), *Soviet Union: Politics, Economics and Society*, London: Pinter.

—— (1986), 'Gorbachov's Politics: Results and Prospects', *Irish Slavonic Studies*, 7, pp. 5-26.

—— (1989), 'Glasnost' and Soviet Politics', *Coexistence* (26), 1989, pp. 317-31.

Hingley, R. (1977), *The Russian Mind*, London: Bodley Head.

Hosking, Geoffrey (1990), *A History of the Soviet Union*, rev. edn, London: Fontana-Collins.

—— (1990), *The Awakening of the Soviet Union*, rev. edn, London: Mandarin.

——, J.Aves and P. Duncan (eds) (1992), *The Road to Post-Communism*, London: Pinter.

Hughes, G. and S. Welfare (1990), *Red Empire: The Forbidden History of the USSR*, London: Weidenfeld & Nicolson.

Igrunov, V. (1988), 'KSI i drugie', *Vek XX i mir* (6), pp. 26-30.

Ikramov, K. (1990), 'O strakhe', *SK*, 2 June.

'Informatsionnoe soobshchenie' (1989), *Lit.*Gaz., 25 January.

'Itogi anketnogo oprosa' (1991), *Golos kommunistov*, 1 (4), p. 3.

Ivanenko, S. (1990), 'They want to restore the Russian monarchy', *MN* (43), 4 November.

Ivanitsky, V. (1990), 'Izbiratel'nye bloki', *Dialog* (3), pp. 47-52.

Ivanov, G. (1989), 'Kto ostalsya za chertoi', *Lit.Gaz.*, 25 January.

Ivanova. L. (1980), *Formirovanie sovetskoi nauchnoi intelligentsii, 1917-1927*, Moscow.

—— (1987), *Sovetskaya intelligentsiya*, Moscow: Politizdat.

Ivanova, N. (1989), 'Zerkalo ili zazerkal'e' in N. Strel'tsova (ed.), *V svoem otechestve*, pp. 150-69.

—— (1990), *Voskreshenie nuzhnykh veshchei*, Moscow: Moskovsky rabochii.

Ivantsov, G. (1990), 'Upryamye voprosy' in S. Yushenkov (ed.), *Neformaly: sotsial'nye initsiativy*.

Ivashko, V. (1991), 'V konfrontatsiyu vstupat' ne sobiraemsya', *SK*, 10 July.

—— (1991), 'Ya za yedinstvo kommunistov', *Lit.Gaz.*, 24 July.

'Izbrannye mesta iz rechei pisatelei' (1989), *Nedelya* (47), 20 November.

Izyumova, N. (1988), 'Unofficial social movements: pros and cons', *MN* (19), 8 May.

—— (1989), 'Camp documentary', *MN* (7), 12 February.

—— (1990), 'LDP set to hold congress in the Kremlin', *MN* (17), 6 May.

'K deyatelyam kul'tury' (1988), *Iskusstvo kino* (11), p. 75.

Kabakov, A. (1989), 'Luzhniki', *MN* (24), 11 June.

Kagarlitsky, Boris (1989), *The Thinking Reed: Intellectuals and the Soviet State: 1917 to the Present*, London and New York: Verso.

—— (1990), *Farewell to Perestroika*, London and New York: Verso.

—— (1990), 'Yeshche odno zharkoe leto' in S. Yushenkov (ed.), *Neformaly: sotsial'nye initsiativy*, pp. 121-35.

'Kakim byt' sovetam' (1988), *Izvestiya*, 26 June.

'Kakim putem my poidem' (1990), *AiF* (21), 26 May.

Kalistratova, S. (1989), 'It was a very difficult time', *MN* (32), 6 August.

Kalugin, O. (1990), 'KGB bez grima', *AiF*, 30 June.

Kanunnikova, V. (ed.), *Yesli po sovesti*, Moscow: Khudozhestvennaya literatura.

Kapelyush, Ya. and A. Kinsbursky (1989), 'Congress of People's Deputies of the USSR', *MN* (29), 16 July.

Karpinsky, Len (1988), 'Pochemu stalinizm ne skhodit so stseny' in Yu. Afanasiev (ed.), *Inogo ne dano*, pp. 648-70.

—— (1989), 'Revolution: disease or recovery?', *MN* (51), 17 December.

—— (1990), 'Too free, too soon', *MN* (17), 21 September.

—— (1990), 'Welcome', *MN* (16), 22 April.

—— (1990), 'It was the very last straw', *MN* (8), 20 July.

Karyakin, Yuri (1988), '"Zhdanovskaya zhidkost'" ili protiv ochernitel'stve' in Yu. Afanasiev (ed.), *Inogo ne dano*, pp. 412-23.

—— (1989), '"Derzhimoda" ili "sokol ty moi sizy"' in N. Strel'tsova (ed.), *V svoem otechestve*, pp. 170-77.

Katsman, I. (1990), 'Karaul ne ustanet zhdat'', *Panorama* (13), December.

Kazutin, D. (1989), 'Surprises of the political Spring', *MN* (12), 19 March.

—— and E. Khamidulin (1989), 'Pluralism abridged?', *MN* (9), 26 February.

—— (1989), 'People of the sixties', *MN* (9), 26 February.

Kerblay, Basile (1983), *Modern Soviet Society*, London: Methuen.

Khanga, E. (1989), 'Non-grata books', *MN* (10), 5 March.

'Khartiya Moskovskogo narodnogo fronta' (1990), *Trezvost' i kul'tura* (6), pp. 30-34.

Khatsenkov, G. (1990), 'Demokraticheskaya partiya Rossii', *Dialog* (12), pp. 33-5.

—— (1990), 'Kakoi byt' Rkp?', *AiF* (16), 21 April.

Khazanov, B. (1991), 'Russkaya intelligentsiya' in T. Notkina (ed.), *Pogruzhenie v tryasinu*, pp. 632-41.

Khasbulatov, Ruslan (1991), *Byurokraticheskoe gosudarstvo*, Moscow: Russkaya entsiklopedia.

—— (1993), *The Struggle for Russia: Power and Change in the Democratic Revolution*, London and New York: Routledge.

Kiselev, A. and A. Mostovshchikov (1987), 'Let's talk on equal grounds: Boris Yeltsin talks with members of the Pamyat' associations', *MN* (20), 17 May.

Kiselyov, S. (1991), 'Coal Miners wouldn't budge', *MN* (14), 7 April.

—— (1991), 'Miners plan for strike for 1 March', *MN* (8), 24 February.

Klyamkin, Igor (1987), 'Kakaya ulitsa vedet k khramu?', *NM* (11), pp. 150-88.

—— (1989), 'What lies ahead?', *MN* (27), 2 July.

—— (1990), 'Logika vlasti i logika oppozitsii' in A. Protashchik (ed.), *Cherez ternii*, pp. 701-19.

Kobo, Kh. (ed.), *Osmyslit' kul't Stalina*, Moscow: Progress.

Kohn, Hans (1963), *Le Pan-Slavisme: son Histoire et son Idéologie*, Paris: Payot.

Kolobaev, Andrei (1989), 'Demokratiya po razresheniyu', *Yunost'* (4), pp. 40-44.

Kolosov, M. (1990), 'Otkrytoe pis'mo Yuriyu Bondarevu', *Ogonek* (1), p. 8.

Komarova, Ye. (1989), 'Problemy vozniknoveniya i razvitiya neformal'nykh obraz- ovanii molodezhi v usloviyakh sotsializma', Moscow: PhD thesis.

Komarovsky, V. and Ye. Dugin (1989), 'Do i posle vyborov', *Izvestiya*, 12 May.

Komarovsky, V. and A. Usol'tser (1989), 'Protivoborstvo?', *AiF* (22), 3 June.

'Kommunisty apparata Rossii' (1990), *AiF* (23), 9 June.

'Kommyunike ob uchreditel'nom s"yezde sotsial-demokraticheskoi assotsiatsii' (1990), *Respublika* (3).

Kondrashov, S. (1989), 'One Humanist's Clairvoyance', *MN* (35), 27 August.

'Konferentsiya bloka "Demokraticheskaya Rossiya"' (1990), *AiF* (14), 7 April.

Kononov, V. (1990), 'Perestroika: molodezh i sotsial'nye intsiativy' in V. Levichev (ed.), *Neformal'naya volna*, pp. 39-48.

Kordonsky, S. (1991), 'Pervy voenny povorot v SSSR' in *Tri dnya*, Moscow: Postfaktum, pp. 70-74.

Kormer, V. (1989), 'Dvoinoe soznanie intelligentsii', *Voprosy filosofii* (9), pp. 65-79.

Korotich, Vitaly (1985), 'O podlinnoi demokratii i pravakh cheloveka', *Pravda*, 15 September.

—— and Cathy Porter (1990), *The Best of Ogonek*, London: Heinemann.

Koval', B. (ed.) (1991), *Rossiya segodnya: politichesky portret v dokumentakh*, Moscow: Mezhdunarodnye otnosheniya.

Kovalevsky, P. (1971), *Zarubezhnaya Rossiya*, Paris: Librairie des Cinq Continents.

Koyré, Alexandre (1976), *La Philosophie et le Problème National en Russie*, rev. edn, Paris: Gallimard.

Kozbanenko, V. (1989), *Komsomol i neformal'nye ob"edineniya molodezhi*, Rostov-on-the-Don.

Krayukhin, S. (1989), 'Back home after 18 Years', *MN* (6), 5 February.

Kropotkin, P. (1978), *Memoirs of a Revolutionist*, rev. edn, London: Folio.

Krotov, N., V. Berezovsky and V. Chervyakov (1991), *Rossiya: partii, assosiatsii, soyuzy, kluby*, 1 (1-2), Moscow: Rau-Press.

Krugly, L. (1987), 'Pokayanie', *Russkaya mysl'*, 23 October.

Krylovsky, V. and K. Zavoisky (1990), 'Antikommunizm - novaya vyveska KPSS?', *Soglasie*, 29 June.

—— (1990), 'S chevo nachinaetsya partiya', *Ekspress-khronika* (41), 9 October.

Kryuchkov, V. (1991), 'Poslednyaya rech' v Kremle', *Den'* (27), 15 December.

'KS. Sotsiologi rekomenduyut: smelei' (1991) in *Tri dnya*, pp. 66-9.

'Kto za chto golosoval' (1990), *AiF* (26), 30 June.

Kudryavtsev, I. (1990), 'Eto vechno novye sotsialisty', *Panorama* (7), July.

—— (1991), 'Vitse-Prezident Rossii dva goda nazad', *Panorama* (28), July.

Kudyukin, A. (1989), 'Iz vsekh pravitelei', *Karetny ryad*, December.

Kudyukin, Pavel (1989), 'Brodskie odezhdy', *Sobesednik* (23), June.

Kuprach, A. (1990), 'Sozdana novaya partiya', *Literaturnaya Rossiya*, 20 April.

Kuptsov, V. (ed.) (1989), *Demokratizatsiya sovetskogo obshchestva*, Moscow: Vysshaya shkola.

Kurashvili, Boris (1988), 'K polnovlastiyu sovetov', *Kommunist* (8), pp. 28-36.

—— (1988), 'Demokratichesky soyuz obshchestvennykh sil: utopia? vozmozhnost'? neobkhodimost'?', *Sovetskaya molodezh*, 27 April.

—— (1988), 'Learning from fraternal countries', *MN* (10), 6 March.

—— (1988), 'Kriticheskaya faza perestroiki' in A. Vyshinsky (ed.), *Pravo i vlast'*, pp. 11-40.

—— (1989), 'At least two candidates', *MN* (8), 19 February.

Kuryanov, S. and G. Ivanov (1988), 'Pervye shagi', *Moskovsky komsomolets*, 9 May.

Kushnerev, S. (1987), 'A vy kto takie?', *Pravda*, 30 March.

Kuteinov, Andrei (1989), 'How the Academy will vote', *MN* (11), 12 March.

Kuvaldin, V. (1989), 'Deceptive simplicity', *MN* (35), 27 August.

Labedz, Leopold (1961), 'The Structure of the Soviet Intelligentsia' in Richard Pipes (ed.), *The Russian Intelligentsia*, pp. 63-79.

Laird, Roy (1970), *The Soviet Paradigm*, London and New York: Collier Macmillan and The Free Press.

Lampert, Nicholas (1979), *The Technical Intelligentsia and the Soviet State*, London: Macmillan.

—— (1990), 'The Socialist Legal State' in M. McCauley (ed.), *Gorbachev and Perestroika*, pp. 116-34.

Lane, David (1985), *State and Politics in the USSR*, Oxford: Basil Blackwell.

—— (1991), 'The Roots of Political Reform: the Changing Structure of the USSR' in C. Merridale and C. Ward (eds), *Perestroika: The Historical Perspective*, pp. 95-115.

—— (1992), *Soviet Society under Perestroika*, rev. edn, London and New York: Routledge.

Lantratov, V. (1989), 'Reformatsiya ili reformizm', *Gorizont* (11), pp. 9-13.

—— (1990), 'Umet' slushat' i slyshat' drug druga' in S. Yushenkov (ed.),

Neformaly: sotsial'nye initsiativy, pp. 220–25.

Laqueur, Walter (1989), *The Long Road to Freedom*, London: Unwin Hyman.

Latsis, Otto (1989), 'Sergo protiv Sergo' in N. Strel'tsova (ed.), *V svoem otechestve*, pp. 121–49.

—— (1989), 'Stalin protiv Lenina' in Kh. Kobo (ed.) *Osmyslit' kul't Stalina*, pp. 215–46.

'The Last Warning' (1990), *MN* (29), 29 July.

Latynina, Alla (1989), 'The climate won't change', *MN* (13), 26 March.

—— (1989), 'About Cinderellas', *MN* (1), 1 January.

Lavrin, Janko (1969), *Russia, Slavdom and the Western World*, London: Bles.

Lavrov, K. (1986), 'Teatr i obshchestvo v epokhu revolutionnykh peremen', *SK*, 6 December.

Legostaev, Valery (1991), 'God 1987 – peremena logiki', *Den'* (14), July.

Levada, Yuri (1989), 'Stalinskie al'ternativy' in Kh. Kobo (ed.), *Osmyslit' kul't Stalina*, pp. 448–59.

—— (1989), 'Question – Answer', *MN* (13), 26 March.

—— (1990), 'The Party's Over', *MN* (9), 27 July.

—— (1991), 'And they still don't understand us', *MN* (38), 22 September.

—— (1992), 'What February left in its wake', *MN* (10), 8 March.

Levanov, Ye. (1987), 'Ucheny idet k "neformalam"', *Komsomolskaya pravda*, 11 December.

Levansky, V., A. Obolensky and G. Tokarevsky (1989), 'Chto dumayut lyudi o vyborakh', *AiF* (10), 11 March.

Levichev, V. (ed.) (1990), *Neformal'naya volna: sbornik nauchnykh trudov*, Moscow.

Levikov, Alexander (1989), 'Are Leningraders any worse?', *MN* (32), 6 August.

Lewytzkyj, Borys (1984), *Politics and Society in Soviet Ukraine*, Edmonton: Canadian Institute for Ukrainian Studies.

Lezov, Sergei (1988), 'Pogromy k tysyachiletiyu', *Strana i mir* (3).

Ligachev, Yegor (1989), *Izbrannye rechi i stat'i*, Moscow: Politizdat.

Likhachev, Dmitri (1989), 'Note on the intellgentsia', *Lit.Gaz.*, 26 April.

—— (1990), 'Sovetovat'sya s sovest'yu', *SK*, 2 June.

—— and Nikolai Samvelin (1990), *Le Retour à l'Homme: Dialogues sur le temps passé, présent, à venir*, Moscow: Progress.

Lisichkin, G. (1989), 'Mify i real'nost'' in Kh. Kobo (ed.), *Osmyslit' kul't Stalina*, pp. 247–83.

—— (1989), 'Nina Andreeva: for and against', *MN* (33), 13 August.

Livshits, Vadim (1990), 'Leningrad: spektr god sputsya', *Panorama* (11), September.

Lomov, V. (1990), 'Studencheskoe dvizhenie v Moskve', *Panorama* (7), July.

Loshak, Viktor (1990), 'New leaders but no plan for Russian CP', *MN* (16), 14 September.

—— (1990), 'Hope', *MN* (8), 20 July.

Losoto, Ye. (1987), 'Slishkom pokhozhe', *Komsomolskaya pravda*, 19 December.

—— (1987), 'V bespamyatstve', *Komsomolskaya pravda*, 22 May.

Lukinikh, N. (1987), 'K zritelyu cherez ternii i lavry', *SK*, 17 February.

Luskanov, V.(1990), 'On the verge', *MN* (28), 22 July.

Lysenko, Vladimir (1989), 'O funktsiyakh partii v sovremennom obshchestve' in A. Zav'yalova, *Postizhenie*, pp. 337–40.

—— (1990), 'Krizis partii i puti vykhoda iz nego', *Politika* (1), pp. 30–41.

—— (1990), 'Ne konfrontatsiya - dialog', *AiF* (11), 17 March.

—— (1990), 'Democratic Platform', *AiF* (21), 26 May.

—— and Shostakovsky, V. (1990), Interview, *Pravda*, 3 March.

Lyubimov, B. (1986), 'V poiskakh radosti', *SK*, 8 April.

McAuley, Mary (1977), *Politics and the Soviet Union*, London: Penguin.

McCauley, Martin (ed.) (1990), *Gorbachev and Perestroika*, London, Macmillan.

Magaril, S. (1990), 'Uchreditel'ny s"yezd sotsial-demokraticheskoi partii Rossiiskoi Federatsii', *Alternativa* (1), 30 May.

Malashenko, Alexei (1992), 'Islam i nastional-kommunizm', *NG*, 21 March.

Malgin, Andrei (1989), 'Non-governmental literature', *MN* (38), 17 September.

Malia, Martin (1961), 'What is the Intelligentsia?' in Richard Pipes, *The Russian Intelligentsia*, pp. 1–18.

Malukhin, V. (1989), 'Debaty pisatelei', *Izvestiya*, 20 January.

Malyakin, Ilya (1990), 'Provintsiya ne prosypaisya', *Panorama* (11), December.

Malyarov, I. (1991), 'My ne dolzhny proigrat'', *Lit.Gaz.*, 20 March.

Malyutin, Mikhail (1988), 'Problemy formirovaniya narodnogo fronta', manuscript.

—— (1988), 'O sotspartii - ne po slukham', *Dialog* (7), pp. 60–63.

—— (1988), 'Neformaly v perestroike: opyt i perspektivy' in Yu. Afanasiev (ed.), *Inogo ne dano*, pp. 210–27.

—— (1989), 'Eti bespokoinye "neformaly"', *Gorizont* (4), pp. 7–12.

—— (1990), 'Sotsial-demokraty i sotsialisty v sovremennoi Rossii', *Gorizont* (8), pp. 16–26.

—— (1990), 'Vybor posle vyborov' in S. Yushenkov (ed.), *Neformaly: sotsial'nye initsiativy*, pp. 75–100.

'Manifest o provozglashenii Sotsial-demokraticheskoi partii Rossiiskoi Federatsii', *Alternativa* (1), 30 May.

Mansurov, V. (1989), 'Obshchestvennoe mnenie o s"yezde narodnykh deputatov SSSR', *AiF* (23), 10 June.

—— (ed.) (1990), *Intelligentsiya o sotsial'no-politicheskoi situatsii v strane*, Moscow: Institut sotsiologii AN SSSR.

—— and S. Bykova (eds) (1991), *Intelligenstiya i perestroika*, Moscow: Institut sotsiologii AN SSSR.

Marsov, V. (1989), 'Who will sit in the Kremlin?', *MN* (16), 16 April.

Martynenko, O. (1989), 'Freedom on a legal basis', *MN* (48), 26 November.

—— (1989), 'Above the conflict', *MN* (49), 3 December.

Masaryk, T.G. (1968), *The Spirit of Russia*, rev. edn, 3 vols, London and Boston: Allen & Unwin.

Materialy Plenuma Tsk KPSS, 5-7 fev. 1990g. (1990), Moscow: Politizdat.

Materialy uchreditel'nogo s"yezda KP RSFSR (1990), Moscow: Politizdat.

Materialy XXVII s"yezda KPSS (1986), Moscow: Politizdat.

Materialy XXVIII s"yezda KPSS (1990), Moscow: Politizdat.

Medvedev, F. (1988), *Trava posle nas*, Moscow: Novosti.

Medvedev, Roy (1977), *On Socialist Democracy*, London: Macmillan.

—— (1985), *On Soviet Dissent: Interviews with Piero Osselino*, New York: Columbia University Press.

—— and Chiesa, G. (1991), *Time of Change*, London and New York: Tauris.

274   *The Rise of the Russian Democrats*

Mel'nikov, I. (1990), 'Byla bor'ba idei', *AiF* (7), 17 February.
'Memorial sovesti' (1988), *Ogonek* (41), p. 25.
Men', Alexander (1989), 'Religiya, kul't lichnosti i sekulyarnoe gosudarstvo' in T. Ryabikova (ed.), *Na puti k svobode sovesti*, pp. 88-113.
—— (1990), 'Poslednee interv'yu o. Alexandra Menya', *Panorama* (13), December.
Menshikova, T. (1990), 'Congress of Democratic Russia Movement', *MN* (43), 4 November.
—— (1991), 'The Kiev Prologue', *MN* (17), 28 April.
Merridale, C. (1991), 'Perestroika and Poltical Pluralism: Past and Prospects' in C. Merridale and C. Ward (eds.), *Perestroika: The Historical Perspective*, pp. 14-34.
—— and C. Ward (eds.), *Perestroika: The Historical Perspective*, London: Edward Arnold.
'Mezhklubnaya partiinaya organizatsiya: informatsiya k razmyshleniyu' (1989), *Gorizont* (10), pp. 7-11.
Migranyan, A. (1988), 'Mekhanizm tormozheniya' in Yu. Afanasiev (ed.), *Inogo ne dano*, pp. 97-121.
Mikko, Marianne (1990), *Konets poslednei imperii: vstrechi s Yuriem Afanasievym*, Riga: Atmoda.
Miloslavsky, L. (1988), 'A place for non-officials', *MN* (40), 2 October.
—— (1989), 'An escort for informals', *MN* (39), 24 September.
Milyukov, Pavel (1930), 'Eurasianism and Europeanism in Russian History' in B.V. Yakovenko (ed.), *Festschrift T.G. Masaryk*, 1, Bonn: F. Cohen, pp. 225-36.
Mindubaev, Zh. (1988), 'Budet Memorial', *Lit.Gaz.* (32), 10 August.
—— (1990), 'Povolzh'e: vchera i zavtra' in V.A. Pechenev (ed.), *Neformaly: kto oni? kuda zovut?*, pp. 134-62.
—— (1990), 'Uroki odnoi otstavki' in V.A. Pechenev (ed.), *Neformaly: kto oni? kuda zovut?*, pp. 216-38.
Mineev, A. (1989), 'Evolution of Social Awareness', *MN* (3), 15 January.
Mitrokin, S. (1991), 'Dvizhenie "Demokraticheskaya Rossiya"', *Panorama* (28), July.
—— (1991), 'Konservativny lager'', *Panorama* (29), September.
Morozov, S. (1990), 'Na ulitsakh i ploshchadakh', *Revolyutsionnaya Rossiya* (6), May.
Morrison, John (1991), *Boris Yeltsin: From Bolshevik to Democrat*, Harmondsworth: Penguin.
Morton, H. (1984), 'The contemporary Soviet city' in H. Morton and R. Stuart (eds), *The Contemporary Soviet City*, London: Macmillan, pp. 3-24.
'Moskovsky partiiny klub' (1989), *Gorizont* (9), pp. 2-9.
Mukhomel', V. (ed.), *SSSR: demografichesky diagnoz*, Moscow: Progress.
Musaelyan, Karina (1990), 'Osoby put'', *Svoboda* (4), May.
—— (1990), 'Trudny put' "Memoriala"', *Narodny deputat* (6), pp. 70-72.
Narodnye deputaty SSSR: spravochnik (1990), Moscow: Vneshtorgizdat.
Nazimova, A. and V. Sheinis (1990), 'Deputatny korpus: chto novogo', *AiF* (17), 28 April.
—— (1990), 'Vybory i vlast'' in V. Mukhomel' (ed.), *SSSR: demografichesky diagnoz*, pp. 652-92.
'Nedelya sovesti' (1988), *Izvestiya*, 24 November.
Neformal'nye dvizheniya i organazitsii (1990), Omsk.

Neformal'nye molodezhnye ob"yedineniya (1989), Odessa.

Neformal'nye ob"yedineniya molodezhi (1988), Kiev.

Nenashev, S. (1990), *S'Affirmer: les Informels de Léningrad*, Moscow: Progress.

Nersesov, Yu. (1990), 'Razbrod i shataniya', *Novaya rech'* (4), October–November.

Nikitina, V. (1990), 'The big nyet', *MN* (9), 27 July.

Notkina, T. (ed.), *Pogruzhenie v tryasinu*, Moscow: Progress.

Nove, Alec (1989), *Glasnost in Action: Cultural Renaissance in Russia*, London and Boston: Unwin Hyman.

Nuikin, Andrei (1988), 'O tsene slova i tsenakh na produkty' in V. Kanunnikova (ed.), *Yesli po sovesti*, pp. 196–211.

—— (1988), 'Plecha i kommunistichesky ideal' in Yu. Afanasiev (ed.), *Inogo ne dano*, pp. 509–18.

—— (1989), 'Slovo o dostoinstve' in N. Strel'tsova (ed.), *V svoem otechestve*, pp. 15–36.

—— (1989), 'Stat' deputatom', *MN* (10), 5 March.

—— (1990), '"Novoe myshlenie" i staraya sovest'' in A. Protashchik (ed.), *Cherez ternii*, pp. 84–105.

'O prakticheskoi rabote po realizatsii reshenii XIX Vsesoyuznoi konferentsii KPSS' (1988), *Pravda*, 31 July.

'O rasstanovke sil v deputatskom korpuse' (1992), *NG*, 1 April.

'Ob ochetakh i vyborakh v partiinykh organizatsiyakh' (1988), *Pravda*, 31 July.

Obolensky, A. (1990), 'Chto den' gryadushchi nam gotovit?' in A. Protashchik (ed.), *Cherez ternii*, pp. 482–509.

Obshchestvennye dvizheniya Leningrada (1989), Leningrad: Sovetskaya sotsiologicheskaya assotsiatsiya.

Okudzhava, Bulat (1989), 'Russian Culture is a source of good', *MN* (41), 8 October.

Okunev, I. (1989), 'Anatoly Rybakov', *Soviet Literature and Art*, Moscow: Novosti, pp. 81–4.

Open letter (signed by Zakharov, Ulyanov *et al.*) in defence of M. Shatrov (1988), *Pravda*, 29 February.

Open letter to Gorbachev (signed by Baklanov, Granin, Klimov *et al.*) (1989), *MN* (1), 1 January.

Orlov, V. (1991), 'Valery Skurlatov's Dirty Work', *MN* (21), 21 July.

—— and I. Yakimov (1990), 'For consolidation but not with the partocracy', *MN* (17), 6 May.

Ostalsky, D. (1989), 'Newspaper strike in Noginsk', *MN* (47), 19 November.

—— (1990), 'Before the Congress', *MN* (16), 22 April.

'Ot politicheskogo monizma k real'nomu plyuralizmu' (1990), in S. Yushenkov (ed.), *Neformaly: sotsial'nye initsiativy*, pp. 56–74.

'Our times' (1989), *MN* (10), 5 March.

Ovcharenko, G. (1988), 'Miting byl zapreshchen', *Pravda*, 24 August.

Ovrutsky, L. (1992), 'Rutskoism', *MN* (12), 22 March.

Parol', V. (1990), 'Mnogopartinost' ili ideologichesky plyuralizm vnutri partii', *Obshchestvennye nauki* (1), pp. 114–23.

'The Parties and Russian reform' (1992), *MN* (4), 26 January.

'Partiya i novye obshchestvennye dvizheniya' in V.A. Pechenev (ed.), *Neformaly:*

kto oni?, pp. 304-26.

'Partiya zelenykh: deklaratsiya printsipov', *Tret'ii put'* (14), November.

Pashkov, M. (1990), '"Zolotoi vek" rossiiskikh neformalykh' in V. Levichev (ed.), *Neformal'naya volna*, pp. 3-11.

Pavlov, Valentin (1993), *Avgust iznutri*, Moscow: Business World.

Pavlovsky, Gleb (1988), 'The last wagon', *MN* (40), 2 October.

Pechenev, V.A. (ed.) (1990), *Neformaly: kto oni? kuda zovut?*, Moscow: Politizdat.

'People before collective farms' (1990), *MN* (37), 23 September.

'Perestroika: obraz mysli i deistvii' (1988), *SK*, 5 May.

Pervy S"yezd narodnykh deputatov SSSR: stenografichesky otchet, 6 vols., Moscow: Izdatel'stvo Verkhnovo Soveta.

Petrichenko, O. (1987), '"Angleter": etyudy i fakty', *Ogonek* (20), May.

Petrov, A. (1990), 'Opinion poll in army', *AiF* (27), 7 July.

Petrov, G. (1987), 'Tak vy probyvaites' k pravde', *SK*, 24 November.

Petrovich, M. (1956), *The Emergence of Russsian Pan-Slavism 1856-1870*, New York: Columbia University Press.

Pipes, Richard (ed.) (1961), *The Russian Intelligentsia*, New York: Columbia University Press.

—— (1961), 'The historical evolution of the Russian intelligentsia' in Richard Pipes (ed.), *The Russian Intelligentsia*, pp. 41-61.

—— (1974), *Russia under the Old Regime*, London and New York: Penguin.

'Pisateli v poderzhku perestroiki' (1989), *Lit.Gaz.*, 15 March.

Piyasheva, L. (1990), 'Democrats look for economic foundations', *MN* (37), 16 September.

Plasky, S. (1988), *Molodezhnye gruppy i ob"yedineniya: prichiny vozniknoveniya i osobennosti deyatel'nosti*, Moscow.

'Platforma Vsesoyuznoi pisatel'skoi assotsiatsii "Aprel"' (1990), *Aprel' Inform* (1-2), 22 March.

'Plenum Voprosov: chto dal'she?' (1988), *Sovetsky ekran* (4), pp. 4-5.

Pochivalov, L. (1990), 'Emigranty' in V. Mukhomel' (ed.), *SSSR: demografichesky diagnoz*, pp. 252-73.

Podshivalov, I. (1990), 'Elected by colleagues', *MN* (16), 22 April.

Polenina, S. (1989), 'Discrimination against women', *MN* (24), 11 June.

Poltoranin, M. (1988), 'Besuch bei Boris Jelzin', *MN* (2).

—— (1989), 'In praise of pedantry', *MN* (4), 22 January.

Pomerants, G. (1981), 'Tsena otrecheniya' in A. Babenyshev (ed.), *Sakharovsky sbornik*, New York: Khronika, pp. 87-103.

—— (1991), 'Zhivye i mertvye idei' in T. Notkina (ed.), *Pogruzhenie v tryasinu*, pp. 311-45.

Ponomarev, L. and V. Shinkarenko (1988), 'Chem silen byurokrat?', *Izvestiya*, 17 May.

—— (1988), 'Kto kogo', *Izvestiya*, 18 May.

Popov, Gavriil (1987), 'S tochki zreniya ekonomista', *Nauka i zhizn'* (4), pp. 54-65.

—— (1988), 'Perestroika upravleniya ekonomikoi' in Yu. Afanasiev (ed.), *Inogo ne dano*, pp. 621-33.

—— (1988), 'Obratnogo khoda ne imeem', *SK*, 7 April.

—— (1989), 'Programma, kotoroi rukovodstvovalsya Stalin' in N. Strel'tsova (ed.), *V svoem otechestve*, pp. 105-20.

—— (1989), 'My - sami', *Ogonek* (6).

—— (1991), 'Zachem G. Popov yedet v Ameriku', *AiF* (7), February.

—— and N. Shmelev (1988), 'Anatomiya defitsita', *Znamya* (5), pp. 158-83.

—— *et al.* (1990), 'Sdelat' osoznanny vybor', *AiF* (15), 14 April.

—— and Anatoly Sobchak (1990), 'Zayavlenie', *AiF* (29), 21 July.

—— and Ye. Yakovlev (1990), 'The Times are getting Tougher', *MN* (42), 28 October.

Popov, M. (1992), 'Kak rozhdalas' Rabochaya partiya', *Narodnaya pravda*, 1 January.

Popov, N. (1990), 'Narod i vlast'' in A. Protashchik (ed.), *Cherez ternii*, pp. 771-87.

—— (1989), 'Obshchestvennoe mnenie i vybory', *Izvestiya*, 22 April.

'Popular Front changes course' (1989), *MN* (26), 25 June.

'Popular Front of Russian Federation formed' (1989), *MN* (44), 29 October.

Portugalov, N. (1989), 'A passion out of control', *MN* (1), 1 January.

—— (1989), 'He's forgotten nothing', *MN* (8), 19 February.

Potanin, V. (1989), 'Sokrovennoe' in V. Stetsenko (ed.), *Pisatel' i vremya*, Moscow: Sovetsky pisatel', pp. 325-37.

Pravda (1989), 13 January, CPSU's election 'manifesto'.

'Predistoriya DS: 1987 i 1988gg.', *Byulleten' soveta partii Demokratichesky Soyuz* (6), pp. 29-33,

'Press-konferentsia "Aprelya"' (1990), *Aprel' Inform* (1-2), 22 March.

Pribylovsky, V. (1990), 'Kem nas pugaet TASS', *Panorama* (13), December.

—— (1991), 'Pouchitel'naya istoriya moskovskogo narodnogo fronta', *Panorama* (28), July.

—— (1991), *Slovar' novykh politicheskikh partii i organizatsii Rossii*, Moscow: Panorama.

—— (1992), 'Bloki i fraktsii rossiiskogo parlamenta', *Panorama* (32), May.

Pringle, Peter (1991), 'Shevardnadze forms democratic force', *The Independent*, 5 July.

'Problemy izucheniya istorii russkoi filosofii i kul'tury' (1988), *Problemy filosofii* (9), pp. 92-162.

Proceedings of the founding conference of the Social Democratic Association, Tallinn, January 1990 (1990), *Otkrytaya zona* (11), January.

Prokhorov, V. and S. Orlov (1990), 'Pervoaprel'skaya partiya', *Panorama* (7), July.

Protashchik, A. (ed.) (1990), *Cherez ternii: prolog: chto dal'she?*, Moscow: Progress.

Proyekty ustava KPSS Moskovskogo i Leningradskogo partiinykh klubov (1990), Moscow: Demokraticheskaya Platforma.

Ra'anan, U. and I. Lukes (eds) (1990), *Gorbachev's USSR: A System in Crisis*, London: Macmillan.

Radzievsky, V. (1990), 'Conservatism retires', *MN* (8-9), 4 March.

—— (1990), 'From the Kremlin to the coalmines', *MN* (15), 14 April.

—— (1991), 'Resounding silence at Kuzbass coal mines', *MN* (12), 24 March.

Rakitsky, B. (1990), 'Putem peremen' in V. Bokarev and D. Polyakova (eds), *Demokratiya – vlast' vsekh i kazhdogo*, pp. 30-35.

Rasshivalova, Ye. and N. Seregin (1991), *Putch: khronika trevozhnykh dnei*, Moscow: Progress.

Razh, G. (1990), 'Rossiya bez tsarya v golove', *Panorama* (12), October.

—— (1991), 'Grazhdanskaya voina yeshche ne segodnya', *Panorama* (15), January.

Razumov, A. *et al.* (1989), *Samodeyatel'nye ob"edineniya molodezhi: voprosy i otvety*, Kiev.

Read, C. (1979), *Religion, Revolution and the Russian Intelligentsia*, London: Macmillan.

'Religiya v SSSR' (1988), *Russkaya mysl'*, 20 May.

'Rezolyutsii s"yezda [sotsial-demokratov]' (1990), *Respublika* (3).

Romanenko, Y. (1991), 'Miners' strike continues', *MN* (10), 10 March.

Romanov, Andrei (1989), 'Difficult ascent', *MN* (3), 15 January.

—— (1989), 'The right to a seat', *MN* (6), 5 February.

—— (1989), 'Without crutches', *MN* (7), 12 February.

—— (1989), 'Breaking one's own rules', *MN* (9), 26 February.

—— (1989), 'Not elected', *MN* (15), 9 April.

—— (1989), 'Money for democracy', *MN* (20), 14 May.

—— (1989), 'Supreme Soviet', *MN* (24), 11 June.

—— (1989), 'Between the two congresses', *MN* (50), 10 December.

—— and V. Shevelev (1989), 'The minority closes ranks', *MN* (32), 6 August.

—— and V. Tretyakov (1989), 'Consolidation through dialogue', *MN* (23), 4 June.

Rossiiskoe khristiansko-demokraticheskoe dvizhenie: sbornik materialov (1990), Moscow: Vybor.

Rothman, S. and G. Breslauer (1978), *Soviet Politics and Society*, St Paul, MN, and New York: West.

Rott, V. (1990), 'O Kh.d.s. Rossii', *AiF* (13), 31 March.

Roxburgh, Angus (1991), *The Second Russian Revolution*, London: BBC Books.

Rozhnovsky, S. (1989), 'Lev Kopelov: a lamb', *MN* (8), 19 February.

Rubinov, Anatoly (1989), 'Kak menya vybrali kandidatom v kandidaty', *Lit.Gaz.*, 1 February.

Rubtsov, A. (1992), 'Democracy as understood in modern Russia', *MN* (4), 26 January.

Rumyantsev, Oleg (1988), *O samodeyatel'nom dvizhenii obshchestvennykh initsiativ*, Moscow: Institut ekonomiki mirovoi sotsialisticheskoi sistemy.

—— (1990), 'Novy etap reformy i zadachi sotsial-demokratii. (Tezisy politicheskogo doklada)', *Respublika*, (3).

—— (1990), 'Pereraspredelitel'naya model', yee protivorechiya i problemy reformirovaniya' in S. Yushenkov (ed.), *Neformaly: sotsial'nye initsiativy*, pp. 203–15.

'Russkaya ideya: problemy kul'tury - problemy kinematografa' (1988), *Iskusstvo kino* (6), pp. 118–31.

Rutland, Peter (1991), 'Labour unrest and movements in 1989 and 1990' in A. Hewett and V. Winston (eds), *Milestones in Glasnost and Perestroyka*, pp. 287–325.

Ryabikova, T. (ed.), *Na puti k svobode sovesti*, Moscow: Progress.

Ryzhkov, Nikolai (1992), *Perestroika: istoriya predatel'stv*, Moscow: Novosti.

Rzhevskaya, Yelena (1989), 'The tragedy of faithful Ruslan', *MN* (4), 22 January.

Sagdeev, R. (1989), 'Worthy choice', *MN* (18), 30 April.

—— *et al.* (1989), 'Letter to editor', *MN* (15), 9 April.

Sakharov, Andrei (1988), 'Neizbezhnost' perestroiki' in Yu. Afanasiev (ed.), *Inogo ne dano*, pp. 122–34.

—— (1990), *Moscow and Beyond*, London: Hutchinson.

—— (1991), *Trevoga i nadezhda*, Moscow: Inter-Verso.

Sakwa, Richard (1990), *Gorbachev and his Reforms*, London and New York: Routledge.

—— (1993), *Russian Politics and Society*, London and New York: Routledge.

Satarov, G. (1991), *Partiinaya zhizn'*. *Rossiya do i posle avgusta*, Moscow (unpublished conference paper).

—— and S. Stankevich (1990), 'Legislators' computerized X-ray photograph', *MN* (31), 12 August.

Schatz, Marshall (1980), *Soviet Dissent in Historical Perspective*, Cambridge: Cambridge University Press.

Schöpflin, George (ed.) (1986), *The Soviet Union and Eastern Europe: A Handbook*, Oxford and New York: Blond.

Sedaitis, J. (1991), 'Worker Activism: politics at the grassroots' in J. Sedaitis and J. Butterfield (eds), *Perestroika from Below: Social Movements in the Soviet Union* pp. 3-17.

—— and J. Butterfield (eds.) (1991), *Perestroika from Below: Social Movements in the Soviet Union*, Boulder, CO: Westview.

Selikhovsky, A. (1990), 'Ob etom pisali vse tsentral'nye gazety', *Krasnaya presnya* (6), February.

Selyunin, V. (1988), 'Istoki' in V. Kanunnikova (ed.), *Yesli po sovesti*, pp. 250-301.

—— (1988), 'Revansh byurokratii' in Yu. Afanasiev (ed.), *Inogo ne dano*, pp. 192-209.

—— (1989), 'Rynok - veliki ob"edinitel' narodov' in N. Strel'tsova (ed.), *V svoem otechestve*, pp. 37-60.

—— (1990), 'Rynok: khimery i real'nosti' in A. Protashchik (ed.), *Cherez ternii*, pp. 132-50.

Semenov, V. *et al.* (eds) (1968), *Klassy, sotsial'nye sloi i gruppy v SSSR*, Moscow: Nauka.

Semenova, L. (1991), 'Politicheskoe soznanie intelligentsii' in V. Mansurov *et al.* (eds), *Intelligentsiya i perestroika*, pp. 13-22.

Semenova, V. (1990), 'Sotsial'no-istoricheskie aspekty problemy neformal'nykh ob"edinenii molodezhi' in V. Levichev (ed.), *Neformal'naya volna*, pp. 27-38.

Semenoy, D. (1991), 'Will the Writers' Union disband itself?', *MN* (34-5), 1 September.

Semina, L. (1990), 'Po zakonam grazhdanskogo vremeni' in V. Pechenev (ed.), *Neformaly: kto oni? kuda zovut?*, pp. 163-86.

Sergeev, I. (1989), 'Obsuzhdaetsya "Znamya"', *Lit.Gaz.*, 1 February.

Sergeyev, V. and N. Biryukov (1993), *Russia's Road to Democracy*, Aldershot: Edward Elgar.

Shabanov, Yu. (1988), 'Saus pikant dlya "demokratii"', *Moskovskaya pravda*, 14 May.

'Shagi k obnovleniyu' (1990), *AiF* (6), 10 February.

Shakhnazarov, G. (1987), 'Learning democracy' in G. Dzyubenko, and G. Kozlova (eds), *USSR: A Time of Change*, pp. 40-47.

Shakhnovsky, V. and A. Bryachikhin (1989), 'Klub v raikome', *Moskovskaya pravda*, 27 July.

Shatrov, M. (1989) and G. Li (eds), *Dal'she ... dal'she ... dal'she: diskussiya vokrug*

odnoi p'esy, Moscow: Knizhnaya palata.
Shchegertsov, V. (1990), 'Politichesky ekstremizm molodezhi' in V. Levichev (ed.), *Neformal'naya volna*, pp. 79-90.
Shchepotkin, V. and I. Karpenko (1990), *Proryv v demokratiyu*, Moscow: Izvestiya.
Sheshma, M. (1990), 'Dialog ili konfrontatsiya' in S. Yushenkov (ed.), *Neformaly: sotsial'nye initsiativy*, pp. 152-89.
Shevardnadze, E. (1991), 'Democracy cannot wait', *The Independent*, 12 August.
Shipler, David (1983), *Russia: Broken Idols, Stolen Dreams*, London and Sydney: Futura.
Shlapentokh, Vladimir (1990), *Soviet Intellectuals and Political Power: The Post-Stalin Era*, London and New York: Tauris.
Shmelev, N. (1987), 'Avansy i dolgi', *NM* (6), pp. 142-58.
—— (1988), 'Novye trevogi' in V. Kanunnikova (ed.), *Yesli po sovesti*, pp. 367-95.
—— (1989), 'Chto mozhet publitsistika?' in N. Strel'tsova (ed.), *V svoem otechestve*, pp. 9-14.
—— and G. Popov (1989), 'Na razvlike dorog. Byla li al'ternativa stalinskoi modeli razvitiya?' in Kh. Kobo (ed.), *Osmyslit' kul't Stalina*, pp. 284-326.
—— (1990), 'Chto zhe dal'she?' in A. Protashchik (ed.), *Cherez ternii*, pp. 535-59.
Shostakovsky, V. (1989), 'Demokraticheskie preobrazovaniya sdelayut partiyu neospornym liderom', *SK*, 7 December.
—— (1990), Speech at the Moscow CP Plenum, *Moskovskaya pravda*, 17 June.
—— and V. Yatskov (1988), 'Demokratizatsiya partii - demokratizatsiya obshchestva', *Kommunist* (6), pp. 31-5.
—— and I. Yakovenko (1990), 'Vozmozhen li vykhod iz krizisa?', *Dialog* (8), pp. 28-31.
Shtukin, V. (1990), 'Prognozy i stavki politicheskogo marketinga', *Moskovskaya pravda*, 22 June.
Shubin, A. (1990), 'Politika i pedagogika: ot Obshchiny - k Konfederatsii anarkho-sindikalistov' in S. Yushenkov (ed.), *Neformaly: sotsial'nye initsiativy*, pp. 101-20.
Sidorov, I. (1988), 'DS: litso, k litsu', *Leningradskaya pravda*, 5 August.
—— (1989), 'Narodny front', *Leningradskaya pravda*, 25 July.
Simanovich, G. (1988), 'Dva goda spustya', *SK*, 11 June.
Simmons, Ernest (1971), 'The Writers' in H.G. Skilling and F. Griffiths (eds), *Interest Groups in Soviet Politics*, pp. 253-90.
'Simvoly slozhnogo vremeni' (1987), *Russkaya mysl'*, 4 December.
Sirotkin, V. (1990), 'Neformaly - za pechatnym stankom', *Nedelya*, 16 January.
Skilling, H.G. (1971), 'Group conflict in Soviet politics: some conclusions' in H.G. Skilling and F. Griffiths (eds), *Interest Groups in Soviet Politics*, pp. 379-416.
—— and F Griffiths (eds) (1971), *Interest Groups in Soviet Politics*, Princeton, NJ: Princeton University Press.
'Slova a sanktsii: venskie soglasheniya i budushchee tsenzury v SSSR' (1989), *Vek XX i mir* (7), pp. 24-32.
Smekhov, V. (1988), 'Skripka mastera', *Teatr* (2), pp. 97-116.
Smirnov, I. (1989), 'Playing with cheats', *MN* (30), 5 August.
Smith, Gordon B. (1992), *Soviet Politics: Struggling with Change*, rev. edn, London:

Macmillan.

Snezhkova, I. (1989), 'Natsional'nye aspekty programm neformal'nykh ob"edinenii', *Obshchestvennye nauki* (6), pp. 110-22.

Sobchak, Anatoly (1989), 'Inter-Regional Group', *MN* (40), 1 October.

—— (1990), 'Stanovlenie novoi politicheskoi sistemy: vlast', partiya i pravo' in A. Vyshinsky (ed.), *Pravo i vlast'*, pp. 145-53.

—— (1991), *Khozhdenie vo vlast'*, Moscow: Novosti.

—— (1991), 'The country won't have another civil war', *MN* (13), 31 March.

Sokolov, Vadim (1986), 'Nachinaetsya s publitsistiki', *Lit.Gaz.*, 15 January.

Solganik, I. (1990), 'S"yezd' komsomola', *AiF* (16), 21 April.

'Sozdan izbiratel'ny blok "Demokraticheskaya Rossiya"' (1990), *Ogonek* (6).

Stankevich, Sergei (1989), 'Tam gde nachinaetsya yedinstvo', *Yunost'* (9), pp. 2-4.

—— (1990), 'Trudnosti stanovleniya demokratii' in S. Yushenkov (ed.), *Neformaly: sotsial'nye initsiativy*, pp. 136-47.

—— (1990), 'KPSS i samostoyatel'nye initsiativy' in S. Yushenkov (ed.), *Neformaly: sotsial'nye initsiativy*, pp. 148-51.

Staravoitova, Galina (1989), 'E pluribus unum' in A. Vyshnevsky (ed.), *V chelovecheskom izmerenii*, pp. 89-117.

—— (1990), 'Tsepi u nas obshche', *AiF* (23), 9 June.

Steele, Jonathan (1994), *Eternal Russia: Yeltsin, Gorbachev and the Mirage of Democracy*, London: Faber.

Stein, A. (1987), 'Moe pokolenie', *SK*, 23 May.

Stepanishin, V. (1989), 'S kem intelligentsiya?', *Vek XX i mir* (12), pp. 7-8.

Stepovoy, A. (1989), 'Kak eto bylo', *Izvestiya*, 18 January.

Strel'tsova, N. (ed.), *V svoem otechestve*, Moscow: Knizhaya palata.

Sudiniev, I. (1987), 'Neformal'nye molodezhnye ob"edineniya: opyt ekspozitsii', *Sotsiologicheskie issledovaniya* (5), pp. 56-62.

—— (1990), 'Nashestvie marsian' in S. Yushenkov (ed.), *Neformaly: sotsial'nye initsiativy*, pp. 4-43.

Surikov, Igor (1990), Interview, *AiF* (6), 10 February.

Szamuely, Tibor (1974), *The Russian Tradition*, London: Fontana.

Tarasov, B. (1991), 'Otchizna zovet', *SR*, 10 July.

Tatu, M. and D. Vernet (1987), 'Un entretien avec le numéro deux soviétique', *Le Monde*, 4 December.

Teague, Elizabeth (1990), 'Perestroika and the Party' in Martin McCauley (ed.), *Gorbachev and Perestroika*, pp. 13-29.

Thaden, Edward (1964), *Conservative Nationalism in Nineteenth Century Russia*, Seattle, WA: University of Washington Press.

'There are no such parties' (1990), *MN* (28), 22 July.

Ticktin, Hillel (c.1975), 'Political Economy of the Soviet Intellectual', *Critique* (2), pp. 6-22.

'To vote or not to vote' (1989), *MN* (13), 26 March.

Tochkin, G. (1992), 'Partii, predstavlennye v deputatskom korpuse Rossii', *Panorama* (32), May.

Tolstaya, Tatiana (1989), 'Intelligentsia and intellectuals', *MN* (32), 6 August.

Tolz, Vera (1990), *The USSR's Emerging Multi-Party System*, New York: Praeger.

Topalov, M (1990), '"Formal'naya" i "neformal'naya" aktivnost' molodezhi' in V.

Levichev (ed.), *Neformal'naya volna*, pp. 152-63.

Toshchenko, Zh., V. Voikov and Ye. Levanov (1990), 'Kommunisty o partii', *AiF* (25), 23 June.

Tovstonogov, G. (1985), 'Razmyshleniya v den' premery', *Lit.Gaz.*, 25 December.

Travkin, N. (1990), 'O demokraticheskoi partii Rossiiskoi Federatsii', *AiF* (20), 19 May.

—— and V. Glotov (1990), 'Kak izbrali predsedatelya', *Ogonek* (24), June.

Treadgold Donald (1973), *The West in Russia and China: Russia: 1472-1917*, 1, Cambridge: Cambridge University Press.

Tretyakov, V. (1989), 'Opposite effect', *MN* (12), 19 March.

—— (1989), 'The Boris Yeltsin Phenomenon', *MN* (16), 16 April.

—— (1989), 'Whose hopes will it justify?', *MN* (24), 11 June.

—— (1989), 'Real democracy', *MN* (8), 19 February.

Trusov, A. (ed.) (1990), 'Neformaly yest'. A chto dal'she?' in V. Pechenev and V. Vyunsky (eds), *Neformaly: kto oni? kuda zovut?*, pp. 241–63.

Tsipko, A. (1990), 'Protivorechiya ucheniya Karla Marxa' in A. Protashchik (ed.), *Cherez ternii*, pp. 60–83.

Tsvigun, S. (1981), 'Podryvnye aktsii - oruzhie imperializma', *Kommunist* (4), pp. 108–19.

—— (1981), 'O proiskakh imperialisticheskikh razvedok', *Kommunist* (14), pp. 88–99.

Tucker, R. (1991), 'What time is it in Russian history?' in C. Merridale and C. Ward (eds), *Perestroika: The Historical Perspective*, pp. 34–46.

Tvorcheskie soyuzy v SSSR. Organizatsionno-pravovye voprosy (1970), Moscow: Institut gosudarstva i prava AN SSSR.

Uglanov, A. (1991), 'Pozitsii proyasnilis', *AiF* (9), March.

Ulyanov, M. (1987), 'Trudny put' k samoupravleniyu', *SK*, 24 October.

—— (1987), 'Now or never' in G. Dzyubenko and G. Kozlova (eds), *USSR: A Time of Change*, pp. 219–31.

Urban, Michael E. (1990), *More Power to the Soviets: The Democratic Revolution in the USSR*, Aldershot: Edward Elgar.

Van Atta, D. (1991), 'Social mobilisation in the Russian countryside' in J. Sedaitis and J. Butterfield (eds), *Perestroika from Below: Social Movements in the Soviet Union*, pp. 43–72.

Van der Heuvel, K. (1989), 'Vocation: Social Critic', *MN* (18), 30 April.

Vasiliev, V. (1990), 'Nadeyus' na intelligentsiyu', *Knizhnoe obozrenie*, 6 July.

Vasilievsky, A. (1990), 'Pora konchat' s sovetami', *Panorama* (11), September.

—— (1990), 'Demokraty', *Panorama* (13), December.

Verkhovsky, A. (1990), 'Problema radikalizma vchera i zavtra', *Panorama* (10), September.

Vernikov, V. (1988), 'Exportnaya glasnost', *Izvestiya*, 3 November.

Veselaya, E. (1989), '*Aprel*: A Writers' Committee in Support of Perestroika', *MN* (12), 19 March.

Vinogradov, Igor (1989), 'Rehabilitating the names', *MN* (24), 11 June.

—— (1989), 'Sketches about Anna Akhmatova', *MN* (28), 9 July.

—— (1989), 'It's a bitter experience', *MN* (7), 12 February.

Vitaliev, Vitaly (1990), *Special Correspondent: Investigating the Soviet Union*,

London: Hutchinson.

Vladimirov, V. (1990), 'Partiya i novye obschestvennye dvizheniya' in V. Pechenev (ed.), *Neformaly: kto oni? kuda zovut?*, pp. 304–26.

Volkov, Leonid (1990), 'Birth or Rebirth?', *MN* (19), 20 May.

Volodin, M. and V. Pribilovsky (1991), 'Novosti partiinogo stroitel'stva', *Panorama* (28), July.

Voronin, V. (1990), 'Tsentristsky blok', *Dialog* (16), pp. 47–50.

Vorontsov, V. (1990), 'Kto i ch'i interesy?', *AiF* (21), 26 May.

Voslensky, M. (1985), *Nomenklatura. Gosudarstvenny klass Sovetskogo Soyuza*, London: Overseas Publications Interchange Ltd.

'Vozzvanie krest'yanskoi partii Rossii' (1990), *Ogonek* (38).

Voznesensky, A. (1988), 'Otvet moemu chitatelyu', *SK*, 11 June.

—— (1989), 'Come back', *MN* (28), 9 July.

'Vsekh poimenno nazvat'' (1989), *Lit.Gaz.*, 1 February.

'Vtoraya konferentsiya Demokraticheskoi platformy', *Rech'* (1), July.

'Vybory narodnykh deputatov' (1989), *Lit.Gaz.*, 22 March.

'Vyderzhki iz stenogrammy pervogo s"yezda DS' (1991), *Byulleten' soveta partii Demokratichesky Soyuz* (6), pp. 22–8.

Vygorbina, A. (1990), 'Mnogopartinost' - uzhe real'nost' sovremennoi politecheskoi zhizni strany', *Obshchestvennye nauki* (3), pp. 74–9.

Vyshinsky, M. (ed.) (1990), *Pravo i vlast'*, Moscow: Progress.

Vyshnevsky, A. (ed.) (1989), *V chelovecheskom izmerenii*, Moscow: Progress.

Vyunitrsky, V. (1990), 'Ot "diki" mnogopartinosti k blokovoi sisteme', *Dialog* (17), pp. 28–36.

Vyzhutovich, V. (1992), 'Despensarizatsiya generala Rutskogo', *Stolitsa* (8), pp. 1–3.

Walicki, A. (1975), *The Slavophile Controversy*, Oxford: Oxford University Press.

Weber, Max (1966), *The City*, New York: Macmillan.

Wheeler, Marcus (1986), 'Ideology and Politics' in G. Schöpflin (ed.), *The Soviet Union and Eastern Europe: A Handbook*, pp. 208–18.

White, Stephen (1979), *Political Culture and Soviet Politics*, London: Macmillan.

—— (1990), *Gorbachev in Power*, Cambridge: Cambridge University Press.

—— (1991), 'Political reform in historical perspective' in C. Merridale and C. Ward (eds), *Perestroika: the Historical Perspective*, pp. 3–14.

XIX Vsesoyuznaya konferentsiya KPSS: *stenografichesky otchet* (1988), Moscow: Politizdat.

Yadov, V. (1989), 'Obshchestvennoe mnenie', *AiF* (22), 3 June.

Yakovenko, Igor (1990), 'People in the square', *MN* (8–9), 4 March.

Yakovlev, Aleksandr (1990), *Realizm – zemlya perestroiki. (Izbrannye rechi i stat'i)*, Moscow: Politizdat.

—— (1991), Interview, *Lit.Gaz.*, 25 December.

—— (1991), *Muki, prochiteniya, bytiya. Perestroika: nadezhdy i real'nosti*, Moscow: Novosti.

—— (1992), *Predislovie, obval, posleslovie*, Moscow: Novosti.

Yakovlev, Anatoly (1989), 'Return from non-existence', *MN* (9), 26 February.

Yakovlev, V. (1987), 'Proshchanie s Bazarovym', *Ogonek* (36).

Yakovlev, Yegor (1989), 'What the bickering is about', *MN* (3), 15 January.

—— (1989), 'Reforming the party', *MN* (36), 3 September.

284   *The Rise of the Russian Democrats*

—— (1990), 'Future is in the hands of the left', *MN* (8), 20 July.
Yakunin, Gleb (1989), 'V sluzhenii kul'tu' in T. Ryabikova (ed.), *Na puti k svobode sovesti*, pp. 172–207.
Yakushkin, D. (1989), 'It's him', *MN* (32), 6 August.
Yanitsky, O. (1986), 'Obshchestvennye initsiativy i samodeyatel'nost' mass', *Kommunist* (8), pp. 61–71.
Yanov, A. (1978), *The Russian New Right: Right Wing Ideologies in the Contemporary Soviet Union*, Berkeley, CA: IIS.
Yanovsky, S. (1989), 'Rozhdenie "Memoriala"', *Ogonek* (6).
Yefimova, L., A. Sobyanin and D. Yuriev (1990), 'Narod i nomenklatura – yediny?', *AiF* (29), 21 July.
Yefremov, Oleg (1986), 'Doverie zritelya', *Pravda*, 21 February.
Yegorov, S. (1990), 'Kak stat' deputatom', *AiF* (15), 14 April.
Yeltsin, Boris (1990), *Against the Grain: An Autobiography*, London: Cape.
—— (1991), 'Iz teleinterv'yu', *AiF* (8), February.
—— and V. Mamedov (1989), 'Why should deputies split', *MN* (32), 6 August.
Yeremin, Vitaly (1990), 'Toska po khozyainu', *Nedelya* (12).
Yerofeev, V. (1989), 'I'll die before I understand it', *MN* (50), 10 December.
Yevtushenko, Yevgeny (1985), 'Kabychevonebyshlisty', *Pravda*, 9 September.
—— (1988), 'Pomogat' perestroike', *Lit.Gaz.*, 2 November.
—— (1989), 'Neskol'ko slov o pis'me semi', *Ogonek* (6).
—— (1989), 'False Alarm', *MN* (6), 5 February.
—— (1989), 'Your plank in the election platform', *MN* (12), 19 March.
—— (1989), 'Stalinizm "po-Platonovu"' in Kh. Kobo (ed.), *Osmylit' kul't Stalina*, pp. 195–212.
—— (1990), *Politika, privilegiya vsekh*, Moscow: Novosti.
Yuriev, D. and A. Sobyanin (1990), 'Politicheskaya temperatura Rossii', *AiF* (37), 15 September.
Yushenkov, S. (ed.) (1990), *Neformaly: sotsial'nye initsiativy*, Moscow: Moskovsky rabochii.
—— (1990), 'Neformal'noe dvizhenie: obshchaya kharakteristika i osnovnye tendentsii razvitiya' in S. Yushenkov (ed.) (1990), *Neformaly: sotsial'nye initsiativy*, pp. 44–55.
Zabastovka: vynuzhdennaya mera zashchity zakonnykh prav, no tot li eto put'? (1989), Moscow: Politizdat.
Zaitsev, I. (1990), 'Chelovecheskoe izmerenie obshchestvennykh problem kak novy faktor politicheskoi deyatel'nosti' in V. Levichev (ed.), *Neformal'naya volna*, pp. 66–78.
Zalygin, Sergei (1987), 'Turnabout' in G. Dzyubenko and G. Kozlova (eds), *USSR: a Time of Change*, pp. 101–24.
—— (1988), 'Nastupaem ili otstupaem?' in Yu. Afanasiev (ed.), *Inogo ne dano*, pp. 228–37.
—— (1989), 'We'll start by publishing *Archipelago*', *MN* (29), 16 July.
—— (1990), 'Ekologiya i obshchestvo' in V. Bokarev and D. Polyakova (eds.), *Demokratiya – vlast' vsekh i kazhdogo*, pp. 38–47.
Zaramensky, I. (1990), 'Opyanenie svobody', *Dialog* (15), pp. 15–21.
Zarechkin, Yuri (1989), 'Posle mitinga', *Lit.Gaz.*, 22 February.

Zaslavskaya, Tatyana (1988), 'Korenny vopros perestroiki', *Izvestiya*, 4 June.
—— (1988), 'O strategii sotsial'nogo upravleniya perestroiki' in Yu. Afanasiev (ed.), *Inogo ne dano*, pp. 9-50.
—— and Ya. Kapelyush (1989), 'Obshchestvennoe mnenie ob itogak s"yezda', *AiF* (26), 1 July.
Zaslavsky, Victor (1982), *The Neo-Stalinist State: Class, Ethnicity and Consensus in Soviet Society*, Armonk, NY: M.E. Sharpe.
Zav'yalova, A. (ed.) (1989), *Postizhenie*, Moscow: Progress.
'Zayavlenie narodnykh deputatov RSFSR-chlenov KPSS' (1990), *AiF* (29), 21 July.
Zernov, N. (1963), *The Russian Religious Renaissance of the Twentieth Century*, London.
Zhavoronkov, Gennadi (1987), 'Neformal'no o neformal'ykh', *MN* (37), 13 September.
—— (1989), 'Sinyavsky in the USSR', *MN* (3), 15 January.
—— (1989), 'For peace and progress', *MN* (6), 5 February.
—— (1989), 'Democracy's salad days', *MN* (47), 19 November.
Zhelnorova, N. and L. Novikova (1989), Interview with Boris Yeltsin, *AiF* (23), 10 June
Zhirinovsky, V. (1990), 'LDPR ot pervogo litsa', *Dialog* (8), 1990, pp. 34-6.
—— (1991), 'My ne pozvolim razrushit' nash dom', *Sovetskaya Rossiya*, 30 July.
'Zhizn' Rossii' (1990), *AiF* (20), 19 May.
Ziegler, Charles (1991), 'Environmental politics and policy under perestroika' in J. Sedaitis and J. Butterfield (eds), *Perestroika from Below: Social Movements in the Soviet Union*, pp. 113-31.
Zinchenko, Z. (1989), 'Without the statute of limitations', *MN* (6), 5 February.
Zinoviev, Aleksandr (1985), 'Ne vse my dissidenty. O sotsial'noi oppozitsii v sovetskom obshchestve', *Kontinent* (44), pp. 175-90.

Index

287